WILLIAM T. MEYER, AIA

ENERGY ECONOMICS AND BUILDING DESIGN

McGRAW-HILL BOOK COMPANY
NEW YORK ST. LOUIS SAN FRANCISCO
AUCKLAND BOGOTÁ HAMBURG
JOHANNESBURG LONDON MADRID MEXICO
MONTREAL NEW DELHI PANAMA PARIS
SÃO PAULO SINGAPORE SYDNEY TOKYO
TORONTO

Library of Congress Cataloging in Publication Data

Meyer, William T.
Energy economics and building design.

1. Architecture and energy conservation—
Economic aspects. I. Title.
NA2542.3.M4 721'.0467 82-56
ISBN 0-07-041751-2 AACR2

1 2 3 4 5 6 7 8 9 0 KPKP 8 9 8 7 6 5 4 3 2

ISBN 0-07-041751-2

The editors for this book were Jeremy Robinson and Beatrice E. Eckes, the designer was Elliot Epstein, and the production supervisor was Teresa F. Leaden. It was set in Caledonia by University Graphics, Inc.

Printed and bound by The Kingsport Press.

CONTENTS

To my parents, William and Eleanor Meyer,
and to Rudolph Meyer and Charlotte Baker,
for their support and encouragement.

PREFACE

There is an almost infinite number of combinations of design alternatives, small and large, that can be assembled to conserve fuel in buildings. That assembly is the responsibility of the building design professions and must address a number of issues. Legally mandated building codes dealing with energy conservation dictate some of this responsibility. The moral commitment of the designer to peers and clients and to the tenets of professionalism dictate the remainder of the responsibility. Designers must design beautiful buildings which also conserve fuel. There is no choice. Technologists may think that the fuel crisis will obviate the need for formal concerns in architecture, but of course it won't. The aesthetists who wish the energy crunch would go away and who fail to consider seriously energy-efficient design approaches are likely to break the law. As some of my colleagues have often said, the concern for energy use in buildings is a forum that provides a basis for and, in fact, demands the breakdown of the polarity between the aesthetic theorists and the rational technologists. The design professions must "get it together" if they are to produce well-designed energy-efficient buildings.

NOTE

This text is meant to be a comprehensive introduction to the art and science of energy-conscious design. For the sake of brevity and simplification, some of the estimating techniques presented here have been abbreviated and others requiring more sophisticated mathematical skills have been eliminated altogether. Throughout the book, however, the reader is referred to experts and texts that can provide the next level of information should the reader desire it.

The material presented in this book will not preclude the need for mechanical engineering input on questions of energy-conscious design. Estimating methods discussed in the following pages are intended to provide approximate answers for use during preliminary and schematic design. They are not intended to yield the ultimate and most accurate projection of energy consumption for an entire building. Engineers and computer programs will still be necessary for that. Rather, it is hoped that this book will enable a designer to ask better-informed questions and permit some early analysis during schematic design so that bounds may be placed on the energy problem and provide more focus to the concerns of energy use in the architectural components of a building.

Also, it should be noted that particularly complex buildings such as hospitals may require mechanical engineering consultation on energy-use architectural issues from the very beginning of design.

And, lastly, the best estimate of energy consumption in a proposed building will frequently come from a comprehensive computer simulation of a building using a well-tested and verified computer program, of which numerous examples are available.

ACKNOWLEDGMENTS

This book was partially supported by a grant from the National Endowment for the Arts (NEA) in Washington, D.C., a federal agency. A number of individuals and other organizations also contributed valuable advice and information to the contents of this project.

I would like in particular to thank Mr. John Leffler, a mechanical engineer in New York City with whom I have taught for several years at Columbia University, whose guidance and review of this book during its preparation have been invaluable. John epitomizes, I think, the new breed of mechanical engineers whom I am encountering ever more frequently: those who understand the entire design and thermal performance of a building and with whom it is a delight to associate as an architect.

Also of particular importance were the association and all of the discussions and interactions with colleagues during my tenure with The Ehrenkrantz Group. I would like to acknowledge especially Ezra Ehrenkrantz, Stephen Weinstein, Peter Kastl, Magnus Magnusson, Michael Golubov, and Tyrone Pike. Richard Holod did many of the drawings in the book and also made valuable contributions as an energy-conscious architect to much of my work with the firm.

My gratitude is also extended to a good friend, Anthony Hoberman of the Alliance Capital Management Corporation, whose comments and suggestions concerning the financial and real estate issues addressed in this book were invaluable.

Research assistance for the chapter dealing with historic precedents in energy-conscious design was ably provided by Phyllis Halpern while she was a student of architecture at Columbia University.

Mr. Frank De Serio, program manager for the U.S. Department of Energy's Solar Cities and Towns Program, endorsed my National Endowment for the Arts fellowship and provided much-needed advice and encouragement.

Mr. Donald Watson, AIA, on the faculty at Yale University and in private practice in Guilford, Connecticut, also supported my NEA fellowship, as did Mr. Fred

Dubin, mechanical engineer and architect in New York City. I am very grateful to both.

Many of the analysis methods presented in this book and accompanying data have been developed by the American Society of Heating, Refrigeration and Air-Conditioning Engineers (ASHRAE). This society has made a major contribution to the knowledge base which all designers of energy-conscious buildings use. The engineers who form part of this society are the experts to whom all other design professionals should turn to get assistance in energy consumption estimating. I am very grateful to ASHRAE for its permission to reproduce the equations and tables presented in the following pages which came from their publications and for the great help this information has been and will be to other energy-concerned building designers.

ONE

INTRODUCTION

BACKGROUND

Fossil fuel shortages and rapidly rising energy costs have been in recent years and are likely to continue to be a critical problem in the United States. Architects, engineers, interior designers, and other building design professionals may play a major role in finding potential solutions to this problem in the sense that their designs will be directly or indirectly responsible for more than 40 percent[1] of the annual energy consumption in the country.

Many architects and interior designers, however, view energy conservation design as a challenge primarily for mechanical engineers. And unless designers preserve the scope of their responsibilities, the subject may indeed become primarily an engineering undertaking. It is clear that a major part of the opportunity for saving fuel in buildings is directly within the traditional domain of architectural and interior design. The architect has almost singular control over the ultimate size of a building as well as over its shape, siting, orientation, spatial arrangement, materials, and many other factors which affect energy use. In effect, an architect controls a building's need for energy; an engineer designs the means to fulfill that need. If the need is small, a building's energy supply systems will use less fuel. If the need is great, no matter what the skill of the engineer, the fuel consumption of a building will remain high.

The most accurate methods of estimating building energy consumption are computer simulation programs. However, the understanding of the output of such programs and, more important, the preparation of designs for saving energy are greatly facilitated by knowledge of the isolated quantities, forces, and economics involved in heat and light movement in buildings. This information, critical to

[1]Richard Stein, *Architecture and Energy*, Anchor Press, Doubleday & Co., Inc., Garden City, N.Y., 1977, p. 14.

intelligent design decision making, is made available to designers in this book in a format specifically tailored to their needs.

The energy-conscious building design decision also has major and unique *economic* implications that are not typically part of traditional design choices. An energy-conserving design saves a client money after construction when a building begins operation. Many times, however, such a design initially costs a client more to build. Designers must understand and be conversant with the first-cost *and* life-cycle cost implications of energy-saving design if they are to communicate with their clients effectively about their proposed design solutions.

The energy-conserving design decision, however, is to some extent no longer a matter of choice for either designers or clients. It has been mandated by most states' new energy conservation building codes. Effective compliance with such codes requires, however, a more exacting knowledge of thermal and luminous transfers in buildings than designers traditionally have possessed. Professionals who are uninformed in energy matters may be restricted, for example, by regulations for items such as facade glass, whereas these may be avoided by designers who can prove that more glass rather than less is energy-conserving in certain circumstances. At the federal level, various energy offices are developing energy consumption standards for buildings. These criteria will give designers greater freedom than existing state energy codes but will be difficult to meet for designers who lack knowledge of energy-conscious design and analysis methods.

Many texts provide some instruction in energy-conscious design. Some of them deal with passive solar design methods; others review design options for a specific building type; still others review design approaches for a specific climate. This book provides, in a single source, most of the principal methods for estimating the energy savings possible in architectural design as well as the means for comparing such benefits with the additional initial costs which often are required.

OBJECTIVES AND SCOPE

The overall objective of this book is to provide a means for improving the effectiveness of energy-related decision making in architectural and interior design. More specifically, the book describes the energy consumption estimating methods which relate to building aspects directly under an architect's or an interior designer's control. It also describes the analysis and evaluation methods which may be used to assess the economic, that is, the life-cycle cost-benefit, implications of energy-conserving architectural and interior designs. As a supplement, a review of a wide range of energy-conserving design approaches is presented along with a description of the basic thermal and luminous energy flows in buildings which such designs affect.

Building elements which architects and designers directly control, including items such as building form and shape, plan arrangement, structure, exterior walls, windows, and interior surface treatment, are addressed in this book. Decision aids for the design of mechanical and electrical systems are *not* presented except for describing the cost savings which an effective architectural design strategy may generate in terms of reduced mechanical-system sizes and installation costs. Energy-conserving mechanical systems are well described in existing texts and typically are controlled in design only peripherally by architects and interior designers.

The calculation methods described in this book focus on decision making by a comparison of costs with benefits. Additional construction costs above established norms that typically are required by an energy-conserving architectural design are compared with the fuel savings generated by such a design in order to determine economic viability. Cost-benefit comparison is presented as a quantitative assessment to be used by designers in conjunction with many qualitative judgments in determining the overall value of a particular design strategy.

The benefits and costs which may accrue to an energy-conscious architectural design are many. Economic benefits include fuel savings, depreciation and interest tax deductions, real estate tax abatements and exemptions, and investment tax credits. Types of costs usually required to achieve such benefits include construction costs, maintenance costs, insurance costs, interest costs, and replacement costs. Methods for comparing benefits with costs include simple and discounted payback period, simple and discounted return on investment, and net present value. All these concepts are described in the following pages.

Commercial buildings in urban settings are emphasized in contrast to the emphasis in most other energy references, which focus on the single-family house. Nonresidential urban buildings typically have huge energy bills for lighting, often substantially higher than for heating and cooling combined. In this case, the light of the sun as well as its heat is an important nondepletable energy resource. For this reason, the book includes a number of methods for estimating natural-light levels inside buildings and describes the costs and technology required to capitalize on daylighting.

A DESIGN EVALUATION PROCESS

A process for evaluating energy-conscious designs is diagramed in Figure 1-1. It begins with the designer identifying comfort needs and climate resources and then proposing a design which will save the building on which he or she is working some amount of fuel. The design may involve the site, the form of the building, the intensity of the use of the building, and/or some aspect of the physical components of the building. An energy-conscious design may reduce a building's need for energy, or it may reduce its dependence on some depletable source of fuel such as oil and make it possible instead to use a renewable source such as the sun or the earth. A description of some of the fuel-saving methods that a designer might employ is presented in Chapter 4. Each method is described in relation to its contribution to the thermal or luminous requirements of a building and to the general design considerations that may be important when a particular design is employed.

The designer must next analyze the proposed design and identify every type of energy flow caused or affected by the design. If the design affects thermal energy flows, the specific type of flow as well as the season in which the flow will occur must be identified. If the design affects the lighting of the building, the source, direction, and intensity of the natural light must be identified. The principles of natural energy flows in buildings are described in Chapter 2.

Once the energy flows have been identified, the designer must select a calculation method to estimate fuel savings. As the reader will see, many architectural designs for saving energy involve more than one type of thermal heat transfer mode to create fuel savings. Furthermore, many cause both thermal and lighting fuel savings.

Most of the thermal estimating methods presented at this stage of the process estimate either the hourly rate of energy flows affected by a design or the overall change in annual energy consumption. Chapters 7, 8, and 9 describe these methods.

The next step of the evaluation process involves translation of the energy flow rates into annual fuel savings. Chapter 6 describes estimating methods for this purpose. The answer at this stage of the analysis will be given in dollars. This will allow the designer to place a value on the fuel savings that his or her design is expected to generate. In other words, the *benefit* expected by the proposed design will be determined. In many cases, however, a design's benefits will cost something to achieve. This cost must be estimated by using normal methods of construction cost estimating. The answer at this stage will be, of course, in dollars as well.

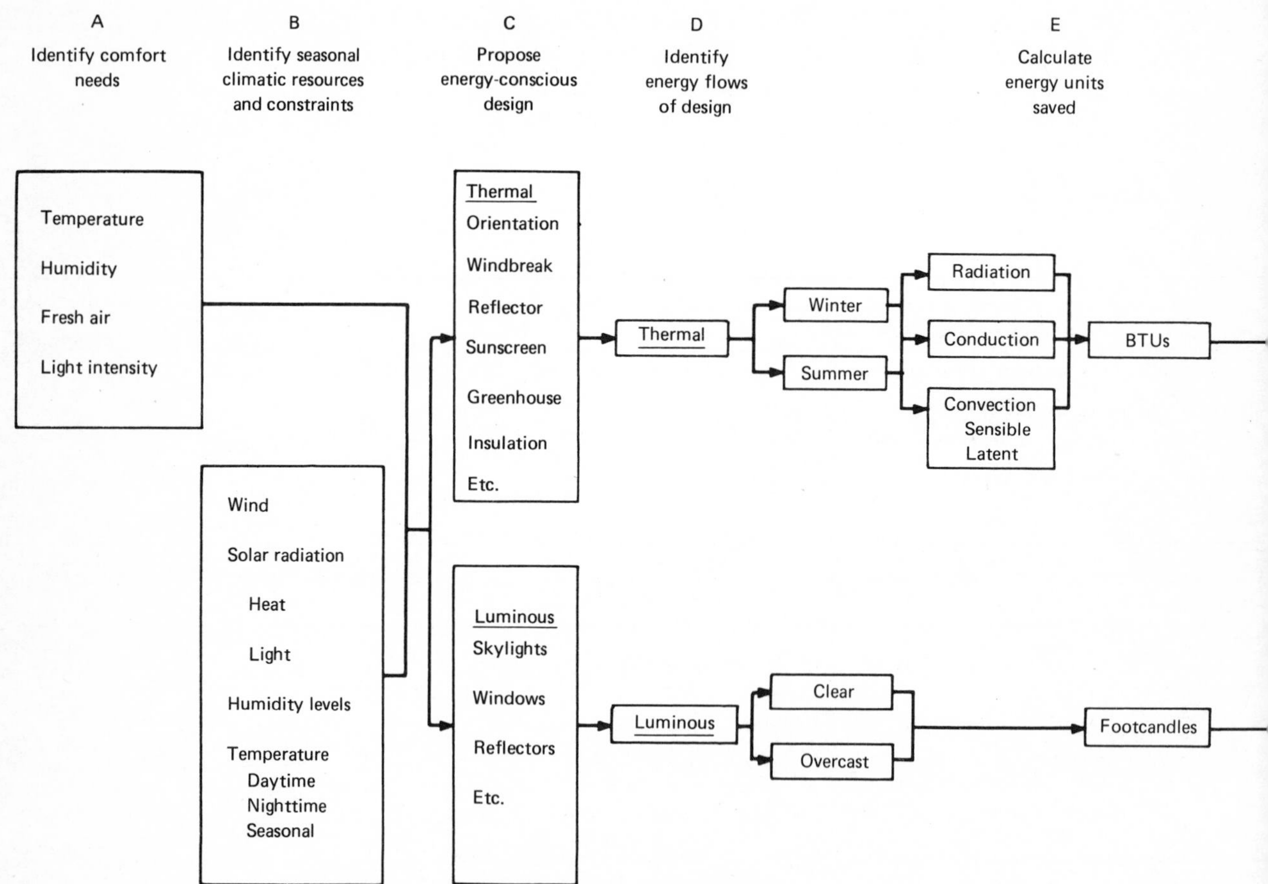

FIGURE 1-1 Process for evaluating energy-conscious building designs.

The last step of the evaluation process is described in Chapter 5. It involves comparing fuel-saving benefits with required construction costs. This chapter describes both simple and more complex methods of calculating payback periods, return on investment, and net present value. The methods presented will allow the designer to acknowledge a number of economic considerations such as depreciation, taxes, financing, and inflation.

The analytic approach which is used in much of this book is called "incremental analysis" or, by some economists, "marginal analysis." That is, the approach is based on estimating the incremental *changes* in the building's fuel consumption and construction costs (and other costs) that energy-conscious designs imply. Changes above and beyond the normal condition are estimated. The normal or base condition used in the analysis is simply the energy use and construction costs that a building would have *without* proposed energy-related design improvements.

The methods described in this book are all usable without computer assistance and without sophisticated mathematical skills. Additional accuracy is possible, of

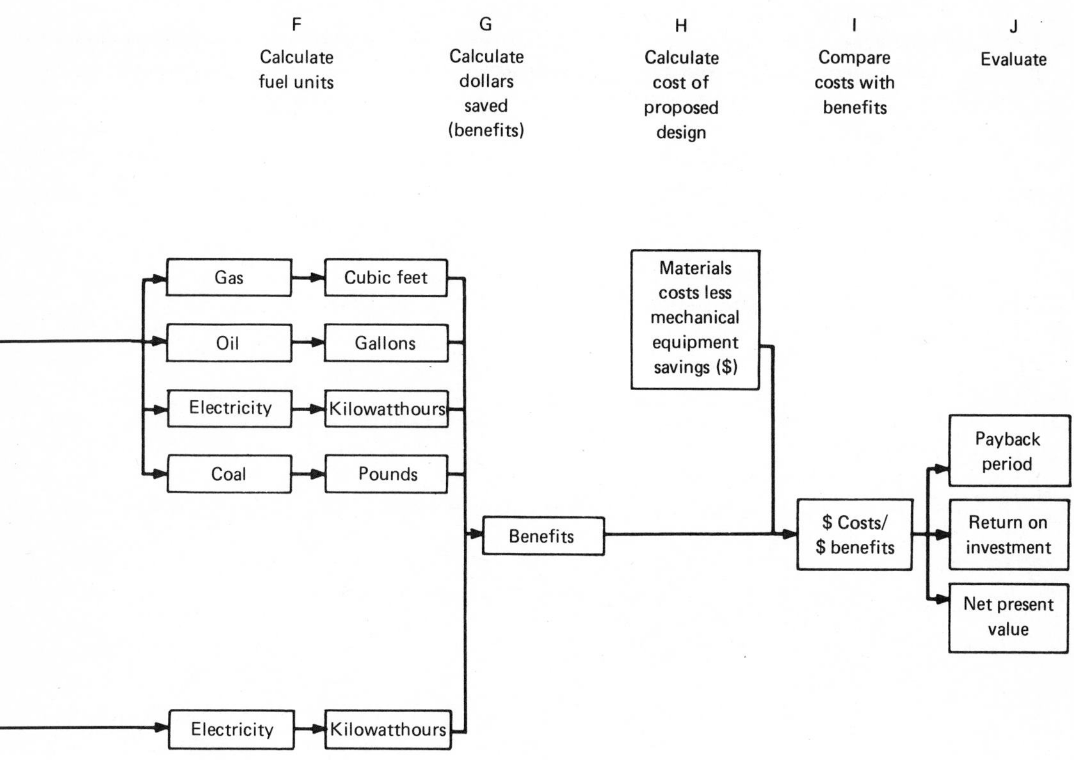

course, with computer use, but the level of accuracy provided by the manual energy estimating methods presented here is commensurate with the accuracy of results from *construction* cost estimating methods. Therefore, until construction cost estimating can become more exact, the methods presented here are quite appropriate for energy-related cost-benefit analysis.

EXAMPLE

The process described above may be illustrated by the following example. A designer proposes to adjust the plan of a proposed office building from the square shape that the client wishes to a rectangle in order to place interior work areas closer to the windows and thereby increase natural-light levels and decrease the need for artificial lighting. The rectangular shape, however, increases the perimeter of the building from 1200 to 1500 linear feet. This creates more surface area to conduct heat out of the building during the winter and into the building during the summer. On the other hand, the increased surface area allows more solar energy to be radiated into the building on the south side in winter. Shading devices already intended for the building keep the sun out of the building in summer. The designer uses methods of estimating winter conductive heat loss and radiative heat gain, summer conductive heat gain, and direct and diffuse natural lighting in the analysis of the proposed design change. The results show that the additional winter heat loss results in a heating expense of $10,000 more per year even with radiative heat gain. Summer air-conditioning costs are $2000 less because of the lower heat load of the lights even though there is a greater conductive heat gain. The lighting analysis shows that electrical savings are $20,000 per year because more lights may be turned off than in the base building design. The summary of the savings is presented below:

Winter heating	−$10,000
Summer air conditioning	+ 2,000
All-year lighting	+ 20,000
Net savings	+$12,000

When analyzing the construction costs of this design, the designer discovers that the increased cost of the exterior wall, foundation, and heating and cooling equipment is $100,000. The designer then moves to the last part of the evaluation. Using a simple approach to cost-benefit analysis, the annual savings are divided by the additional construction costs:

Benefits	$ 12,000/year
Costs	÷ 100,000
	0.12, or 12 percent/year

By this process, it is determined that the simple return on investment generated by the design is 12 percent. The designer is aware that this simple analysis ignores the time value of money and future increases in fuel prices among other things, but the client wishes to consider the results at this stage. After a review, the client states that 12 percent is a somewhat higher percentage than that which other opportunities for investment will yield at an equivalent risk and has concluded that the proposed design is acceptable.

The designer's analysis provides the client with a way of assessing an investment in an energy-saving design in a manner compatible with normal investment decision making.

The decision by the client may be made quickly, and the designer may then proceed with completion of the building project.

Most of the examples presented in this book focus on expressing the results of a thermal or luminous analysis in a cost-benefit ratio of some form. In the following chapters, therefore, basic information dealing with cost-benefit analysis is presented first so that later examples can use cost-benefit concepts with the full understanding of the reader.

TWO

BASIC ENERGY CONSIDERATIONS

To identify the energy flows affected by a particular design approach (Step D, Figure 1-1), it will be necessary for a designer to understand some of the thermal and luminous principles which govern the behavior of architectural environments. A designer must be able to identify these flows so that he or she may properly select the correct method or methods for estimating fuel-saving benefits. Also, of course, knowledge of the laws of thermodynamics and lighting will help a designer to create more energy-effective designs.

In general terms, there are three types of thermal flows and two types of luminous flows in buildings:

1 Thermal energy flows

a. Conduction

b. Convection

c. Radiation

2 Luminous energy flows

a. Direct

b. Indirect

The physical principles which govern these flows will be described in the following paragraphs. The flows will be discussed separately, but in fact most building-related designs affect multiple types of energy flows at the same time. Placing a skylight in a building, for example, will affect primarily four types of energy flow in the building: thermal conduction, thermal radiation, diffuse light, and direct light (see Figure 2-1).

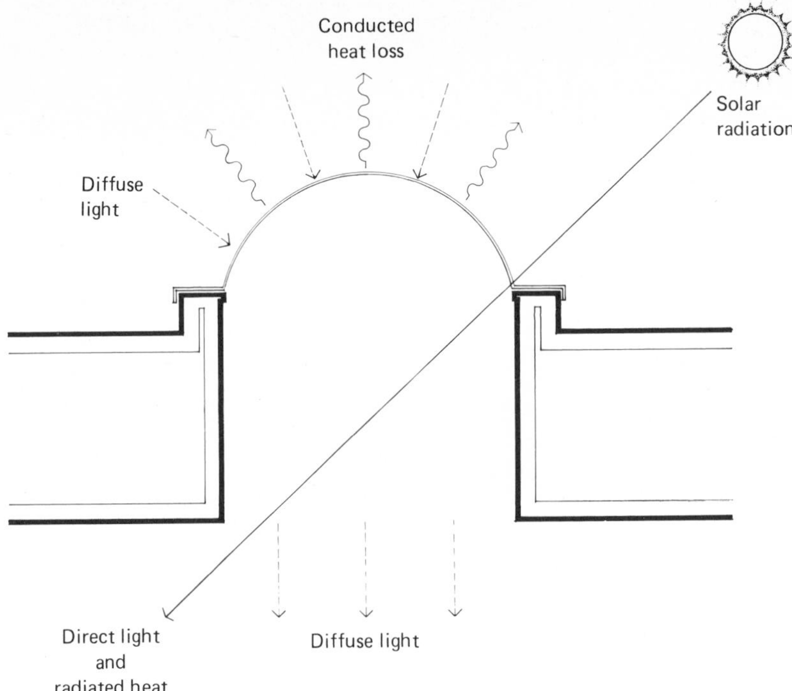

FIGURE 2-1 **Thermal and luminous energy flows through a skylight.**

THERMAL ENERGY

Thermal energy is measured in terms of British thermal units (Btus). A British thermal unit is defined as the amount of heat required to heat one pound of water one degree Fahrenheit at 65°F and at one standard atmosphere. It is transferred from one location to another by three ways: conduction, convection, and/or radiation.

Thermal energy moves from one mass to another whenever the temperatures of the two differ. The direction of the energy movement is from the higher temperature zone to the lower temperature zone. The speed, or rate, at which the energy transfer occurs is usually a function of the *amount* of temperature difference.

Conduction

Conducted thermal energy is transported between parts of a continuum, or mass, owing to the transfer of kinetic energy between particles at the atomic level, typically through a solid such as a metal (see Figure 2-2). Materials which are good conductors of electricity are also typically good conductors of heat. Conduction is the means by which heat flow can occur in solid materials.[1]

[1] *Energy Conservation Design Manual,* Energy Resources Conservation and Development Commission, Sacramento, Calif., 1978, p. 3–2.

Conductivity varies with temperature, although within normal climatic temperature ranges it is usually assumed to be constant. In pure metals, for example, thermal conductivity decreases slightly with temperature increases, and for insulating materials it increases slightly with temperature increases.

Conductivity is measured by so-called *R* values and *U* values and is expressed in terms of a rate of heat flow per unit of temperature over a given cross-sectional area of material.

The basic relationship between critical variables which describes the physical phenomenon of thermal conduction is presented below:

$$q = U \times A \times (t_w - t_c) \tag{2-1}$$

in units,

$$\text{Btu/h} = \text{Btu/(h}\cdot{}^\circ\text{F}\cdot\text{ft}^2) \times \text{ft}^2 \times {}^\circ\text{F}$$

where q = rate of conducted heat flow, Btu/h
U = air-to-air heat transfer coefficient of the material through which heat is being conducted, Btu/(h·°F·ft²)
A = cross-sectional area of material, ft²
t_w = temperature of air next to the warmer surface of the conducting material, °F
t_c = temperature of air next to the cooler surface of the conducting material, °F

This equation will be transformed into a more commonly used version in Chapter 7.

The thermal conductivity of a solid material is often related to its density. Less dense materials such as Styrofoam or fiberglass have low conductivity, while denser materials such as steel or glass have high thermal conductivities.

A designer can cause a change in conductive heat flow by changing any of the values of the critical dependent variables in the above equation. To *decrease* conduction, the heat transfer coefficient *U* of an object may be *decreased*, the area *A* may be *decreased*, the thickness may be *increased*, the cooler temperature condition may be *increased*, or the warmer temperature condition may be *decreased*.

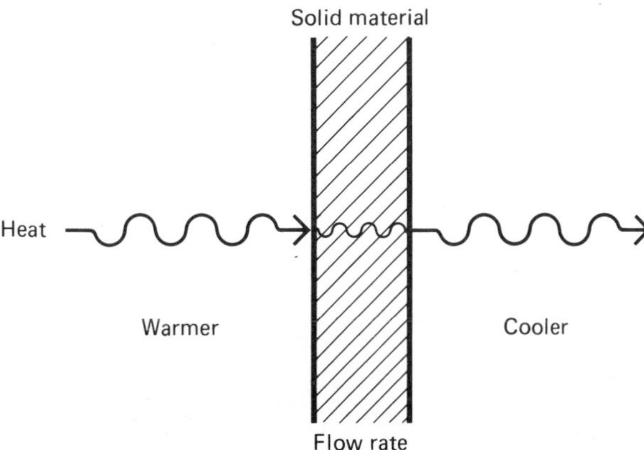

FIGURE 2·2 Conducted heat transfer. Flow rate depends on the area, thickness, and conductivity of the material and the temperature differences between the two sides.

Convection

In general terms, convection is the movement of heat through fluids or gases. Heat transfer by convection typically occurs in a room of a building when air passes over a solid surface of a different temperature or when warmer air moves to a position where colder air exists (Figure 2-3). If the motion of air is caused by some mechanical or artificial means such as a fan or by a pressure difference such as wind, it is called "forced convection." If the movement of air is caused by a density difference due to a temperature difference (for example, warm air rising), the phenomenon is called "natural convection." For example, warm air introduced at the floor of a room will rise to the top of the room and set up air currents or eddies; heat introduced at the top of a room will stay at the top and not result in as much air movement or, hence, heat transfer.

Convection heat transfer, as defined in this book, includes the phenomenon in buildings that has been traditionally called infiltration. It will be linked also to the phenomenon of cooling by evaporation when air moves across a surface and causes a change of state in the moisture on the surface (such as a person's skin).

The rate of fluid-solid convection is a function of the area and shape of the surface of the solid body over which a fluid such as air moves and the temperature difference between the fluid and the solid. Temperature difference is, in general terms, a "potential" difference in the same way as voltage is a potential difference in electricity. And, as in electricity, energy flow is proportional to the difference in potential of such forces.

Convection between air and a surface may be described in more formal terms by the following equation:

$$q = h \times A \times (t_a - t_s) \qquad (2\text{-}2)$$

in units,

$$\text{Btu/h} = \text{Btu/(h}\cdot{}^\circ\text{F}\cdot\text{ft}^2) \times \text{ft}^2 \times {}^\circ\text{F}$$

where q = rate of convective heat flow, Btu/h

h = film conductance of the surface over which air is moving and through which heat is being transferred, Btu/(h·°F·ft²)

A = area of surface over which air is passing, ft²

t_a = temperature of air, °F

t_s = temperature of the surface, °F

Note that Equation (2-2) is similar in form to the equation for conducted heat transfer.

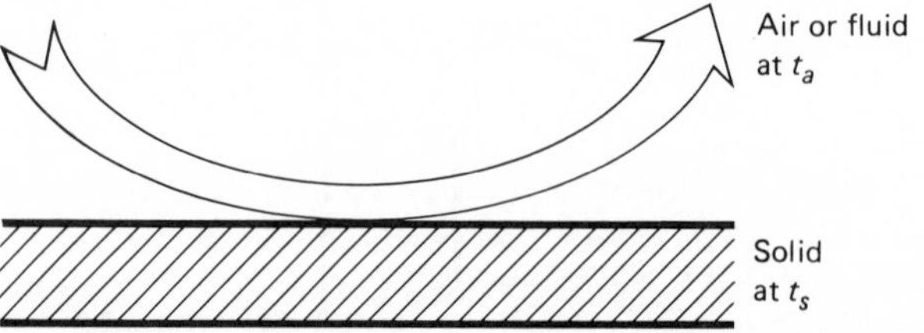

FIGURE 2-3 Convected heat transfer between air and a solid surface.

Convection heat transfer solely *within* air may be described by the following equation:

$$q = c \times V \times d(t_1 - t_2) \tag{2-3}$$

in units,

$$\text{Btu/h} = \text{Btu/(lb}\cdot{}^\circ\text{F)} \times \text{ft}^3 \times \text{lb/ft}^3 \times {}^\circ\text{F}$$

where q = rate of convective heat flow, Btu/h
c = specific heat of air, 0.24 Btu/(lb·°F)
V = volume of air being moved, ft^3/h
d = density of air (assume 0.075 lb/ft^3)
t_1 = temperature of air at location 1, °F
t_2 = temperature of air at location 2, °F

Radiation

Heat transfer can also take place between two bodies even when there is no solid or fluid connection between them. This process is called, of course, radiation. In this case, energy is transmitted through space either by electromagnetic waves or by photons, depending on which scientific theory is accepted.

Heat transfer takes place through a change in energy form: from internal energy at the source to electromagnetic energy or photons for transmission, then back to internal energy at the receiver. Radiation is distinguished from conduction and convection in that it doesn't depend on the presence of an intermediate material as a carrier. It is, however, impeded by such a material.

A person standing at one end of a room with a metal floor below and a stove at the other end would be receiving heat by all three thermal heat transfer processes. Heat would be conducted through the metal floor, convected by moving air currents, and radiated from the stove to the person's skin (Figure 2-4).

The primary radiation sources with which architectural designers must deal are the *sun's* radiation and the thermal radiation between human beings and architectural surfaces.[2]

Heat transfer by radiation depends on the surface condition of both the emitting material and the receiving material. The concepts which help to describe the radiation-related properties of such surfaces are emissivity, absorptivity, reflectivity, and transmissivity.

Emissivity, designated by ϵ, is the ability of a material and its surface to radiate or emit energy. Rough surfaces emit radiation better than highly polished surfaces.

Absorptivity (α), as one might expect, is the ability of a material and its surface to absorb heat. In opaque materials, whatever energy is not absorbed is reflected so that the two concepts represent mutually exclusive phenomena. In terms of reflectivity (ρ), the more dense and smooth a surface, the more reflective it is. In terms of color, darker colors are more absorptive than lighter colors. For example,

[2]The latter is part of a phenomenon called "mean radiant temperature" and is beyond the scope of this book.

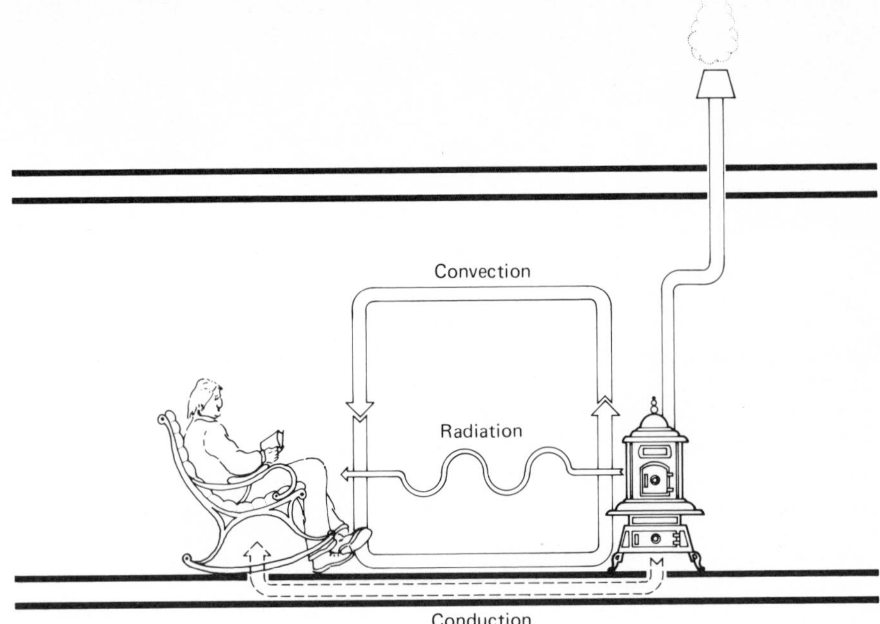

FIGURE 2-4 Radiated, conducted, and convected heat transfer.

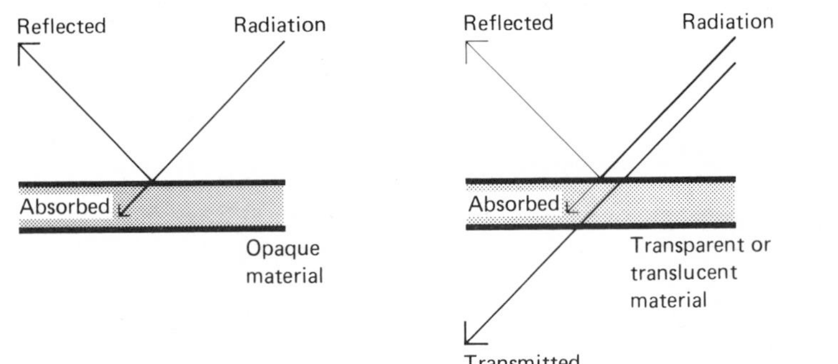

FIGURE 2-5 Reflection, absorption, and transmission in opaque and transparent materials.

a material painted with flat black paint will absorb 90 percent of the solar radiation that falls on it, whereas aluminized Mylar film absorbs only a small percentage. (Table 7-21 in Chapter 7 shows the relative absorptance of various materials.)

If a material is translucent or transparent, a third phenomenon takes place: transmission of the radiation (τ). Thus, thermal energy striking such a surface will be partially reflected, partially absorbed, and partially transmitted (see Figure 2-5). The relationship between these three variables is expressed below:[3]

$$\rho + \alpha + \tau = 1 \tag{2-4}$$

where ρ = reflectance of radiated energy *from* a surface, no units
α = absorptance of radiated energy *by* a surface, no units
τ = transmittance of radiated energy *through* a surface material, no units

[3]Ibid., p. 3–8.

Transmission of heat through glass causes a particularly useful change in the energy transferred. Glass is not a good transmitter of thermal radiation, but it is a good transmitter of light. In a greenhouse, for example, sunlight passes easily through the glass walls and gets absorbed by opaque materials within the greenhouse. The thermal energy that these materials emit back to the glass is partly absorbed by the glass and *not* transmitted directly. The absorbed heat in the glass, of course, eventually conducts its way to the outer surface of the glass, where it is finally emitted to the outside. This phenomenon has been termed the "greenhouse effect" and has become the basis for a number of fuel-saving design strategies discussed in Chapter 7 (see Figure 2-6).

Since solar radiation is one of the major radiation sources discussed in this book, some of its characteristics relative to building applications need to be reviewed. The earth moves around the sun once a year, rotating around its axis once every 24 hours. The axis is tilted at a 23.5° angle relative to the sun (see Figure 2-7). As one can see, the tilted axis of the earth causes the sun to strike the northern hemisphere at a relatively low angle (or altitude) in the winter and a relatively high angle in the summer. (For exact sun angles at various times of day and year and location, see Table 7-14 in Chapter 7.) This axis tilt also causes the sun to appear to "rise" in the *north*east in the summer months in the northern hemisphere and in the *south*east during the winter. The angle of the sun with respect to due south is called the sun's azimuth (see also Table 7-14 for azimuth angles).

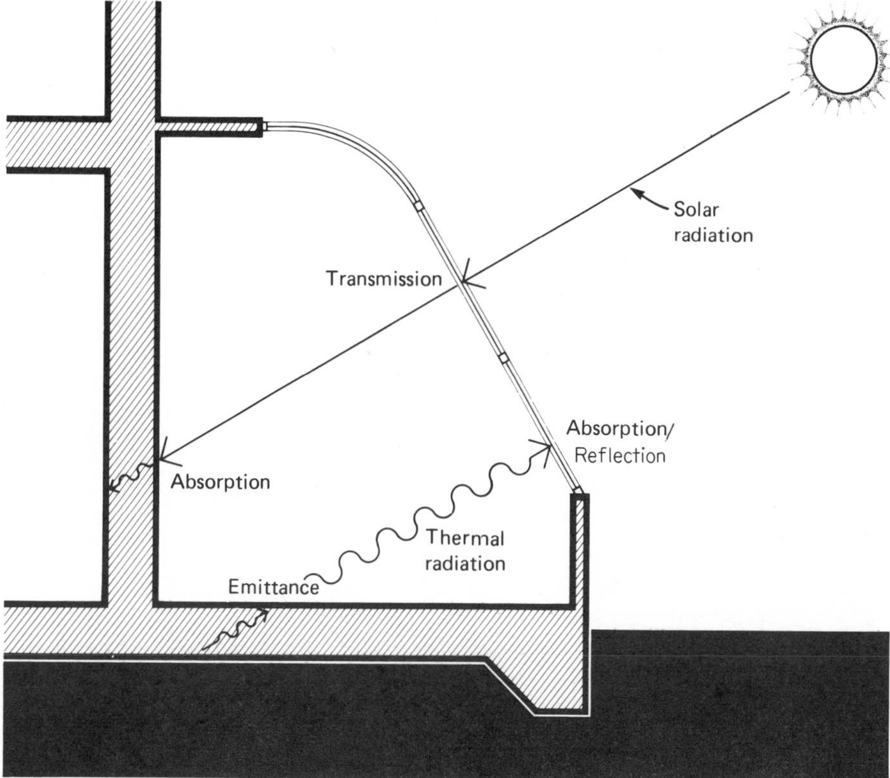

FIGURE 2-6 Light and heat radiation in greenhouses.

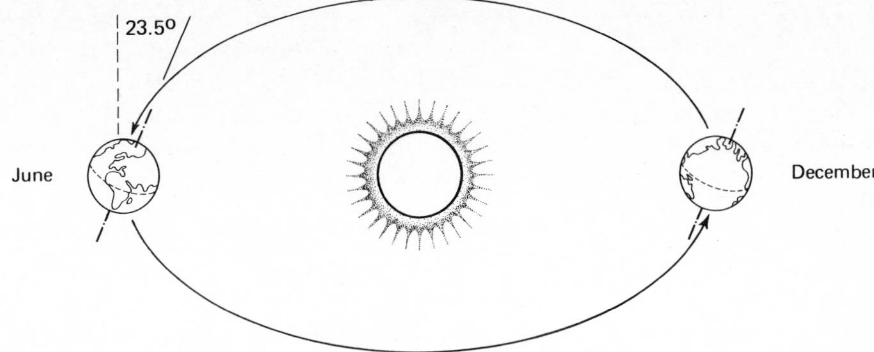

FIGURE 2-7 The earth's tilt in its orbit around the sun.

The angle of incidence is the angle of the sun's rays with respect to a line perpendicular to the surface that the rays strike (see Figure 2-8). This angle is calculated for the designer in most of the tables that need to be used for estimating natural-light intensity (see Table 10-7). The examples presented later in this book will show how the angle-of-incidence information may be used in an energy consumption estimate.

The formal expression of the physical characteristics of radiation is presented below. Note that, unlike convection or conduction, the heat transfer rate in radiation increases with the temperature difference to the *fourth* power, or much more rapidly than with the other two thermal transfer modes.

$$q = \sigma \times \epsilon \times A(t_1^4 - t_2^4) \tag{2-5}$$

in units,

$$\text{Btu/h} = \text{Btu/(h}\cdot\text{ft}^2\cdot{}^\circ\text{F)} \times \text{ft}^2 \times {}^\circ\text{F}$$

where q = rate of radiative heat flow, Btu/h
σ = Stefan-Boltzmann constant, 1.7135×10^{-9}, Btu/(h·ft²·°F)
ϵ = emittance of surface, no units
A = area of radiating surface, ft²
t_1 = absolute temperature of the radiating body, °F
t_2 = surface temperature of the absorbing body, °F

LUMINOUS ENERGY

Light is measured by a *lumen*, which is defined as the light emitted by a single candle. The intensity of that light is a function of the distance from the light source. The intensity of light one foot away from a candle on a surface one foot square is called a *footcandle*. In other words:

$$1 \text{ fc} = 1 \text{ lm/ft}^2$$

Light energy striking an opaque surface is partly absorbed and partly reflected. Light striking a translucent or transparent surface is partly absorbed, partly transmitted, and partly reflected. Light which enters a building space becomes heat as soon as it is absorbed by surfaces within the space.

Sunlight, or solar radiation, is about one-half visible energy, or light, and one-half invisible energy. The invisible portion is made up of shorter wavelengths called ultraviolet and longer wavelengths called infrared. When both visible and invisible solar radiation is absorbed by a material, it becomes heat.

Natural light for a building, as described in greater detail in Chapter 10, comes directly and indirectly from the sun. Direct solar illumination is not, of course, obstructed in its path from the sun to a building. Its angle of arrival on a building's surface varies constantly, as described above in the subsection "Radiation." Intensity of direct sunlight can be greater than 9000 footcandles.

Indirect natural light is sunlight which has been reflected off particles and surfaces before it reaches a building. There are two basic categories of indirect sunlight: skylight and ground-reflected light. Skylight is sunlight which has been reflected off particles in the atmosphere. Ground-reflected light is sunlight reflected off the surfaces of objects resting on the ground plane, including buildings, trees, lakes, pavements, and many others. Indirect sunlight rarely gets above intensities of 1000 footcandles.

Light, as does any form of radiation, behaves according to the inverse-square law. This law states that the illumination intensity, usually measured in footcandles, or lumens per square foot, varies inversely with the square of the distance

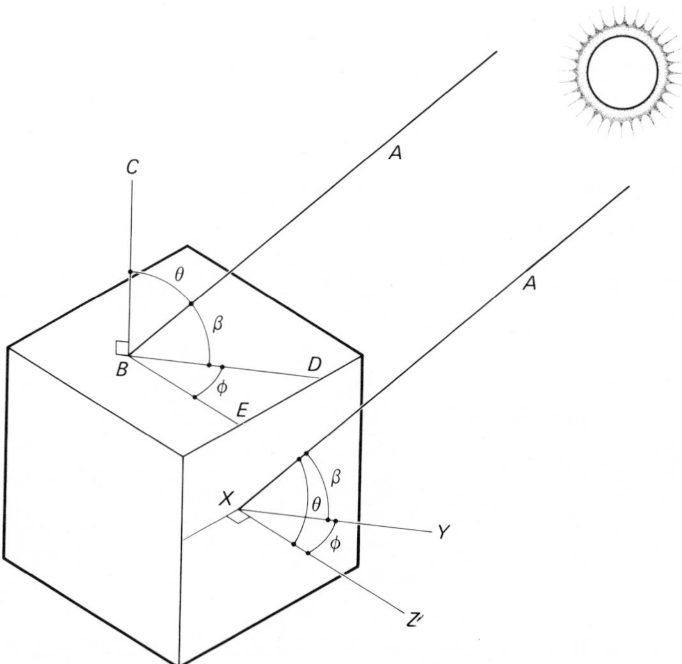

FIGURE 2-8 Solar angles. Symbols: β = solar altitude; ϕ = solar azimuth; θ = angle of incidence. For horizontal surfaces, β = solar altitude = $\angle ABD$; ϕ = solar azimuth = $\angle DBE$; θ = angle of incidence = $\angle ABC$; $\cos\theta = \sin\beta$; and angle of incidence and solar altitude = 90°. For vertical surfaces, β = solar altitude = $\angle AXY$; ϕ = solar azimuth = $\angle YXZ$; θ = angle of incidence = $\angle AXZ$.

between the source and the surface being measured. If the surface is perpendicular to the light, the law takes the following form:

$$E = I/d^2 \tag{2-6}$$

in units,

$$\text{lm/ft}^2 = \text{lm} \div \text{ft}^2$$

where E = intensity of surface illumination, lm/ft^2
I = intensity of the light source, lm
d = distance between the source and a plane illuminated by the source, ft

Light also behaves according to the cosine law. This law states that illumination intensity varies according to the cosine of the angle of incidence with a surface. The angle of incidence is the angle between a line perpendicular to a surface and the light (for example, the cosine of 0° is 1).

This means that when the angle of incidence is other than 0° or when light is falling at an angle other than perpendicular to a plane, the inverse-square law takes the following form:

$$E = \frac{I}{d^2} \cos\theta \tag{2-7}$$

in units,

$$\text{lm/ft}^2 = \text{lm} \div \text{ft}^2$$

where θ = angle of incidence of light falling on a surface, no units

The diagram in Figure 2-9 shows graphically the relationship between these variables. In terms of another distance, h, which is perpendicular to the plane of illumination,

$$\text{Cos}\,\theta = h/d, \text{ or } d = h/\cos\theta$$

Substituting $d = h/\cos\theta$ in the inverse-square law, the equation for that law in terms of height h becomes

$$E = \frac{I\cos\theta}{h^2/\cos^2\theta} = \frac{I\cos^3\theta}{h^2} \tag{2-8}$$

This equation is called the cosine-cubed law.

The application of these general equations in estimating change in the rate of heat or light transfer in buildings is presented in Chapters 6 through 10.

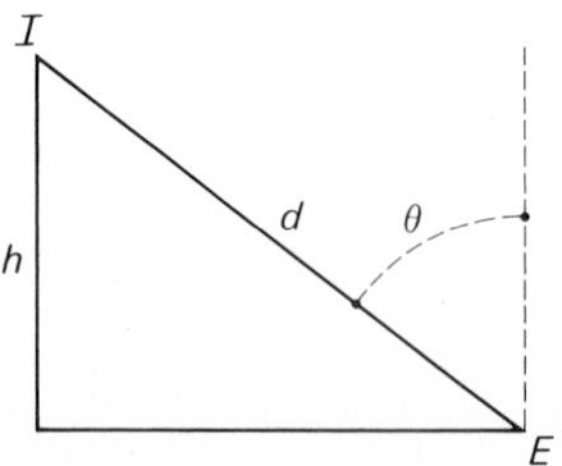

FIGURE 2-9 The inverse-square law and the cosine-cubed law.

$$E = \frac{I}{d^2}\cos\theta \qquad \cos\theta = h/d$$

$$d = h/\cos\theta \qquad E = \frac{I\cos^3\theta}{h^2}$$

BIBLIOGRAPHY

ASHRAE Handbook and Product Directory—1977 Fundamentals Volume, American Society of Heating, Refrigerating and Air-Conditioning Engineers, Inc., New York, 1977.

Energy Conservation Design Manual, Energy Resources Conservation and Development Commission, Sacramento, Calif., 1978.

Mazria, Edward: *The Passive Solar Energy Book*, Rodale Press, Inc., Emmaus, Pa., 1979.

Ozisik, M. Necati: *Basic Heat Transfer*, McGraw-Hill Book Company, New York, 1977.

Recommended Practice of Daylighting, Illuminating Engineering Society of North America, New York, 1979.

THREE

HISTORICAL ENERGY-CONSCIOUS DESIGN

This chapter documents some of the work of formally trained architects in their attempts to design energy-conscious buildings. It deals with "high-style" architecture, not with the work of indigenous populations. The latter has been reviewed and described by many other authors who wrote about building approaches such as the pueblos of the southwestern American Indian tribes, the igloos of the Eskimos, and the underground houses of African peoples. Most of this work, however, was an architecture of climatic extremes. Many of the designers who might be tempted to read this book will be confronted with much more moderate climatic contexts. The historical examples that are presented here, therefore, were selected because they were designed for more middle-of-the-road climates. In some cases, the designer seemed to know something about energy use in buildings. In other cases, an architectural form that had potential for conserving energy was developed but was used incorrectly by the original designer, suggesting no energy-conscious intention. Such examples are presented here because they represent part of a formal tradition that designers can draw upon in their attempts to design for energy conservation.

OVERHANGS AS PORTICOES, LOGGIAS, AND PORCHES

Some form of exterior shading device on buildings has been used by architects for centuries. The energy-saving and/or comfort-providing benefit of such a device is created because of the manner in which the sun's altitude varies between summer and winter in latitudes substantially north or south of the equator such as those found in most of Europe, Australia, and the United States. At 40° north latitude, in New York, for example, the sun at twelve o'clock noon in June is at 72° from the horizontal plane, whereas at the same time in December it is only 27° from the horizontal. A properly dimensioned south-facing window will let the winter

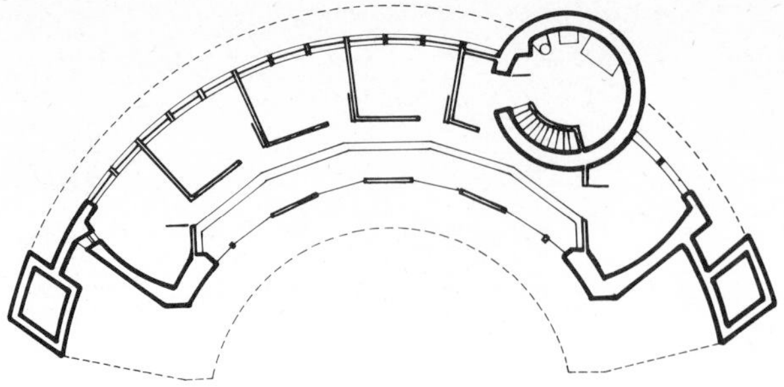

Second-Floor Plan

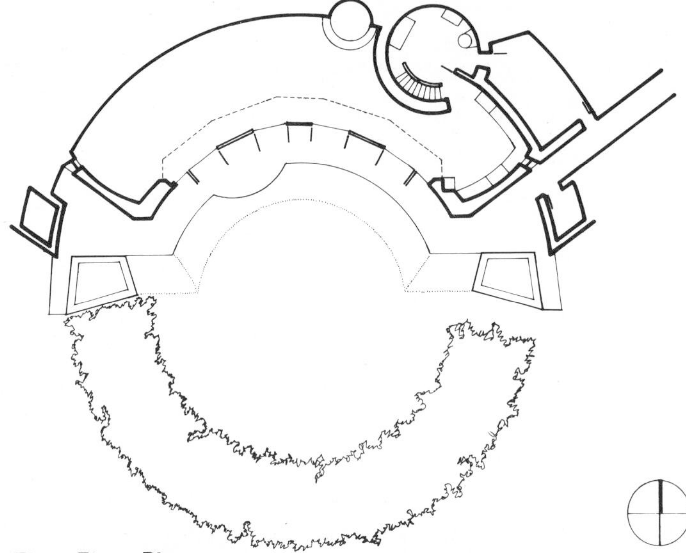

First-Floor Plan

FIGURE 3-1 Plans and photograph of Jacobs House Number II, in Middleton, Wisconsin, by Frank Lloyd Wright, 1943. [*Plans drawn by the author. Photograph: Ezra Stoller, Copyright © ESTO.*]

sun into a building to help heat the interior and, during the summer, will keep the sun out when it is undesirable for human comfort. This architectural device is present in much of Frank Lloyd Wright's work, of course, but it can take a number of different forms.

The house in Figure 3-1 is Wright's Jacobs House Number II, in Middleton, Wisconsin. The overhang shades the curved south-facing glass facade. The house also has a number of other energy-conscious design features worth noting. The main living spaces all face south, while auxiliary spaces such as bathrooms are placed on the north side. The house is curved to the south, reflecting the apparent rotation of the sun in the sky. It is not clear that the curve increases the overall collection of solar radiation by the house when compared with a straight south-

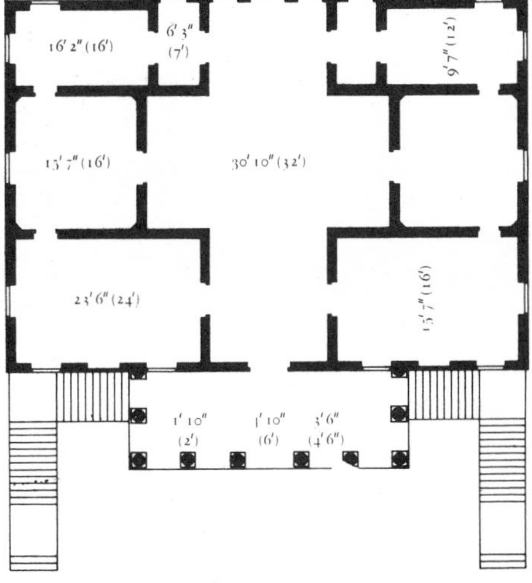

FIGURE 3-2 Plan and photograph of Villa Foscari, by Andrea Palladio, sixteenth century. [*Plan: James S. Ackerman,* Palladio, *Penguin Books, Inc., New York, 1976. Photograph: Phyllis Massar, New York.*]

facing facade, but it probably doesn't decrease the sun's input either, and it adds other desirable features to the design of the house. Lastly, the house is enclosed by earth on the north, east, and west exposures. This reduces winter heat loss and summer heat gain through the exterior walls by providing a constant outside temperature of about 50°F. (See Chapter 9 for a more detailed discussion of earth-covered buildings.

Andrea Palladio also made a very formal element out of an overhang in many of his buildings. The use of a portico, or entry porch, as a shading device is illustrated in his Villa Foscari (Figure 3-2). Here, the windows of some of the rooms adjacent to the portico are shaded, while others are not. The architect undoubtedly had greater concern for the porch as a means for designating the entrance to the building than as a means for shading, although both benefits were provided.

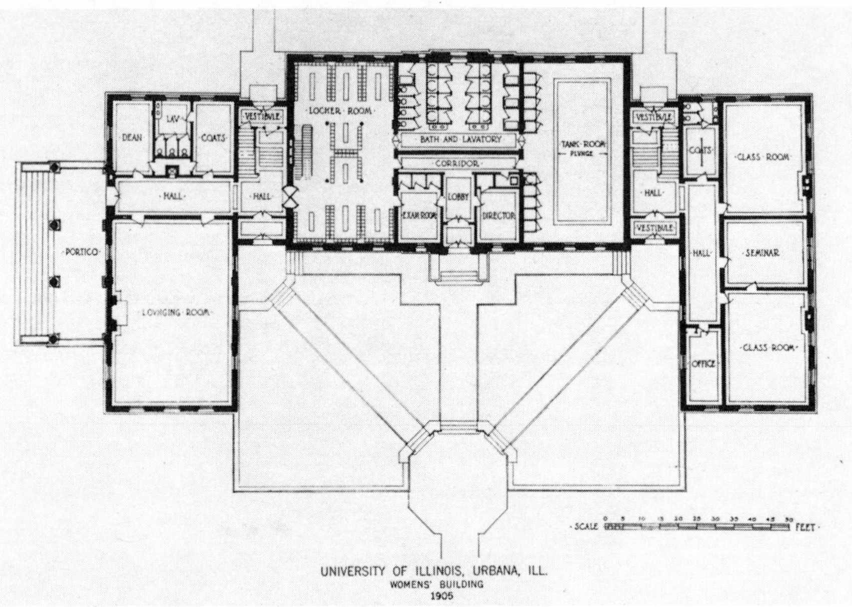

FIGURE 3-3 Plan and photograph of the Women's Building, University of Illinois, Urbana, Illinois, by McKim, Mead and White, 1905. *[Reprinted by Benjamin Blom, Inc., 1973. Distributed by Arno Press, Inc.]*

Later, nineteenth- and early-twentieth-century architects used the overhang portico in a manner similar to Palladio's designs. Figure 3-3 shows a college building by McKim, Mead and White with a colonnaded portico shading its entrance facade.

The use of an overhang as a loggia, or an exterior circulation zone, is illustrated in Palladio's design for the loggia around the Palazzo della Ragione in Vicenza (Figure 3-4). In the Mediterranean climate, the loggia provides an effective shad-

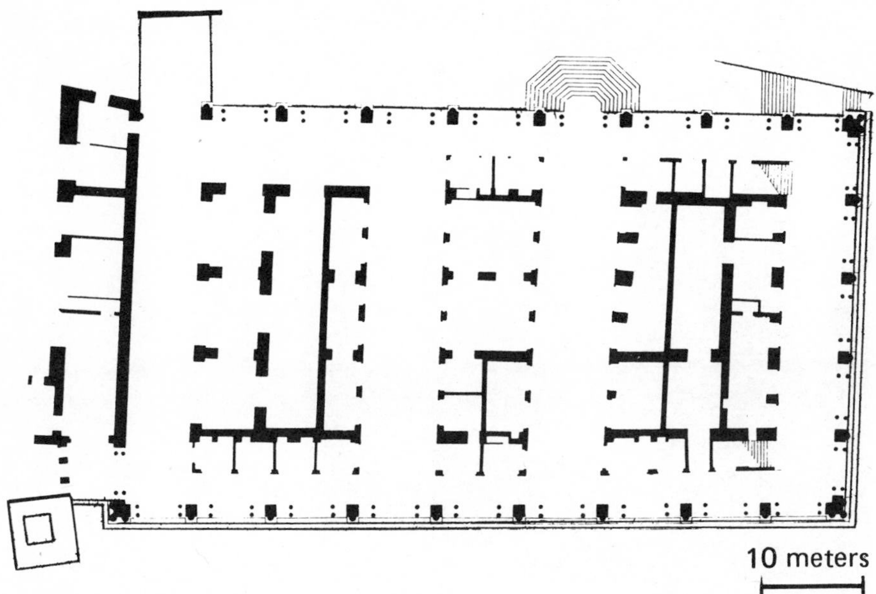

FIGURE 3-4 Plan and photograph of the loggia for the Palazzo della Ragione, in Vicenza, Italy, by Andrea Palladio, designed 1546–1549. [*Plan: James S. Ackerman,* Palladio, *Penguin Books, Inc., New York, 1976. Photograph: Phyllis Massar, New York.*]

ing of the building's facades. The loggia was also called a piazza, terrace, or veranda in later American architecture.

The Georgian houses of the southern United States, with their extensive verandas as shown in Figure 3-5, are good examples of porch applications. Other veranda designs are present in a Victorian-style house designed by McKim,

FIGURE 3-5 **Photograph of a nineteenth-century house in Charleston, South Carolina.** [*Charles W. Moore, Gerald Allen, and D. Lyndon,* The Place of Houses, *Holt, Rinehart and Winston, Inc., New York, 1974, p. 196.*]

FIGURE 3-6 **Photograph of a Victorian house for Charles G. Francklyn in Elberon, New Jersey, by McKim, Mead and White, 1876.** [*Arnold Lewis (intro.),* American Victorian Architecture, *Dover Publications, Inc., New York, 1975, p. 100.*]

Mead and White (Figure 3-6) and the shingle-style design by Arthur Rich (Figure 3-7).

The earlier historical examples did not always create an energy-conscious solution. Sometimes, for example, the overhang-and-balcony combination was on the north side. Sometimes it was too deep to admit the winter sun. Nevertheless, the design precedent was established by these early styles and incorporated into a formal design approach that is part of an architectural heritage from which designers might draw in efforts to make contemporary buildings more energy-efficient.

This design approach was used, more recently for example, in a house designed by the author in 1978 for builder markets in the northeastern United States (Figure 3-8). In this case, the overhang-and-balcony combination is placed only on the south side and is dimensioned specifically to shade during the summer and admit the sun's rays during the winter.

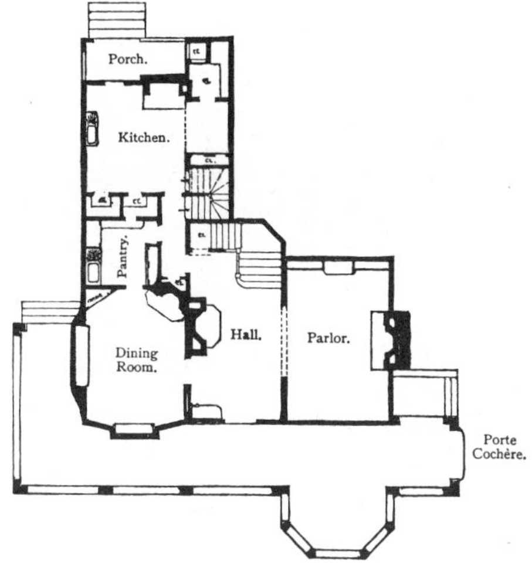

FIGURE 3-7 Plan and photograph of a shingle-style house in Port Chester, New York, by Arthur Rich, 1885. [*Vincent Scully, Jr.,* The Shingle Style and the Stick Style, *Yale University Press, New Haven, Conn., 1955*]

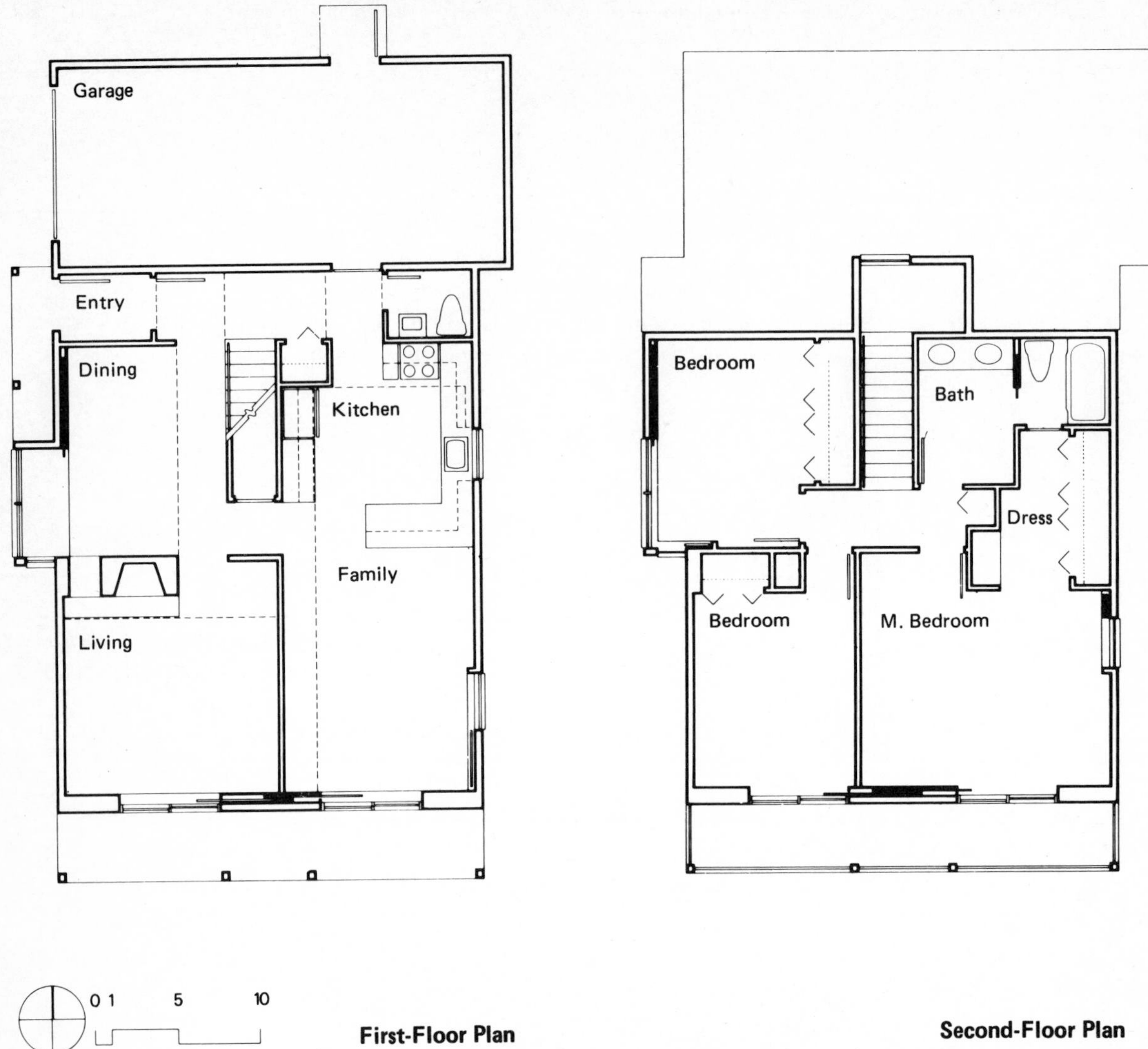

FIGURE 3-8 **Plans and photograph of a house designed for Exxon Enterprises, Inc., in Washington Township, New Jersey, by William Meyer and Carl Meinhardt while principals of The Ehrenkrantz Group, 1977.** [*Photograph by the author. Drawings: The Ehrenkrantz Group.*]

This house also happens to recall the saltbox form of early New England houses. If the "lean-to" portion of this form faces north, the long, sloping roof has the potential of deflecting northerly prevailing winter winds, while the higher south facade may be glazed for solar heat gain.

LANTERNS, BELVEDERES, AND CLERESTORIES

Another building form that is a highly visible part of the American architectural heritage is a small, sometimes glassed-in room that appears on the peaks of roofs.

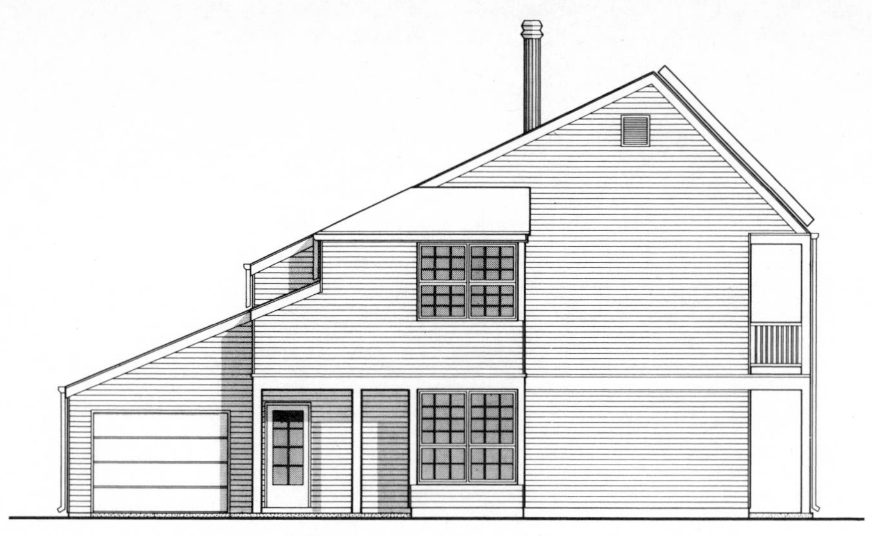

Front Elevation

It resembles a belfry on a church and often appears on barns as well as on residential and sometimes commercial buildings. Its decorative purpose seems to be the visual terminus of and emphasis to the top of a pitched-roof structure. Its original functional purpose was usually to provide ventilation to the attic below the roof.

This roof ornament may be seen in its glassed-in form on a house in Brunswick, Maine (Figure 3-9), or on a house in West Salem, Wisconsin (Figure 3-10), both of which have unknown architects but are clearly patterned after the formal styles of their east coast and European predecessors.

FIGURE 3-9 **Photograph of a house in Brunswick, Maine, with a roof belvedere.** [*Photograph by the author.*]

FIGURE 3-10 Photograph of a house in West Salem, Wisconsin, with a roof belvedere. [*Photograph by the author.*]

Designs by some of the American architects of the nineteenth and early twentieth centuries which have rather ornate lanterns include the auditorium building for Vassar College (Figure 3-11) by McKim, Mead and White.

The belvedere, particularly with glass walls, has fuel-saving and comfort-providing potential. If the belvedere is connected not only to the attic but to the living spaces below, it will provide a means for increasing natural ventilation in a number of ways. First, the high position of the belvedere will provide an opening for the warmest air in the structure to escape during the summer. Also, when there are summer breezes, the belvedere will provide an additional outlet, facilitating movement of air through the spaces of the building (Figure 3-12).

When the sun strikes the south-facing glass of a belvedere, another phenomenon takes place. Solar radiation will heat the surfaces on the inside of the belvedere. Painting these surfaces a dark color will, of course, add to solar absorption. The heated surfaces will be in contact with air, and convection will be established. Warmer air will rise to the peak of the belvedere and escape to the outside. This will leave a partial vacuum, that is, a lowered-pressure area in the belvedere, which will be quickly filled by higher-pressure air from the rooms below. As long as the sun shines, movement of air within the building up and out the belvedere will occur. This sun-induced convection will help to make the occupants of the building feel cooler because the moving air will cause evaporation to occur on their skin. The cooling effect of the evaporation will make the air temperature level tolerable inside the building during the summer and reduce the need for air conditioning.

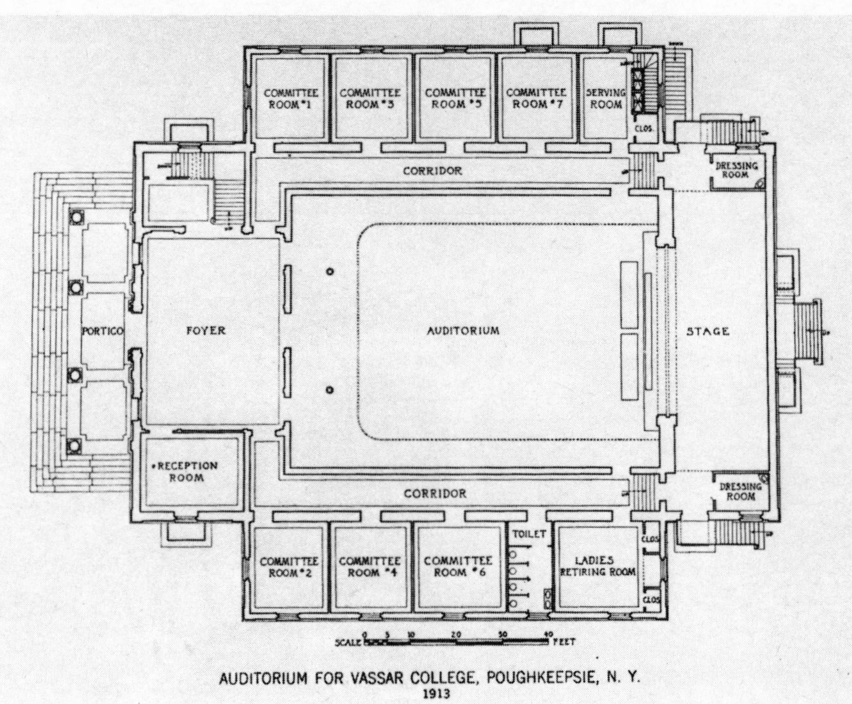

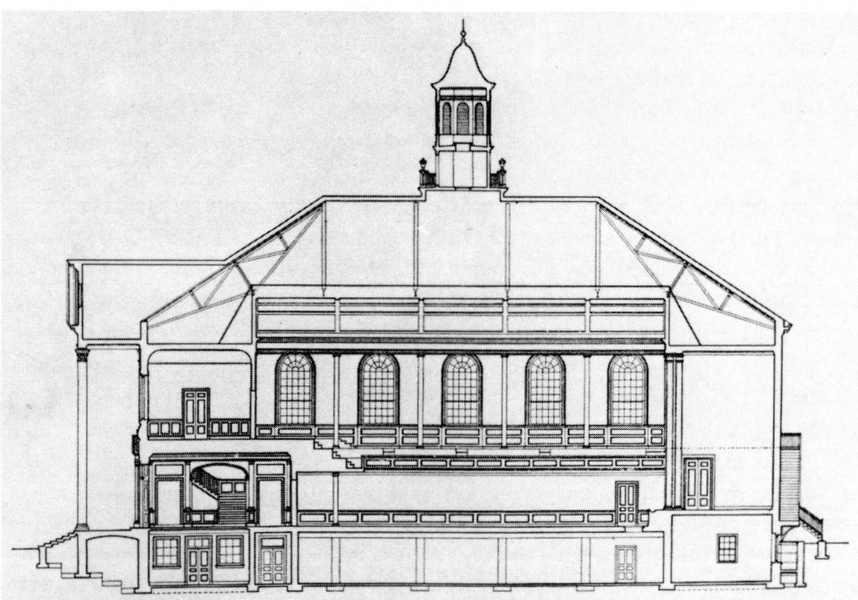

AUDITORIUM FOR VASSAR COLLEGE, POUGHKEEPSIE, N. Y.
1913

FIGURE 3-11 Drawings and photograph of the auditorium building for Vassar College, by McKim, Mead and White, 1913. [*Reprinted by Benjamin Blom, Inc., 1973. Distributed by Arno Press, Inc.*]

Fuel savings will occur, of course, only if the building is air-conditioned. An analysis of the thermal benefits of a belvedere will show that an air conditioner will need to be on for less time during the summer than it would be if a belvedere weren't part of the structure. An air conditioner might need to come on, for example, only after the outside air temperature reaches 90°F instead of 85°, depending on the level of humidity, of course. Chapter 8 will present methods for estimating the cooling benefits provided by a belvedere.

The drawings in Figure 3-12 show how a belvederelike design might be incorporated into a townhouse design. In this case, the belvedere occurs over the stairwell, providing an open vertical path through the building for solar-induced and wind-induced air movement during the summer months.

The high space which is required for a belvedere to operate is a potential detriment during the heating season. Warm air will rise to the top of the high space and remain there. With no adjustment for this problem, fuel would be consumed in such a design only to provide heat for a space which has no functional use. This problem may be minimized by a number of different approaches. The warm air at the top of the belvedere may be moved by fans and ducts to other spaces in the dwelling which need heat. Such mechanical equipment, of course, requires additional investment. Alternatively, old-fashioned exposed ceiling fans may be used to drive the warm air at the top of the high space down to the lower occupied portions of the building. Such fans are much less expensive than ductwork and provide an opportunity for improving summer comfort as well. It should also be

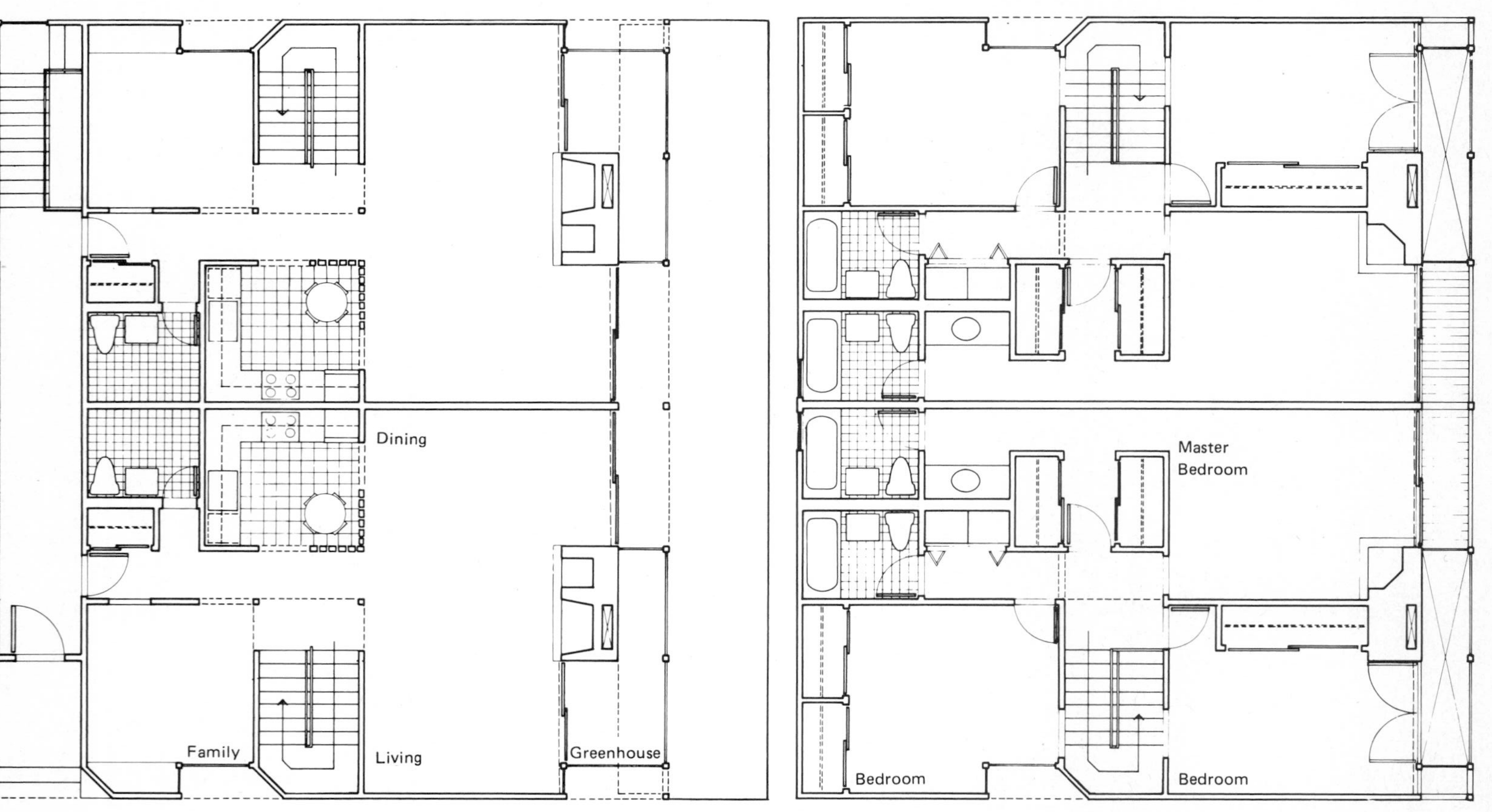

Ground-Floor Plan

Second-Floor Plan

FIGURE 3-12 Drawings of a house with a belvedere design in Brookside, New York, designed for Carl Kahmi by William Meyer and Peter Wormser, 1979. [*Drawings by L. F. Tantillo.*]

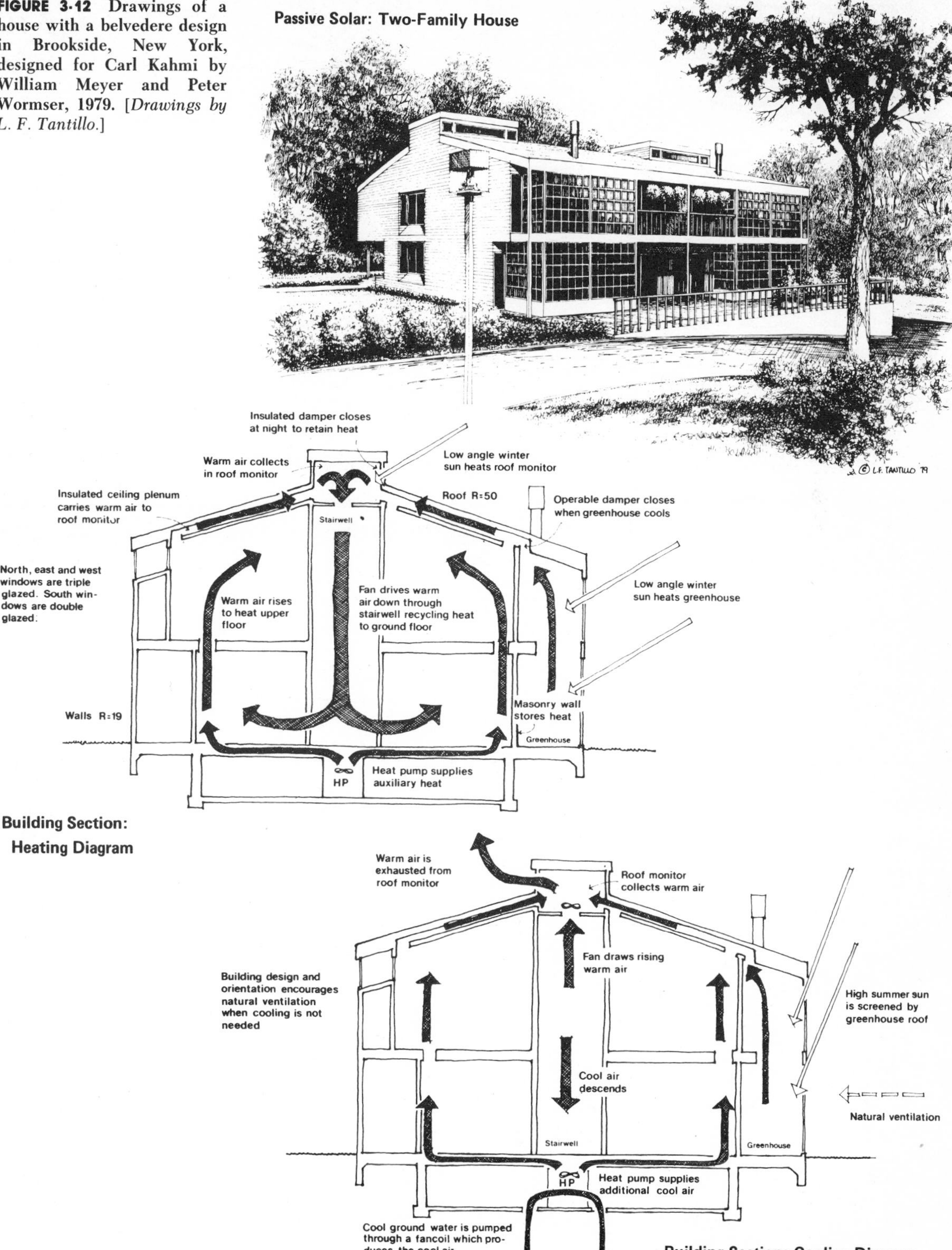

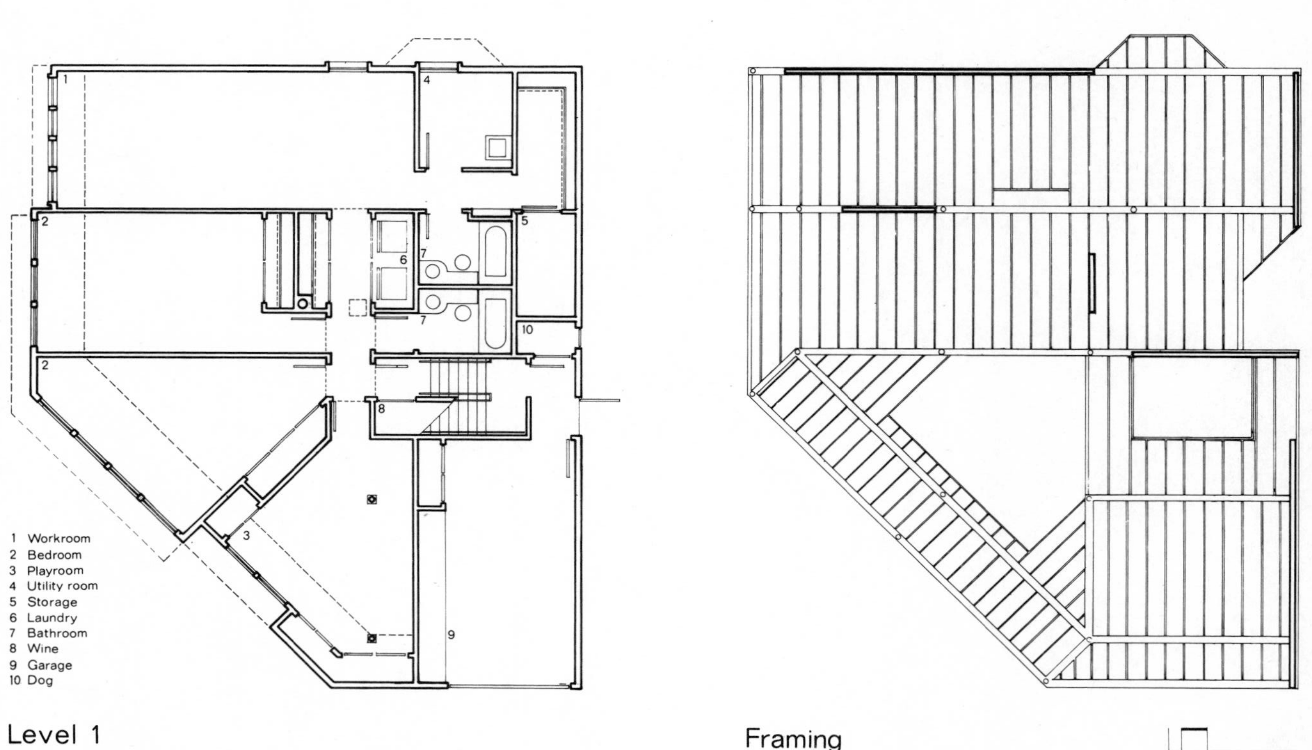

FIGURE 3-13 Drawings of a house using both belvedere and porch elements in Palo Alto, California, designed for Tom and Sharon Wagner by William Meyer.

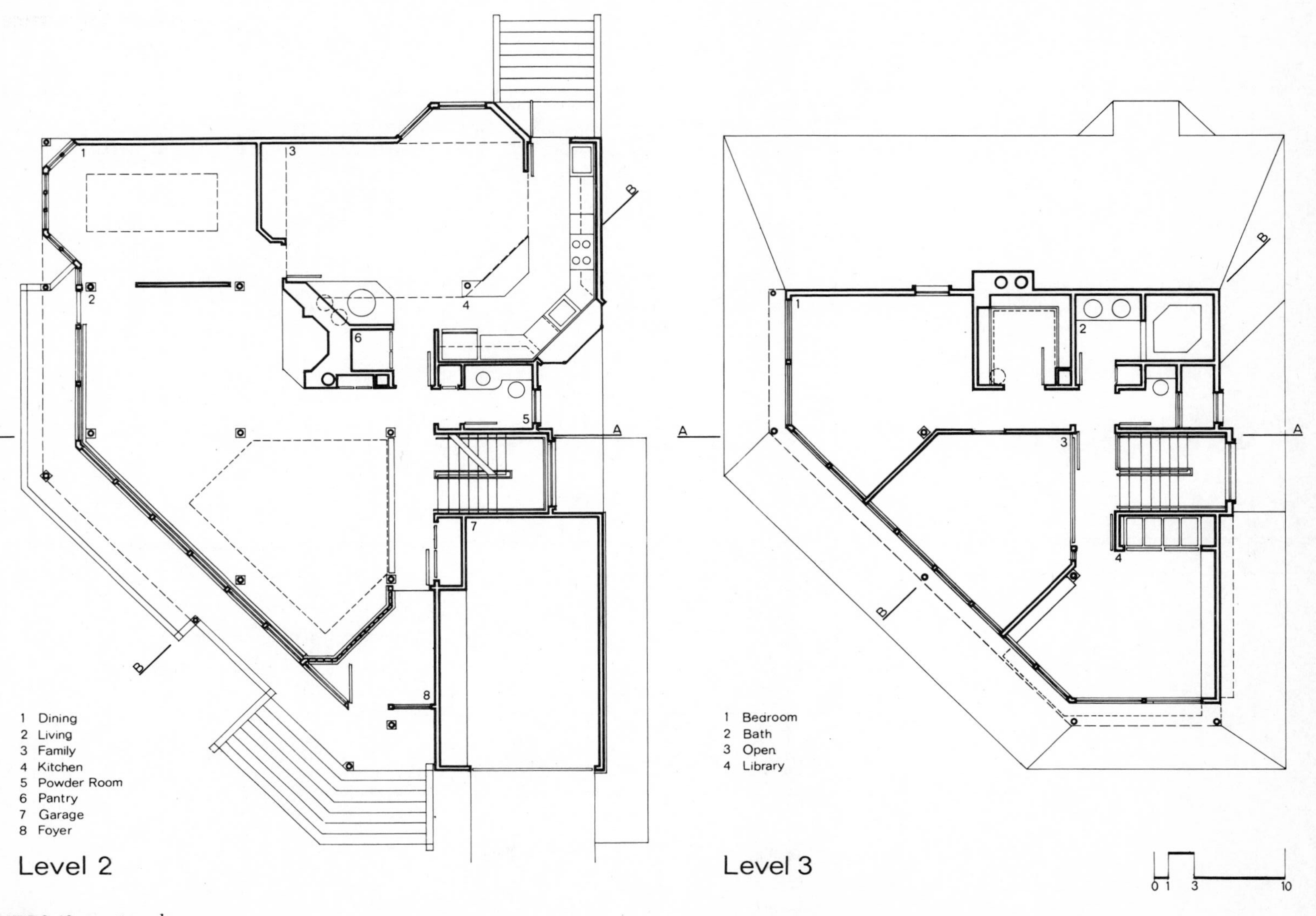

FIGURE 3-13, *continued.*

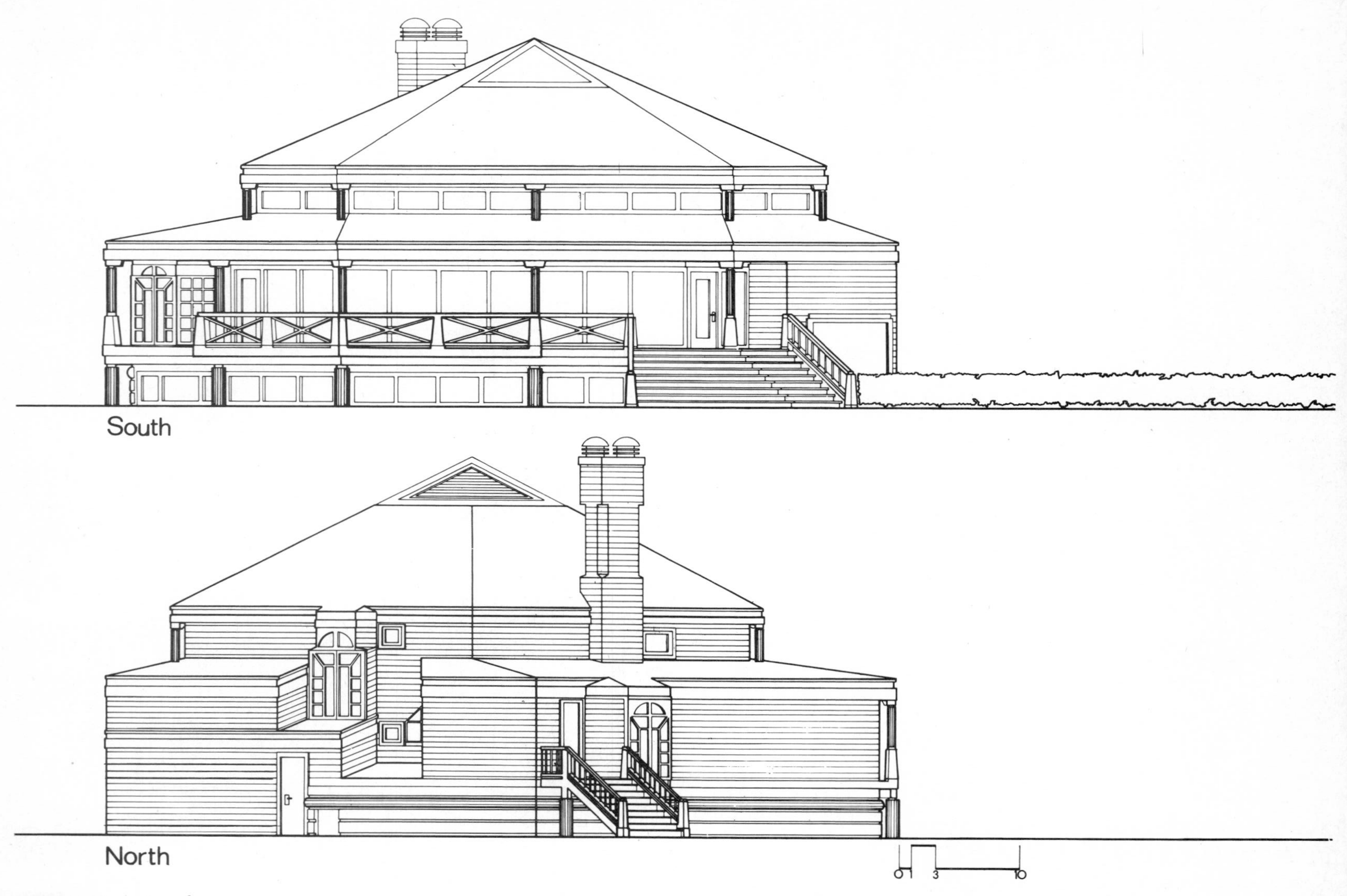

FIGURE 3-13, *continued.*

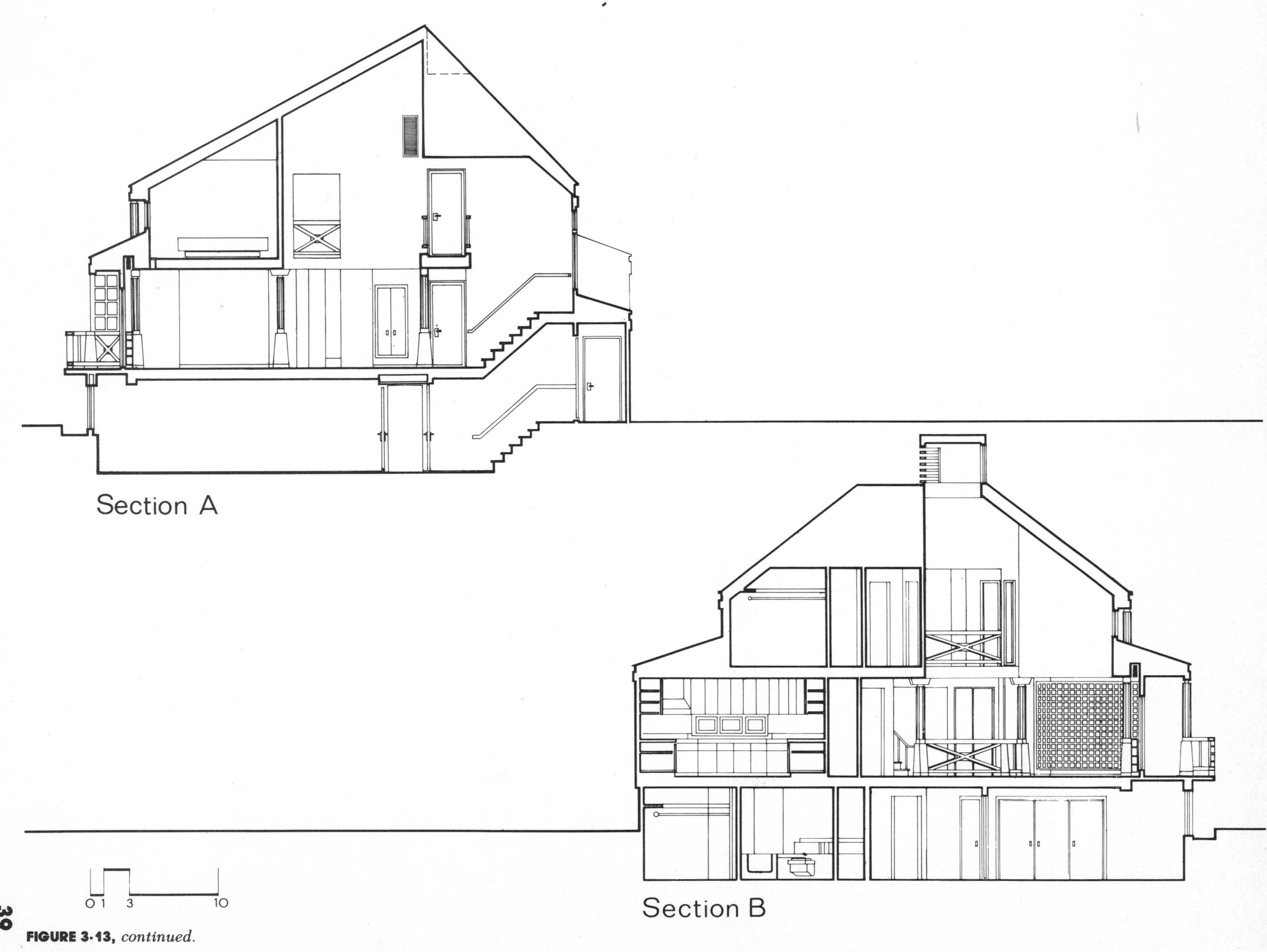

FIGURE 3-13, *continued.*

pointed out that the exhaust vent on the north side of the belvedere should be open in summer but closed and insulated in winter.

Figure 3-13 illustrates the construction of belvedere and porch elements in a design for a single-family house in California. This design also uses the earth to temper the thermal environment around the lower level of the house.

These past design approaches are presented here simply to encourage designers to be aware of their architectural heritage and to continue to learn from energy-related designs which have been developed in earlier periods. The chapters which follow will present quantitative methods for estimating the thermal and luminous benefits which the designs described in this chapter and many others will yield.

BIBLIOGRAPHY

Ackerman, James S.: *Palladio,* Penguin Books, Inc., New York, 1976.

Lewis, Arnold (intro.): *American Victorian Architecture,* Dover Publications, Inc., New York, 1975.

A Monograph of the Works of McKim, Mead and White, 1879–1915, Benjamin Blom, Inc., New York, 1973.

Moore, Charles W., Gerald Allen, and D. Lyndon: *The Place of Houses,* Holt, Rinehart and Winston, Inc., New York, 1974.

Scully, Vincent, Jr.: *The Shingle Style and the Stick Style,* Yale University Press, New Haven, Conn., 1955.

FOUR

DESIGN ALTERNATIVES

A range of designs which architects and interior designers may consider for reducing energy consumption in buildings is presented in the following pages.[1] Each of these examples is described in terms of the type of energy flow that it affects:

1 Thermal energy

a. Conducted

b. Convected

c. Radiated

2 Luminous energy

Some designs affect more than one type of energy flow. Others create a reduction in one energy flow while creating an increase in another. Later chapters in this book will describe methods of quantifying these changes. The goal of this chapter is simply to help designers identify which type of flow is affected by their plans and in what manner.

The design alternatives described here are organized and presented in terms of the aspect of a building's form, materials, structure, or enclosure that each encompasses. The general classification of these design options is as follows:

1 Landscape

2 Building form

[1]Some of the material presented here was first prepared by the author for the Pennsylvania Avenue Development Corporation's *Energy Guidelines* in the spring of 1980. At that time, the author was a vice president of The Ehrenkrantz Group. The work was carried out under a subcontract to The Ehrenkrantz Group from TAMS, Inc., in Washington, D.C.

3 Building components

a. Wall exteriors

b. Walls

c. Glazing

d. Roofs

e. Basements

f. Interiors

g. Entries

Most of the designs presented here take different forms depending on the type of building with which they are used. The main component of residential energy costs is heating, while in office buildings the main energy consumer is often lighting. Because of these basic differences in energy use, energy-saving designs for the form and facade of residential buildings will frequently differ from those for office buildings.

A horizontal louver, for example, on a residential south-facing window will reduce energy consumption most if it simply shades the window during the air-conditioning season. The same design on an office building may well decrease energy consumption more if it reflects light on the interior ceiling of an office, thereby reducing the need for electricity for artificial lighting.

Comments on the residential and/or office applicability of each design are presented in the following pages together with possible problems which may be encountered when employing a particular design.

LANDSCAPE

Ground Reflectance-Absorptance

Ground surface treatments may be designed to balance the amount of light and solar heat that enters a building with the building's thermal and luminous needs.

1 ***Thermal effects***

Conduction: None.

Convection: None.

Radiation: Increased winter solar heat gain.

2 ***Luminous effects.*** Increased natural light will be reflected to the building interior.

3 ***Design considerations.*** For office building uses, the designer should consider providing light-colored ground surfaces for buildings with interior daylight controls[2] and dark-colored surfaces for buildings without such controls.

[2]Daylight controls will dim fluorescent lights in response to changing natural-light levels. See Chapter 10.

For residential uses, designers should consider providing dark surfaces immediately adjacent to windows while providing lighter colors farther away. This will reflect low-angle winter sun onto the window while absorbing and preventing reflections of higher-angle summer sun. Care should be taken, however, to make sure that sol-air temperatures[3] near adjacent walls are not increased to undesirable levels.

Trees

Trees may be used to shade buildings and alter wind patterns.

1 ***Thermal effects***

Conduction: None.

Convection: Reduced winter infiltration heat loss.

Radiation: Reduced winter and summer solar heat gain.

2 ***Luminous effects.*** Undesirable reductions in natural light may occur.

3 ***Design considerations.*** For office buildings, light is more valuable than heat in many cases, and care should be taken to prevent trees from reducing available natural light. Designers should consider using trees only on western sides to provide partial shading of windows during the summer.

For residential uses, deciduous trees may be used on the south, east, and west sides of a building so that the summer sun is shaded from the building when the trees are fully leaved. Coniferous trees may be used on the north and west sides to act as winter windbreaks.

Earth Berms

Deep enclosures of earth may be used against the north and possibly the east and west sides of a building for insulation and to provide a warmer-than-air exposure during the winter and a cooler-than-air exposure during the summer.

1 ***Thermal effects***

Conduction: Reduced winter heat loss and summer heat gain.

Convection: Reduced infiltration losses and gains.

Radiation: Elimination of sol-air temperature effects on walls covered by earth.

2 ***Luminous effects.*** None.

3 ***Design considerations.*** Steep berms will require some means of erosion prevention. Walls next to berms will require waterproofing.

[3]See Chapter 8 for a more detailed discussion of sol-air temperatures.

Buried Structures

Building space may be placed below grade to reduce exposure to outdoor air temperature extremes.

1 *Thermal effects*

Conduction: Reduced winter heat loss and summer heat gain.

Convection: Reduced winter and summer infiltration heat losses and gains.

Radiation: Elimination of roof and wall sol-air temperature conditions.

2 ***Luminous effects.*** Access to natural light requires the use of devices such as skylights, heliostats, reflectors, and/or lenses.

3 ***Design considerations.*** Buried structures often require stronger construction and more expensive waterproofing and dampproofing. Ventilation, natural light, and lack of views are major design concerns. Covering the top of structures with earth is often not cost-effective since it adds little insulating value but substantially increases structural costs.[4]

Buried Ventilation Ducts

Underground ductwork, sometimes called "cool pipes," may be used to provide cooled ventilation air during summer months by causing warm outside air to pass underground before entering a building. Figure 4-1 shows sections through a house which uses a cool pipe for summertime ventilation.

1 *Thermal effects*

Conduction: None.

Convection: Cooled air provided to building interiors.

Radiation: None.

2 ***Luminous effects.*** None.

3 ***Design considerations.*** Underground ducts need to be closed off during winter months. Also, moisture and odor controls may be a problem.

BUILDING FORM

Atriums

Atriums, or light courts, may be provided on the interior of deep office buildings. They are particularly applicable to buildings equipped with daylighting controls. Figure 4-2 shows a design for a large mixed-use atrium building.

[4]See Chapter 9 for an example calculation of this condition.

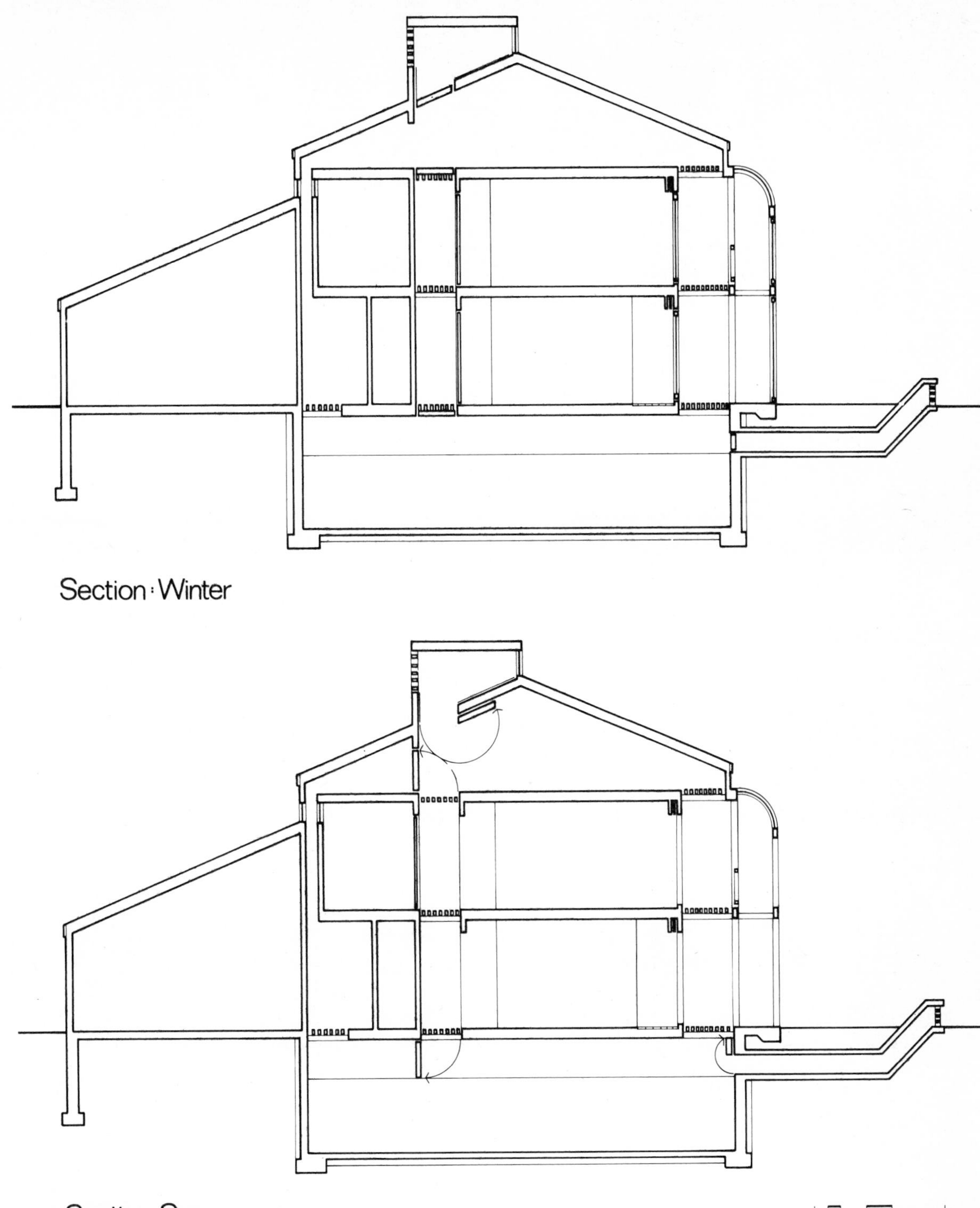

FIGURE 4·1 Sections showing a house with underground ductwork for summer cooling, designed by William Meyer for John Orlando, Foxboro, Massachusetts, 1979.

1 ***Thermal effects***

Conduction: In glazed atriums, reduced exterior surface exposure to outside air conditions.

Convection: Solar stack effects may enhance summer ventilation. See section "Roofs" below for a more detailed discussion of solar stack effects.

Radiation: Winter solar heat gains to the building may be increased.

2 ***Luminous effects.*** Atriums provide an effective means of getting natural light into the interior of buildings.

3 ***Design considerations.*** Use of atriums will cause increased building volume, which, while not necessarily requiring space conditioning, is likely to increase construction costs and require large land parcels.

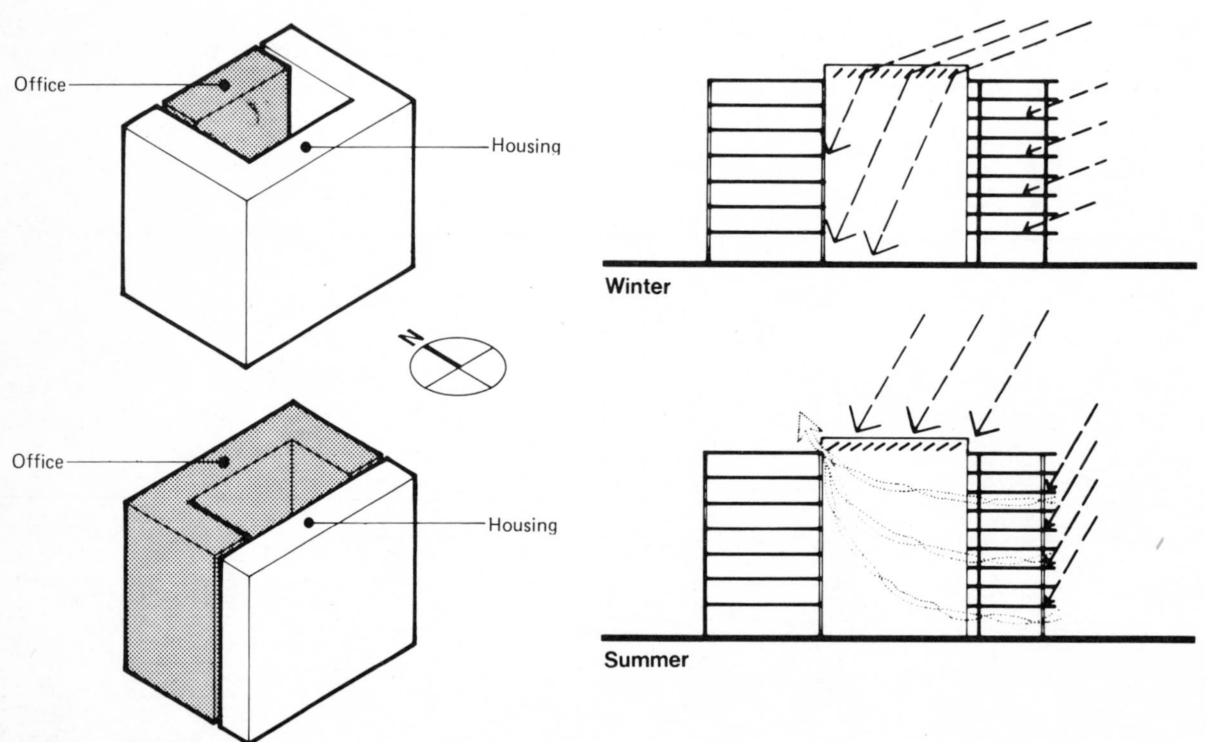

FIGURE 4-2 Axonometrics and sections of atrium design for an office-residential complex in Washington, D.C., designed by William Meyer, while a principal of The Ehrenkrantz Group, for the Pennsylvania Avenue Development Corporation under a subcontract with TAMS, Inc. [*Drawings and design assistance by Richard Holod.*]

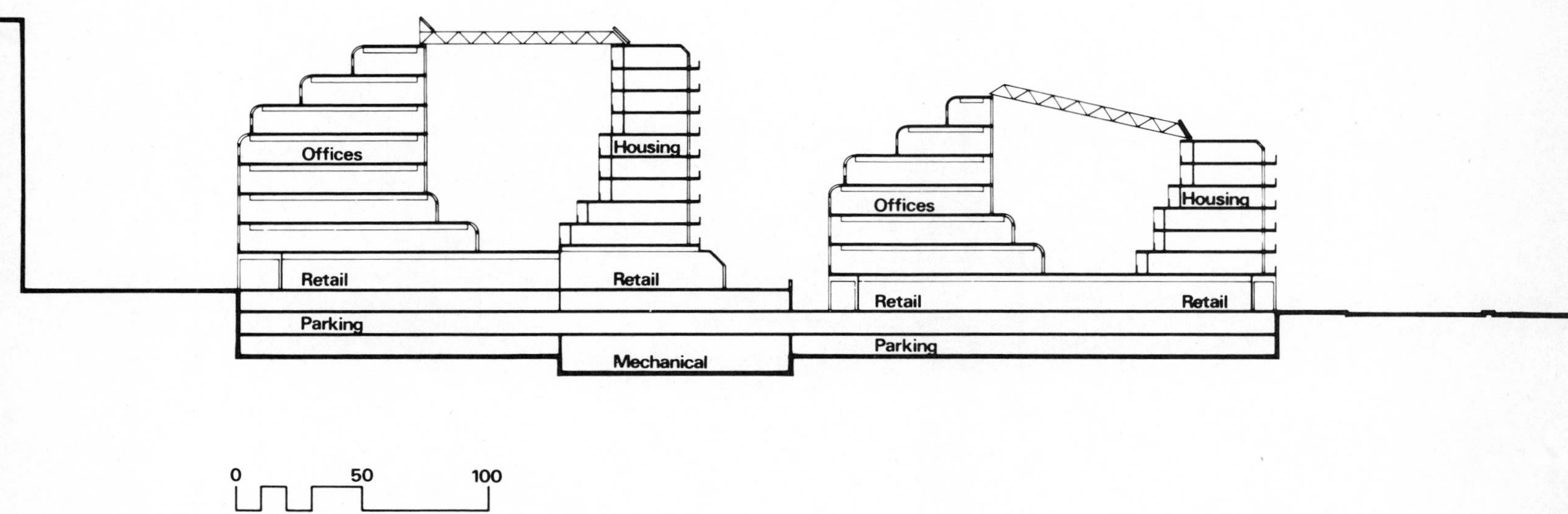

SECTION

FIGURE 4-2, *continued.*

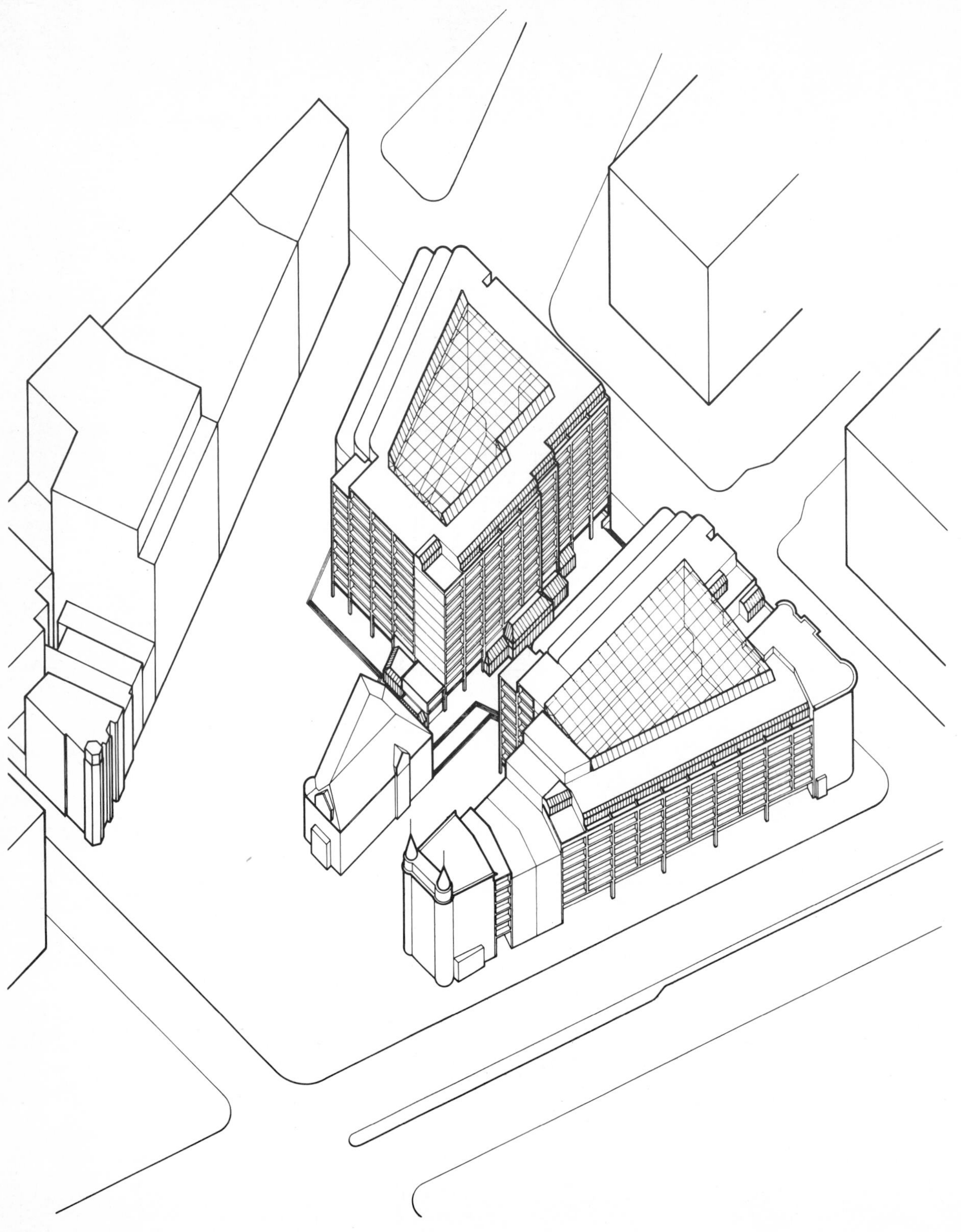

FIGURE 4-2, *continued.*

Configuration

The length, width, and height of a building may be proportioned to reduce overall fuel consumption. Figure 4-3 indicates a design for a townhouse which uses a minimum-perimeter octagon shape in plan.

1 ***Thermal effects***

Conduction: Reduced surface-to-volume ratios will reduce heat gain and loss.

Convection: Reduced north-side surface area may reduce winter infiltration heat losses.

Radiation: Increased south-facing surface area will increase winter solar heat gain and summer heat gain also if not shaded.

2 ***Luminous effects.*** *Increased* surface-to-volume ratios will increase access to natural light.

3 ***Design considerations.*** If lighting controls which dim artificial lights in response to natural lighting are used in an office building, a long, narrow building with more perimeter access to outside light may use less electricity. On the other hand, a building with no daylighting controls may best be configured in a shape which minimizes the exterior surface.

Orientation

The rooms of a building may be oriented so that the natural forces of sunlight and wind may offset dependence on depletable energy sources.

1 ***Thermal effects***

Conduction: None.

Convection: Rooms facing prevailing wind directions will have access to natural cooling and ventilation during summer months.

Radiation: Rooms with windows facing south will have high levels of winter solar heat gain.

2 ***Luminous effects.*** Rooms facing south will have access to direct sunlight for interior lighting.

3 ***Design considerations.*** In office uses, orientation is a function of building plan, shape, and daylighting controls. Square plan shapes with daylighting controls, for example, are often not particularly sensitive to orientation, while rectangular plan shapes without daylighting controls are best oriented with the long sides facing north and south.

In residential uses, however, all major living spaces such as dining rooms, family rooms, bedrooms, and living rooms should face south. All ancillary spaces such as hallways, bathrooms, garages, and utility rooms should face north. Fig-

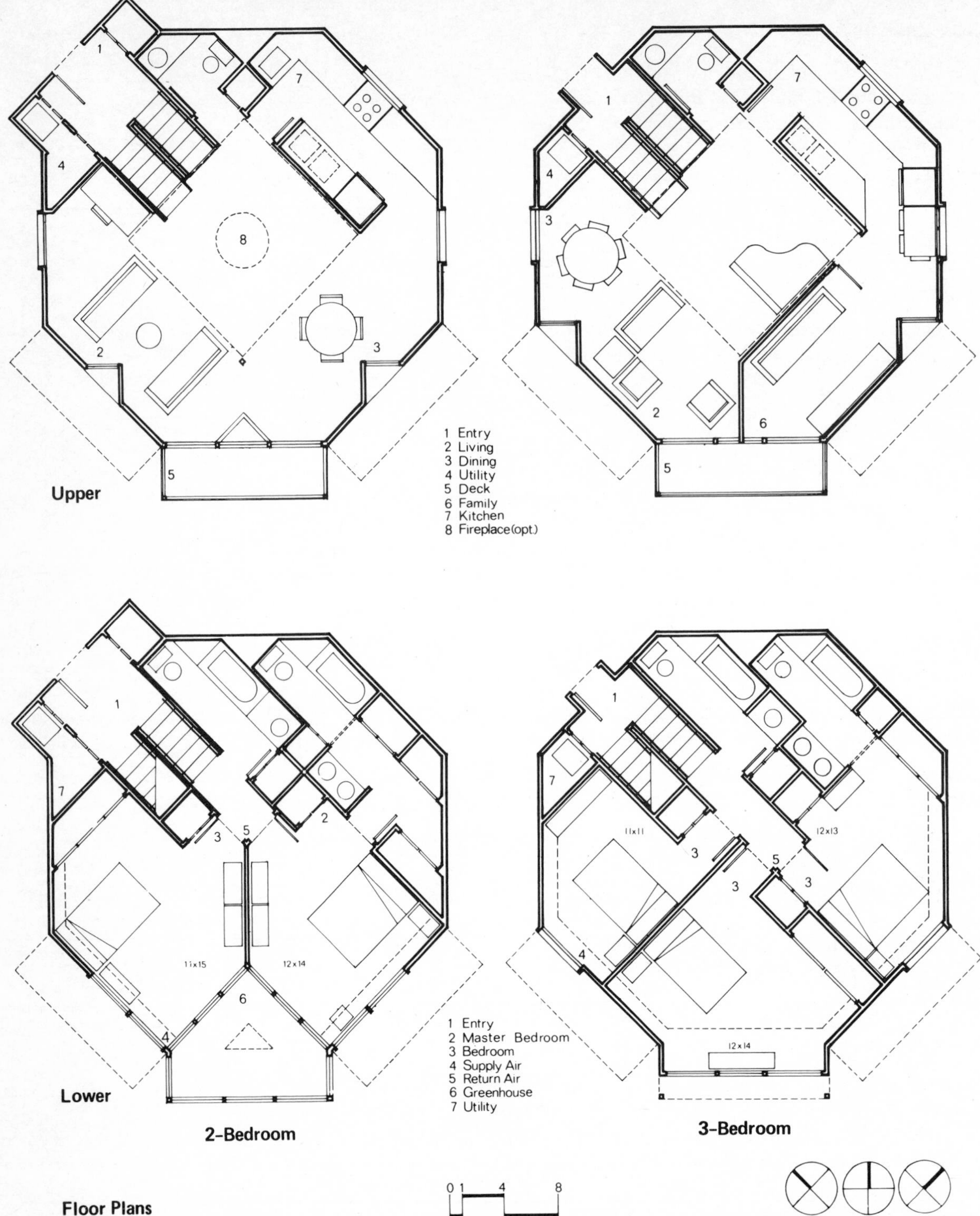

FIGURE 4-3 Plans, section, and axonometrics of an octagon design for row housing, designed by William Meyer for a private developer, 1981.

Attached: 8 D. U./Acre

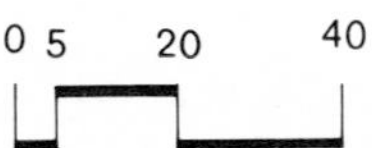

Site Plan

FIGURE 4-3, *continued.*

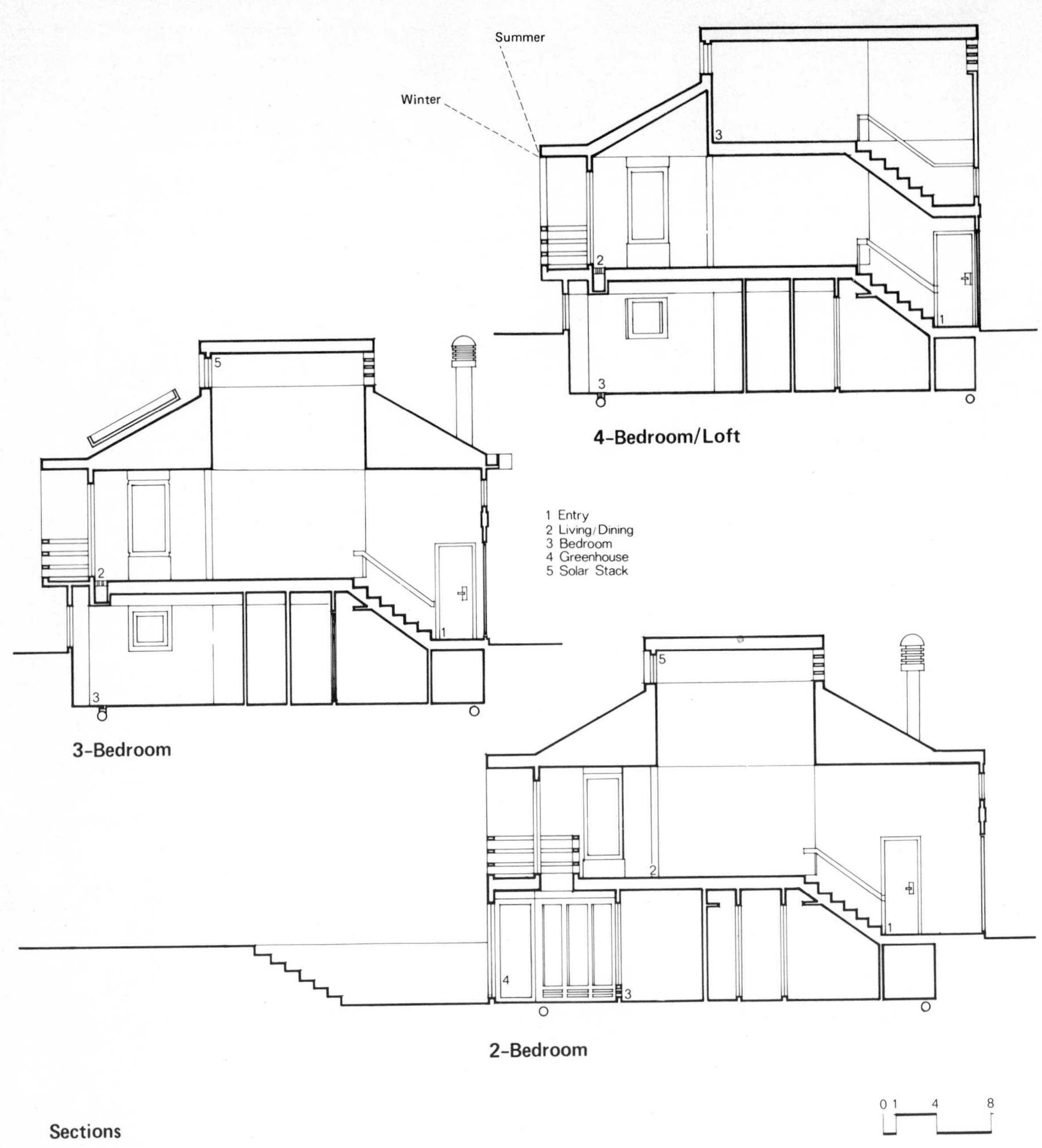

Sections

FIGURE 4-3, *continued.*

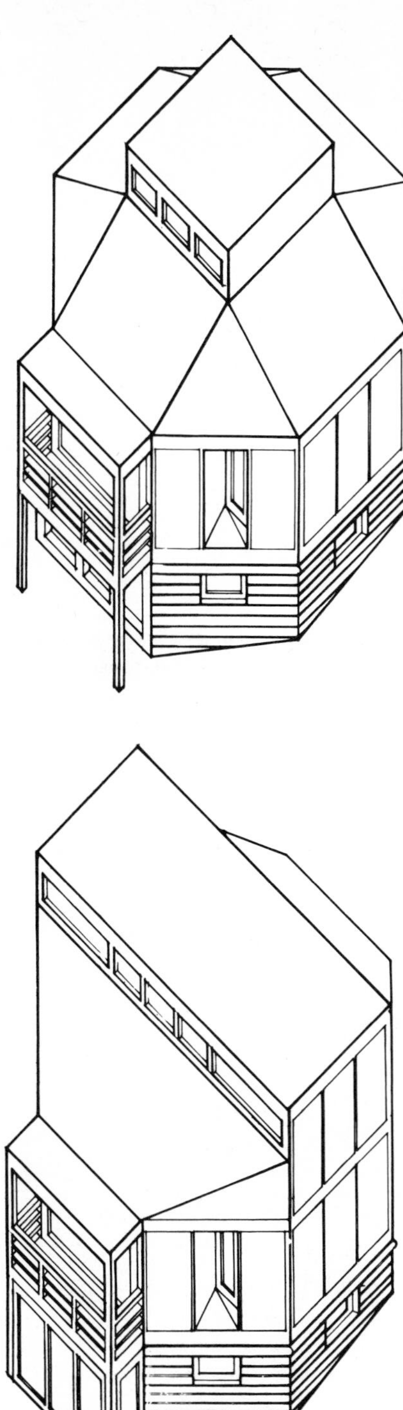

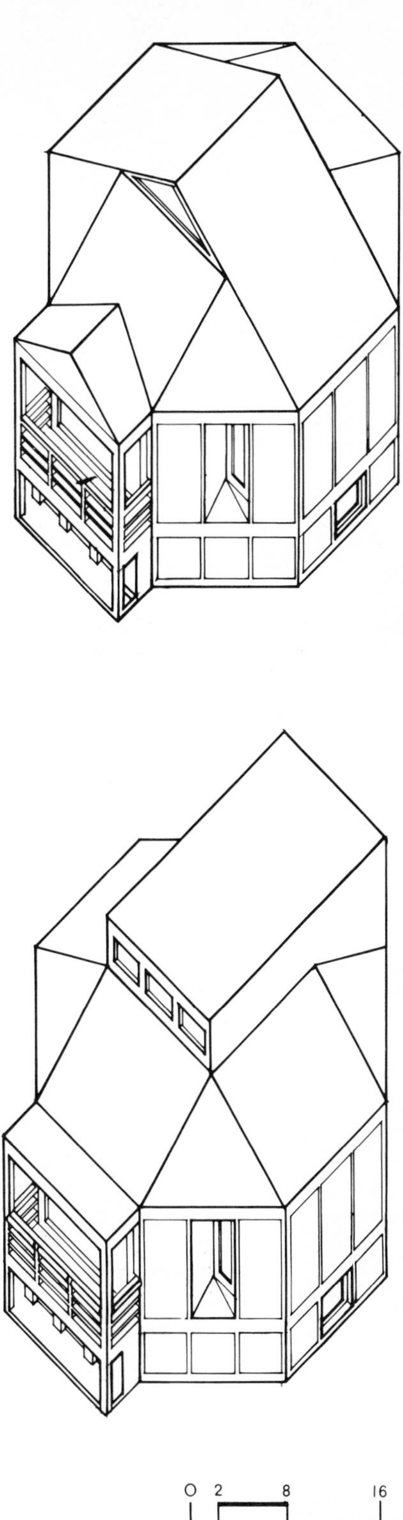

Axonometrics

FIGURE 4-3, *continued.*

ure 4-4 presents plans for a house which carries out this orientation consideration.

Furnishings in rooms with direct sunlight should be designed to resist fading.

WALL EXTERIORS

Exterior Shading Devices

Exterior shading devices may be designed to control direct sunlight.

1 ***Thermal effects***

Conduction: Minor conduction may occur through the shading device to the building.

Convection: None.

Radiation: Reduced summertime solar heat gain.

2 ***Luminous effects.*** Light reflected from the top of exterior shading designs may help to increase interior lighting levels.

3 ***Design considerations.*** For office buildings, horizontal shading devices might shade the perimeter rooms of the south side from the summer sun while reflecting sunlight into the interior zones of the building for natural lighting. On the east and west sides, vertical louvers might keep out direct sun in the summer but admit the winter sun. (See Figure 4-5.)

For residential uses, a shading device should admit the winter sun but keep out the summer sun. Also, the top of a horizontal shade should minimize the reflection of sunlight to the dwelling's interior.

In cold climates, exterior shading devices should be designed to deal with snow and ice buildup. They should also be designed to minimize unwanted summertime conducted heat through the shade attachment to the building mass.

Reflectors

Reflectors may be used on the south side of a building to increase the amount of sunlight available.

1 ***Thermal effects***

Conduction: None.

Convection: None.

Radiation: Increased winter solar heat gain.

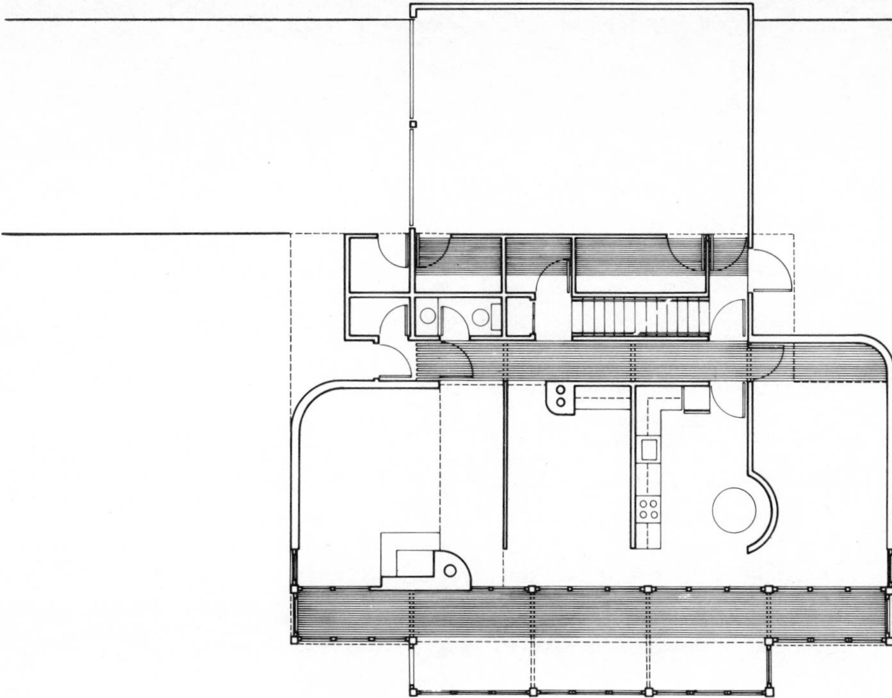

First-Floor Plan

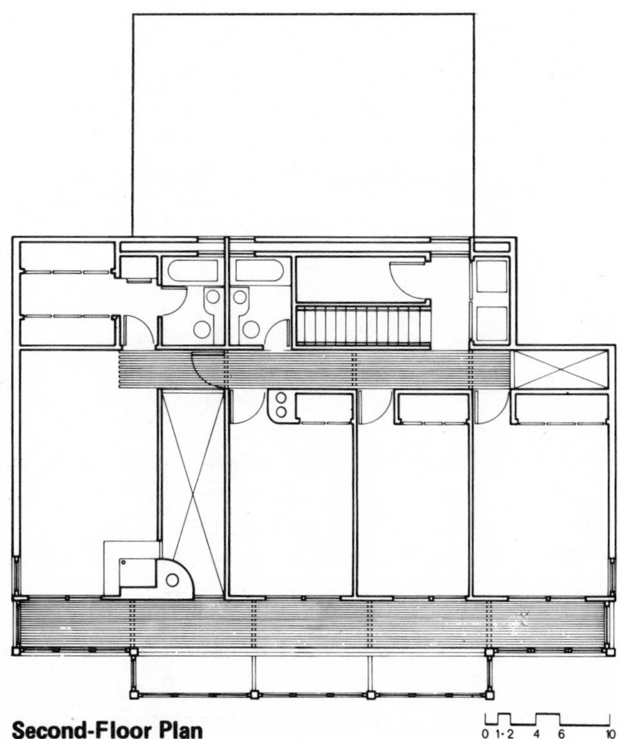

Second-Floor Plan

FIGURE 4-4 Plans for a house with south-facing room orientation, designed by William Meyer for John Orlando, Foxboro, Massachusetts, 1979.

2 ***Luminous effects.*** Increased natural light for building interiors.

3 ***Design considerations.*** In residential building, reflectors should focus solar radiation onto absorbing materials within a building's interior, where it will be converted into heat. The main concern here is to prevent re-reflection of sunlight back out of a building.

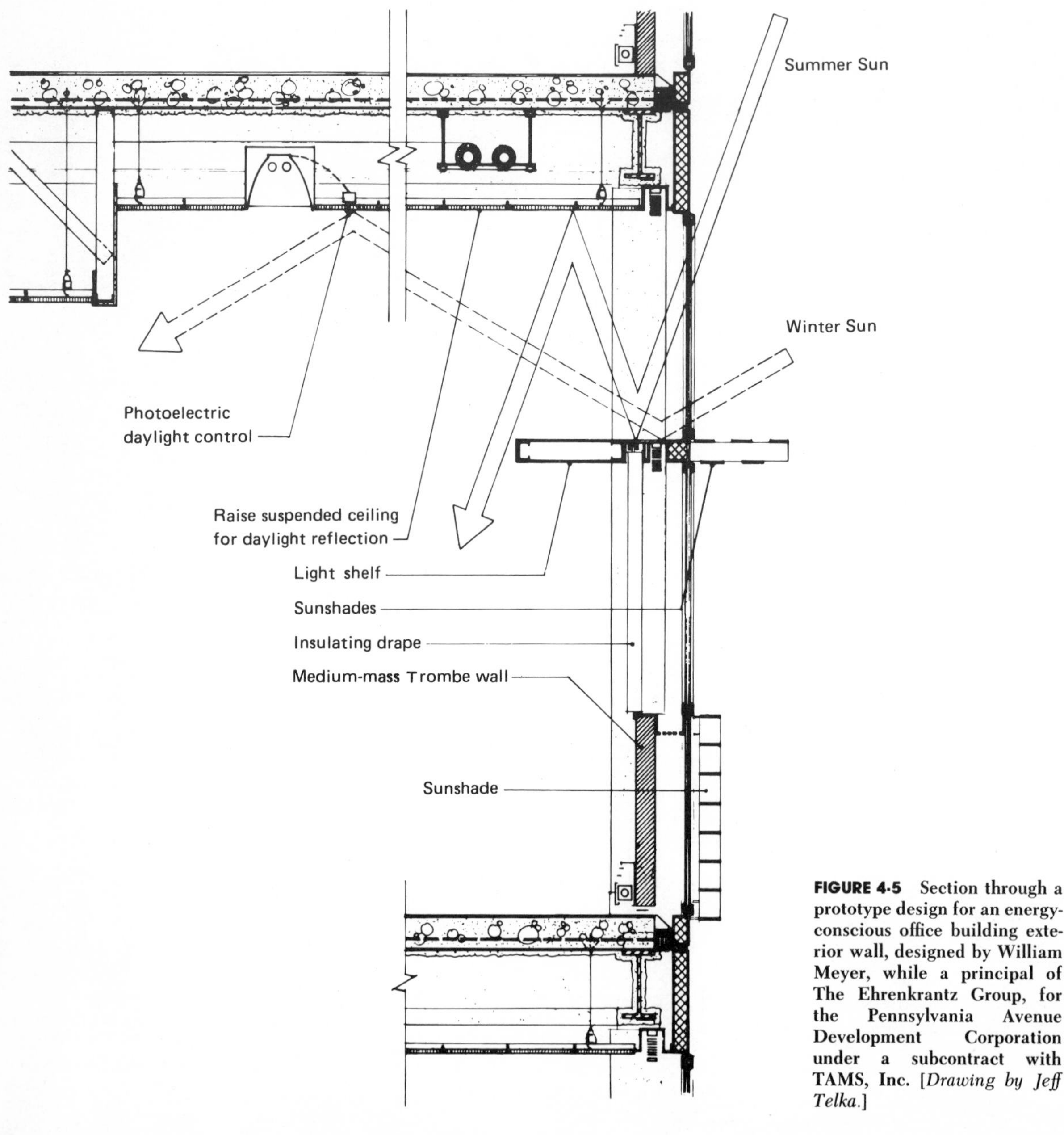

FIGURE 4-5 Section through a prototype design for an energy-conscious office building exterior wall, designed by William Meyer, while a principal of The Ehrenkrantz Group, for the Pennsylvania Avenue Development Corporation under a subcontract with TAMS, Inc. [*Drawing by Jeff Telka.*]

Trombe Walls or Air Collectors

Use glass and masonry in a "Trombe" wall configuration to provide solar heat to interior zones (see Figure 4-5).

1 *Thermal effects*

Conduction: Glass enclosure will lower conducted heat loss and gain through a masonry wall.

Convection: Air between the glass and masonry will be heated by the solar-heated masonry. It will then rise and pass through vents which may be provided at the top of the masonry into the adjacent room.

Radiation: Solar radiation will pass through the glass and be absorbed by the masonry. The absorbed radiation will slowly pass through the masonry and heat it. The heated masonry, in turn, will radiate to other surfaces in the adjacent room.

2 ***Luminous effects.*** Natural lighting is precluded by this design unless water is substituted for masonry or unless the Trombe design is coordinated with windows.

3 ***Design considerations.*** For office building uses, a Trombe wall should extend only up to desk height so that natural light may penetrate the space. Some mass may be needed to prevent overheating in adjacent rooms and to lag the solar heat into evening hours. If overheating does not occur, it may be desirable to minimize the mass of the wall because of the added structural requirements imposed by the weight of the wall.

For residential uses, a Trombe wall may extend up to the ceiling provided it does not conflict with desirable views. In this case, the masonry (water may also be used) should store heat for use in evening hours or on the next day. In some cases, it may be more effective to prevent convection from occurring by omitting dampers from the top and bottom of the wall. Overheating problems may be minimized with this approach. If dampers are used, they should be designed to prevent back drafts.

Greenhouses

In a residential building, a greenhouse may be used on the south side to collect solar radiation and provide a transition living space and plant-growing area. See Figure 4-6 for an example of a house with a greenhouse integrated into the south facade.

1 *Thermal effects*

Conduction: Winter heat loss may be reduced by the additional air space and glazing provided by adding a greenhouse to a building's exterior.

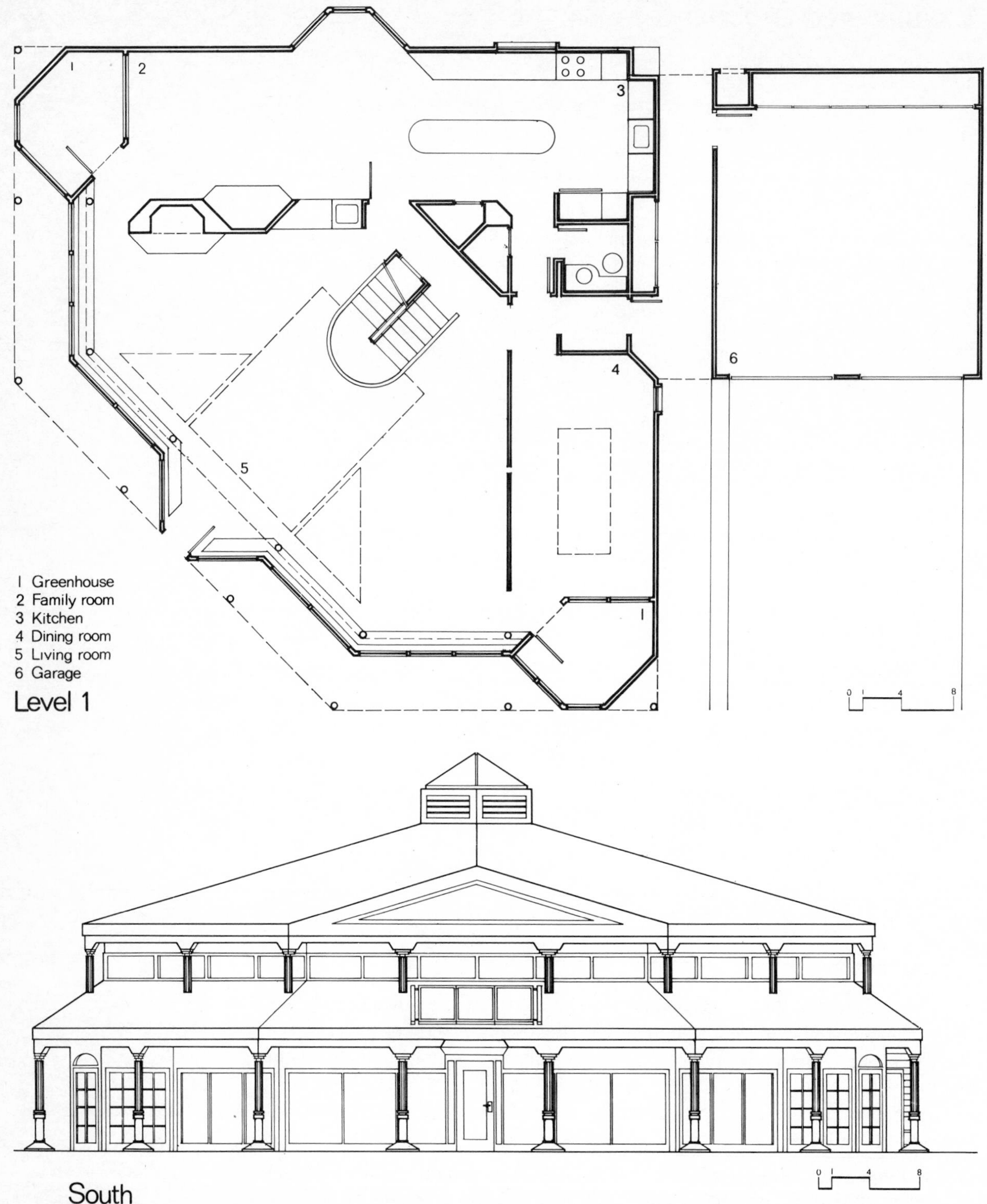

FIGURE 4-6 Plan and elevation of a house with two greenhouses, designed by William Meyer for Thomas and Sharon Wagner, Palo Alto, California, 1981.

Convection: Hot air at the top of a greenhouse may flow into adjacent rooms, with cooler return air passing from the rooms back into the lower levels of the greenhouse. In this manner, a natural thermosiphon may be established.

Radiation: Solar radiation will pass through the greenhouse glass, heating the interior surfaces of the greenhouse. The absorbed solar radiation will become heat which is blocked from reradiation to the outdoors by the glass.

2 ***Luminous effects.*** None.

3 ***Design considerations.*** If a greenhouse is used only periodically as a living space when temperatures permit, the rest of the dwelling should be separated from the greenhouse by a solid or glazed wall in order to maintain interior comfort levels. A greenhouse should not be expected to provide conditions comfortable for year-round living unless it is insulated at night and on cloudy days and shaded during the summer. Screens may replace glass for the summertime use of a greenhouse.

WALLS

Wall Insulation

Insulation in walls above the levels required by energy conservation codes is often cost-effective.

1 ***Thermal effects***

Conduction: Winter heat loss and summer heat gain will be reduced.

Convection: None.

Radiation: None.

2 ***Luminous effects.*** None.

3 ***Design considerations*** Insulation placed on or near the outside wall surface may help to decrease temperature swings on the interior of the building because the entire mass of the building will be providing thermal inertia.

Wall Color

A color which provides a compatible link between climatic forces and building fuel consumption should be used for walls of buildings.

1 ***Thermal effects***

Conduction: None.

Convection: None.

Radiation: Color affects the radiative reflectance and absorptance of a surface, that is, its ability either to reflect or to absorb solar heat.

2 ***Luminous effects.*** None.

3 ***Design considerations.*** For office buildings, this frequently means a light, reflective color because cooling costs are often greater than heating costs. For residential buildings, it may mean a dark, absorbing color since heating costs usually dominate.

Wall Surface Treatment

Exterior surface treatments for walls should match energy needs with natural thermal forces.

1 ***Thermal effects***

Conduction: Rough surfaces have greater film coefficients than smooth surfaces.

Convection: Rough surfaces have greater convection heat transfer potential than smooth surfaces.

Radiation: Density of surface increases reflectivity; rough surfaces have greater emittance potential than smooth surfaces.

2 ***Luminous effects.*** None.

3 ***Design considerations.*** Residential buildings may benefit from rough wall surfaces; smooth, dense surfaces may be more appropriate for office buildings.

GLAZING

Glazing Area

The glazing area should be balanced with the building's luminous and thermal needs.

1 ***Thermal effects***

Conduction: Larger glazing areas will increase the overall thermal conductivity of a wall.

Convection: Larger glazing areas may result in increased frame infiltration.

Radiation: Larger glazing areas will increase winter solar heat gains and, if unshaded, summer solar heat gains as well.

2 ***Luminous effects.*** Larger glass areas will increase the amount of natural light reaching interior areas.

3 ***Design considerations.*** An office building equipped with daylight controls may have lower fuel consumption if its glass area is increased. A commercial

building without daylight controls is likely to have lower fuel consumption if its glass area is reduced.

A residential building may need very little glass on the north side but large amounts on the south side for solar radiative heat gain during the winter.

Glazing Insulation

Double glazing or triple glazing may be more cost-effective than single glazing.

1 ***Thermal effects***

   Conduction: Increased glass layers will decrease conductivity.

   Convection: None.

   Radiation: Increased glass layers will decrease solar radiation transmission.

2 ***Luminous effects.*** Multiple layers of glass may decrease natural-light transmission.

3 ***Design considerations.*** An office building may, because of setback temperatures during evening and weekend periods in winter, require less glazing insulation than a residential structure.

   Most residential buildings benefit from triple glazing except on the south side, where three layers of glass may excessively reduce transmission of winter solar heat gain, in which case double glazing may be more appropriate.

Glazing Transmission

Glazing transmission qualities, that is, transmission qualities of tinted or reflective glass, should be adjusted to balance energy requirements for lighting, air conditioning, and heating.

1 ***Thermal effects***

   Conduction: None.

   Convection: None.

   Radiation: Reduced glass transmission levels will reduce solar heat gain.

2 ***Luminous effects.*** Tinted or reflective glass reduces the intensity of the natural light which enters interior spaces.

3 ***Design considerations.*** Residential buildings should have clear glass because heating costs dominate annual energy consumption and interior lighting needs are relatively minor. Clear glass will help to maximize winter solar heat gain. Office buildings *with* daylight controls should also have clear glass.

Window Operation

Providing operable windows will increase summer ventilation and potentially reduce air-conditioning costs.

1 ***Thermal effects***

Conduction: None.

Convection: Summer access to breezes will be increased, as will be infiltration heat gains and losses through the cracks between windows and frames.

Radiation: None.

2 ***Luminous effects.*** None.

3 ***Design considerations.*** In office buildings, operable windows may allow outside air to be used in the spring and fall in lieu of using the heating, ventilating, and air-conditioning (HVAC) systems. Particulates in the outside air may increase cleaning costs inside the building, however, and additional exhaust ductwork may be required in particularly deep buildings to facilitate natural ventilation. Also, HVAC system balancing may be much more difficult and expensive with operable windows.

Residential buildings typically have adequate numbers of operable windows. Care should be taken so that air movements caused by summer winds through such windows maximize air movements within rooms in order to increase summer comfort levels.

If operable windows are used, adequate weatherstripping should be provided.

Glazing Tilt

The angle of glazing should be set to control access to solar radiation.

1 ***Thermal effects***

Conduction: None.

Convection: None.

Radiation: Solar heat gain per unit of glass area is increased as the glass surface draws nearer to being perpendicular to the angle of the sun.

2 ***Luminous effects.*** Interior light intensities will also be increased as the average of incidence of sunlight on glazing approaches 90°.

3 ***Design considerations.*** In office buildings, the tilt of the glass may work best at less than a 90° altitude so that direct summer radiation is excluded and direct winter sun may still enter. (This provides essentially the same effect as an overhang.)

In residential buildings, a tilt of more than 90° altitude may be beneficial so that the glass is more nearly perpendicular to the winter sun.

Solar Stack Effect

Providing south-facing glazing and absorber plates along with exhaust outlets at the top of tall interior spaces (stacks) will facilitate air movement within the spaces.

1 *Thermal effects*

Conduction: None.

Convection: Solar radiation entering through the top of the stack will heat surfaces surrounding the stack. Air moving across these surfaces will in turn be heated. The heated air will rise and leave the stack through exhaust outlets. Air from lower areas will then move up to replace the exhausted air, and convection currents will start up. The convection air movement will cause an evaporative cooling effect on inhabitants of spaces adjacent to the lower portions of the stack.

Radiation: Solar radiation provides the motive force behind the convection currents. With no exhaust of the heated air, the solar radiation heat gains will remain inside the stack. This may be of benefit, of course, during winter months if the heat is moved by forced convection down to rooms under the stack.

2 ***Luminous effects.*** If office uses are adjacent to the stack, the sunlight entering the top of the stack may be of benefit for natural lighting.

3 ***Design considerations.*** This concept may be integrated into atrium designs or interior courtyards of office buildings. Stair shafts of single-family attached residential buildings may also benefit from the concept. (See Figures 4-1, 4-2, 4-3, 4-6, and 3-12.)

Roof Color

Roof color may help to reduce overall fuel consumption.

1 *Thermal effects*

Conduction: Solar radiation on dark-colored roofs may increase sol-air temperatures, which in turn may increase conductive heat gains.

Convection: None.

Radiation: Darker colors will be more absorptive; lighter colors, more reflective.

2 ***Luminous effects.*** None.

3 ***Design considerations.*** For office buildings, it may be appropriate to use a light color in order to reduce the building's air-conditioning costs, which typically are greater than the heating costs. For residential buildings, a dark color may be more appropriate because heating costs dominate.

Rooftop Greenhouse

A greenhouse on the roof of a multifamily residential structure may help to reduce fuel consumption (see Figure 4-7).

1 *Thermal effects*

Conduction: Heat loss and gain through the roof will be reduced by the addition of a rooftop structure.

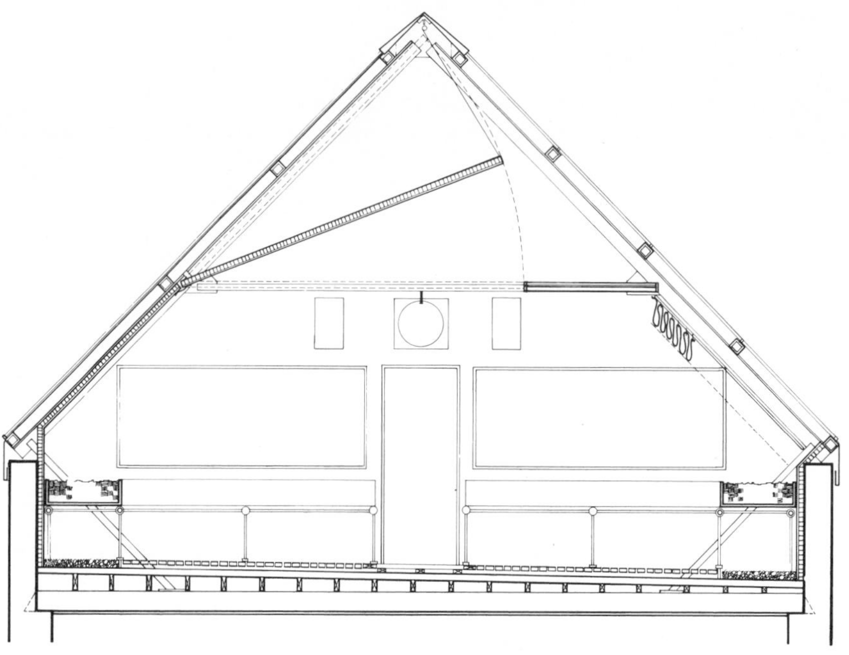

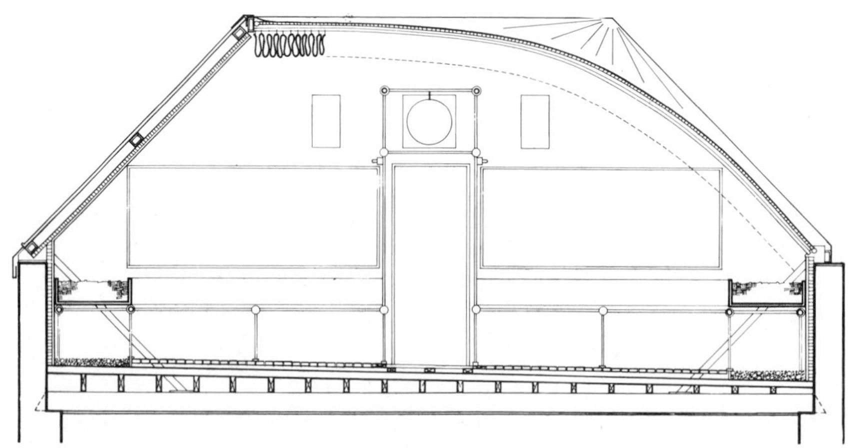

FIGURE 4-7 Sections through designs for energy-conscious rooftop greenhouses, designed by Michael Golubov while a project manager with The Ehrenkrantz Group, William Meyer, principal in charge, under a contract with the Northeast Solar Energy Center, 1980. Project consultants included Geiger-Berger Associates, P.C., Goldman Sokolow Copeland, Michael Bobker, and Jan Johnson. [*Drawings by James Czajka.*]

Convection: Some summer ventilation may be encouraged through the building by venting of the warm air in the greenhouse and establishment of a solar stack effect.

Radiation: Solar radiation collected by the greenhouse may help to reduce the building's heating requirements.

2 ***Luminous effects.*** Natural light will facilitate plant growth in the greenhouse.

3 ***Design considerations.*** The greenhouse and its contents, if used for plant growing, will impose an additional structural load on the building. Also, building height restrictions in urban areas must be considered. The ductwork and fans required for providing heated air from the greenhouse to the building may not be cost-effective. Night insulation may be required to reduce nocturnal conducted heat loss.

Roof Skylights

Skylights used for the natural lighting of the top floor of a multistory building or in a one-story building may have positive thermal and luminous effects (see Figure 4-8).

1 ***Thermal effects***

Conduction: Heat loss during the winter and heat gain during the summer will increase unless nocturnal insulation is used.

Convection: There will be little convection change unless operable glass is used and summer ventilation is encouraged by opening the skylight during the cooling season.

Radiation: Winter and summer solar heat gains will occur unless shading is part of the design.

2 ***Luminous effects.*** Natural light from skylights is a desirable source of light for reducing artificial lighting in floors immediately below skylights.

3 ***Design considerations.*** In office buildings, skylights should be spaced so that adequate lighting is provided while balancing brightness, controlling glare, reducing solar heat gain during the summer, and minimizing winter heat losses. South-facing clerestories and deep-well dome skylights insulated at night are good examples.

In residences, the effect of natural light is not as important as is the solar heat gain during the winter. Incorporation of thermal storage capacity under the skylight may be beneficial. South-facing clerestories with night insulation are also good examples of this application.

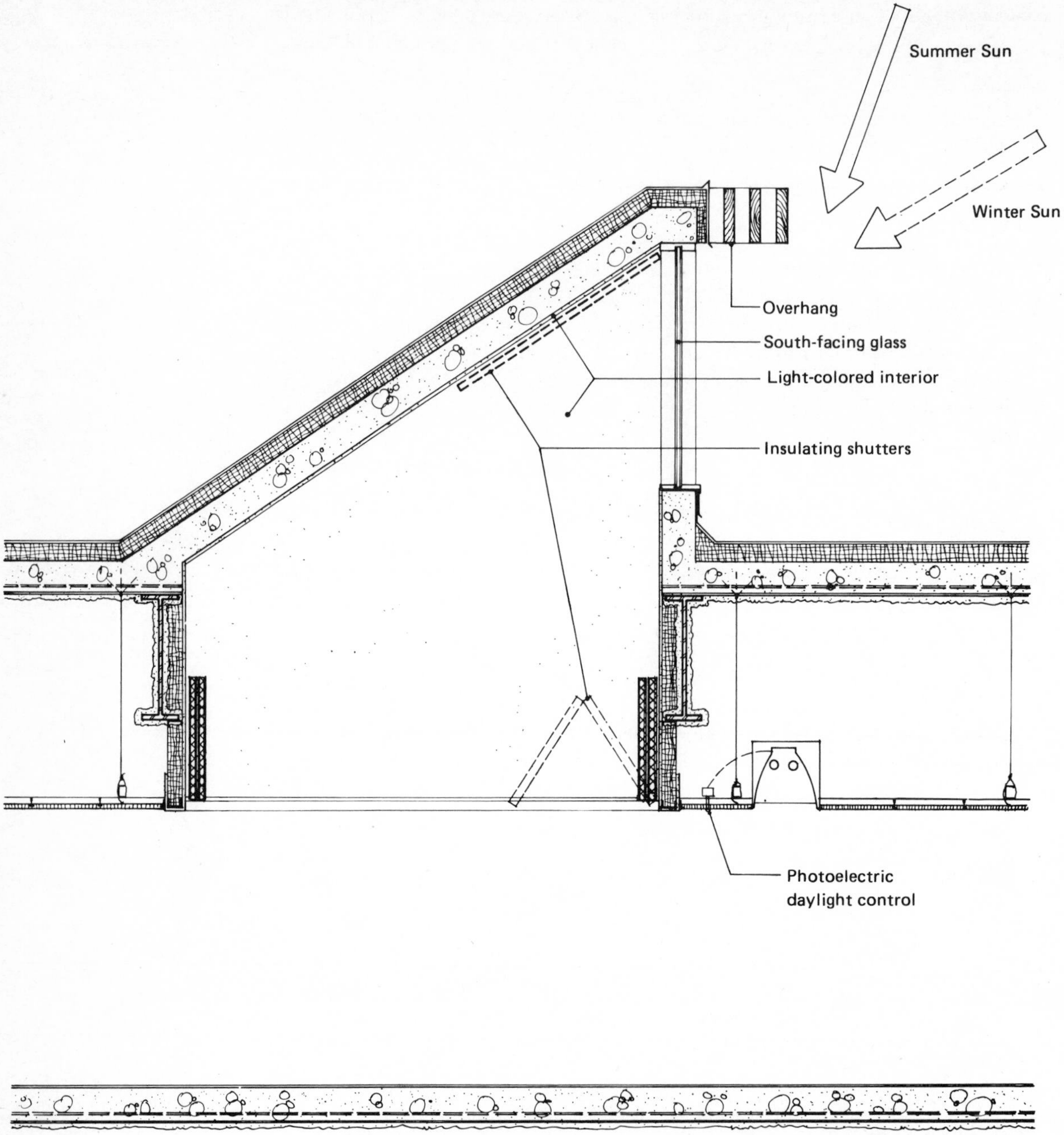

Summer Sun

Winter Sun

Overhang

South-facing glass

Light-colored interior

Insulating shutters

Photoelectric daylight control

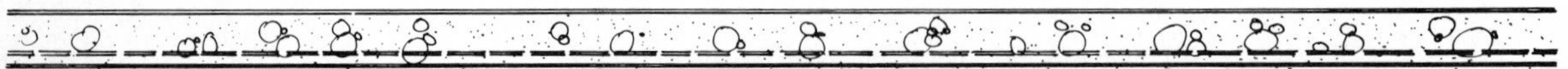

FIGURE 4-8 Section through an energy-conscious clerestory skylight, designed by William Meyer, while a principal of The Ehrenkrantz Group, for the Pennsylvania Avenue Development Corporation under a subcontract with TAMS, Inc. [*Drawing by Jeff Telka.*]

Roof Insulation

Insulation above levels required by existing energy conservation codes may be cost-effective.

1 ***Thermal effects***

Conduction: Heat gains and losses will be reduced.

Convection: None.

Radiation: None.

2 ***Luminous effects.*** None.

3 ***Design considerations.*** The physical depth of a roof structure may limit additional insulation. Insulation placed in or near the outside roof surface may help to decrease temperature swings on the interior of the building because the mass of the roof structure will be enclosed by the insulation.

Roof Ponds

Pools of water on metal deck roofs of residential structures with insulating panels will increase winter and summer energy savings. This design was originally developed by Harold Hay of Los Angeles.

1 ***Thermal effects***

Conduction: When insulating panels cover the water pond, heat loss to the exterior will be reduced.

Convection: Warm air inside the dwelling during the summer day will transfer its heat to the metal deck ceiling by convection.

Radiation: During the winter, solar heat gained by the roof pond will be radiated by the metal deck to the living space below. During the summer, the roof pond will radiate heat to the cold night sky, increasing heat loss from the dwelling and causing it to be cooler.

2 ***Luminous effects.*** None.

3 ***Design considerations.*** Roof ponds will impose greater dead loads and seismic loads on structures. Also, care must be taken in designing movable insulating panels so that their continued operation will not be interrupted by climatic forces such as snow and wind or by mechanical failures.

Double Roofs

In hot, humid climates, “double” roofs may be used to increase summer comfort conditions.

1 ***Thermal effects***

Conduction: None.

Convection: Solar heat gains on the top layer of the roof will be removed by air moving between the two roofs.

Radiation: Sol-air temperature effects on conducted heat gain will be minimized.

2 ***Luminous effects.*** None.

3 ***Design considerations.*** Care should be taken to screen the openings between the two roof layers to prevent access to rodents and foreign objects such as leaves.

Solar Optics

Solar optics systems including heliostats, lenses, and mirrors may provide daylight effectively to interior spaces (see Figure 4-9).

1 ***Thermal effects***

Conduction: Use of lenses which concentrate and direct natural-light streams to building interiors will result in a reduced glass area in exterior walls and lower conducted heat losses and gains through windows.

Convection: None.

Radiation: Use of "cool" mirrors which separate the infrared (heat) portions from the visible portions of the natural-light spectrum will facilitate reductions of unwanted summer solar heat gain in interior spaces.

2 ***Luminous effects.*** Natural lighting combined with dimming controls on artificial lighting systems will reduce electrical energy consumption.

3 ***Design considerations.*** Heliostats require motor-driven parts, which must be protected by light-emitting enclosures to minimize interference by exterior conditions of rain, wind, dirt, and other factors.

BASEMENTS

Thermal storage mass may be provided in basement areas (see Figure 4-1).

1 ***Thermal effects***

Conduction: None.

Convection: Air moving across and/or through thermal storage mass may lose or gain heat, depending on relative temperatures.

Radiation: None.

Left, heliostat sends light through lens allowing reduction in window size. Right, solar optics applied horizontally to a single-story building and below, vertically to a multistory building.

Polar axis
Mirror
Lens
Optical axis
Heliostat
Coupling lens
Mirror
Lens 3
Lens 4
Cold mirror
Solar cell

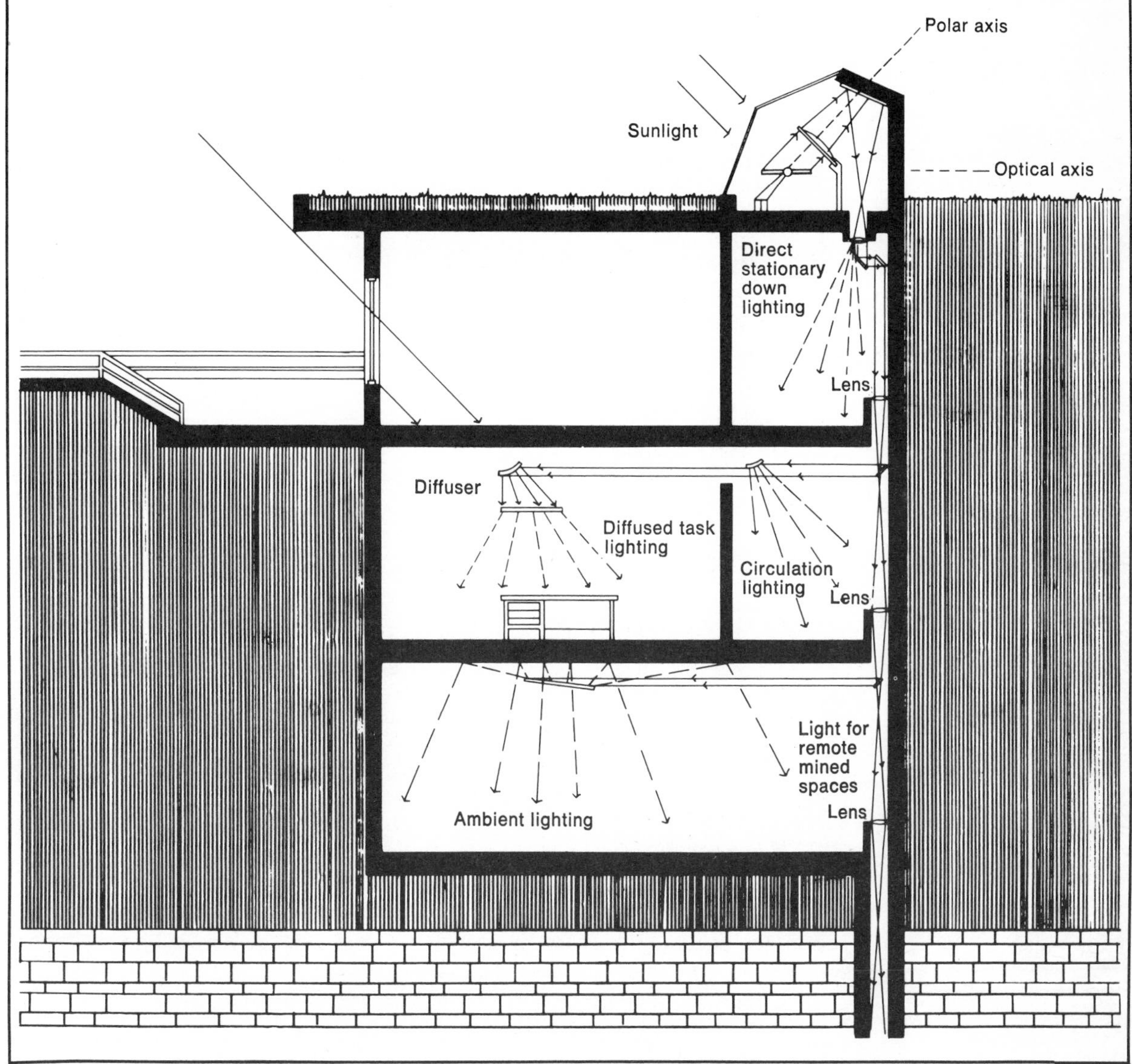

FIGURE 4·9 Diagrams of a solar optics light projection system. [*David Bennett and David Eijadi, "Solar Optics: Projecting Light into Buildings,"* AIA Journal, *March 1980, p. 73.*]

2 ***Luminous effects.*** None.

3 ***Design considerations.*** Rocks, earth, or water vessels may be used for thermal storage. Air must move down to the storage location and back to the living space for heat transfer to occur. Odor control may be a problem.

INTERIORS

General

In office buildings, if daylight controls are used, interiors should be light in color, fabrics should be ultraviolet-resistant, and partitions should be of glass, low in height, or nonexistent.

1 ***Thermal effects.*** None.

2 ***Luminous effects.*** Light-colored interiors will increase the reflectance of natural light from windows and skylights and result in a wider distribution of daylight. This will provide a greater opportunity for reductions in artificial-lighting consumption.

3 ***Design considerations.*** Glass or low partitions will provide much less interruption of natural-light penetration into a space than will full-height opaque partitions. If opaque partitions must be used, they should be placed perpendicular to exterior walls.

Insulating Shades

Insulating materials may be moved across glazing during winter nights. Such devices may take the form of insulating drapery, roll-down shades, or sliding or hinged shutters.

1 ***Thermal effects***

Conduction: Nighttime winter heat loss will be reduced.

Convection: Convection between the glazing and the nocturnal insulation, if allowed to occur, will substantially reduce the effectiveness of the insulation. Convection may be minimized by a seal at the top or bottom (or both) ends of the insulation edge.

Radiation: None.

2 ***Luminous effects.*** None.

3 ***Design considerations.*** Nocturnal glazing insulation may not be as effective in office buildings as in residential buildings because setting back night temperatures to 50 or 55°F will reduce the indoor-outdoor temperature difference and the opportunity for fuel savings.

Interior Window Shading

In office buildings equipped with daylight controls, interior shading devices may control glare and maximize penetration of natural light to the interior of the building (see Figure 4-5).

1 ***Thermal effects.*** None.

2 ***Luminous effects.*** Natural-light levels will be higher farther away from the source of the light, thus providing opportunities for greater artificial-lighting savings.

3 ***Design considerations.*** Devices which may have some value are inverted venetian blinds and light shelves. Blinds may not be able to control glare as well as light shelves can.

Ceiling Heights

If daylight controls are used in office buildings, suspended ceilings in exterior zones may be raised to increase the depth of ceiling-reflected natural light (see Figure 4-5).

1 ***Thermal effects.*** None.

2 ***Luminous effects.*** Natural-light levels will be more evenly distributed in rooms adjacent to a window. Light intensities will be greater farther away from a window and, if coordinated with light shelves, less intense next to a window.

3 ***Design considerations.*** Exterior zones of office buildings typically have perimeter mechanical systems at or near floor level and *not* in the ceiling, thus reducing the need for low, suspended ceilings near window areas.

Recessed Windows

Moving a window into a space, thus creating an overhang, will, if the recess is dimensioned properly, reduce fuel consumption for summer cooling. In addition, on east and west facades a vertical shading plane will be established and will help shade early-morning or late-afternoon summer sun. (See Figure 4-10.)

1 *Thermal effects*

Conduction: None.

Convection: None.

Radiation: Summer solar heat gains will be reduced by the shading effect of the recessed window.

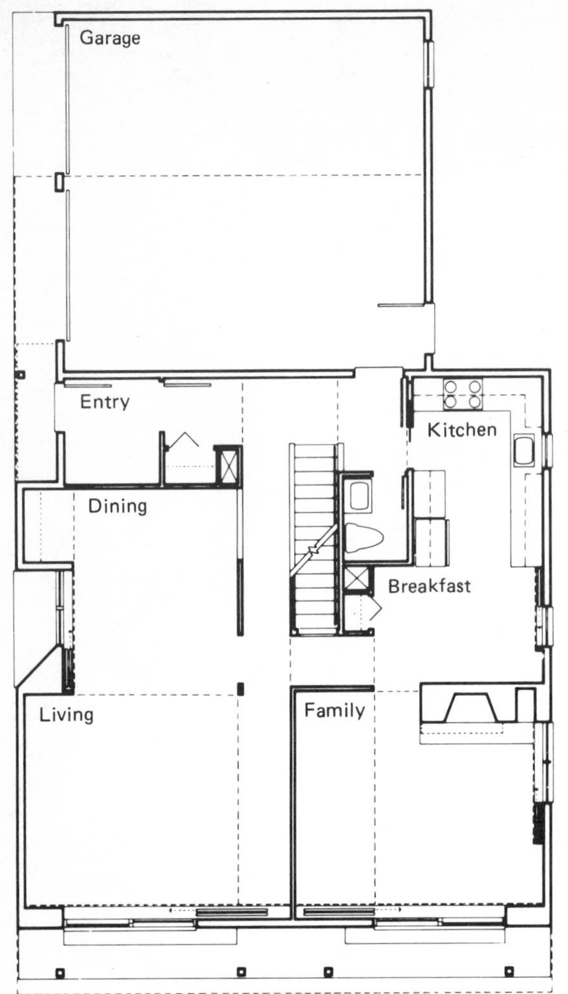

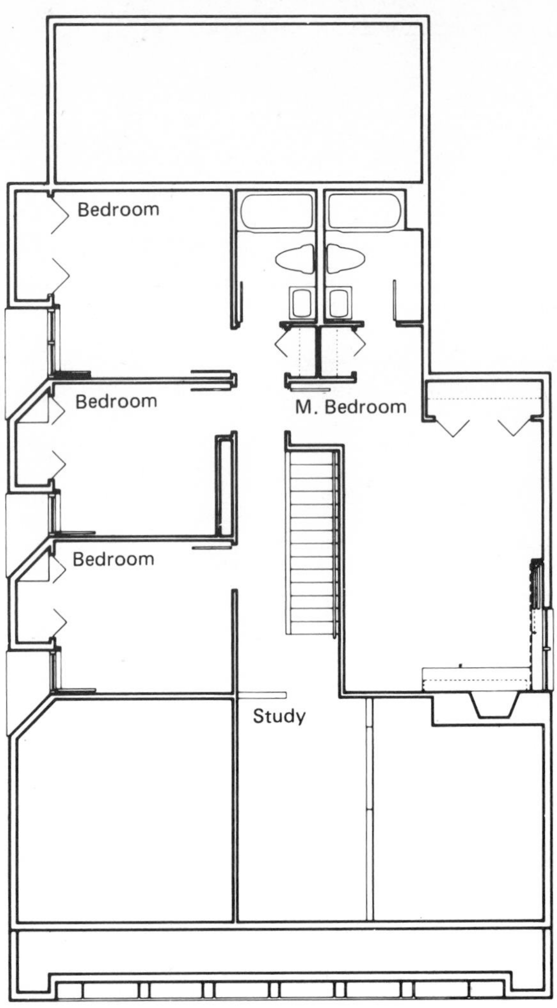

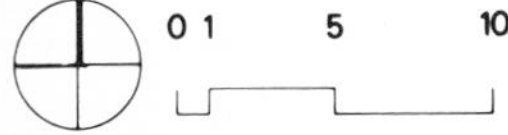

First-Floor Plan

Second-Floor Plan

Front Elevation

FIGURE 4·10 Plans and elevation of a house with recessed windows, designed by William Meyer and Carl Meinhardt, while principals of The Ehrenkrantz Group, for Exxon Enterprises, Inc., for a site in Foxboro, Massachusetts, 1978.

2 ***Luminous effects.*** Natural-light intensities on the interior during the cooling season will be somewhat reduced by recessed windows unless light shelves or other reflecting devices are provided.

3 ***Design considerations.*** Recessed windows provide interior designers with opportunities for summer shading design without altering building exteriors.

ENTRIES

Entry designs such as vestibules will reduce energy consumption.

1 ***Thermal effects***

Conduction: None.

Convection: Infiltration heat losses and gains will be reduced.

Radiation: None.

2 ***Luminous effects.*** None.

3 ***Design considerations.*** In office buildings, using either double banks of swinging doors with a vestibule in between or revolving doors will help reduce fuel consumption.

In residential buildings, storm doors or double-door vestibules are appropriate.

FIVE

LIFE-CYCLE COST-BENEFIT ANALYSIS

The designer of an energy-conscious building is often faced with a dilemma: the design saves the client money through fuel reductions, but the building costs more as a result. The questions that immediately arise are: "Is it worth it to my client to pay more initially to save more later? If so, how much more should my client pay before the design ceases to become worthwhile?"

In the simplest terms, the methods used to assess the worthiness of an investment are two: payback period and return on investment. One is the reciprocal of the other. But sometimes a more sophisticated analysis is warranted. The example presented below shows how a simple cost-benefit analysis may be made and what its limitations are.

A designer of a development of single-family houses proposes to use triple glazing on each house instead of double glazing. His energy analysis involves identifying the types of thermal flows which will be affected by the triple glazing. He finds that winter conductive heat loss will be reduced, as will summer conductive heat gain. He also sees that on the south side of the house, as well as on the east and west sides to some extent, winter radiative heat gain is reduced somewhat by the additional layer of glass, which lowers the overall solar heat transmission qualities of the windows. The houses have overhangs over the south-, east-, and west-facing windows, so there is no significant summertime solar radiation on the windows. Also, the change in available natural light is not significant because little artificial lighting will be used in the houses during the daytime.

The designer's calculation of the monetary value of the changes in the energy flows of a typical house in the development is as follows from a homeowner's point of view:

Reduction in winter conductive heat loss	\$50
Reduction in winter radiative heat gain	− 10
Reduction in summertime heat gain	+ 10
Net savings	\$50/year

The designer's estimate of the cost of *adding* triple glazing to each house is \$700.

The last step in the designer's analysis is to compare the added construction cost with the fuel savings benefits. Two methods are used for initial comparison. The designer divides the additional, or *incremental,* construction cost C_0 by the fuel savings benefits B_t to obtain a simple payback period:[1]

$$\text{Simple payback period} = \frac{\text{cost}}{\text{annual benefits}} = \frac{C_0}{B_t} = \frac{\$700}{\$50/\text{year}} = 14 \text{ years} \tag{5-1}$$

A homeowner is usually more accustomed to evaluating investments based on rate of return, however. This measure, as mentioned earlier, is the reciprocal of the payback calculation. It is calculated by dividing annual fuel savings B_t by initial construction costs C_0.

$$\text{Simple return on investment} = \frac{\text{annual benefits}}{\text{cost}} = \frac{B_t}{C_0} = \frac{\$50/\text{year}}{\$700} = 0.07/\text{year} = 7 \text{ percent/year} \tag{5-2}$$

The designer asks his client what the homeowners' *normal* return on investment is. The client answers that his market usually expects to get 12 percent per year before taxes but that because the people to whom he sells are in the 50 percent bracket, the return amounts to 6 percent after taxes. The 7 percent return on investment of the triple glazing exceeds 6 percent per year, and on that basis the designer suggests that the homeowners would be wise to invest in the design modification.

The client quite appropriately points out that he would like the designer to consider some other things in the analysis before finally deciding whether or not to accept triple glazing. In particular, he wants to know how escalation of fuel prices, income taxes, and financing will affect the return-on-investment analysis.

The analysis required to consider these issues involves two basic types of measures of economic change: escalation rates and discount rates.

ESCALATION RATES (r_e)

An escalation rate is the annual compounded rate of change with which prices increase. Table 5-1 presents escalation rates which were prevalent for various kinds of prices in the early 1980s in the United States. Fuel oil, for example, is assumed to increase in price by 9 percent per year. This assumption may be varied depending on economic conditions and/or the designer's expectations of future inflation.

[1] C_0 means the incremental *cost* in the beginning of the project, that is, Year 0. B_t means *benefits* over some period of time, where time is designated by the letter t. The time period typically used is a year, and the year used for simple cost-benefit analysis is often the base year, Year 0.

TABLE 5-1 Escalation Rate Assumptions

	Percent per year	
	Escalation including inflation	Escalation after deducting for inflation
General inflation	8	0
Oil	9	1
Electricity	12	4
Gas	10	2
Steam	12	4
Labor for operation and maintenance	8	0
Materials for operation and maintenance	8	0

SOURCE: Estimates prepared by the author.

If fuel oil savings created by an energy-conserving design are expected to be \$50 in Year 0 (that is, the present), the savings in the following year (Year 1) will be 9 percent more, or

Year 1: $1.09 \times \$50 = \$54.50$

The next year, the savings will increase by another 9 percent. This time using the previous year's cost as a base,

Year 2: $1.09 \times \$54.50 = \$59.41$

This may also be written as

Year 2: $1.09 \times (1.09 \times \$50) = \$59.41$

The third year's savings will be

Year 3: $1.09 \times \$59.41 = \$64.75$

or Year 3: $1.09 \times [1.09\,(1.09 \times \$50)] = \$64.75$

The results of this escalation of fuel prices, over a 15-year period for the example discussed, are presented in column A of Table 5-2.

Year 3 may also be written as

$$1.09 \times 1.09 \times 1.09 \times 50 = \$64.75$$

or

$$1.09^3 \times 50 = \$64.75$$

or

$$(1 + 0.09)^3 \times 50 = \$64.75$$

The escalation rate r_e in this example is 0.09, and the base-year benefits B_0 are \$50. The benefits in the third year B_3 are \$64.75. Given these designations, the above equation becomes:

$$(1 + r_e)^3 \times B_0 = B_3$$

If we let t equal time in years, the general form of the equation then becomes:

$$B_t = (1 + r_e)^t \times B_0 \qquad (5\text{-}3)$$

TABLE 5-2 Example Cash Flows Resulting from Adding Triple Glazing to a Single-Family House [construction cost: \$700 for triple glazing (C_0); energy savings: \$50 for base year (B_0)]

Year	(A) Fuel savings escalated at 9 percent (B_t)	(B) Discount factor at 6 percent	(C) Discounted savings (A) × (B) (B_d)	(D) Cumulation of (C)	(E) Discount factor at 10 percent	(F) Discounted savings (A) × (E)
1	\$ 55	0.943	\$ 52		0.909	\$ 50
2	59	0.890	53	\$105	0.826	49
3	65	0.840	55	160	0.751	49
4	71	0.792	56	216	0.683	48
5	77	0.747	58	274	0.621	48
6	84	0.705	59	333	0.564	47
7	91	0.665	61	394	0.513	47
8	100	0.627	63	457	0.467	47
9	109	0.592	65	522	0.424	46
10	118	0.558	66	588	0.386	46
11	129	0.527	68	656	0.350	45
12	141	0.497	70	726 (>700)	0.319	45
13	153	0.469	72		0.290	44
14	167	0.442	74		0.263	44
15	182	0.417	76		0.239	43
Total	\$1601		\$948			\$698 (≅\$700)

Simple payback = \$700 ÷ \$50/year = 14 years
Discounted payback* = 12 years
Simple return = \$50/year ÷ \$700 = 7 percent/year
Discounted return* = 10 percent
Net present value* = \$948 − \$700 = \$248

*Explained in subsections "Discounted Payback Period," "Discounted Rate of Return on Investment," and "Net Present Value."

SOURCE: Compiled by the author.

in units,

$$\$/\text{year} = \$/\text{year}$$

where t = time in years
B_t = benefits in year t, \$/year
B_0 = benefits in base year, \$/year
r_e = escalation rate, no units

DISCOUNT RATES (r_d)

A "discount rate" is the return on investment that an investor typically makes, or requires from, his or her normal investment opportunities. It varies depending on the investment sophistication and opportunities available to the investor, his or her income tax bracket, and the risk associated by the investor with a particular investment. If an investment is made in an energy-conserving building design, the design must yield at least the same rate of return as other investment opportunities of *equivalent risk* available to an investor if it is to be economically worthy of investment.

If an investor's normal return was 6 percent per year, he or she could invest \$50 today and expect to receive \$53 at the end of one year or \$56.18 at the end of the second year. If, for example, the same investor provided professional services worth \$50 to a client but the client couldn't pay for those services for 1 year, the client should eventually pay \$53 to the investor since that is what \$50 would be worth 1 year away if invested at 6 percent per year. In other words, the "present value" of the \$53 received 1 year in the future is \$50 today, given a 6 percent annual average return-on-investment rate, or "discount" rate.

The above example may be illustrated numerically as follows:

$$1.06 \times \$50 = \$53$$

$$\text{Therefore} \quad \$50 = \$53/1.06 = \$53 \times 1/1.06$$

$$\text{or} \quad \$50 = \$53 \times 0.943$$

where 0.943 is called a "discount factor" and is equal to 1/1.06 (see Table 5-3 for a comprehensive list of discount factors).

Similarly, if

$$1.06 \times 1.06 \times \$50 = \$56.18$$

$$\text{then} \quad \$50 = \$56.18/1.06^2 = \$56.18 \times 1/1.06^2$$

$$\text{or} \quad \$50 = \$56.18 \times 0.890$$

That is, the present value of \$56.18 received 2 years in the future, given a 6 percent annual discount rate, is \$50. In this case, 0.890 is the 6 percent discount factor for 2 years in the future and is equal to $1/1.06^2$.

Generalizing in the same manner as in the section "Escalation Rates,"

$$\text{in units,} \quad B_d = \frac{B_t}{(1 + r_d)t} \tag{5-4}$$

$$\$/\text{year} = \$/\text{year}$$

where t = time, years
B_d = discounted incremental benefits in the base year, \$/year
B_t = incremental benefits in year t, \$/year
r_d = discount rate, no units

The discount rate for individuals assumed for most of the examples in this book is 6 percent per year. This is an aftertax rate of return, one that an individual might expect to get, for example, from investing in tax-exempt bonds in times of moderate interest rates.

In the example of triple glazing, a 6 percent discount rate was used to discount or reduce the value of the future cash benefits of the fuel savings as shown in Table 5-2. Column B has discount factors for a 6 percent discount rate. These were computed as follows:

$$\text{Year 1: } 1/1.06 = 0.943$$

$$\text{Year 2: } 1/1.06^2 = 0.890$$

$$\text{Year 3: } 1/1.06^3 = 0.840$$

TABLE 5-3 Discount Factors: Present Value of $1 Received at the End of a Period

Years hence	Percent										
	1	2	4	6	8	10	12	14	15	16	18
1	0.990	0.980	0.962	0.943	0.926	0.909	0.893	0.877	0.870	0.862	0.847
2	0.980	0.961	0.925	0.890	0.857	0.826	0.797	0.769	0.756	0.743	0.718
3	0.971	0.942	0.889	0.840	0.794	0.751	0.712	0.675	0.658	0.641	0.609
4	0.961	0.924	0.855	0.792	0.735	0.683	0.636	0.592	0.572	0.552	0.516
5	0.951	0.906	0.822	0.747	0.681	0.621	0.567	0.519	0.497	0.476	0.437
6	0.942	0.888	0.790	0.705	0.630	0.564	0.507	0.456	0.432	0.410	0.370
7	0.933	0.871	0.760	0.665	0.583	0.513	0.452	0.400	0.376	0.354	0.314
8	0.923	0.853	0.731	0.627	0.540	0.467	0.404	0.351	0.327	0.305	0.266
9	0.914	0.837	0.703	0.592	0.500	0.424	0.361	0.308	0.284	0.263	0.225
10	0.905	0.820	0.676	0.558	0.463	0.386	0.322	0.270	0.247	0.227	0.191
11	0.896	0.804	0.650	0.527	0.429	0.350	0.287	0.237	0.215	0.195	0.162
12	0.887	0.788	0.625	0.497	0.397	0.319	0.257	0.208	0.187	0.168	0.137
13	0.879	0.773	0.601	0.469	0.368	0.290	0.229	0.182	0.163	0.145	0.116
14	0.870	0.758	0.577	0.442	0.340	0.263	0.205	0.160	0.141	0.125	0.099
15	0.861	0.743	0.555	0.417	0.315	0.239	0.183	0.140	0.123	0.108	0.084
16	0.853	0.728	0.534	0.394	0.292	0.218	0.163	0.123	0.107	0.093	0.071
17	0.844	0.714	0.513	0.371	0.270	0.198	0.146	0.108	0.093	0.080	0.060
18	0.836	0.700	0.494	0.350	0.250	0.180	0.130	0.095	0.081	0.069	0.051
19	0.828	0.686	0.475	0.331	0.232	0.164	0.116	0.083	0.070	0.060	0.043
20	0.820	0.673	0.456	0.312	0.215	0.149	0.104	0.073	0.061	0.051	0.037
21	0.811	0.660	0.439	0.294	0.199	0.135	0.093	0.064	0.053	0.044	0.031
22	0.803	0.647	0.422	0.278	0.184	0.123	0.083	0.056	0.046	0.038	0.026
23	0.795	0.634	0.406	0.262	0.170	0.112	0.074	0.049	0.040	0.033	0.022
24	0.788	0.622	0.390	0.247	0.158	0.102	0.066	0.043	0.035	0.028	0.019
25	0.780	0.610	0.375	0.233	0.146	0.092	0.059	0.038	0.030	0.024	0.016
26	0.772	0.598	0.361	0.220	0.135	0.084	0.053	0.033	0.026	0.021	0.014
27	0.764	0.586	0.347	0.207	0.125	0.076	0.047	0.029	0.023	0.018	0.011
28	0.757	0.574	0.333	0.196	0.116	0.069	0.042	0.026	0.020	0.016	0.010
29	0.749	0.563	0.321	0.185	0.107	0.063	0.037	0.022	0.017	0.014	0.008
30	0.742	0.552	0.308	0.174	0.099	0.057	0.033	0.020	0.015	0.012	0.007
40	0.672	0.453	0.208	0.097	0.046	0.022	0.011	0.005	0.004	0.003	0.001
50	0.608	0.372	0.141	0.054	0.021	0.009	0.003	0.001	0.001	0.001	

SOURCE: R. N. Anthony, *Management Accounting: Text and Cases*, Richard D. Irwin, Inc., Homewood, Ill., 1969.

These values are presented in Table 5-3 so that they need not be calculated each time.

The *present value* of each cash flow in column A was found by multiplying each cash flow by a corresponding discount factor in column B. The resulting values for each year are presented in column C.

The total of the cash flows in column C is $948. In general terms, a sum of annual discounted cash flows may be written as follows:

$$\text{Total } B_d = \sum_{t=1}^{n} \frac{B_t}{(1 + r_d)^t} \tag{5-5}$$

20	22	24	25	26	28	30	35	40	45	50
0.833	0.820	0.806	0.800	0.794	0.781	0.769	0.741	0.714	0.690	0.667
0.694	0.672	0.650	0.640	0.630	0.610	0.592	0.549	0.510	0.476	0.444
0.579	0.551	0.524	0.512	0.500	0.477	0.455	0.406	0.364	0.328	0.296
0.482	0.451	0.423	0.410	0.397	0.373	0.350	0.301	0.260	0.226	0.198
0.402	0.370	0.341	0.328	0.315	0.291	0.269	0.223	0.186	0.156	0.132
0.335	0.303	0.275	0.262	0.250	0.227	0.207	0.165	0.133	0.108	0.088
0.279	0.249	0.222	0.210	0.198	0.178	0.159	0.122	0.095	0.074	0.059
0.233	0.204	0.179	0.168	0.157	0.139	0.123	0.091	0.068	0.051	0.039
0.194	0.167	0.144	0.134	0.125	0.108	0.094	0.067	0.048	0.035	0.026
0.162	0.137	0.116	0.107	0.099	0.085	0.073	0.050	0.035	0.024	0.017
0.135	0.112	0.094	0.086	0.079	0.066	0.056	0.037	0.025	0.017	0.012
0.112	0.092	0.076	0.069	0.062	0.052	0.043	0.027	0.018	0.012	0.008
0.093	0.075	0.061	0.055	0.050	0.040	0.033	0.020	0.013	0.008	0.005
0.078	0.062	0.049	0.044	0.039	0.032	0.025	0.015	0.009	0.006	0.003
0.065	0.051	0.040	0.035	0.031	0.025	0.020	0.011	0.006	0.004	0.002
0.054	0.042	0.032	0.028	0.025	0.019	0.015	0.008	0.005	0.003	0.002
0.045	0.034	0.026	0.023	0.020	0.015	0.012	0.006	0.003	0.002	0.001
0.038	0.028	0.021	0.018	0.016	0.012	0.009	0.005	0.002	0.001	0.001
0.031	0.023	0.017	0.014	0.012	0.009	0.007	0.003	0.002	0.001	
0.026	0.019	0.014	0.012	0.010	0.007	0.005	0.002	0.001	0.001	
0.022	0.015	0.011	0.009	0.008	0.006	0.004	0.002	0.001		
0.018	0.013	0.009	0.007	0.006	0.004	0.003	0.001	0.001		
0.015	0.010	0.007	0.006	0.005	0.003	0.002	0.001			
0.013	0.008	0.006	0.005	0.004	0.003	0.002	0.001			
0.010	0.007	0.005	0.004	0.003	0.002	0.001	0.001			
0.009	0.006	0.004	0.003	0.002	0.002	0.001				
0.007	0.005	0.003	0.002	0.002	0.001	0.001				
0.006	0.004	0.002	0.002	0.002	0.001	0.001				
0.005	0.003	0.002	0.002	0.001	0.001	0.001				
0.004	0.003	0.002	0.001	0.001	0.001					
0.001										

where the variables and units are the same as in Equation (5-4), except that n = number of years, that is, the useful life of the item generating the cash flows.

In Table 5-2, B_d is represented by column C, where each cash flow has been calculated as follows:

Year 1: $B_d = 55/1.06 = 52$

Year 2: $B_d = 59/1.06^2 = 53$

Year 3: $B_d = 65/1.06^3 = 55$

Year 4: $B_d = 71/1.06^4 = 56$

. . . .

. . . .

. . . .

$$\text{Year 15: } B_c = 182/1.06^{15} = 76$$

$$\text{Total } B_d = \sum_{t=1}^{15} \frac{B_t}{(1 + 0.06)^t} = 948$$

A period of 15 years was used in the analysis because that is the estimated life of the triple-glazing design with no residual value at the end of that period. The useful life of a building component should determine the length of the analysis period unless assumptions are made concerning sale price and/or residual value (see section "Comprehensive Cash-Flow Projections").

METHODS FOR EVALUATING ENERGY-CONSERVING DESIGNS

The financial community uses a number of methods for determining whether or not a particular investment is worth making. These include:

- Simple payback period
- Discounted payback period
- Simple rate of return on investment
- Discounted rate of return on investment
- Net present value

In all cases, *incremental* costs above the normal cost of building to achieve a lower level of fuel consumption will be treated as cash *outflows*. These include one-time costs such as construction costs as well as recurring costs such as maintenance costs and interest. Such costs will be designated, as mentioned earlier, by a C.

Lower fuel costs will be treated as fuel savings and for the purpose of analysis will be called cash *inflows*. Such savings, or benefits, will be designated by a B and will include income tax–related savings as well as fuel savings.

Simple Payback Period

This measure is calculated, as described earlier, by dividing the additional construction costs in the base year by the fuel savings expected at the end of the first year of operation:

$$\text{Simple payback period} = C_0 \div B_t = \frac{\$}{\$/\text{year}} = \text{years} \tag{5-1}$$

In the triple-glazing example,

$$\text{Simple payback period} = \$700 \div \$50/\text{year} = 14 \text{ years}$$

If this is compared with the simple payback of an investment yielding 6 percent per year, or $42 the first year,

$$\text{Simple payback} = \$700 \div \$42/\text{year} = 16.7 \text{ years}$$

The payback period is shorter for the investment in triple glazing than for the investor's typical investment opportunity of equivalent risk; therefore, the triple glazing may be selected as a worthwhile, or *cost-effective*, investment. Another way of describing this situation is the following. On the basis of the simple-payback-period evaluation method and a required return on investment of 6 percent per year, triple glazing is a cost-effective energy conservation design strategy.

The drawback of the simple payback method is that it ignores all future costs and benefits which may be expected by the owner after the first year of operation. This disadvantage makes the simple payback period a relatively crude measure of value.

Discounted Payback Period

The discounted payback period is the number of years k that it takes for the following condition to be satisfied:

$$C_0 = \sum_{t=1}^{k} \frac{B_t - C_t}{(1 + r_d)^t} \tag{5-6}$$

in units,

$$\$ = \$$$

where t = time, years
C_0 = incremental construction costs of the design being analyzed in the base year, $
C_t = incremental costs occurring in year t, $/year
B_t = incremental benefits or savings occurring in year t, $/year
k = year in which payback occurs
r_d = discount rate, no units

A design strategy is considered cost-effective, that is, worth investing in, if its discounted payback period is less than its useful life. Table 5-2 shows that in column C the value of C_0, or $700, is reached in the twelfth year.

In other words, the discounted payback period, for that example, is 12 years, while the useful life is estimated to be 15. It may be concluded, therefore, that the triple glazing is cost-effective. This method also ignores all cash flows which occur after the year in which payment occurs and is not recommended for rigorous analysis.

Simple Rate of Return on Investment

This ratio, as mentioned earlier, may be calculated by dividing the first complete annual fuel savings by the incremental construction cost associated with a particular design strategy:

$$\text{Simple rate of return} = B_t/C_0 = \frac{\$/\text{year}}{\$} = \text{percent/year} \qquad (5\text{-}2)$$

In the triple-glazing example,

$$\text{Simple rate of return} = \$50 \div \$700/\text{year} = 7.1 \text{ percent/year}$$

Since 7.1 percent is greater than 6 percent, the investor's normal return, the triple glazing is judged cost-effective by this method as well.

As with the simple-payback-period method, this method ignores all future cash flows.

Discounted Rate of Return on Investment

The discounted rate of return is that discount rate which creates the following condition:

$$\sum_{t=0}^{n} \frac{B_t - C_t}{(1 + r_d)^t} = 0 \qquad (5\text{-}7)$$

or in simple cases, in which no annual costs are associated with a design,

$$\sum_{t=1}^{n} \frac{B_t}{(1 + r_d)^t} - C_0 = 0 \qquad (5\text{-}8)$$

The units are the same as in Equation (5-6), except that n is equal to the number of years of useful life of the asset generating the cash flow.

In the triple-glazing example, the discounted rate of return was the discount rate which, when applied to the cash benefits B_t in column A, resulted in a sum of $700 over the 15-year period. This rate can be found only by *trial and error*. In Table 5-2, column F is a set of cash flows which are the result of discounting column A cash flows by a 10 percent rate. The sum of the cash flows in column F is $698, which is very close to $700. The conclusion in the example, therefore, is that the discounted rate of return is approximately 10 percent per year. When this is compared with the investor's normal 6 percent per year, the triple glazing appears to be a worthwhile investment; that is, it's cost-effective.

This method is recommended because it accounts for *all* cash flows over the life of the investment. When cash flows do not vary evenly from year to year, however, it sometimes produces multiple answers or answers which lead to an incorrect decision. The occurrence is rare, however, in cash flows created by buildings.

Net Present Value

An investment is worth making if the net present value of all cash inflows and outflows generated by it is greater than zero. That is, if

$$\sum_{t=0}^{n} \frac{B_t - C_t}{(1 + r_d)^t} > 0 \qquad (5\text{-}9)$$

or in simple cash flows, in which no annual costs are associated with a design,

$$\sum_{t=1}^{n} \frac{B_t}{(1 + r_d)^t} - C_0 > 0 \tag{5-10}$$

The units here are the same as in Equations (5-6) and (5-7).

In the triple-glazing example, from column C of Table 5-2 the sum of the cash flows discounted at 6 percent is $948.

In this example, there are no C_t beyond Year 0; there is only C_0. Therefore,

$$\$948 - \$700 = \$248$$

or

$$\sum_{t=1}^{15} \frac{B_t}{(1 + 0.06)^t} - \$700 = \$248$$

or

$$\sum_{t=1}^{n} \frac{B_t}{(1 + r_d)^t} - C_0 > 0$$

In other words, since the net present value is positive ($248 is greater than zero), the investment in triple glazing may be judged cost-effective. The benefits exceed the costs.

This method is the most rigorous under any conditions of cash flow and is regarded by most experts as the most reliable for decision-making purposes. It is also, however, the least well understood by the general public.

COMPREHENSIVE CASH-FLOW PROJECTIONS

Up to this point, emphasis in this presentation has been placed on future cash flows which consist primarily of fuel savings. There are many more, of course. The annual cash flows resulting from an *architectural* energy conservation design may be designated as follows:

Annual cash flow $= B_t - C_t$ (that is, incremental benefits each year minus incremental costs each year)

where B_t = fuel savings + income tax savings

C_t = mortgage payments + maintenance costs + insurance + property taxes

Income Tax Effects

The fuel savings and income tax savings depend on the income and *ownership status* of the investor. Income tax savings occur because a number of items are deductible from a building owner's gross income.

Deductible items for a single-family homeowner-occupant, under current tax laws,[2] include:

- Interest on mortgage
- Property tax

[2]These are allowable deductions related to *federal* income taxes and to *most* state and municipal income taxes. The reader should check local income tax laws, however, to ensure accuracy for a particular locale.

Deductible items for an owner of a building for business or investment purposes include:

- Interest on mortgage
- Property tax
- Fuel costs
- Maintenance costs
- Insurance
- Depreciation

For the investor who lives in a single-family house, the annual cash flows affected by energy-conscious improvements in architectural design are presented below. Cash outflows are designated as negative and inflows as positive.

$$\begin{aligned}\text{Annual cash flow } (B_t - C_t) = {} & + \text{fuel savings } (B_t) \\ & - \text{mortgage principal repayment} \\ & - \text{maintenance costs} \\ & - \text{insurance} \\ & - (1 - tx) \text{ property tax}^3 \\ & - (1 - tx) \text{ mortgage interest}\end{aligned}$$

For the investor in rental dwelling units or other building types owned and operated as a business or investments,

$$\begin{aligned}\text{Annual cash flow} = {} & + (1 - tx) \text{ fuel savings} \\ & - \text{mortgage interest} \\ & - \text{maintenance costs} \\ & - \text{insurance} \\ & - \text{property tax} \\ & + tx \text{ depreciation} \\ & - \text{mortgage principal repayment}\end{aligned}$$

Note that because of the tax-deductible nature of fuel costs for the second type of investor the fuel costs displaced by an energy-conserving strategy are worth *aftertax* $(1 - tx)$ fuel savings. In other words, if an investor were in the 25 percent bracket, the actual aftertax cash savings related to reduced fuel consumption would be worth only 75 percent of the before-tax savings.

The reader should also be aware that property taxes in most states are not levied against those portions of a building which are considered energy-conservative.

Depreciation Effects

Depreciation is typically a noncash "expense"; that is, it does not involve a cash outlay: it only helps to reduce income taxes. Depreciation in real estate is a deduc-

[3] tx = income tax rate; the discussion which follows explains the $(1 - tx)$ factor.

tion allowable by the Internal Revenue Service when gross income is computed for income tax purposes. Lower gross income means lower income taxes. In fact, however, most buildings actually appreciate in value. Depreciation, therefore, is usually an expense *only* for tax purposes; it typically does not involve a cash outlay. It generates, rather, a cash *inflow* in terms of income tax savings.

"Straight-line depreciation" is computed as the cost of the installation C_0 divided by the expected life n of the system (C_0/n). The cash savings resulting from depreciation are calculated by multiplying the income tax rate by the depreciation. For example, if an investor has a taxable income of $10,000, a tax bracket of 25 percent, and $1000 of depreciation available from a building, the following calculations illustrate the cash savings to be derived from the depreciation deduction:

Gross income × tax rate = income tax before depreciation

$10,000 × 0.25 = $2500

(Gross income − depreciation) × tax rate = income tax after depreciation

($10,000 − $1000) × 0.25 = $2250

Tax before depreciation − tax after depreciation = tax savings due to depreciation

$2500 − $2250 = $250

Or tax savings due to depreciation could also be calculated more directly:

Depreciation × tax rate = tax savings due to depreciation

$1000 × 0.25 = $250

Interest

The real cost of interest decreases because it is deductible from gross income for purposes of computing income taxes. If, for example, an investor has $10,000 of taxable income, an income tax rate of 25 percent, and an interest deduction of $600, then

Gross income × tax rate = income tax before interest deduction

$10,000 × 0.25 = $2500

(Gross income − interest) × tax rate = income tax after interest deduction

($10,000 − $600) × 0.25 = $2350

Tax before interest deduction − tax after interest deduction

= value of interest deduction

$2500 − $2350 = $150

Tax savings due to interest deductions could also be calculated more directly:

Interest deduction × tax rate = value of interest deduction

$600 × 0.25 = $150

Therefore, the actual, or aftertax, cost of interest

= interest − (value of interest deduction)

or = interest − (interest × tax rate)

or = interest (1 − tax rate)

= \$600 (1 − 0.25)

= \$450

EXAMPLE

The above considerations may be illustrated by continuing the triple-glazing example for two different ownership conditions. In the first case, the owner will be assumed to live in the house. In the second case, the house will not be inhabited by the owner but rather will be operated as a business investment and rented to other people.

The useful as well as the depreciable life of the windows is assumed to be 15 years. Maintenance and insurance costs are disregarded in this example for purposes of simplification.

In both cases, the building owner finances the installation of the storm windows *as part of* the general construction of the house. The terms of the mortgage that the owner has negotiated with his lender are listed below along with assumptions for depreciation method, income tax bracket, discount rate, real estate tax rates, and residual value.

Initial cost of storm windows C_0	\$700
Downpayment of 30 percent of C_0	\$210
Base-year fuel savings B_0	\$50
Property tax	Assume \$0
Maintenance costs	Assume \$0
Discount rate	0.06
Fuel escalation rate	0.09
Owner's income tax bracket	25 percent
Owner's discount rate	6 percent
Depreciation method	Straight-line
Mortgage loan (\$700 − \$210)[4]	\$490
Depreciation (\$700 ÷ 15 years)	\$46.47/year
Insurance	Assume \$0
Mortgage interest	8¾ percent
Mortgage term	20 years
Mortgage constant[5]	10.6 percent
Mortgage down payment	30 percent
Real estate taxes	None
Residual value at end of assumed useful life	None
Location	New York City

The schedule of payments per \$1 of mortgage principal amount based on the terms listed above is presented in Table 5-4. These figures may be employed to calculate the amount of interest and principal of any size of mortgage by using the figures in the table as a

[4]Incremental amount of increase in principal of mortgage loan applicable to energy-saving components, less the down payment.

[5]A mortgage "constant" is a fixed payment made by a mortgagee each year to pay off both the principal and the interest of a mortgage. (See also the explanation in Table 5-4.)

TABLE 5-4 Example Mortgage Amortization Schedule [amount, $1; constant, 10.6 percent (0.1060) per year; interest, 8 3/4 percent (0.0875) per year; term, 20 years]

Year	Interest	Principal	Balance at end of year
1	0.0875	0.0185	0.9815
2	0.0859	0.0210	0.9614
3	0.0841	0.0219	0.9395
4	0.0822	0.0238	0.9157
5	0.0801	0.0258	0.8898
6	0.0779	0.0281	0.8617
7	0.0754	0.0306	0.8311
8	0.0727	0.0332	0.7978
9	0.0698	0.0362	0.7616
10	0.0666	0.0394	0.7222
11	0.0632	0.0428	0.6794
12	0.0594	0.0466	0.6328
13	0.0554	0.0506	0.5822
14	0.0509	0.0551	0.5271
15	0.0461	0.0599	0.4672
16	0.0409	0.0652	0.4021
17	0.0352	0.0708	0.3313
18	0.0290	0.0770	0.2543
19	0.0223	0.0837	0.1706
20	0.0149	0.0910	0.0796
	0.007	0.0796	

Illustration of the constant-payment principal and interest components:

Constant payment	= $490 × 0.1060 =		$51.94
Interest in Year 1	= $490 × 0.0875 =	$42.87	
Principal in Year 1	= $490 × 0.0185 =	9.07	
			$51.94
Interest in Year 2	= $490 × 0.0859 =	$42.09	
Principal in Year 2	= $490 × 0.0201 =	9.85	
			$51.94

proportionality factor. The figures are valid, of course, only for the 8¾ percent interest rate and 10.6 percent constant payment.

As can be seen from the solutions presented in Tables 5-5 and 5-6, the homeowner condition provides a somewhat better return-on-investment situation (17 percent per year) than does the house which is rented to a tenant (14 percent per year). The reason is that deductible fuel costs do not provide as great a benefit for the rental condition as in the homeowner situation. In Year 1, aftertax fuel savings for the homeowner are $55, whereas they are only $41 for the rental situation: a $14 difference. The possibility of depreciating the value of the investment helps offset this difference but not completely. In Year 1, the value of the depreciation for the rental situation is only $12.

Residual Value

Another concept that needs to be reviewed is residual, or salvage, value. Single-family houses, as in the previous examples, typically are sold every 5 years or so. How does one acknowledge this event in a discounted-cash-flow analysis?

TABLE 5-5 Solution 1: House Owned and Occupied by an Individual (C_0 = $210)

Year	B_t Fuel savings escalated at 9 percent	$-C_t$ Mortgage principal	$-C_t$ Interest × (1 − 0.25)	$= (B_t - C_t)$ Net savings	$\times \frac{1}{(1 + r_d)^t}$ Discount factor at 6 percent	$= B_d$ Discounted net savings at 6 percent rate
1	$ 55	$ 9	$ 32	$ 14	0.943	$ 13
2	59	10	32	17	0.890	15
3	65	11	31	23	0.840	19
4	71	12	30	29	0.792	23
5	77	13	29	35	0.747	26
6	84	14	29	41	0.705	29
7	91	15	28	48	0.665	32
8	100	16	27	57	0.627	36
9	109	18	26	65	0.592	38
10	118	20	24	74	0.558	41
11	129	21	23	85	0.527	45
12	141	23	22	96	0.497	48
13	153	25	20	108	0.469	51
14	167	27	19	121	0.442	53
15	182	29	17	136	0.417	57
16	199	32	15	152	0.394	60
17	216	35	13	168	0.371	62
18	236	38	11	187	0.350	65
19	257	41	8	208	0.331	69
20	280	45	5	230	0.312	72
		36	3			
Total		$490	$444			$854

Discounted payback period = 8.5 years
Net present value = $644 for a 20-year analysis period ($854 − $210)
$316 for a 15-year analysis period ($526 − $210)
Discounted rate of return = 17 percent per year for a 15-year analysis period

Year	Cumulated discounted net savings	$(B_t - C_t)$ Net savings	$\times \frac{1}{(1 + r_d)^t}$ Discount factor at 17 percent*	$= B_d$ Discounted net savings
1		$ 14	0.855	$ 12
2	$ 28	17	0.731	12
3	47	23	0.624	14
4	70	29	0.534	15
5	96	35	0.456	16
6	125	41	0.390	16
7	157	48	0.333	16
8	193	57	0.285	16
9	231	65	0.243	16
10	272	74	0.208	15
11	317	85	0.152	13
12	365	96	0.130	12
13	416	108	0.111	12
14	469	121	0.095	11
15	526	136	0.081	11
				$207 (≅$210)

*By trial and error 17 percent was found to be that discount rate which when applied to the "net savings" cash flows yielded a discount sum over a 15-year period equal (approximately) to the original cost of the investment: $207 ≅ $210.

TABLE 5-6 Solution 2: House Owned by an Individual and Rented to a Tenant (C_0 = \$210)

Year	B Fuel savings escalated at 9 percent (1 − 0.25)	$-C_t$ Interest × (1 − 0.25)	$-C_t$ Mortgage principal	$+B_t$ Depreciation × 0.25	$= (B_t - C_t)$ Net savings	$\times \frac{1}{(1+r_d)^t}$ Discount factor at 6 percent	$= B_d$ Discounted net savings
1	\$ 41	\$ 32	\$ 9	\$12	\$ 12	0.943	\$ 11
2	44	32	10	12	14	0.890	12
3	49	31	11	12	19	0.840	16
4	53	30	12	12	23	0.792	18
5	58	29	13	12	28	0.747	21
6	63	29	14	12	32	0.705	23
7	68	28	15	12	37	0.665	25
8	75	27	16	12	44	0.627	28
9	82	26	18	12	50	0.592	30
10	89	24	20	12	57	0.558	32
11	97	23	21	12	65	0.527	34
12	106	22	23	12	73	0.497	36
13	115	20	25	12	82	0.469	38
14	125	19	27	12	91	0.442	40
15	137	17	29	12	103	0.417	43
16	149	15	32		102	0.394	40
17	162	13	35		114	0.371	42
18	177	11	38		128	0.350	45
19	193	8	41		144	0.331	48
20	210	5	45		160	0.312	50
		3	36				
Total		\$444	\$490				\$632

Discounted payback period = 10 years
Net present value = \$422 for a 20-year analysis period (\$632 − \$210)
\$197 for a 15-year analysis period (\$407 − \$210)
Discounted rate of return = 14 percent per year for a 15-year analysis period

Year	Cumulated discounted net savings	$(B_t - C_t)$ Net savings	$\times \frac{1}{(1+r_d)^t}$ Discount factor at 14 percent	$= B_d$ Discounted net savings
1		\$ 12	0.877	\$ 11
2	\$ 23	14	0.769	11
3	39	19	0.675	13
4	57	23	0.592	14
5	78	28	0.519	15
6	101	32	0.456	15
7	126	37	0.400	15
8	154	44	0.351	15
9	184	50	0.308	15
10	216	57	0.270	15
11	250	65	0.237	15
12	286	73	0.208	15
13	324	82	0.182	15
14	364	91	0.160	15
15	407	103	0.140	14
				\$213 (≅\$210)

Assume, for example, that an investor-owned house is sold in the seventh year. The question that must first be answered is: "What is the value of the triple glazing in that year?" A number of alternative methods may be used to make that determination:

- Book value
- Replacement cost
- Capitalized income

Which method is used is up to the reader. The problem is, of course, that if the house is sold, it is difficult to say how much the triple glazing will contribute to the sale price. To conduct a cost-benefit analysis which involves the sale of a building as an event sometime in the future, however, an analyst must be able to prepare an estimate of the price that the building might be expected to sell for on the basis of an accepted estimating method.

Book value is the original value of the item in question, typically the construction cost minus the depreciation taken up to the time of sale. In the triple-glazing, example, the book value may be calculated as follows:

		Book value in each year
Construction cost	$700	
Less depreciation in Year 1 ($700 ÷ 15)	(47)	$653
Year 2	(47)	606
Year 3	(47)	559
Year 4	(47)	512
Year 5	(47)	465
Year 6	(47)	418
Year 7	(47)	371

Book value is not usually used directly as an estimate of the future sales price that a building or a building component might yield. As mentioned earlier in this chapter, building construction usually increases rather than decreases in value. Book value is used, however, to estimate the *income tax* required on the profit made on the sale of a building. This is illustrated below.

Replacement cost may be used to estimate residual value for items that do not lose their value with time. It would not be appropriate, however, for items such as pumps or fans which actually wear out with use over time. Replacement cost may be calculated by increasing the initial construction cost by the rate of inflation assumed in the analysis; for example,

Initial construction cost	$ 700
Inflation over 7 years at 9 percent per year (1.09^7)	× 1.83
Replacement cost	$1280

Capitalizing income is another method of establishing value for an asset. Income, in the triple-glazing example used in this chapter, is assumed to be the aftertax fuel savings generated by the triple glazing. Capitalizing means converting a flow of income into its capital or investment equivalent. In other words, for the triple glazing one should ask: "How much would a prudent investor pay for a series of annual payments of $37 received in perpetuity? ($37 is the net savings in Year 7 from Table 5-6. The sum for which $37/*year* represents a 6 percent aftertax return on investment is the answer:

$$\text{Capitalized income} = \frac{\$37/\text{year}}{0.06/\text{year}} = \$617$$

Selling an asset that has been depreciated for more than its depreciated value (or book value) creates a profit which is subject to income tax.[6] In the triple-glazing example, we will assume that the asset is sold after being held for more than 1 year (7 years, in fact). This means that it is taxed at one-half the normal income tax rate, or what is known as the "capital gains rate."[7] When the capitalized-income method of calculating residual value is used, the income tax at the time of sale on the triple glazing will be:

Residual value (sales price)	$617	
Less book value	371	
Taxable income	$246	
Capital gains tax rate (0.25 × 0.50)	×0.125	
Income tax owed on sale	$ 31	
Aftertax residual value	$586	($617 − $31)

If we assume sale of the house in the seventh year and ownership of the house by an investor, the discounted-cash-flow and cost-benefit analysis for the triple glazing takes the form presented in Table 5-7.

Note that if a sale is assumed, the mortgage balance as well as the income taxes owed on the profit from the sale must be deducted from the salvage value.

The results of the sale in the seventh year as shown in Table 5-7 indicate that discounted payback can be achieved in the seventh year instead of in 10 years, as indicated in the preceding analysis (Table 5-6). Assumption of a sale is not often made in energy-conscious design analysis but it may give a client an answer to the question of what the implications of a sale may be on his or her investment.

MECHANICAL-SYSTEM EQUIPMENT SAVINGS

In general, design approaches which create savings in fuel consumption by involving some change in the architectural aspects or components of a building increase overall construction cost. Those designs which reduce the *peak* heating or cooling load of a building, however, reduce the *size* of the boiler or chiller required to

[6]Except, of course, for the homeowner, who is not allowed to use depreciation as a deduction in calculating income tax owed.

[7]The capital gains rate has recently been lowered to 40 percent instead of one-half the nominal tax rate and may in the future be changed again. The reader should check with an accountant on the rates to stay current.

TABLE 5-7 Example Cash Flows for a House Owned and Occupied by an Individual Acknowledging Salvage Value (C_0 = $210)

Year	B_t Savings escalated at 9 percent	$-\ C_t$ Mortgage principal	$-\ C_t$ Interest × (1 − 0.25)	$+\ B_t$ Depreciation × 0.25	$= (B_t - C_t)$ Net savings	Aftertax mortgage value	Mortgage balance	Net proceeds from sale	$\times \frac{1}{(1+r_d)^t}$ Discount factor at 6 percent	$= B_d$ Discounted net savings at 6 percent
1	$55	$9	$32	$12	$12				0.943	$ 11
2	59	10	32	12	14				0.890	12
3	65	11	31	12	19				0.840	16
4	71	12	30	12	23				0.792	18
5	77	13	29	12	28				0.747	21
6	84	14	29	12	32				0.705	23
7	. .	. .	. .	. .	. .	$586	$421	$165	0.665	110
										$211 (≅$210)

Discounted payback period = 7 years
Net present value at 6 percent discount rate = $1 after 7 years ($211 − $210)
Discounted rate of return = 6 percent per year for a 7-year analysis period

satisfy that load. A peak heating load is the need for heat which a building experiences at the coldest time of the year. Actually, it's the "statistically" coldest time of the year, that is, the temperature above which a local climate remains during 97.5 or 99 percent of the time, depending on how conservative the designer wants to be. (See Table 6-3.) Adding insulation to a building, for example, will reduce the peak heating load. Adding more south-facing glass to increase winter daytime solar heat gain will reduce energy consumption but will not reduce the peak heating load because the coldest time of the winter will still occur at night.

Peak thermal loads are expressed in terms of Btus per hour and are represented by q. More discussion of this variable and its related measure of overall energy consumption Q is presented in Chapter 6.

For those design approaches which reduce a building's peak heating or cooling load, that is, designs which reduce a building's need for heating or cooling at the coldest or warmest outdoor temperatures of the surrounding climate, a saving in installed cost of mechanical equipment will be realized. This saving is, of course, a nonrecurring construction cost saving, not an annual operations saving. In other words, in the terms used in the previous sections of this chapter, mechanical-system size reductions are an incremental benefit which occurs in Year 0 and are represented by B_0.

For greatest accuracy, a designer should consult a mechanical engineer for estimates of equipment size reductions which might result if peak loads are reduced because of an architectural design improvement. In lieu of that, Table 5-8 may be used to approximate these savings. The base year for the costs in this table is 1980. Estimates for later years should be increased to account for inflation.

EXAMPLE

The designer of an apartment building finds that additional insulation in the outside wall of her building will reduce annual energy consumption by $2500 per year after taxes, cost $9000 to implement, reduce the peak heating load by 100,000 Btu/h, and reduce the peak cooling load by 5.5 tons.

TABLE 5-8 **Savings Due to Cooling and Heating Equipment Size Reductions** (base year, 1980)

Cooling equipment		Cost increments
Commercial buildings		$450/ton*
Residential buildings		$520/ton
		NOTE: Peak cooling loads must be reduced by at least 5 tons before savings can occur.

Heating equipment	Peak load	Cost increments
Houses	±100,000 Btu/h	$14 for each 1000 Btu/h
Medium-size apartment and commercial buildings	±500,000 Btu/h	$8 for each 1000 Btu/h
Large commercial buildings	±3,000,000 Btu/h	$6.75 for each 1000 Btu/h
		NOTE: Peak heating load must be reduced by 10,000 Btu/h before savings can occur.

*A ton is equal to 12,000 Btus per hour. It is the amount of heat required to melt 1 ton of ice.

The value of the reduction in the size of the heating equipment is estimated below on the basis of savings of $8 for each 1000 Btu/h of load reduction, as listed in Table 5-8:

$$B_0 = 100{,}000 \text{ Btu/h} \times \$8/1000 \text{ Btu/h}) = \$800$$

The value of the reduction in the cooling equipment size is estimated as follows, on the basis of $520/ton of load decrease:

$$B_0 = 5.5 \text{ tons} \times \$520/\text{ton} = \$2860$$

The initial cost of installing the insulation, adjusted by the lower equipment saving, is, therefore:

Insulation cost	$9000
Heating equipment savings	(800)
Cooling equipment savings	(2860)
Net installation cost C_0	$5340

A simple cost-benefit analysis yields the following:

$$\text{Simple payback period} = \frac{\$5340}{\$2500/\text{year}} = 2.1 \text{ years}$$

$$\text{Simple return on investment} = \frac{\$2500/\text{year}}{\$5340} = 46.8 \text{ percent/year}$$

As shown above, acknowledgment of mechanical-equipment size reductions can have a significant impact on the cost-effectiveness of architectural energy-conscious design.

DEMAND CHARGES

An economic impact of changes in peak loads, besides mechanical-equipment cost implications, is the effect on cooling-season electricity demand charges. During the summer, electric utility companies typically charge customers[8] not only for the amount of electricity that is used but also for the size of the greatest demand for electricity that a building will make. The units for overall electrical consumption are dollars per kilowatthour, while the units for demand charges are usually dollars per kilowatt-month. Demand charges are levied if a building's peak cooling load demand occurs during the time of day when other buildings make peak demands and when, as a result, the electric utility experiences its peak loadings.

EXAMPLE

In the example presented above, if demand charges are $20 per kilowatt-month, the cooling-system power requirement is 1.2 kilowatts per cooling ton, and the cooling season is 4 months long, the following would be the impact of demand charge reductions on the overall cost-effectiveness of the insulation:

$$\begin{aligned}\text{Demand charge reduction} &= \$20/(\text{kW}\cdot\text{month}) \times 5.5 \text{ T} \times 1.2 \text{ kW/T} \\ &\quad \times 4 \text{ months/year} \\ &= \$528/\text{year}\end{aligned}$$

[8]Demand charges are typically levied on large buildings only. Single-family houses are usually exempt from such charges.

If the building owner is in a 45 percent income tax bracket, the aftertax value of these savings is:

$$B_t = \$528/\text{year}\ (1 - 0.45)$$
$$= \$290/\text{year}$$

The overall savings for the year would then be

$$B_t = \$2500/\text{year} + \$290/\text{year}$$
$$= \$2790/\text{year}$$

The cost-effectiveness of the insulation including the impact of demand charges is revised as follows:

$$\text{Simple payback period} = \frac{\$5340}{\$2790/\text{year}} = 1.9 \text{ years}$$

$$\text{Simple return on investment} = \frac{\$2790/\text{year}}{\$5340} = 52.2 \text{ percent}$$

SUMMARY

The principal equations presented in this chapter are summarized in Table 5-9. The level of detail that a designer should use in conducting a cost-benefit analysis is a function of the complexity of the design being analyzed and many other factors.

An abbreviated cost-benefit analysis approach will be used in the examples presented in the chapters which follow. This approach acknowledges only *major* costs and benefits which will occur in the *initial* years of the life of an energy-saving design. Specifically, the following factors will be considered:

- First year's fuel savings
- Income tax savings due to fuel savings
- Mechanical-equipment size reductions
- Electricity demand charges
- Income tax credits
- Construction costs

TABLE 5-9 Summary of Equations to be Used for Cost-Benefit Analysis

5-1	Simple payback period $= \dfrac{C_0}{B_t}$
5-2	Simple return on investment $= \dfrac{B_t}{C_0}$
5-6	Discounted payback period, k: $C_0 = \sum_{t=1}^{k} \dfrac{B_t - C_t}{(1 + r_d)^t}$
5-7	Discounted return on investment, r_d: $\sum_{t=1}^{n} \dfrac{B_t - C_t}{(1 + r_d)^t} = 0$
5-9	Net present value $= \sum_{t=0}^{n} \dfrac{B_t - C_t}{(1 + r_d)^t} > 0$

This simplified cost-benefit analysis approach will yield an approximate answer which, if considerably above or below a break-even point, may provide a sufficient basis for decision making. If, however, the answer obtained from this method is inconclusive, a more extensive discounted-cash-flow analysis may be necessary.

BIBLIOGRAPHY

Johnson, Robert W.: *Capital Budgeting,* Wadsworth Publishing Company, Inc., Belmont, Calif., 1970.

SIX

THERMAL BENEFITS

To perform a cost-benefit analysis as part of deciding whether or not an energy-saving design is worth implementing, the benefits of such a design must be estimated. Many energy-conscious designs may have both lighting benefits and thermal benefits, as discussed in earlier chapters. This chapter, however, will review methods for estimating thermal benefits only.

Two types of thermal benefits will be discussed:

- Heating benefits
- Cooling benefits

Various approaches will be presented for estimating each type of thermal transfer. Also, the discussion will emphasize some of the factors that a designer must consider, depending on whether residential or nonresidential buildings are being analyzed.

HEATING BENEFITS

The heating fuel savings which a design may create are related not only to reduced heat requirements but also to the heat content of the fuel source being used, the type and operating efficiency of the heating system being employed, and the cost of the fuel.

The general form of the equation which may be used to estimate heating benefits B_h is the following:[1]

$$B_h = \frac{C_f \times \Delta Q_h}{n \times v} \qquad (6\text{-}1)$$

[1]SOURCE: *ASHRAE Handbook and Product Directory—1980 Systems Volume*, American Society of Heating, Refrigerating and Air-Conditioning Engineers, Inc., New York, 1980, p. 4.38. Reprinted by permission.

in units,

$$\$/\text{year} = \frac{\$/\text{fuel unit} \times \text{Btu/year}}{\text{Btu/fuel unit}}$$

where B_h = benefits in terms of heating savings, \$/year
C_f = cost of fuel; \$/fuel unit, e.g., \$/gal, \$/ft^3, or \$/kWh
ΔQ_h = heat saved during heating season, Btu/year [See Equation (7-8).]
v = heating value of fuel being used, Btu/fuel unit, e.g., Btu/gal, Btu/ft^3, or Btu/kWh (See Table 6-1 for numerical values of heat equivalents for various types of fuel.)
n = heating system seasonal efficiency including considerations of full-load efficiency, part-load efficiency, oversizing, and efficiency decreases caused by various energy-conserving devices (Fuel-fired equipment may be assumed to operate between 0.55 and 0.65 and electric resistance heating at 1.00 in lieu of more accurate estimates provided by mechanical engineers.)

EXAMPLE

Suppose, for example, that the designer of an apartment building proposes to increase the amount of insulation in its roof so that an additional 20 million Btus can be saved each year over and above fuel consumption associated with the normal insulation level used by the client. The added cost of the extra insulation is \$900. The building is heated with Number 2 fuel oil at a cost of \$1.50 per gallon. The client asks the designer whether or not the proposal is cost-effective.

The heating benefit may be calculated as follows:

$$B_h = \frac{\$1.50/\text{gal} \times 20 \text{ million Btu/year}}{0.65 \times 139{,}400 \text{ Btu/gal}} = \$331/\text{year} \tag{6-1}$$

To adjust these savings to reflect the effect of fuel savings as a deductible item from gross income in computing income taxes, the calculation is adjusted by assuming a 45 percent tax bracket:

$$B_h = \$331/\text{year} \times (1 - 0.45) = \$182/\text{year}$$

A simple cost-benefit analysis of just the heating fuel savings shows the following:

$$\text{Simple payback period} = \frac{\$900}{\$182/\text{year}} = 4.9 \text{ years}$$

$$\text{Simple return on investment} = \frac{\$182/\text{year}}{\$900} = 20.2 \text{ percent/year}$$

Since 20 percent is higher than the client's required return on investment, the design is judged to be cost-effective even though the savings created by the extra insulation during the summer cooling season have not yet been accounted for.

If a fuel-based (i.e., gas or oil) heating system delivers fewer Btus to a building each year because of a design improvement in the energy efficiency of the building, it usually means that the electrically operated fans and pumps which are part of the system's heat generation and distribution equipment will operate less frequently and consume less electricity.

TABLE 6-1 Heat Equivalents of Various Fuels

Fuel	Heat equivalent
Coal*	
Anthracite	12,700 Btu/lb
Semianthracite	13,600 Btu/lb
Low-volatile bituminous	14,350 Btu/lb
Medium-volatile bituminous	14,000 Btu/lb
High-volatile bituminous A	13,800 Btu/lb
High-volatile bituminous B	12,500 Btu/lb
High-volatile bituminous C	11,000 Btu/lb
Subbituminous B	9,000 Btu/lb
Subbituminous C	8,500 Btu/lb
Lignite	6,900 Btu/lb
Oil*	
Grade 1	137,000–132,900 Btu/gal
Grade 2	141,800–137,000 Btu/gal
Grade 4†	148,100–143,100 Btu/gal
Grade 5L	150,000–146,800 Btu/gal
Grade 5H	152,000–149,400 Btu/gal
Grade 6†	155,900–151,300 Btu/gal
Electricity*	3,413 Btu/kWh
Gases*	
Natural gas	
I high-inert type	958–1,051 Btu/ft^3
II high-methane type	1,008–1,071 Btu/ft^3
III high-Btu type	1,071–1,124 Btu/ft^3
Commercial propane	2,500 Btu/ft^3
Commercial butane	3,200 Btu/ft^3
Commercial propane-air and butane-air mixtures	500–1,800 Btu/ft^3
Wood‡	8,000–10,000 Btu/lb

*SOURCE: *ASHRAE Handbook and Product Directory—1977 Fundamentals Volume*, American Society of Heating, Refrigerating and Air-Conditioning Engineers, Inc., New York, 1977, pp. 14.3, 14.5, and 14.8. Reprinted by permission.

†In some urban areas such as New York City, restrictions on the sulfur content of Numbers 4 and 6 oil for air pollution reasons will reduce their heat content to approximately 140,000 Btus per gallon.

‡SOURCE: Bruce N. Anderson, *Solar Energy: Fundamentals in Building Design*, McGraw-Hill Book Company, New York, 1977.

For estimating these electrical savings, the designer may assume that 2 kilowatthours of electricity is saved for every 1 million Btus of fuel saved. The equation representing this relationship is as follows:

$$B_e = C_e \times 2 \times \Delta Q_h \div 10^6 \tag{6-2}$$

in units,

$$\$/\text{year} = \$/\text{kWh} \times \text{kWh} \times \text{Btu/year} \div \text{Btu}$$

where B_e = electrical benefit of reduced fan and pump operation, \$/year
C_e = cost of electricity, \$/kWh
ΔQ_h = heat saved during heating season, Btu/year [See Equation (7-8).]

EXAMPLE

In the example presented above, the heating savings amounted to 20 million Btus. Thus the electrical benefit B_e in terms of reduced fan and pump operation would be

$$B_e = 2 \text{ kWh} \times (20 \text{ million Btu/year} \div 1 \text{ million Btu}) = 40 \text{ kWh/year}$$

If electricity cost $0.15 per kilowatthour, the electrical savings would be

$$B_e = \$0.15/\text{kWh} \times 40 \text{ kWh/year} = \$6/\text{year, or } \$3/\text{year after tax}$$

The total savings would then be

B_e	$3/year
B_h	$182/year
Total B	$185/year

The revised cost-benefit results would then be

$$\text{Simple payback} = \frac{\$900}{\$185/\text{year}} = 4.9 \text{ years}$$

$$\text{Simple return on investment} = \frac{\$185/\text{year}}{\$900} = 20.6 \text{ percent/year}$$

Degree-Day Method

To estimate thermal benefits for simple residential and light commercial buildings, it is sometimes useful to use a measure of climate called a "degree-day" (°F·day).

A degree-day is the number of degrees between 65° and the average temperature of a particular day during a heating season.[2] The 65° temperature represents the outdoor air temperature around a building below which a building's heating system will go on in order to keep the indoor temperature at a constant 70°F. When the outdoor temperature is 65° or above, internal heat sources are assumed to provide for a 5° temperature rise between the outside and the inside of the building. In other words, internal heat loads from people and lights are assumed to suffice to keep a building above 70°F when the temperature is 65°F outside. This is true of most residential buildings and of some small commercial buildings, but it is not true of larger commercial buildings with substantially larger internal heat loads. For buildings in that category, another method, presented below in the subsection "Bin-Hour Methods," should be used.

For example, suppose that on December 5 of a particular year the average outside air temperature is 20°F. The number of degree-days that day would be 65° − 20°F = 45°F × 1 day = 45°F·day. Similar calculations have been made for each day during the heating season. The data presented in Table 6-2 represent average monthly and yearly summaries of degree-days for selected American and Canadian cities.

Calculating heating benefits by using the degree-day method requires an adjustment to the general equation presented earlier [Equation (6-1)]. The new form[3]

[2]Degree-days are counted, of course, only when the average temperature is below 65°F.

[3]SOURCE: *ASHRAE Handbook and Product Directory—1980 Systems Volume,* American Society of Heating, Refrigerating and Air-Conditioning Engineers, Inc., New York, 1980, p. 4.38. Reprinted by permission.

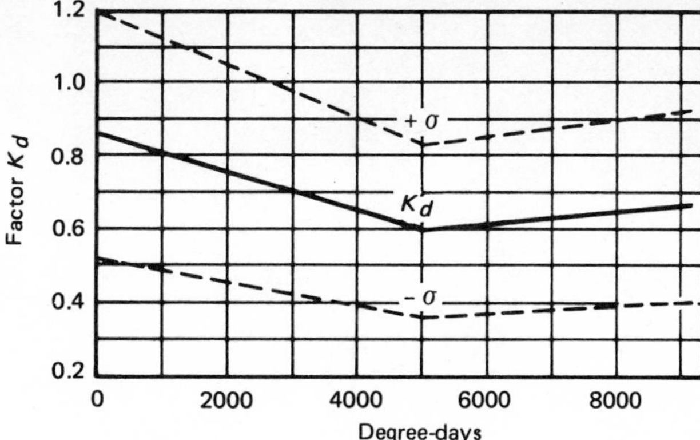

FIGURE 6-1 Correction factor K_d versus degree-days (σ = standard deviation). [ASHRAE Handbook and Product Directory—1980 Systems Volume, *American Society of Heating, Refrigerating and Air-Conditioning Engineers, Inc., New York, 1980, p. 4.38. Reprinted by permission.*]

becomes

$$B_h = \frac{C_f \times \Delta q_h \times \text{DD} \times 24}{(t_i - t_o) \times n \times v} \times K_d \qquad (6\text{-}3)$$

in units,

$$\$/\text{year} = \frac{\$/\text{fuel unit} \times \text{Btu/h} \times (°\text{F}\cdot\text{day})/\text{year} \times \text{h/day}}{°\text{F} \times \text{Btu/fuel unit}}$$

where b_h = benefits in terms of heating savings, \$/year
C_f = cost of fuel, \$/fuel unit
Δq_h = change in peak heat loss rate at a selected winter temperature, Btu/h [See Equation (7-6).]
t_i = indoor winter design temperature, typically 70°F
t_o = outdoor winter design temperature, typically the design (peak) dry-bulb temperature at the 97.5 percentile[4] level, °F (See Table 6-3.)
n = aggregate seasonal heating system efficiency, 0.55 to 0.65 for fuel-fired equipment and 1.00 for electric resistance systems [See also Equation (6-1).]
v = heating value of fuel being used, Btu/fuel unit (See Table 6-1.)
K_d = correction factor for 65°F degree-days (In newer housing internal gains are sufficient to offset a home's heat loss at average daily temperatures somewhat below 65°, so Figure 6-1 should be used to interpolate a correction for this condition.)

The designer should note that the energy-saving measure used with Equation (6-3) is a measure of a reduction of *peak* heat load q, not a measure of reduction in *annual* heating consumption Q, used in Equation (6-1).

EXAMPLE

For example, a designer of a house in the New York City suburbs creates on the northwest side of the house a windbreak such that average wind speeds adjacent to that portion of

[4]A temperature at the 97.5 percentile level in the United States means that during 97.5 percent of the time in the winter months of December, January, and February temperatures are higher than that level.

TABLE 6-2 Average Monthly and Yearly Heating Degree-Days for Cities in the United States and Canada (base, 65°F)

Station	Average winter temperature*	July	August	September	October	November	December	January	February	March	April	May	June	Yearly total
Fairbanks, Alaska	6.7	171	332	642	1,203	1,833	2,254	2,359	1,901	1,739	1,068	555	222	14,279
Phoenix, Arizona	58.5	0	0	0	22	234	415	474	328	217	75	0	0	1,765
Los Angeles, California	60.3	0	0	6	31	132	229	310	230	202	123	68	18	1,349
San Francisco, California	55.1	192	174	102	118	231	388	443	336	319	279	239	180	3,001
Denver, Colorado	40.8	0	0	90	366	714	905	1,004	851	800	492	254	48	5,524
Washington, D.C.	45.7	0	0	33	217	519	834	871	762	626	288	74	0	4,224
Miami, Florida	71.1	0	0	0	0	0	65	74	56	19	0	0	0	214
Atlanta, Georgia	51.7	0	0	18	124	417	648	636	518	428	147	25	0	2,961
Honolulu, Hawaii	74.2	0	0	0	0	0	0	0	0	0	0	0	0	0
Chicago, Illinois (O'Hare)	35.8	0	12	117	381	807	1,166	1,265	1,086	939	534	260	72	6,639
New Orleans, Louisiana	61.8	0	0	0	12	165	291	344	241	177	24	0	0	1,254
Boston, Massachusetts	40.0	0	9	60	316	603	983	1,088	972	846	513	208	36	5,634
Minneapolis, Minnesota	28.3	22	31	189	505	1,014	1,454	1,631	1,380	1,166	621	288	81	8,382
Kansas City, Missouri	43.9	0	0	39	220	612	905	1,032	818	682	294	109	0	4,711
New York, New York (La Guardia)	43.1	0	0	27	223	528	887	973	879	750	414	124	6	4,811

Houston, Texas	62.0	0	0	0	0	165	288	363	258	174	30	0	0	1,278
Seattle, Washington	46.9	50	47	129	329	543	657	738	599	577	396	242	117	4,424
Edmonton, Alberta	....	74	180	411	738	1,215	1,603	1,810	1,520	1,330	765	400	222	10,268
Vancouver, British Columbia	....	81	87	219	456	657	787	862	723	676	501	310	156	5,515
Winnipeg, Manitoba	....	38	71	322	683	1,251	1,757	2,008	1,719	1,465	813	405	147	10,679
Fredericton, New Brunswick*	....	78	68	234	592	915	1,392	1,541	1,379	1,172	753	406	141	8,671
St. John's, Newfoundland*	....	186	180	342	651	831	1,113	1,262	1,170	1,187	927	710	432	8,991
Fort Norman, Northwest Territories	....	164	341	666	1,234	1,959	2,474	2,592	2,209	2,058	1,386	732	294	16,109
Halifax, Nova Scotia	....	58	51	180	457	710	1,074	1,213	1,122	1,030	742	487	237	7,361
Ottawa, Ontario	....	25	81	222	567	936	1,469	1,624	1,441	1,231	708	341	90	8,735
Toronto, Ontario	....	7	18	151	439	760	1,111	1,233	1,119	1,013	616	298	62	6,827
Charlottetown, Prince Edward Island	....	40	53	198	518	804	1,215	1,380	1,274	1,169	813	496	204	8,164
Montreal, Quebec*	....	9	43	165	521	882	1,392	1,566	1,381	1,175	684	316	69	8,203
Regina, Saskatchewan	....	78	93	360	741	1,284	1,711	1,965	1,687	1,473	804	409	201	10,806
Dawson, Yukon Territory	....	164	326	645	1,197	1,875	2,415	2,561	2,150	1,838	1,068	570	258	15,067

*The data for these normals were from the full 10-year period 1951–1960, adjusted to the standard normal period 1931–1960, for the period from October to April inclusive.

SOURCE: *ASHRAE Handbook and Product Directory—1980 Systems Volume*, American Society of Heating, Refrigerating and Air-Conditioning Engineers, Inc., New York, 1980, pp. 43.2–43.7. Reprinted by permission.

TABLE 6-3 Climatic Conditions

Station	Latitude		Longitude		Winter: Design dry-bulb, percent		Summer: Design, dry-bulb and mean coincident wet-bulb, percent			Summer: Mean daily range	Summer: Design wet-bulb, percent		
	Degrees	Minutes	Degrees	Minutes	99	97.5	1	2.5	5		1	2.5	5
United States°													
Fairbanks, Alaska	64	5	147	5	−51	−47	82/62	78/60	75/59	24	64	62	60
Phoenix, Arizona	33	3	112	0	31	34	109/71	107/71	105/71	27	76	75	75
Los Angeles, California	34	0	118	1	37	40	93/70	89/70	86/69	20	72	71	70
San Francisco, California	37	5	122	3	38	40	74/63	71/62	69/61	14	64	62	61
Denver, Colorado	39	5	104	5	−5	1	93/59	91/59	89/59	28	64	63	62
Andrews Air Force Base, Washington, D.C.	38	5	76	5	10	14	92/75	90/74	87/73	18	78	76	75
Miami, Florida	25	5	80	2	44	47	91/77	90/77	89/77	15	79	79	78
Atlanta, Georgia	33	4	84	3	17	22	94/74	92/74	90/73	19	77	76	75
Honolulu, Hawaii	21	2	158	0	62	63	87/73	86/73	85/72	12	76	75	74
Chicago, Illinois	42	0	87	5	−8	−4	91/74	89/74	86/72	20	77	76	74
New Orleans, Louisiana	30	0	90	2	29	33	93/78	92/78	90/77	16	81	80	79
Boston, Massachusetts	42	2	71	0	6	9	91/73	88/71	85/70	16	75	74	72
Minneapolis–St. Paul, Minnesota	44	5	93	1	−16	−12	92/75	89/73	86/71	22	77	75	73
Kansas City, Missouri	39	1	94	4	2	6	99/75	96/74	93/74	20	78	77	76
New York, New York (La Guardia)	40	5	73	5	11	15	92/74	89/73	87/72	16	76	75	74
Houston, Texas	29	5	95	2	28	33	97/77	95/77	93/77	18	80	79	79
Seattle, Washington	47	4	122	2	22	27	85/68	82/66	78/65	19	69	67	65
Canada													
Edmonton, Alberta	53	34	113	31	−29	−25	85/66	82/65	79/63	23	68	66	65
Vancouver, British Columbia	49	11	123	10	15	19	79/67	77/66	74/65	17	68	67	66
Winnipeg, Manitoba	49	54	97	14	−30	−27	89/73	86/71	84/70	22	75	73	71
Fredericton, New Brunswick	45	52	66	32	−16	−11	89/71	85/69	82/68	23	73	71	70
St. John's, Newfoundland	47	37	52	45	3	7	77/66	75/65	73/64	18	69	67	66
Fort Smith, Northwest Territories	60	1	111	58	−49	−45	85/66	81/64	78/63	24	68	66	65
Halifax, Nova Scotia	44	39	63	34	1	5	79/66	76/65	74/64	16	69	67	66
Toronto, Ontario	43	41	79	38	−5	−1	90/73	87/72	85/71	20	75	76	73
Charlottetown, Prince Edward Island	46	17	63	8	−7	−4	80/69	78/68	76/67	16	71	70	68
Montreal, Quebec	45	28	73	45	−16	−10	88/73	85/72	83/71	17	75	74	72
Regina, Saskatchewan	50	26	104	40	−33	−29	91/69	88/68	84/67	26	72	70	68
Whitehorse, Yukon Territory	60	43	135	4	−46	−43	80/59	77/58	74/56	22	61	59	58

Other Countries

Station	Latitude and Longitude	Winter: Mean of annual extremes	Winter: Percent 99	Winter: Percent 97½	Summer: Design dry-bulb, percent 1	2½	5	Outdoor daily range (°F)	Design wet-bulb, percent 1	2½	5
Buenos Aires, Argentina	34°35′S/58°29′W	27	32	34	91	89	86	22	77	76	75
Melbourne, Australia	37°49′S/144°58′E	31	35	38	95	91	86	21	71	69	68
Sydney, Australia	33°52′S/151°12′E	38	40	42	89	84	80	13	74	73	72
Brasília, Brazil	15°52′S/47°55′W	46	49	51	89	88	86	17	76	75	75
Pôrto Alegre, Brazil	30°02′S/51°13′W	32	37	40	95	92	89	20	76	76	75
Rio de Janeiro, Brazil	22°55′S/43°12′W	56	58	60	94	92	90	11	80	79	78
Rangoon, Burma	16°47′N/96°09′E	59	62	63	100	98	95	25	83	82	82
Santiago, Chile	33°27′S/70°42′W	27	32	35	90	89	88	32	71	70	69
Shanghai, China	31°12′N/121°26′E	16	23	26	94	92	90	16	81	81	80
Bogotá, Colombia	4°36′N/74°05′W	42	45	46	72	70	69	19	60	59	58
Havana, Cuba	23°08′N/82°21′W	54	59	62	92	91	89	14	81	81	80
Quito, Ecuador	0°13′S/78°32′W	30	36	39	73	72	71	32	63	62	62
Addis Ababa, Ethiopia	9°02′N/38°45′E	35	39	41	84	82	81	28	66	65	64
Marseille, France	43°18′N/5°23′E	23	25	28	90	87	84	22	72	71	69
Paris, France	48°49′N/2°29′E	16	22	25	89	86	83	21	70	68	67
Berlin, Germany	52°27′N/13°18′E	6	7	12	84	81	78	19	68	67	66
Munich, Germany	48°09′N/11°34′E	−1	5	9	86	83	80	18	68	66	64
Athens, Greece	37°58′N/23°43′E	29	33	36	96	93	91	18	72	71	71
Bombay, India	18°54′N/72°49′E	62	65	67	96	94	92	13	82	81	81
Calcutta, India	22°32′N/88°20′E	49	52	54	98	97	96	22	83	82	82
Djakarta, Indonesia	6°11′S/106°50′E	69	71	72	90	89	88	14	80	79	78
Manokwari, Indonesia	0°52′S/134°05′E	70	71	72	89	88	87	12	82	81	81
Teheran, Iran	35°41′N/51°25′E	15	20	24	102	100	98	27	75	74	73
Baghdad, Iraq	33°20′N/44°24′E	27	32	25	113	111	108	34	73	72	72
Dublin, Ireland	53°22′N/6°21′W	19	24	27	74	72	70	16	65	64	62
Jerusalem, Israel	31°47′N/35°13′E	31	36	38	95	94	92	24	70	69	69
Milan, Italy	45°27′N/09°17′E	12	18	22	89	87	84	20	76	75	74
Rome, Italy	41°48′N/12°36′E	25	30	33	94	92	89	24	74	73	72
Tokyo, Japan	35°41′N/139°46′E	21	26	28	91	89	87	14	81	80	79
Seoul, Korea	37°34′N/126°58′E	−1	7	9	91	89	87	16	81	79	78
Singapore	1°18′N/103°50′E	69	71	72	92	91	90	14	82	81	80
Mexico City, Mexico	19°24′N/99°12′W	33	37	39	83	81	79	25	61	60	59
Monterrey, Mexico	25°40′N/100°18′W	31	38	41	98	95	93	20	79	78	77
Christ Church, New Zealand	43°32′S/172°37′E	25	28	31	82	79	76	17	68	67	66
Oslo, Norway	59°56′N/10°44′E	−2	0	4	79	77	74	17	67	66	64

TABLE 6-3 Climatic Conditions (*cont.*)

Other Countries

		Winter			Summer						
		Mean of annual extremes	Percent		Design dry-bulb, percent			Outdoor daily range (°F)	Design wet-bulb, percent		
Station	Latitude and Longitude		99	97½	1	2½	5		1	2½	5
Karachi, Pakistan	24°48′N/66°59′E	45	49	51	100	98	95	14	82	82	81
Riyadh, Saudi Arabia	24°39′N/46°42′E	29	37	40	110	108	106	32	78	77	76
Johannesburg, South Africa	26°11′S/78°03′E	26	31	34	85	83	81	24	70	69	69
Madrid, Spain	40°25′N/3°41′W	22	25	28	93	91	89	25	71	69	67
Taipei, Taiwan	25°02′N/121°31′E	41	44	47	94	92	90	16	83	82	81
Istanbul, Turkey	40°58′N/28°50′E	23	28	30	91	88	86	16	75	74	73
Leningrad, U.S.S.R.	59°56′N/30°16′E	−14	−9	−5	78	75	72	15	65	64	63
Moscow, U.S.S.R.	55°46′N/37°40′E	−19	−11	−6	84	81	78	21	69	67	65
Belfast, United Kingdom	54°36′N/5°55′W	19	23	26	74	72	69	16	65	64	62
Glasgow, United Kingdom	55°52′N/4°17′W	17	21	24	74	71	68	13	64	63	61
London, United Kingdom	51°29′N/00°00′	20	24	26	82	79	76	16	68	66	65
Caracas, Venezuela	10°30′N/66°56′W	49	52	54	84	83	81	21	70	69	69
Saigon, Vietnam	10°47′N/106°42′E	62	65	67	93	91	89	16	85	84	83
Kimshasa, Zaire	4°20′S/15°18′E	54	60	62	92	91	90	19	81	80	80

*Percentage of winter design data for the United States shows the percentage of the 3-month period December through February. Percentage of summer design data shows the percentage of the 4-month period June through September.

SOURCE: *ASHRAE Handbook and Product Directory—1977 Fundamentals Volume*, American Society of Heating, Refrigerating and Air-Conditioning Engineers, Inc., New York, 1977, pp. 23.3–23.22.

the house are reduced in winter, thus reducing at peak load the rate of infiltration heat loss by 4000 Btus per hour. The house is heated by natural gas at 1000 Btus per cubic foot at a cost of \$0.007 per cubic foot. The cost of the windbreak planting is \$1200.

From Tables 6-2 and 6-3 the following data are obtained:

Degree-days for New York (La Guardia) = 4811 °F·days

Design dry-bulb temperature (97.5 percent, La Guardia) = 15°F

With this information, the following calculation may be made:

$$B_h = \frac{\$0.007/\text{ft}^3 \times 4000\ \text{Btu/h} \times 4811\ (°\text{F}\cdot\text{days})/\text{year} \times 24\ \text{h/day} \times 0.63}{(70°\text{F} - 15°\text{F}) \times 0.65 \times 1000\ \text{Btu/ft}^3}$$

$$= \$56.97/\text{year} \qquad (6\text{-}3)$$

The electrical power saving for reduced operation of fans and pumps at \$0.14 per kilowatthour is

$$B_e = \$0.14/\text{kWh} \times 2\ \text{kWh} \times 4000\ \text{Btu/h} \times \frac{4811\ (°\text{F}\cdot\text{days})/\text{year} \times 24\ \text{h/day}}{70°\text{F} - 15°\text{F}} \div 10^6$$

$$= \$2.35/\text{year}$$

The total heating savings are

B_h	\$56.97/year
B_e	\$ 2.35/year
B_{total}	\$59.32/year

A simple cost-benefit analysis yields the following:

$$\text{Simple payback period} = \frac{\$1200}{\$59/\text{year}} = 20.3\ \text{years}$$

$$\text{Simple return on investment} = \frac{\$59/\text{year}}{\$1200} = 4.9\ \text{percent/year}$$

The return on investment for this design strategy is below the client's required return and is considered insufficient by the designer.

The reader is again cautioned that this particular method is a simplified estimating approach which is appropriate only for residential buildings in which thermal loads are primarily due to the outside climate. An estimating procedure for more thermally complex buildings such as offices with substantial internal heat loads will be presented next.

Bin-Hour Methods

Degree-day data describing climatic temperature conditions do not describe variations in temperature conditions within a 24-hour period. Thus, it is not possible to estimate the heating savings for design strategies which are in effect during part of the day, such as glazing insulation used during evening hours or lighting controls in effect during daytime hours. Design strategies which attempt to reduce heating energy consumption in buildings that have variations in interior temperature within a 24-hour period are also not easily estimated by using degree-day data.

Office buildings are an example of a building type in which interior temperatures are usually lowered to around 55°F during unoccupied hours on evenings and weekends.

As a result, another type of data called "bin-hour data" may be used for estimating heating and cooling savings from designs which operate under these conditions. The reader should note that bin data are in units of °*F*·*hours*, as compared with °*F*·*days* for degree-day data.

Table 6-4 contains bin-hour data for various temperature ranges, or bins, and for various intervals during the day for each month during the heating season for a number of cities.[5] The vertical coordinate of the table contains temperature ranges in 5°F increments. The horizontal coordinate represents three time intervals over a 24-hour period for each month:

2 A.M.–9 A.M.

10 A.M.–5 P.M. (10:00–17:00)

6 P.M.–1 A.M. (18:00–1:00)

Depending on the type of design being analyzed, the designer may wish to regroup the data into different time categories.

Table 6-5 shows bin-hour data for former Mitchel Air Force Base, in Nassau County, New York, regrouped to reflect daily time intervals for 8 A.M. to 11 P.M. and 11 P.M. to 7 A.M. These periods represent the daily schedule of waking and sleeping hours of a typical residence.

Table 6-6 shows how bin-hour data for Mitchel Air Force Base may be reorganized to reflect daily time intervals of 8 A.M. to 6 P.M. and 6 P.M. to 8 A.M. These are the daily occupied and nonoccupied periods for a typical office building. Other adjustments made in the table reflect the fact that office buildings are occupied for only 5 of the 7 days of a week. These reorganized bin-hour data may be used to evaluate a number of design strategies for residential and commercial buildings.

EXAMPLE

Suppose, for example, that an interior designer proposes to a client who owns a single-family house in New York that insulating shutters be installed so that, at night when the family is asleep, the windows may be closed off to reduce winter heat loss by conduction. The following information is gathered by the designer for evaluation of the proposal:

U of windows[6]	0.62
U of shutters and windows	0.10
ΔU	0.52

Heating system	Oil-fired furnace
Fuel cost	$1.50/gal
Window and shutter area	360 ft^2
Cost of shutter	$5/ft^2

[5]Bin-hour data for other cities may be obtained from Ecodyne Corporation, *Weather Data Handbook*, McGraw-Hill Book Company, New York, 1980.

[6]For a detailed description of U values, see Chapter 7.

The following calculations provide an estimate of the value of the heating fuel savings due to moving the interior shutters across the windows at night:

$$\text{Difference in } U \text{ value, } \Delta U = 0.52 \text{ Btu/(h}\cdot{}^\circ\text{F}\cdot\text{ft}^2)$$

$$\begin{aligned}\text{Heating savings, } \Delta Q &= 0.52 \text{ Btu/(h}\cdot{}^\circ\text{F}\cdot\text{ft}^2) \\ &\quad \times 360 \text{ ft}^2 \times 49{,}780\ ({}^\circ\text{F}\cdot\text{h})/\text{year} \\ &= 9{,}318{,}816 \text{ Btu/year [See Equation (7-8).]}\end{aligned}$$

$$B_h = \frac{\$1.50/\text{gal} \times 9{,}318{,}816 \text{ Btu/year}}{0.55 \times 139{,}400 \text{ Btu/gal}} = \$182/\text{year} \qquad (6\text{-}1)$$

$$C_0 = \$360/\text{ft}^2 \times \$5/\text{ft}^2 = \$1800$$

A simple cost-benefit analysis yields the following:

$$\text{Simple payback period} = \frac{\$1800}{\$182/\text{year}} = 9.9 \text{ years}$$

$$\text{Simple return on investment} = \frac{\$182/\text{year}}{\$1800} = 10.1 \text{ percent/year}$$

An analysis, however, of the impact of the shutters on change in the peak heating load yields the following:

$$\begin{aligned}\Delta q_h &= 0.52 \text{ Btu/(h}\cdot{}^\circ\text{F}\cdot\text{ft}^2) \times 360 \text{ ft}^2 \times (70^\circ\text{F} - 15^\circ\text{F}) \\ &= 10{,}296 \text{ Btu/h [See Equation (7-6).]}\end{aligned}$$

Using data in Table 5-8, construction cost decreases owing to reduction in the size of heating equipment may be estimated:

$$B_0 = \$14/1000 \text{ Btu/h} \times 10{,}296 \text{ Btu/h} = \$144$$

The reduced installation cost of the shutters, given the credit due to the reduced cost of the heating system, is calculated below:

$$C_0 = (\$1800 - \$144) = \$1656$$

A revised cost-benefit analysis yields the following:

$$\text{Simple payback period} = \frac{\$1656}{\$182/\text{year}} = 9.1 \text{ years}$$

$$\text{Simple return on investment} = \frac{\$182}{\$1656} = 11 \text{ percent/year}$$

The cost-effectiveness of the shutters is, of course, improved with the heating system installation cost credit.

As mentioned earlier, bin data may also be used for analyzing structures such as office buildings with dominant internal loads. First, the reader should be aware of the internal thermal loads in office buildings which are only roughly acknowledged in degree-day data. These loads are:

- People (see Table 6-7)
- Lights
- Solar radiation
- Equipment (interior zones, primarily)

(Cont. on p. 129)

TABLE 6-4 Bin-Hour Weather Data for Selected Cities

LOS ANGELES INTERNATIONAL AIRPORT, CALIFORNIA

Latitude, 33°56′N; longitude, 118°24′W; elevation, 97 feet)

Mean frequency of occurrence of dry-bulb temperature (°F) with mean coincident wet-bulb temperature (°F) for each dry-bulb temperature range

Temperature range	Observation hour group 01 to 08	09 to 16	17 to 24	Total observation	MCWB	Observation hour group 01 to 08	09 to 16	17 to 24	Total observation	MCWB	Observation hour group 01 to 08	09 to 16	17 to 24	Total observation	MCWB
	May					June					July				
105/109															
100/104															
95/99		0		0	63		0		0	63		0		0	68
90/94		0		0	60		0		0	61		0		0	70
85/89	0	1		1	58	0	1	0	1	64	0	3		3	68
80/84	0	2	0	2	57	0	1	0	1	66	0	15	1	16	69
75/79	0	6	1	7	60	0	22	1	23	65	3	62	6	71	67
70/74	1	34	3	38	61	3	66	12	81	63	21	117	41	179	65
65/69	6	103	19	128	58	25	113	53	191	61	104	47	117	268	63
60/64	72	91	100	263	56	139	37	141	317	58	104	3	77	184	59
55/59	126	11	114	251	54	68	1	33	102	55	16		6	22	56
50/54	39	0	11	50	50	5		0	5	51	0			0	53
45/49	2		0	2	45	0			0	47					
	November					December					January				
105/109															
100/104															
95/99		0		0	60										
90/94		1		1	60		0		0	59					
85/89		4		4	59		0		0	55		0		0	60
80/84		10	0	10	56		5		5	56		3		3	57
75/79	0	19	1	20	56		10	0	10	54		7	0	7	55
70/74	0	30	5	35	57		19	2	21	53		16	1	17	54
65/69	5	61	22	88	56	0	40	8	48	53		29	5	34	53
60/64	34	78	80	192	55	10	82	36	128	53	3	60	26	89	52
55/59	86	32	97	215	52	51	69	106	226	52	33	85	86	204	51
50/54	80	4	31	115	48	92	20	78	190	48	83	38	89	210	48
45/49	31	1	5	37	43	73	2	16	91	43	81	10	33	124	43
40/44	4			4	38	19	0	2	21	38	39	1	8	48	39
35/39	0			0	33	2			2	32	9		0	9	33
30/34						0			0	29	0			0	28

Observation hour group 01 to 08	09 to 16	17 to 24	Total observation	MCWB	Observation hour group 01 to 08	09 to 16	17 to 24	Total observation	MCWB	Observation hour group 01 to 08	09 to 16	17 to 24	Total observation	MCWB
August					**September**					**October**				
						0		0	73					
						1		1	72		1		1	67
	0		0	71		2	0	2	69		1		1	65
	0		0	70	0	1	0	1	69	0	3		3	63
	1	0	1	70	0	5	1	6	68	0	4	0	4	62
0	16	0	16	69	2	17	2	21	68	1	10	2	13	62
2	70	6	78	67	5	49	9	63	66	1	22	3	26	63
21	121	45	187	65	16	93	35	144	64	6	65	13	84	62
119	37	132	288	63	69	63	98	230	62	34	100	64	198	61
100	2	63	165	60	122	8	91	221	60	97	40	127	264	58
6		1	7	57	26	0	4	30	56	88	2	37	127	55
					0			0	53	21		1	22	50
										0			0	43

01 to 08	09 to 16	17 to 24	Total observation	MCWB	01 to 08	09 to 16	17 to 24	Total observation	MCWB	01 to 08	09 to 16	17 to 24	Total observation	MCWB	01 to 08	09 to 16	17 to 24	Total observation	MCWB
February					**March**					**April**					**Annual total**				
																0		0	73
																2		2	70
																3	0	3	67
	0		0	63							0		0	59	0	5	0	5	65
	1		1	59		1		1	56		1		1	62	0	22	1	23	64
	2	0	2	57		3		3	56		4	0	4	62	3	88	5	96	64
	6	0	6	56		6	0	6	55	0	6	2	8	61	11	285	29	325	64
	15	1	16	54	0	15	2	17	56	1	20	4	25	59	69	611	164	844	63
2	32	6	40	53	2	41	7	50	55	3	51	12	66	58	369	717	543	1629	60
5	72	30	107	53	5	95	31	131	54	24	114	45	183	55	715	682	847	2244	57
48	71	95	214	52	61	71	116	248	52	113	41	141	295	53	722	383	836	1941	53
83	23	75	181	48	108	16	82	206	49	81	3	35	119	50	592	104	402	1098	48
66	2	16	84	43	61	0	9	70	44	17	0	1	18	45	331	15	80	426	43
19		1	20	38	10		1	11	40	0			0	41	91	1	12	104	39
1			1	34	1			1	37						13		0	13	33
															0			0	28

TABLE 6-4 Bin-Hour Weather Data for Selected Cities (*cont.*)

MIAMI, FLORIDA
READINGS TAKEN AT HOMESTEAD AIR FORCE BASE*

(Latitude, 25°29′N; longitude, 80°24′W; elevation, 7 feet)

Mean frequency of occurrence of dry-bulb temperature (°F) with mean coincident wet-bulb temperature (°F) for each dry-bulb temperature range

Temperature range	Observation hour group 01 to 08	09 to 16	17 to 24	Total observation	MCWB	Observation hour group 01 to 08	09 to 16	17 to 24	Total observation	MCWB	Observation hour group 01 to 08	09 to 16	17 to 24	Total observation	MCWB
	May					**June**					**July**				
95/99															
90/94		1		1	74		7	0	7	78		9	0	9	78
85/89		37	3	40	75	2	91	14	107	77	5	174	35	214	77
80/84	13	138	48	199	73	49	107	93	249	75	89	50	136	275	76
75/79	104	60	134	298	71	136	27	108	271	73	143	13	71	227	74
70/74	97	10	55	162	69	52	8	25	85	71	11	2	5	18	71
65/69	27	1	7	35	64	1		0	1	66					
60/64	7		1	8	59										
55/59	1			1	55										
50/54															
	November					**December**					**January**				
95/99															
90/94															
85/89		4		4	75		0		0	71					
80/84	0	69	5	74	72		24	0	24	72		21	1	22	71
75/79	29	109	69	207	70	5	89	24	118	69	1	76	16	93	69
70/74	86	35	106	227	67	60	64	85	209	66	42	67	75	184	66
65/69	69	12	38	119	63	58	37	68	163	62	71	39	78	188	63
60/64	34	6	13	53	58	44	19	37	100	58	50	20	40	110	58
55/59	12	3	7	22	52	35	9	21	65	53	36	15	21	72	53
50/54	7	2	2	11	47	26	4	10	40	48	25	7	11	43	48
45/49	2	0	1	3	43	12	1	3	16	43	12	3	5	20	43
40/44	1		0	1	37	5	0	1	6	39	8	1	3	12	38
35/39						2	0	0	2	35	3	0	0	3	34
30/34											0			0	32

*Comparative Design Data

	Elevation, ft	Winter 97½ percent	Summer, percent Dry-bulb, 2½ percent	Wet-bulb, 2½ percent
Miami Airport, Florida	7	47°F	90°F	79°F
Homestead Air Force Base	7	46°F	90°F	79°F

Observation hour group			Total observation	MCWB	Observation hour group			Total observation	MCWB	Observation hour group			Total observation	MCWB					
8	09 to 16	17 to 24			01 to 08	09 to 16	17 to 24			01 to 08	09 to 16	17 to 24							
August					**September**					**October**									
	0		0	80															
	18	1	19	78		10	1	11	78		0		0	77					
4	168	35	207	78	2	132	18	152	77	0	56	3	59	76					
9	46	132	267	76	67	71	123	261	76	23	124	70	217	74					
1	14	74	229	74	143	24	88	255	74	102	52	115	269	72					
4	2	6	22	72	28	3	10	41	71	80	13	48	141	69					
										30	3	11	44	63					
										9	0	2	11	59					
										2		0	2	55					
										0			0	47					
February					**March**					**April**					**Annual total**				
																0		0	80
											1		1	76		46	2	48	78
	2		2	74		5	0	5	73		18	3	21	74	13	687	111	811	77
	36	3	39	72		53	7	60	72	1	84	16	101	72	331	823	634	1788	75
9	65	30	104	69	12	87	45	144	69	42	109	90	241	70	867	725	864	2456	72
48	49	65	162	67	78	60	94	232	66	108	24	101	233	67	704	337	675	1716	67
46	35	54	135	62	68	23	60	151	62	57	4	24	85	63	427	154	340	921	63
42	18	41	101	58	41	13	24	78	57	23	0	5	28	58	250	76	163	489	58
37	13	18	68	53	22	6	14	42	52	8		1	9	54	153	46	82	281	53
23	5	9	37	48	19	1	4	24	47	1		0	1	49	101	19	36	156	48
13	1	4	18	43	8	0	0	8	44	0			0	44	47	5	13	65	43
5	0	0	5	39	1		0	1	39						20	1	4	25	38
1			1	34	0			0	37						6	0	0	6	35
															0			0	32

CHICAGO—O'HARE INTERNATIONAL AIRPORT, ILLINOIS

(Latitude, 41°59′N; longitude 87°54′W; elevation, 658 feet)

Mean frequency of occurrence of dry-bulb temperature (°F) with mean coincident wet-bulb temperature (°F) for each dry-bulb temperature range

Temperature range	May: Observation hour group 01 to 08	09 to 16	17 to 24	Total observation	MCWB	June: Observation hour group 01 to 08	09 to 16	17 to 24	Total observation	MCWB	July: Observation hour group 01 to 08	09 to 16	17 to 24	Total observation	MCWB
100/104							0		0	77		0		0	78
95/99							1	0	1	78		1	0	1	78
90/94		2	0	2	71		13	2	15	74		12	1	13	76
85/89		9	2	11	70	0	31	10	41	72	1	43	10	54	73
80/84	0	21	7	28	68	4	43	21	68	69	4	67	29	100	70
75/79	3	32	15	50	64	17	43	32	92	67	23	58	48	129	68
70/74	12	33	23	68	61	36	42	44	122	64	56	43	64	163	66
65/69	25	34	29	88	59	50	29	44	123	61	78	17	57	152	63
60/64	31	31	32	94	55	50	20	38	108	57	54	4	28	86	59
55/59	38	33	39	110	51	37	11	27	75	53	23	0	7	30	55
50/54	46	29	39	114	47	30	5	17	52	49	8		2	10	50
45/49	44	17	35	96	43	13	0	6	19	45	1		0	1	45
40/44	30	5	20	55	39	3		1	4	40					
35/39	16	2	6	24	35	0			0	36					
30/34	3		0	3	31										
25/29															
20/24															
15/19															

Observation hour group		Total observation	MCWB	Observation hour group			Total observation	MCWB	Observation hour group			Total observation	MCWB
09 to 16	17 to 24			01 to 08	09 to 16	17 to 24			01 to 08	09 to 16	17 to 24		
August				**September**					**October**				
2		2	75		2		2	73					
17	2	19	75		8	1	9	73		0		0	66
31	7	38	73	0	15	3	18	72		2		2	70
55	21	79	71	0	24	8	32	69		11	1	12	66
66	42	126	68	7	35	16	58	66	0	16	3	19	63
48	64	162	66	19	47	30	96	63	2	26	9	37	61
23	60	151	63	33	50	45	128	60	9	37	20	66	59
6	34	96	59	48	35	53	136	57	23	38	30	91	55
0	13	46	55	43	19	40	102	53	32	37	41	110	51
	4	19	50	42	5	25	72	49	38	36	43	117	47
	1	5	46	26	1	13	40	45	49	24	42	115	44
		1	42	14	0	6	20	41	37	13	28	78	39
				5		2	7	36	29	7	18	54	35
				1		0	1	32	20	1	8	29	30
									6		3	9	26
									2		0	2	21
									0			0	18

TABLE 6-4 Bin-Hour Weather Data for Selected Cities (*cont.*)

CHICAGO—O'HARE INTERNATIONAL AIRPORT, ILLINOIS

(Latitude, 41°59′N; longitude 87°54′W; elevation, 658 feet)

Mean frequency of occurrence of dry-bulb temperature (°F) with mean coincident wet-bulb temperature (°F) for each dry-bulb temperature range

Temperature range	Observation hour group 01 to 08	Observation hour group 09 to 16	Observation hour group 17 to 24	Total observation	MCWB	Observation hour group 01 to 08	Observation hour group 09 to 16	Observation hour group 17 to 24	Total observation	MCWB	Observation hour group 01 to 08	Observation hour group 09 to 16	Observation hour group 17 to 24	Total observation	MCWB
	November					December					January				
100/104															
95/99															
90/94															
85/89															
80/84															
75/79		1		1	66										
70/74		3	1	4	61										
65/69	1	8	2	11	58							0		0	63
60/64	5	11	8	24	56	0	1	0	1	54		0	0	0	58
55/59	9	20	13	42	51	0	3	2	5	53	0	1	1	2	55
50/54	10	27	19	56	47	2	7	4	13	48	1	2	1	4	50
45/49	22	38	29	89	43	4	10	6	20	43	2	5	3	10	44
40/44	33	35	38	106	38	9	21	13	43	39	4	13	5	22	39
35/39	39	36	43	118	34	28	36	34	98	34	17	34	26	77	34
30/34	46	28	35	109	30	46	52	52	150	30	45	56	54	155	30
25/29	38	17	27	82	25	42	41	44	127	25	41	40	41	122	25
20/24	18	9	14	41	20	35	27	27	89	21	34	29	30	93	20
15/19	10	3	7	20	16	22	17	18	57	16	26	22	23	71	16
10/14	5	2	4	11	11	19	14	17	50	11	20	17	19	56	11
5/9	2	1	2	5	6	12	9	12	33	6	18	15	18	51	6
0/4	2	0	1	3	1	11	5	9	25	1	16	8	15	39	1
−5/−1	1		0	1	−3	8	3	6	17	−3	11	4	7	22	−3
−10/−6						5	1	3	9	−8	7	2	3	12	−8
−15/−11						3	0	1	4	−13	4	1	1	6	−13
−20/−16						1		0	1	−17	1	0		1	−17
−25/−21											0			0	−21

February					March					April					Annual total				
Observation hour group					Observation hour group					Observation hour group									
01 to 08	09 to 16	17 to 24	Total observation	MCWB	01 to 08	09 to 16	17 to 24	Total observation	MCWB	01 to 08	09 to 16	17 to 24	Total observation	MCWB					
																0		0	77
																6	0	6	76
																52	6	58	74
											1	0	1	65	1	132	32	165	72
						0		0	62		4	1	5	64	11	225	88	324	70
						0		0	61		9	3	12	63	68	260	159	487	67
						2	0	2	57	1	18	8	27	60	176	262	243	681	64
	0		0	60	0	3	1	4	55	6	19	11	36	57	270	220	269	759	61
	1	0	1	55	0	5	3	8	53	13	24	18	55	54	280	176	244	700	57
1	2	1	4	52	3	9	5	17	50	14	25	22	61	50	233	160	211	604	52
1	4	2	7	47	4	15	8	27	46	25	33	32	90	46	222	163	196	581	47
2	8	4	14	43	10	22	14	46	42	35	39	36	110	42	212	164	189	565	43
4	18	10	32	38	15	39	27	81	37	44	37	49	130	38	194	181	197	572	38
18	42	30	90	34	41	57	51	149	34	50	23	35	108	34	243	237	245	725	34
53	57	61	171	30	72	50	69	191	30	33	7	20	60	30	319	251	299	869	30
45	37	46	128	25	41	24	36	101	25	14	1	5	20	25	227	160	202	589	25
30	21	28	79	21	31	14	17	62	21	4	0	1	5	20	154	100	117	371	21
23	13	16	52	16	16	5	9	30	16	1		0	1	16	98	60	73	231	16
16	9	8	33	11	9	1	4	14	11						69	43	52	164	11
9	5	8	22	6	3	0	1	4	6						44	30	41	115	6
8	5	6	19	1	3	0	0	3	2						40	18	31	89	1
7	2	4	13	−4	0	0		0	−3						27	9	17	53	−3
5	0	1	6	−8	0			0	−7						17	3	7	27	−8
1	0	0	1	−13											8	1	2	11	−13
0			0	−16											2	0	0	2	−17
															0			0	−21

TABLE 6-4 Bin-Hour Weather Data for Selected Cities (*cont.*)

HOUSTON, TEXAS—ELLINGTON AIR FORCE BASE

(Latitude, 29°37′N; longitude, 95°10′W; elevation, 40 feet)

Mean frequency of occurrence of dry-bulb temperature (°F) with mean coincident wet-bulb temperature (°F) for each dry-bulb temperature range

Temperature range	Observation hour group			Total observation	MCWB	Observation hour group			Total observation	MCWB	Observation hour group			Total observation	MCWB
	01 to 08	09 to 16	17 to 24			01 to 08	09 to 16	17 to 24			01 to 08	09 to 16	17 to 24		
	May					**June**					**July**				
100/104												0		0	80
95/99		0		0	78		4	0	4	78		16	2	18	79
90/94		4	1	5	76		56	7	63	77		87	19	106	78
85/89		52	6	58	74	4	103	36	143	76	5	93	44	142	77
80/84	4	103	32	139	72	28	48	64	140	75	39	34	80	153	76
75/79	50	57	82	189	71	100	19	92	211	73	148	13	89	250	74
70/74	95	21	79	195	69	83	9	34	126	70	51	4	13	68	70
65/69	55	9	33	97	64	21	1	5	27	65	4	0	1	5	65
60/64	27	2	13	42	59	3	0	1	4	59	1			1	59
55/59	15	1	2	18	54	1			1	54					
50/54	3		0	3	50										
45/49	0			0	48										
40/44															
35/39															
	November					**December**					**January**				
100/104															
95/99															
90/94															
85/89		2		2	71										
80/84		20	1	21	71		1		1	69		2	0	2	70
75/79	4	48	10	62	69		19	1	20	68		12	1	13	68
70/74	19	45	32	96	66	6	33	14	53	66	2	28	10	40	65
65/69	38	40	47	125	63	21	38	28	87	63	21	28	26	75	63
60/64	37	30	42	109	58	31	41	40	112	58	24	32	28	84	58
55/59	32	24	35	91	53	33	38	43	114	53	26	34	36	96	53
50/54	36	18	35	89	48	35	32	42	109	48	29	36	43	108	48
45/49	35	8	22	65	44	42	25	41	108	44	33	28	37	98	43
40/44	22	4	10	36	39	36	13	23	72	39	42	24	32	98	39
35/39	10	1	4	15	34	26	6	12	44	35	33	14	23	70	34
30/34	5	0	0	5	30	13	2	4	19	30	24	6	9	39	29
25/29	0			0	26	4	0	1	5	25	10	3	3	16	25
20/24						1	0		1	21	3	1	2	6	20
15/19											2	0	0	2	15

Observation hour group (01 to 08)	09 to 16	17 to 24	Total observation	MCWB	01 to 08	09 to 16	17 to 24	Total observation	MCWB	01 to 08	09 to 16	17 to 24	Total observation	MCWB
August					**September**					**October**				
	1	0	1	77		0		0	77					
	15	2	17	78		2	0	2	77		0		0	78
	81	16	97	78		29	2	31	77		2		2	77
3	90	38	131	77	0	89	20	109	76		34	2	36	74
3	41	81	155	76	14	67	54	135	75	1	65	13	79	72
2	17	95	264	74	92	35	94	221	73	17	65	43	125	69
5	3	14	72	71	79	14	50	143	70	47	39	68	154	67
5	1	1	7	65	35	4	16	55	64	58	25	51	134	63
4		0	1	59	14	1	3	18	59	48	12	36	96	58
)			0	55	5	0	1	6	56	36	5	22	63	53
					0		0	0	49	26	2	10	38	49
					0			0	45	11	0	2	13	45
										2		0	2	40
										1			1	37

(01 to 08)	09 to 16	17 to 24	Total observation	MCWB	01 to 08	09 to 16	17 to 24	Total observation	MCWB	01 to 08	09 to 16	17 to 24	Total observation	MCWB	01 to 08	09 to 16	17 to 24	Total observation	MCWB
February					**March**					**April**					**Annual total**				
																1	0	1	77
																37	4	41	78
											0		0	74		259	45	304	78
	0		0	66		0		0	70		4	0	4	73	12	467	146	625	76
	3	0	3	69		7	1	8	67		50	6	56	71	119	441	332	892	74
	10	1	11	67		30	6	36	66	10	82	36	128	70	573	407	550	1530	72
2	26	10	38	65	8	54	25	87	65	72	53	82	207	68	519	329	431	1279	68
9	34	24	77	62	34	52	50	136	62	53	31	55	139	63	364	263	337	964	63
9	35	30	84	57	44	42	55	141	57	41	14	35	90	58	290	209	283	782	58
7	38	40	105	53	45	27	44	116	52	35	5	18	58	53	255	172	241	668	53
1	34	44	119	48	41	17	32	90	47	17	1	6	24	48	228	140	212	580	48
9	21	37	97	43	34	11	23	68	43	10		1	11	44	204	93	163	460	43
7	14	22	73	39	24	5	9	38	39	2			2	38	165	60	96	321	39
2	6	11	39	35	13	1	3	17	34	0			0	37	105	28	53	186	34
4	2	4	20	30	4	0	0	4	30						60	10	17	87	30
4	0	0	4	26	0			0	26						18	3	4	25	25
															4	1	2	7	20
															2	0	0	2	15

TABLE 6-4 Bin-Hour Weather Data for Selected Cities (*cont.*)

SEATTLE NAVAL AIR STATION, WASHINGTON

(Latitude, 47°41′N; longitude, 122°15′W; elevation, 47 feet)

Mean frequency of occurrence of dry-bulb temperature (°F) with mean coincident wet-bulb temperature (°F) for each dry-bulb temperature range

Temperature range	Observation hour group 01 to 08	09 to 16	17 to 24	Total observation	MCWB	Observation hour group 01 to 08	09 to 16	17 to 24	Total observation	MCWB	Observation hour group 01 to 08	09 to 16	17 to 24	Total observation	MCWB
	May					**June**					**July**				
95/99		0		0	65		0		0	67		0	0	0	79
90/94		0		0	67		1	0	1	69		2	1	3	72
85/89		1	0	1	65		2	2	4	68		9	5	14	69
80/84		5	2	7	64		7	4	11	66		20	13	33	67
75/79		8	4	12	62	0	16	10	26	64	0	31	25	56	65
70/74		16	9	25	60	1	33	21	55	61	2	53	41	96	62
65/69	1	32	21	54	57	6	55	41	102	58	15	63	55	133	60
60/64	6	53	39	98	54	30	66	65	161	56	70	52	72	194	57
55/59	33	66	65	164	52	103	47	69	219	54	131	17	33	181	54
50/54	98	50	69	217	49	92	12	26	130	50	29	1	2	32	51
45/49	81	15	34	130	45	9	0	1	10	47	1		0	1	48
40/44	28	1	4	33	41										
35/39	2		0	2	37										
	November					**December**					**January**				
95/99															
90/94															
85/89															
80/84															
75/79															
70/74															
65/69		0		0	56										
60/64	0	3	1	4	54		0		0	52		0		0	51
55/59	4	24	8	36	52	0	4	2	6	52		4	1	5	50
50/54	37	74	54	165	49	18	39	24	81	49	9	21	14	44	48
45/49	77	73	86	236	45	64	79	74	217	45	42	64	57	163	45
40/44	66	43	60	169	40	68	68	73	209	40	72	80	76	228	40
35/39	38	15	24	77	36	58	39	53	150	36	72	50	64	186	36
30/34	13	5	4	22	32	27	13	17	57	31	29	16	22	67	31
25/29	2	1	1	4	25	7	3	2	12	27	12	9	9	30	25
20/24		1	1	2	19	2	1	2	5	20	6	3	5	14	20
15/19	2	0	1	3	16	1	2	1	4	15	5	1	1	7	16
10/14	0			0	14	1	1	1	3	11	0			0	13
5/9						0			0	8					

NOTE: MCWB = mean coincident wet-bulb temperature.

SOURCE: Ecodyne Corporation, *Weather Data Handbook*, McGraw-Hill Book Company, New York, 1980 (for all cities except New York).

Observation hour group					Observation hour group					Observation hour group				
1 o 8	09 to 16	17 to 24	Total observa- tion	MCWB	01 to 08	09 to 16	17 to 24	Total observa- tion	MCWB	01 to 08	09 to 16	17 to 24	Total observa- tion	MCWB
August					September					October				
	1	0	1	69										
0	1	0	1	67		0	0	0	70					
	5	2	7	68		1	0	1	67					
	17	9	26	66		5	2	7	65		0		0	67
	30	19	49	64		16	5	21	64		1	0	1	64
1	54	38	93	62	0	31	15	46	62		5	1	6	60
0	66	62	138	60	2	56	37	95	59		19	4	23	58
8	58	81	227	58	39	70	78	187	57	7	49	24	80	56
0	16	35	171	55	101	48	76	225	54	40	77	73	190	53
8	0	3	31	51	78	12	25	115	51	90	67	92	249	50
1			1	48	18	1	2	21	47	80	24	46	150	46
					1			1	43	29	5	8	42	42
										3	0	0	3	38

February					March					April					Annual total				
																1	0	1	71
															0	4	1	5	70
																18	9	27	68
																54	30	84	66
											1	0	1	59	0	103	63	166	64
	0		0	56		0		0	55		4	1	5	58	4	196	126	326	62
	1	0	1	55		3	1	4	54		12	4	16	55	34	307	225	566	59
	3	1	4	52		9	3	12	52	0	21	12	33	52	240	384	376	1000	57
1	13	5	19	50	0	23	9	32	49	2	50	32	84	50	535	389	408	1332	53
1	40	25	76	48	6	57	36	99	47	24	81	71	176	47	520	454	441	1415	49
3	73	68	184	44	49	86	87	222	44	99	56	83	238	44	564	471	538	1573	45
7	60	74	211	40	102	53	78	233	40	87	13	32	132	41	530	323	405	1258	40
1	27	40	128	36	67	15	28	110	36	26	0	5	31	37	327	146	214	687	36
4	6	9	39	31	22	2	4	28	31	1		0	1	33	116	42	56	214	31
5	1	2	8	25	1	1	1	3	26						27	15	15	57	25
2	1	0	3	19	1		0	1	20						11	6	8	25	20
1	0	0	1	16											9	3	3	15	16
															1	1	1	3	12
															0			0	8

TABLE 6-4 **Bin-Hour Weather Data for Selected Cities** *(cont.)*

MITCHEL AIR FORCE BASE, NASSAU COUNTY, NEW YORK

Mean frequency of occurrence of dry-bulb temperature (°F) with mean coincident wet-bulb temperature (°F) for each dry-bulb temperature range

Temperature range	Observation hour group 01 to 08	Observation hour group 09 to 16	Observation hour group 17 to 24	Total observation	MCWB	Observation hour group 01 to 08	Observation hour group 09 to 16	Observation hour group 17 to 24	Total observation	MCWB	Observation hour group 01 to 08	Observation hour group 09 to 16	Observation hour group 17 to 24	Total observation	MCWB
	May					June					July				
100/104							0		0	80		1		1	77
95/99							2	0	2	78		4		4	75
90/94		0		0	74	0	7	1	8	75	1	16	1	18	74
85/89		4		4	70	2	22	3	27	72	3	45	5	53	72
80/84	0	11	1	12	67	6	41	8	55	69	14	74	22	110	70
75/79	2	24	3	29	64	17	58	26	101	67	43	73	66	182	68
70/74	8	41	13	62	61	40	51	50	141	64	92	28	101	221	67
65/69	22	59	28	109	59	59	36	68	163	62	63	5	42	110	63
60/64	43	51	52	146	56	66	17	54	137	58	27	1	10	38	59
55/59	62	36	69	167	52	36	6	23	65	54	5	1	1	7	55
50/54	61	15	56	132	48	13	0	7	20	50					
45/49	35	7	22	64	44	1			1	46					
40/44	15	0	4	19	40										
35/39	0			0	33										
30/34															
	November					December					January				
100/104															
95/99															
90/94															
85/89															
80/84															
75/79															
70/74		1		1	56										
65/69	1	9	0	10	58		0		0	58					
60/64	8	23	9	40	57	0	2	1	3	55					
55/59	21	48	28	97	53	5	13	6	24	53		1		1	52
50/54	34	46	44	124	47	11	23	10	44	48	4	6	2	12	49
45/49	42	48	47	137	42	15	32	22	69	43	8	23	8	39	44
40/44	47	35	46	128	38	33	51	43	127	38	19	36	25	80	38
35/39	46	19	39	104	34	53	50	54	157	34	40	55	55	150	34
30/34	27	9	20	56	29	48	34	45	127	29	52	62	59	173	29
25/29	9	1	6	16	24	34	23	32	89	24	50	32	48	130	24
20/24	4	1	1	6	19	25	13	19	57	19	33	21	25	79	19
15/19	1			1	15	16	6	13	35	15	25	10	17	52	15
10/14						7	1	2	10	10	11	2	8	21	11
5/9						1		1	2	6	5	0	1	6	6
0/4						0			0	1	1			1	2
−5/−1															

NOTE: MCWB = Mean coincident wet-bulb temperature.

SOURCE: Departments of the Air Force, the Army, and the Navy, *Engineering Weather Data*, Washington, June 1967.

August

Observation hour group 09 to 16	17 to 24	Total observation	MCWB
3		3	75
8	0	8	74
35	2	39	73
66	15	90	71
73	61	173	69
44	85	204	67
16	59	144	63
3	22	64	59
	4	19	55
		0	51

September

Observation hour group 01 to 08	09 to 16	17 to 24	Total observation	MCWB
	0		0	77
0	2		2	74
0	7	0	7	73
1	29	2	32	71
12	58	17	87	68
41	58	52	151	66
50	49	57	156	61
52	28	60	140	58
48	8	32	88	53
23	1	16	40	49
10		4	14	44
3		0	3	39
0			0	37

October

Observation hour group 01 to 08	09 to 16	17 to 24	Total observation	MCWB
	5	0	5	71
1	15	1	17	66
7	26	9	42	65
16	50	21	87	60
36	61	47	144	57
46	47	55	148	52
52	28	50	130	48
46	12	40	98	43
30	4	19	53	39
13	0	6	19	35
1	0	0	1	30

February

Observation hour group 09 to 16	17 to 24	Total observation	MCWB
0		0	57
1	0	1	53
6	1	7	50
15	5	23	47
32	15	59	42
50	36	112	38
53	59	161	33
35	55	142	29
16	26	80	24
8	13	43	20
5	7	24	15
2	5	13	10
1	2	6	6
0	0	1	1
		0	−4

March

Observation hour group 01 to 08	09 to 16	17 to 24	Total observation	MCWB
	1		1	52
	3	0	3	53
0	7	0	7	51
2	16	2	20	47
7	29	15	51	46
18	50	31	99	41
43	50	56	149	37
69	50	72	191	34
57	27	44	128	29
31	13	19	63	24
16	2	8	26	19
5	0	1	6	15
0			0	11

April

Observation hour group 01 to 08	09 to 16	17 to 24	Total observation	MCWB
	0		0	66
	3	0	3	64
0	7	1	8	59
1	14	2	17	58
2	20	6	28	55
9	33	14	56	53
22	40	32	94	51
53	48	54	155	47
59	51	63	173	43
52	18	48	118	38
31	4	16	51	34
10	2	4	16	30
0		0	0	23
1		0	1	20

Annual total

01 to 08	09 to 16	17 to 24	Total observation	MCWB
	1		1	78
	9	0	9	76
1	33	2	36	74
6	111	11	128	71
31	230	49	310	69
114	306	175	595	66
264	264	312	840	62
284	247	280	811	59
280	227	266	773	56
258	218	251	727	52
259	211	257	727	48
244	255	248	747	43
269	249	278	796	38
304	233	304	841	34
247	169	230	646	29
163	86	133	382	24
102	44	67	213	19
59	21	38	118	15
24	4	15	43	11
9	2	4	15	6
2	0	0	2	1
				−4

TABLE 6-5 Degree-Hours for South-Facing Walls, a 70°F Indoor Temperature, and Nonsleeping and Sleeping Periods in Residential Occupancies, Mitchel Air Force Base, Nassau County, New York, Heating Season

Average bin temperature (°F)	Difference from 70°F (A)	Sol-air temperature adjustment* (°F) (B)	Hours of occurrence (nonsleeping) 7–10 A.M. (C)	10 A.M.–6 P.M. (D)	6–11 P.M. (E)	(°F·h)/year (without sol-air adjustment) [A·(C·D·F)]	(°F·h)/year (with sol-air adjustment) [B (C + D)] + (A·E)	Hours of occurrence (sleeping) 11 P.M.–2 A.M.	2–7 A.M.	Total hours (F)	(°F·h)/year (A·F)
67	3	. .	1	32	4	111	12	2	2	4	12
62	8	. .	6	66	15	696	120	9	11	20	160
57	13	. .	19	124	43	2,418	559	26	50	76	988
52	18	4	42	167	81	5,220	2,294	49	88	137	2,466
47	23	9	58	236	116	9,430	5,314	70	128	198	4,554
42	28	14	83	240	159	13,496	8,974	95	171	266	7,448
37	33	19	108	231	184	17,259	12,513	111	187	298	9,834
32	38	24	92	169	142	15,314	11,660	85	135	220	8,360
27	43	29	61	85	82	9,804	7,760	49	101	150	6,450
22	48	34	38	45	41	5,952	4,790	25	62	107	5,136
17	53	39	22	21	24	3,551	2,949	14	37	51	2,703
12	58	44	9	5	9	1,334	1,138	5	15	20	1,160
7	63	49	3	1	3	441	385	1	6	7	441
2	68	54	1	0	. .	68	54	. .	1	. .	68
						85,094	58,522				49,780

*$t_{sa} = t_o + [92\ \text{Btu/(h·ft}^2) \times 0.15]$
$= t_o + 14°F$

[Figure 8-1 with average solar radiation data from Table 7-13 adjusted to Btu/(h·ft²)]

SOURCE: Calculated by author from data in Table 6-4.

TABLE 6-6 Degree-Hours for South-Facing Walls, a 70°F Indoor Temperature during Occupied Periods, a 55°F Indoor Temperature during Unoccupied Periods in Nonresidential Buildings, Mitchel Air Force Base, Nassau County, New York, Heating Season

Average bin temperature (°F)	Difference from 70°F (A)	Sol-air temperature adjustment* (B)	Occupied period: hours of occurrence (8–10 A.M.)	+	(10 A.M.–6 P.M.)	Total hours (C)	Adjustment for 5-day week (D)	(°F·h)/year (without sol-air temperature) (A·C·D)	(°F·h)/year (with sol-air temperature) (B·C·D)	Difference from 55°F (E)	Sol-air temperature adjustment (F)	Unoccupied period: hours of occurrence (6 P.M.–10 A.M.)	—	8–10 A.M. × adjustment for 5-day week† (G)	10 A.M.–6 P.M. × adjustment for 2 days per week‡ (H)	(°F·h)/year (without sol-air temperature) E·(G + H)	(°F·h)/year (with sol-air temperature) (G·E) + (H·F)
67	3	..	1	+	32	33	.714	71	.....	..	..	...					
62	8	..	4	+	66	70	.714	400	.....	..	..	...					
57	13	..	13	+	124	137	.714	1,272	.....	..	..	...					
52	18	4	28	+	167	195	.714	2,506	557	3	..	242	—	(28 × 0.714) = 222	(167 × 0.286) = 48	810	666
47	23	9	39	+	236	275	.714	4,516	1,767	8	..	340	—	(39 × 0.714) = 312	(236 × 0.286) = 68	3,040	2,497
42	28	14	55	+	240	295	.714	5,898	2,949	13	..	474	—	(119 × 0.714) = 389	(240 × 0.286) = 69	5,954	5,057
37	33	19	72	+	231	303	.714	7,139	4,110	18	4	583	—	(146 × 0.714) = 479	(231 × 0.286) = 66	9,810	8,882
32	38	24	62	+	169	231	.714	6,267	3,958	23	9	473	—	(118 × 0.714) = 389	(169 × 0.286) = 48	10,051	9,376
27	43	29	41	+	85	126	.714	3,868	2,609	28	14	293	—	(73 × 0.714) = 241	(85 × 0.286) = 24	7,420	7,085
22	48	34	25	+	45	70	.714	2,399	1,699	33	19	167	—	(42 × 0.714) = 137	(45 × 0.286) = 13	4,950	4,766
17	53	39	15	+	21	36	.714	1,362	1,002	38	24	97	—	(24 × 0.714) = 80	(21 × 0.286) = 6	3,268	2,891
12	58	44	6	+	5	11	.714	456	346	43	29	39	—	(10 × 0.714) = 32	(5 × 0.286) = 1	1,419	1,411
7	63	49	2	+	1	3	.714	135	105	48	34	13	—	(3 × 0.714) = 11	(1 × 0.286) = 0	528	531
2	68	54	0	+	0	0	.714	0	0	53	39	2	—	(1 × 0.714) = 1	0 0	53	68
								36,289	19,102							47,303	43,230

*$t_{sa} = t_o + [92\ \text{Btu}/(\text{h}\cdot\text{ft}^2) \times 0.15]$
$= t_o + 14°\text{F}$
(Figure 8-1 with average solar radiation data from Table 7-13)

†5/7 = 0.714.

‡2/7 = 0.286.

SOURCE: Calculated by author from data in Table 6-4.

TABLE 6-7 Rates of Heat Gain from Occupants of Conditioned Spaces*

Degree of activity	Typical application	Total heat adults, male			Total heat adjusted†			Sensible heat			Latent heat		
		Watts	Btu/h	kcal/h	Watts	Btu/h	kcal/h	Watts	Btu/h	kcal/h	Watts	Btu/h	kcal/h
Seated at rest	Theater, motion picture	115	400	100	100	350	90	60	210	55	40	140	30
Seated, very light work, writing	Offices, hotels, apartments	140	480	120	120	420	105	65	230	55	55	190	50
Seated, eating	Restaurant‡	150	520	130	170	580‡	145	75	255	60	95	325	80
Seated, light work, typing	Offices, hotels, apartments	185	640	160	150	510	130	75	255	60	75	255	65
Standing, light work or walking slowly	Retail store, bank	235	800	200	185	640	160	90	315	80	95	325	80
Light benchwork	Factory	255	880	220	230	780	195	100	345	90	130	435	110
Walking, 2 mph, light machine work	Factory	305	1040	260	305	1040	260	100	345	90	205	695	170
Bowling§	Bowling alley	350	1200	300	280	960	240	100	345	90	180	615	150
Moderate dancing	Dance hall	400	1360	340	375	1280	320	120	405	100	255	875	220
Heavy work, heavy machine-work, lifting	Factory	470	1600	400	470	1600	400	165	565	140	300	1035	260
Heavy work, athletics	Gymnasium	585	2000	500	525	1800	450	185	635	160	340	1165	200

*Tabulated values are based on 78°F room dry-bulb temperature. For 80°F room dry-bulb temperature, the total heat remains the same, but the sensible heat value should be decreased by approximately 8 percent and the latent heat values increased accordingly.

†Adjusted total heat gain is based on normal percentage of men, women, and children for the application listed, with the postulate that the gain from an adult female is 85 percent of that for an adult male and that the gain from a child is 75 percent of that for an adult male.

‡Adjusted total heat value for eating in a restaurant, includes 60 Btu/h for food per individual (30 Btu sensible and 30 Btu latent).

§For bowling, figure one person per alley actually bowling and all others as sitting (400 Btu/h) or standing and walking slowly (790 Btu/h).

NOTE: All values are rounded to the nearest 5 W or kcal/h or to the nearest 10 Btu/h.

SOURCE: *ASHRAE Handbook and Product Directory—1977 Fundamentals Volume*, American Society of Heating, Refrigerating and Air-Conditioning Engineers, Inc., New York, 1977, p. 25.17. Reprinted by permission.

Second, the way in which such buildings behave thermally and are conditioned mechanically must be understood. Typically, there are an interior heating, ventilating, and air-conditioning (HVAC) zone and an exterior or perimeter HVAC zone. The exterior zone is frequently assumed to be a perimeter strip of space about 15 feet from the exterior wall. This zone is subject to the varying thermal zones of the exterior climate as well as to loads from people and lights. The interior zone is dominated by the thermal loads of equipment as well as by loads from people and lights and is affected relatively little by climatic forces. Interior spaces are typically conditioned by all-air HVAC systems, while exterior zones are usually conditioned by air-water systems such as induction or fan-coil systems.

Architects can easily effect changes in the energy consumption of the exterior zone but can have very little impact on the fuel and energy expenses of the interior zone. The analysis method presented in the following paragraphs focuses, therefore, on the exterior zone only.

The fundamental approach for evaluating wintertime thermal benefits for the exterior zones of nonresidential buildings is based on estimating the balance of daytime thermal gains and losses contributed by both external climatic and internal thermal forces. The method allows the designer to acknowledge that the internal heat gains during a winter day are significant and often exceed heat losses, while nighttime internal heat gains, particularly in the exterior zone, are negligible, with heat losses dominating.

This analysis method ignores, however, the thermal storage effect of the building's structure. The quantification of this effect is beyond the scope of this book and, while of some value, will not increase significantly the benefits of energy-saving architectural design improvements. This is due, among other reasons, to the unoccupied status of a commercial building at night and also to the effect of an all-air HVAC system on constant recirculation of air throughout the building and the tendency of this to minimize local structural thermal storage.

EXAMPLE

Assume, for example, that an architect wishes to increase the insulation in the south-facing exterior wall of the office building she is developing. The design may be analyzed as follows:

U wall before	0.20 Btu/(°F·h·ft^2)
U wall after	0.10 Btu/(°F·h·ft^2)
ΔU	0.10 Btu/(°F·h·ft^2)
Heating fuel	Oil
Fuel cost	$1.60/gal
Electricity cost	$0.14/kWh
Insulation cost	$0.60/ft^2
Cooling system	Central water-cooled system, 75 tons
Lighting system	2.5 W/ft^2
Solar transmittance (clear 1/4-in insulating glass)	0.59

Assume a 10-foot-long portion of wall:

Wall area	70 ft^2
Window area	40 ft^2
Crack length (fixed window)	34 ft

Assume, also, that the 10-foot length of south-facing wall represents 1 percent of the entire south wall of the building.

Daytime solar and internal heat gains:

Lighting (See also Chapter 10.)

$$q = 2.5\ \text{W/ft}^2 \times 150\ \text{ft}^2 \times 3.413\ \text{Btu/Wh}$$
$$= 1280\ \text{Btu/h}$$ [See Equation (10-2).]

or, assuming 9 h/day, 5 days/week, and a 6-month heating season,

$$Q = 1{,}497{,}600\ \text{Btu/year}$$

People[7]

$$q = [150\ \text{ft}^2 \div (100\ \text{ft}^2/\text{person})] \times 255\ \text{Btu/(h}\cdot\text{person)}$$
$$= 383\ \text{Btu/h}$$

or $Q = 447{,}525$ Btu/year

Solar[8]

$$q_h = 943\ \text{Btu/(day}\cdot\text{ft}^2) \times 40\ \text{ft}^2 \times 0.59$$
$$= 22{,}255\ \text{Btu/day}$$
$$Q_h = 2{,}893{,}250\ \text{Btu/year}$$

Total internal and solar heat gains = 4,838,275 Btus per year.

Daytime heat losses:[9]

Conduction through walls

$$\text{Old } Q_h = 0.20\ \text{Btu/(h}\cdot{}^\circ\text{F}\cdot\text{ft}^2) \times 19{,}102\ ({}^\circ\text{F}\cdot\text{h})/\text{year} \times 70\ \text{ft}^2$$
$$= 267{,}428\ \text{Btu/year}$$ [See Equation (7-8).]
$$\text{New } Q_h = 0.10\ \text{Btu/(h}\cdot{}^\circ\text{F}\cdot\text{ft}^2) \times 19{,}102\ ({}^\circ\text{F}\cdot\text{h})/\text{year} \times 70\ \text{ft}^2$$
$$= 133{,}714\ \text{Btu/year}$$

Conduction through windows

$$Q_h = 0.58\ \text{Btu/(h}\cdot{}^\circ\text{F}\cdot\text{ft}^2) \times 40\ \text{ft}^2 \times 36{,}289\ ({}^\circ\text{F}\cdot\text{h})/\text{year}$$
$$= 841{,}905\ \text{Btu/year}$$

Convection: infiltration through window frames

$$Q_h = 0.018\ \text{Btu/(}{}^\circ\text{F}\cdot\text{ft}^3) \times [3\ \text{ft}^3/(\text{h}\cdot\text{ft}) \times 34\ \text{ft}] \times 36{,}289\ ({}^\circ\text{F}\cdot\text{h})/\text{year}$$
$$= 66{,}627\ \text{Btu/year}$$ [See Equation (7-8).]

[7]The figure of 255 Btu/(h·person) is taken from Table 6-7. For typical buildings use sensible heat of people only for heating-season analyses and both sensible and latent heat for cooling-season analyses. If a building's HVAC system has a humidifier, include latent heat with heating-season calculations.

[8]The figure of 943 Btu/(day·ft²) is taken from Table 7-13, averaged for 6 months, November through April.

[9]The figures of 19,102 (°F·h)/year and 36,289 (°F·h)/year are taken from Table 6-6. For infiltration calculations use degree-hour data without the sol-air temperature adjustment.

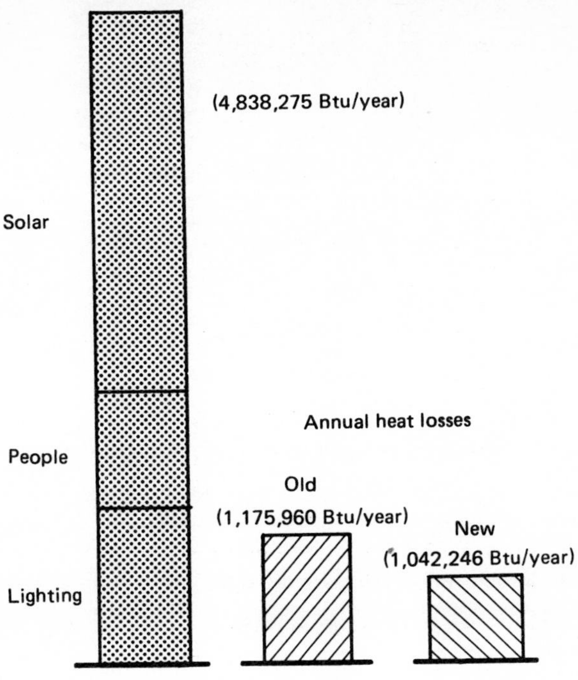

FIGURE 6-2 Analysis of the winter daytime thermal balance for the south-facing exterior zone of an office building in New York City.

Total heat losses:

Old = 1,175,960 Btu/year

New = 1,042,246 Btu/year

The results of this analysis are displayed in Figure 6-2. The daytime heat gains in the exterior zone on the south facade of this building far exceed the daytime heat losses. Added insulation will be of no value during this period of the day. In fact, added insulation may actually increase energy consumption if refrigeration is needed to get rid of the excess heat caused by internal and solar gains which might have been allowed to escape if the insulation had been less resistive. Refrigeration may not be needed, of course, if outside air is used for cooling in lieu of refrigeration, something often done during the winter months. (As a generalization, a designer may conclude, of course, that the effectiveness of designs for improving the thermal performance of the exterior facades of large nonresidential buildings frequently depends on orientation and/or control of solar heat gain.)

During the night and on weekends in the exterior zone, the lights are off, the people are gone, and the sun has set; so there are no significant heat gains. The benefit of added insulation may be calculated directly:[10]

$$\Delta Q_h = 0.10 \text{ Btu/(h}\cdot{}^\circ\text{F}\cdot\text{ft}^2) \times 70 \text{ ft}^2 \times 43{,}230 \ ({}^\circ\text{F}\cdot\text{h})/\text{year}$$

$$= 302{,}610 \text{ Btu/year [See Equation (7-6).]}$$

[10]The figure of 43,230 (°F·h)/year is taken from Table 6-6.

The dollar value of this saving is calculated below:

$$B_h = \frac{\$1.60/\text{gal} \times 302{,}610\ \text{Btu/year}}{0.60 \times 140{,}000\ \text{Btu/gal}} \qquad (6\text{-}1)$$

$$= \$5.76/\text{year}$$

Since the portion of the wall analyzed here represents 1 percent of the entire wall of the building, the impact of the insulation on the mechanical equipment size may be analyzed as follows:

$$\Delta q_h = 0.10 \times 70\ \text{ft}^2 \times (70°\text{F} - 15°\text{F})\ \text{[See Equation (7-6).]}$$

$$= 385\ \text{Btu/h}$$

or for the entire building,

$$= 385 \times 100 = 38{,}500\ \text{Btu/h}$$

This building is classified as a medium-size commercial building. Using data from Table 5-8, the following provides an estimate of the equipment size reduction cost savings:

$$B_0 = (38{,}500\ \text{Btu/h} \div 1000\ \text{Btu/h}) \times \$8$$

$$= \$308$$

or for each 10-foot strip of south wall,

$$= (\$308 \div 100) = \$3.08$$

The estimate of the fuel savings created during the summer by the extra insulation is calculated in the next section of this chapter.

COOLING BENEFITS

Designs such as overhangs for south-facing residential windows which reduce summer heat gain or roof monitor designs which increase natural ventilation will decrease a building's need for air conditioning. The value of such designs is due to a reduction in the cost of electrical consumption by air-conditioning systems. If a building is not air-conditioned, of course, designs such as those mentioned above will increase summer *comfort* conditions but will not have any impact on energy conservation.

The designer must consider what impact his or her design will have on the number of hours during which the air-conditioning system will be on, the peak cooling load, or the overall summer cooling load.

Equivalent Full-Load Hour Method

The general form for a relatively simple but somewhat inaccurate method which may be used to estimate air-conditioning savings is presented below:[11]

$$B_c = P \times C_e \times T \times (\Delta q_c \div 12{,}000) \qquad (6\text{-}4)$$

[11]SOURCE: *ASHRAE Handbook and Product Directory—1980 Systems Volume*, American Society of Heating, Refrigerating and Air-Conditioning Engineers, Inc., New York, 1980, p. 43.10. Reprinted by permission.

TABLE 6-8 Electrical Power Required to Operate Various Types and Sizes of Cooling Systems

System	Compressor, kW/ton [kWh/(ton·h)]
Window units	1.46
Through-wall units	1.64
House: central air	1.49
Central	
3–5 tons, air-cooled	1.20
25–100 tons, air-cooled	1.18
25–100 tons, water-cooled	0.94
Over 100 tons	0.79

SOURCE: *ASHRAE Handbook and Product Directory—1980 Systems Volume,* American Society of Heating, Refrigerating and Air-Conditioning Engineers, Inc., New York, 1980, p. 43.10. Reprinted by permission.

in units,

$$\$/\text{year} = \text{kW/ton} \times \$/\text{kWh} \times \text{h/year} \times [\text{Btu/h} \div 12{,}000\ \text{Btu/(ton}\cdot\text{h)}]$$

where B_c = benefit of reduced cooling energy consumption, \$/year

P = power required to operate the air-conditioning system, kW/ton (Air-conditioning systems have different power requirements depending on size and type. Designer should refer to Table 6-8 for specific values.)

C_e = cost of electricity, \$/kWh

T = equivalent full-load hours[12] for an air-conditioning system, h/year (Designer may refer to Table 6-9 for normal air-conditioning full-load operating hours in various locations. The general rule of thumb for using the table is to assume that residential buildings will be at the higher end of the scale and commercial buildings at the lower end.)

Δq_c = change in design (peak) cooling load, Btu/h [See Equation (8-1). Typically this figure must be adjusted (as is indicated in the equation) to units used for cooling loads which are called "tons," where 1 ton = 12,000 Btu/h, or 1 ton·h = 12,000 Btu.]

The reader should be cautioned that this method is not particularly accurate for *either* residential or commercial buildings unless more precise data concerning equivalent full-load hours for various building types are available from local sources.

[12]An air-conditioning system will *actually* operate for many more hours each season than the equivalent full-load hour data indicate. Cooling system *operating time* has been translated in these data into full-load hours *equivalent* in terms of energy consumption because data describing cooling system full-load performance have traditionally been more readily available.

TABLE 6-9 Estimated Equivalent Rated Full-Load Hours of Operation for Properly Sized Equipment during Normal Cooling Season

City	Hours*	City	Hours*
Albuquerque, New Mexico	800–2200	Indianapolis, Indiana	600–1600
Atlantic City, New Jersey	500–800	Little Rock, Arkansas	1400–2400
Birmingham, Alabama	1200–2200	Minneapolis, Minnesota	400–800
Boston, Massachusetts	400–1200	New Orleans, Louisiana	1400–2800
Burlington, Vermont	200–600	New York, New York	500–1000
Charlotte, North Carolina	700–1100	Newark, New Jersey	400–900
Chicago, Illinois	500–1000	Oklahoma City, Oklahoma	1100–2000
Cleveland, Ohio	400–800	Pittsburgh, Pennsylvania	900–1200
Cincinnati, Ohio	1000–1500	Rapid City, South Dakota	800–1000
Columbia, South Carolina	1200–1400	St. Joseph, Missouri	1000–1600
Corpus Christi, Texas	2000–2500	St. Petersburg, Florida	1500–2700
Dallas, Texas	1200–1600	San Diego, California	800–1700
Denver, Colorado	400–800	Savannah, Georgia	1200–1400
Des Moines, Iowa	600–1000	Seattle, Washington	400–1200
Detroit, Michigan	700–1000	Syracuse, New York	200–1000
Duluth, Minnesota	300–500	Trenton, New Jersey	800–1000
El Paso, Texas	1000–1400	Tulsa, Oklahoma	1500–2200
Honolulu, Hawaii	1500–3500	Washington, D.C.	700–1200

*The number to the left of the dash is typical of commercial buildings; the number to the right is for residential uses.

SOURCE: *ASHRAE Handbook and Product Directory—1980 Systems Volume*, American Society of Heating, Refrigerating and Air-Conditioning Engineers, Inc., New York, 1980, p. 43.11. Reprinted by permission.

EXAMPLE

An architect proposes to have overhangs placed over the south-facing windows of a house. The overhangs will be dimensioned so that the direct summer sun will not enter the house through the windows. The information required to analyze this design is as follows:

Reduced peak cooling load[13]	Δq = 11,800 Btu/h
Air-conditioning system: summer equivalent full-load hours	1000 h
Air-conditioning system type	Central air
Electrical cost	\$0.15/kWh
Cost of overhang	\$550

An analysis of the value of the overhang is presented below:

$$\begin{aligned} B_c &= 1.49\ \text{kW/ton} \times \$0.15/\text{kWh} \times 1000\ \text{h/year} \\ &\quad \times [11{,}800\ \text{Btu/h} \div 12{,}000\ \text{Btu/(ton}\cdot\text{h)}] \\ &= \$220/\text{year} \end{aligned} \tag{6-4}$$

A simple cost-benefit analysis may next be conducted:

$$\text{Simple payback period} = \frac{\$500}{\$220/\text{year}} = 2.3\ \text{years}$$

$$\text{Simple return on investment} = \frac{\$220/\text{year}}{\$500} = 44\ \text{percent/year}$$

The overhang is clearly worth constructing.

[13]Chapter 8 will describe how Δq may be calculated for summer radiative heat gain.

Bin Method

A more sophisticated method for estimating cooling savings in *non*residential buildings involves the use of bin data. It is based on the following assumptions. As noted in the subsection "Bin-Hour Methods," which delineates the analysis of nonresidential *heating* benefits, architectural energy-saving designs are assumed to affect primarily the exterior 15-foot zone of a commercial building and to have negligible effects on the energy consumption of the interior zone. Therefore, equipment loads are ignored.

Two other assumptions are made in this analysis approach. First, it is assumed that unless the building is a hospital or a building with a similar operating schedule, the air-conditioning system does not operate during the evening or the weekend hours. Second, it is assumed that the building's refrigeration equipment begins operating when the outside air temperature rises above 65°F. While there is still a need for cooling the building interior at outside temperatures *below* 65°F because of internal heat loads, it is assumed that this need is accommodated by so-called "economizer cycles." Such systems use outside air for cooling instead of electrically induced cooling by refrigeration.

Bin data for use in this analysis approach must be reorganized, as was done in "Bin-Hour Methods," to differentiate weekday from nighttime and weekend occupancy schedules and also to reflect the 65°F set point for the cooling system and an 80°F indoor summertime temperature (see Table 6-10).

Equation (6-4) may take the following form for use with bin-hour data in an analysis of cooling savings in nonresidential buildings:

$$B_c = P \times C_e \times (\Delta Q_c \div 12{,}000) \tag{6-5}$$

in units,

$$\$/\text{year} = \text{kWh/(ton}\cdot\text{h)} \times \$/\text{kW} \times [\text{Btu/year} \div \text{Btu/(ton}\cdot\text{h)}]$$

TABLE 6-10 Degree-Hours for South-Facing Walls, an 80°F Indoor Temperature, and 65°F Cooling System Set-Point Temperature on Weekdays in Nonresidential Buildings, Mitchel Air Force Base, Nassau County, New York, Cooling Season

Average bin temperature	Difference from 80°F (A)	Sol-air adjustment* (B)	Hours of occurrence (8–10 A.M.)	+ (10 A.M.–6 P.M.)	Total hours (C)	Adjustment for 5-day week (D)	(°F·h)/year (without sol-air temperature) (A·C·D)	(°F·h)/year (with sol-air temperature) (B·C·D)
102	22	37	...	1	1	0.714	16	26
97	17	32	...	9	9	0.714	109	206
92	12	27	...	33	33	0.714	283	636
87	7	22	2	109	111	0.714	555	1744
82	2	17	8	210	218	0.714	311	2646
77	−3	12	28	262	290	0.714	−621	2485
72	−8	7	62	181	243	0.714	−1388	1215
67	−13	2	60	106	166	0.714	−1541	237
			160	911	1071		−2276	9195

* $t_{sa} = t_o + [101 \text{ Btu/(h}\cdot\text{ft}^2) \times 0.15]$

(Figure 8-1 with data from Table 7-13)

SOURCE: Calculated by author from *Air Force Manual*, AFM 88-8, U.S. Air Force, Washington, 1976, chap. 6.

where all variables are the same as in Equation (6-4) except for ΔQ_c = change in overall *annual* cooling load, Btu/year [see Equation (8-2)]. P = for seasonal energy consumption analysis, power required to operate the air-conditioning system, kWh(ton·h) (See Table 6-8.)

EXAMPLE

Given the data in Table 6-10, the analysis of added insulation in the south-facing wall of the office building analyzed in the previous section may be completed as follows. (Specific techniques used below without detailed explanation are presented and discussed in the remaining chapters of this book.)

Conduction through the walls:

$$\Delta Q_c = 0.10 \text{ Btu/(°F·ft}^2\text{·h)} \times 70 \text{ ft}^2 \times 9195 \text{ (°F·h)/year}$$

$$= 64{,}365 \text{ Btu/year [See Equation (8-2).]}$$

The dollar value of this saving may be calculated as follows:

$$B_c = 0.94 \text{ kWh/(ton·h)} \times \$0.14\text{/kWh}$$

$$\times [64{,}365 \text{ Btu/year} \div 12{,}000 \text{ Btu/(ton·h)}] \qquad (6\text{-}5)$$

$$= \$0.71\text{/year}$$

The impact of the insulation on the peak cooling load is calculated below:

$$\Delta q_c = 0.10 \text{ Btu/(°F·h·ft}^2) \times 70 \text{ ft}^2 \times 22\text{°F}$$

$$= 154 \text{ Btu/h [See Equation (8-1).]}$$

or for the entire building,

$$= (154 \times 100) = 15{,}400 \text{ Btu/h, or } 1.28 \text{ tons}$$

This is not enough to effect a size reduction in the cooling equipment, so no equipment cost savings are possible here.

An estimate of the reduction in demand charges due to the peak load reduction is presented below:

$$B_c = 0.94 \text{ kW/ton} \times 1.28 \text{ tons} \times \$20\text{/(kW·month)} \times 3 \text{ months/year}$$

$$= \$72.19\text{/year}$$

or for the 10-ft-long wall,

$$B_c = \$72.19\text{/year} \div 100 = \$0.72\text{/year}$$

The combined saving for both seasons is summarized below:

Winter (B_h)	\$5.76/year
Summer (B_c)	\$1.43/year (\$0.72 + \$0.71)
Total (B_T)	\$7.19/year

In a building operated as a business, however, as discussed in Chapter 5, fuel expenses are deductible from gross income in computing income taxes. This means that the fuel savings calculated above are not as valuable and must be adjusted to an aftertax basis. For a 45 percent corporate income tax bracket, an aftertax adjustment may be made as follows:

$$B_T = \$7.19/\text{year} \times (1 - 0.45)$$
$$= \$3.95/\text{year}$$

The cost of the insulation is calculated below:

$$C_0 = 70 \text{ ft}^2 \times \$0.60/\text{ft}^2$$
$$= \$42$$

By adjusting for the heating equipment size reduction, this becomes

$$C_0 = (\$42 - \$3.08) = \$38.92$$

A simple cost-benefit analysis yields the following:

$$\text{Simple payback period} = \frac{C_0}{B_t} = \frac{\$38.92}{\$3.95/\text{year}} = 9.9 \text{ years}$$

$$\text{Simple return on investment} = \frac{B_t}{C_0} = \frac{\$3.95/\text{year}}{\$38.92} = 10.1 \text{ percent/year}$$

The design approach appears to be not quite cost-effective if the building owner's required return on investment is assumed to be at least 12 percent per year. A more detailed discounted-cash-flow analysis would be required to make a final recommendation in this case.

The equations presented in this chapter are summarized in Table 6-11.

It is important to emphasize that the energy saving which an architectural design may generate in a building is highly dependent on the type of mechanical heating and cooling system. The nature of the saving for more complex systems involving equipment not reviewed in the preceding pages, such as heat pumps, is best estimated by a mechanical engineer. The methods presented here and the mechanical systems they represent are valid within the limits of the context they represent. Expert consultation should be retained for energy analysis questions beyond these limits.

TABLE 6-11 **Summary of Equations to Be Used for Estimating Heating Benefits and Cooling Benefits**

Heating benefits	$B_h = \dfrac{C_f \times \Delta Q_h}{n \times v}$	6-1 General form for residential and commercial buildings
	$B_h = \dfrac{C_f \times \Delta q_h \times \text{DD} \times 24}{(t_i - t_o) \times n \times v} \times K_d$	6-3 Degree-day data for residential buildings
	$B_e = C_e \times 2 \times \Delta Q_c \div 10^6$	6-2 Fan and pump savings
Cooling benefits	$B_c = P \times C_e \times T \times (\Delta q_c \div 12{,}000)$	6-4 Equivalent full-load hour data for residential and commercial buildings
	$B_c = P \times C_e \times (\Delta Q_c \div 12{,}000)$	6-5 Bin-hour data for commercial buildings

BIBLIOGRAPHY

Anderson, Bruce N.: *Solar Energy: Fundamentals in Building Design*, McGraw-Hill Book Company, New York, 1977.

ASHRAE Handbook and Product Directory—1977 Fundamentals Volume, American Society of Heating, Refrigerating and Air-Conditioning Engineers, Inc., New York, 1977.

ASHRAE Handbook and Product Directory—1980 Systems Volume, American Society of Heating, Refrigerating and Air-Conditioning Engineers, Inc., New York, 1980.

Ecodyne Corporation: *Weather Data Handbook*, McGraw-Hill Book Company, New York, 1980.

Engineering Weather Data, Departments of the Air Force, the Army, and the Navy, Washington, July 1978.

SEVEN

WINTER HEATING SAVINGS

This chapter presents methods for estimating the thermal value of fuel savings during the winter heating season. These savings are expressed in terms of the following variables:

q = Btu/h, typically the peak thermal load

or Q = Btu/year, representing annual thermal energy use

These values will provide some of the input required by the estimating methods presented in Chapter 6, which translated the thermal value of heating savings into dollar values.

Heating savings may be achieved by developing designs which intervene in some way with one of the three basic methods of heat transfer:

- Conduction
- Convection
- Radiation

The following sections present methods for estimating heating savings caused by changes in each of these thermal transfer modes.

CONDUCTION: CHANGES IN WINTER TRANSMISSION HEAT LOSS

Designs which reduce conductive heat losses in a building may be analyzed by the methods presented in this section. These include approaches which slow down heat flow conducted from the inside of a building through its exterior envelope to the outside. Wall insulation, roof insulation, glazing insulation, and reductions in the area of the envelope and the area of glazing within that envelope are examples of designs which reduce conducted heat loss. (See Chapter 4, "Design Alternatives," for additional examples.)

The designer is cautioned, however, to be comprehensive in his or her analysis of any particular design approach. For example, a design which minimizes conductive heat losses may not minimize overall fuel consumption for a building because it precludes more valuable savings through some other mode such as the use of natural lighting or increased winter solar radiation.

As mentioned in Chapter 2, conductive heat transfer moves from conditions of higher temperature to conditions of lower temperature. The rate at which the heat moves between those two conditions depends on the magnitude of the difference between the temperatures as well as on other physical conditions. If there is no difference between the temperatures of the two conditions, there will be no heat transfer from one condition to the other. Conductive heat transfer rates are also directly proportional to the area of the material perpendicular to the direction of heat flow through which the heat must travel as well as to the conductivity of the material. Conductive heat flow rates are inversely proportional, however, to the length of travel between two differing temperature conditions. These considerations may be expressed in the following form:

$$q = k(A/L)(t_i - t_o) \tag{7-1}$$

in units,

$$\text{Btu/h} = \text{Btu/[h}\cdot\text{ft}^2\cdot(^\circ\text{F/ft})] \times \text{ft}^2/\text{ft} \times {}^\circ\text{F}$$

where q = heat flow rate, Btu/h
A = mean cross-sectional area perpendicular to heat flow, ft^2
L = mean length of heat flow path (thickness through a material), ft
k = thermal conductivity, Btu/[h·ft^2·(°F/ft)]
t_i = temperature of inside conditions, °F
t_o = temperature of outside conditions, °F

Designers and engineers have developed some concepts which make analysis of conductive heat flow rates somewhat simpler. They have introduced the concept of R values,[1] in which, for a given material,

$$R = L/k \tag{7-2}$$

in units,

$$(\text{ft}^2\cdot{}^\circ\text{F}\cdot\text{h})/\text{Btu} = \text{ft} \div \text{Btu/[h}\cdot{}^\circ\text{F}\cdot(\text{ft}^2/\text{ft})]$$

where the variables are the same as above except

R = thermal resistance, (ft^2·°F·h)/Btu

By substituting Equation (7-2) in Equation (7-1), the heat transfer rate may be expressed as follows:

$$q = A/R(t_i - t_o) \tag{7-3}$$

[1]See Tables 7-1 through 7-5 for R values and other thermal resistance–related data.

Length of travel L is sometimes reduced to a smaller unit, typically 1 inch, in practice. For example, from Table 7-3 the R value of *1 inch* of expanded polyurethane is 6.25 $(\text{ft}^2 \cdot {}^\circ\text{F} \cdot \text{h})/\text{Btu}$.

The overall R value of a material other than 1 inch in thickness is found by multiplying the actual thickness in inches by the R value of the material. For example, 2¾ inches of expanded polyurethane would have the following R value:

$$R = 2.75 \text{ in} \times 6.25\ ({}^\circ\text{F} \cdot \text{ft}^2 \cdot \text{h})/\text{Btu in}$$

$$= 17.19\ ({}^\circ\text{F} \cdot \text{ft}^2 \cdot \text{h})/\text{Btu}$$

When heat transfer crosses more than one material, the overall rate of heat transfer may also be calculated. For example, a given material designated by the number 1 may have an R value designated by R_1. The rate of heat flow conducted through 1 inch of that material may be designated as follows:

$$q = A/R_1(t_i - t_o)$$

For three different materials designated 1, 2, and 3, subjected to an indoor temperature designated by a next to material 1 and to an outdoor temperature of d next to material 3 (Figure 7-1), the following equation describes the heat flow through the composite material:

$$q = A(t_a - t_d) \times \frac{1}{R_1 + R_2 + R_3} \qquad (7\text{-}4)$$

In practice, it has become convenient to use another concept to simplify the analysis further. This concept is called a U value, and it equals the following in

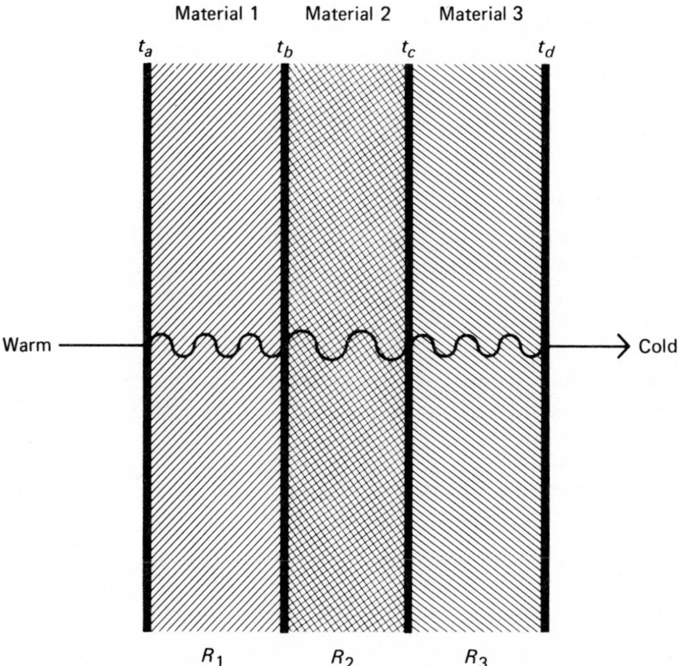

FIGURE 7-1 Section through three different materials, showing conduction of heat from one temperature condition to another.

the example above:

$$U = \frac{1}{R_1 + R_2 + R_3}$$

in units,

$$\text{Btu}/(°\text{F}\cdot\text{h}\cdot\text{ft}^2) = 1 \div [(°\text{F}\cdot\text{h}\cdot\text{ft}^2)/\text{Btu}]$$

The U value is often called the "overall coefficient of conducted heat transfer" or sometimes the "thermal transmittance value." Thus, if the U value is used in Equation (7-4), the equation becomes:

$$q_{\text{total}} = A(t_a - t_d) \times U$$

or as it is more commonly written,

$$q = U \times A(t_a - t_d) \quad \text{or} \quad q = U \times A(t_i - t_o) \tag{7-5}$$

in units,

$$\text{Btu/h} = \text{Btu}/(\text{h}\cdot°\text{F}\cdot\text{ft}^2) \times \text{ft}^2 \times (°\text{F} - °\text{F})$$

where q = heat transfer rate, Btu/h
U = overall coefficient of conducted heat transfer, Btu/(h·°F·ft²) (See Tables 7-3, 7-4, and 7-5.)
A = mean cross-sectional area perpendicular to heat flow, ft²
t_i = temperature of inside surface, °F
t_o = temperature of outside surface, °F

In this book, the primary concern will be with analysis of the *change* or improvement in the heat flow rate which a change in insulation may have on a building. As a result, Equation (7-5) will be modified and used as follows:

$$\Delta q_h = \Delta(U \times A)(t_i - t_o) \tag{7-6}$$

The units are the same as in Equation (7-5), and

Δq_h = *change* in heat flow rate during the heating season, Btu/year
Δ = change in a quantity due, in this book, to an architectural design change
U = overall coefficient of conducted heat transfer because of change in insulation or materials for a building, Btu/(°F·h·ft²)
A = surface area, ft²

Equation (7-6) may also be modified further to reflect *annual* heat transfer rates (Q, Btu/year) instead of *hourly* heat transfer rates (q, Btu/h):

$$Q_h = U \times A \times \text{DH}_h \tag{7-7}$$

$$\text{or} \quad \Delta Q_h = \Delta(U \times A) \times \text{DH}_h \tag{7-8}$$

in units,

$$\text{Btu/year} = \text{Btu}/(\text{h}\cdot\text{ft}^2\cdot°\text{F}) \times \text{ft}^2 \times (°\text{F}\cdot\text{h})/\text{year}$$

where U, Δ, and A have been defined previously and

Q_h = annual energy consumption during heating season, Btu/year
ΔQ_h = change in annual heating season energy consumption, Btu/year
DH_h = bin-hour data reflecting annual heating season outdoor climatic and indoor temperature conditions, (°F·h)/year

The new variable here, of course, is DH, or degree-hours per year. As shown in Chapter 6, data expressed in these units are particularly useful in analyzing buildings in which indoor temperature conditions vary during the day or week and indoor heat loads are substantial, as is typical of most nonresidential buildings.

The reader should note that when Δq_h is calculated as in Equation (7-6), it represents a change in *peak* winter heat load. When ΔQ_h is calculated by using Equation (7-8), however, it represents a change in *annual* energy consumption and as such should account for another phenomenon, sol-air temperature, described in greater detail in Chapter 8. The outside surface temperature of a wall is higher than the air temperature surrounding the wall *if* the sun is shining on it. Because the peak winter heat load usually occurs at night or on cloudy days, the sol-air temperature is not a factor for that situation. Annual winter heating expenditures are obviously a function of both cloudy and sunny conditions and daytime as well as nighttime conditions. The sun shining on building surfaces will reduce overall winter conducted heat loss because of the sol-air temperature phenomenon. (Tables 6-5 and 6-6 show how heating-season degree-hour data may be adjusted to account for this.)

Occasionally, two other concepts are used in analyzing conductive heat transfer. In analyzing the wall of a building, for example, the air molecules next to the surface of the wall on the inside and outside surfaces help to slow down the rate of heat transfer. This phenomenon depends not on the thickness of the wall but on the speed of the air and the emittance (see Chapter 2) of the surface, that is, its ability to radiate heat.

The value of the air film in the heat conduction process is designated by the variable h and is called the film, or surface, conductance. Its units are the same as a U value: Btu/(°F·h·ft²); they are the reciprocal of an R value.

Table 7-1 lists values for surface conductances under various conditions of surface emittance and air speed.

Some materials such as concrete block have nonuniform cross sections. Thus, an R value for a particular inch of the material is not the same as the next inch. Therefore, an overall measure of the heat transfer capability of the material itself is used. This is called its "conductance" and is designated by the variable C. Its units are also the same as the U value [Btu/(°F·h·ft²)]. Because it is a measure of a specific material as is the R value, the two values are essentially reciprocals of one another; that is,

$$C = 1/R$$

The difference between the U value and the C value is simply that U is a measure of a *group* of materials acting together while C is a measure of only *one* of those materials.

TABLE 7-1 **Surface Conductances and Resistances for Air** [All conductance values expressed in Btu/(h·ft²·°F)]

Section A: Surface conductances and resistances*

Position of surface	Direction of heat flow	Surface emittance: Nonreflective, $\epsilon = 0.90$		Reflective, $\epsilon = 0.20$		Reflective, $\epsilon = 0.05$	
		h_1	R	h_1	R	h_1	R
Still air							
Horizontal	Upward	1.63	*0.61*	0.91	*1.10*	0.76	*1.32*
Sloping	Upward	1.60	*0.62*	0.88	*1.14*	0.73	*1.37*
Vertical	Horizontal	1.46	*0.68*	0.74	*1.35*	0.59	*1.70*
Sloping	Downward	1.32	*0.76*	0.60	*1.67*	0.45	*2.22*
Horizontal	Downward	1.08	*0.92*	0.37	*2.70*	0.22	*4.55*
Moving air (any position)							
15-mph wind (for winter)	Any	6.00	0.17				
7.5-mph wind (for summer)	Any	4.00	0.25				

Section B: Reflectivity and emittance values of various surfaces and effective emittances of air spaces

Surface	Reflectivity, percent	Average emittance, ϵ	Effective emittance of air space: One surface emittance, ϵ; the other, 0.90	Both surfaces emittances, ϵ
Aluminum foil, bright	92–97	0.05	0.05	0.03
Aluminum sheet	80–95	0.12	0.12	0.06
Aluminum-coated paper, polished	75–84	0.20	0.20	0.11
Steel, galvanized, bright	70–80	0.25	0.24	0.15
Aluminum paint	30–70	0.50	0.47	0.35
Building materials: wood, paper, masonry, nonmetallic paints	5–15	0.90	0.82	0.82
Regular glass	5–15	0.84	0.77	0.72

*Conductances are for surfaces of the stated emittance facing virtual black-body surroundings at the same temperature as the ambient air. Values are based on a surface-air temperature difference of 10°F and for surface temperature of 70°F.

NOTE: A surface cannot take credit for both an air space resistance value and a surface resistance value. No credit for an air space value can be taken for any surface facing an air space of less than ½ in.

SOURCE: *ASHRAE Handbook and Product Directory—1977 Fundamentals Volume*, American Society of Heating, Refrigerating and Air-Conditioning Engineers, Inc., New York, 1977, p. 22.11. Reprinted by permission.

For a wall of one material of conductivity k, thickness or length L, and surface conductance coefficients h_i and h_o:

$$\begin{aligned} & \quad\text{inside air film} \quad \text{wall} \quad \text{outside air film} \\ R_{total} &= 1/h_i + L/K + 1/h_o \\ &= 1/h_i + R + 1/h_o \\ U &= 1/R_{total} \end{aligned}$$

For a wall with an air space of conductance c between two materials:

$$\begin{aligned} & \quad\text{inside air film} \quad \text{wall} \quad \text{air space} \quad \text{wall} \quad \text{outside air film} \\ R_{total} &= 1/h_i + L_1/K_1 + 1/c + L_2/K_2 + 1/h_o \\ &= 1/h_i + R_1 + 1/c + R_2 + 1/h_o \\ U &= 1/R_{total} \end{aligned}$$

EXAMPLE

If a designer wishes to analyze the impact of 1 inch of Styrofoam on the outside of a single-family house in which the Styrofoam replaces plywood sheathing, the analysis would take the following form.

Figure 7-2 indicates the construction of the two walls, one with the Styrofoam and the other without. The difference in U values of the two walls is

U with Styrofoam	0.085 Btu/(°F·h·ft²)
U without Styrofoam	0.061 Btu/(°F·h·ft²)
ΔU	0.024 Btu/(°F·h·ft²)

Other relevant data for completion of the evaluation include the following:

Location	New York City
Heating fuel	Oil
Styrofoam cost	\$0.80/ft² (including cost of diagonal bracing)
Plywood cost	\$0.60/ft²
Wall area	1700 ft²
Air conditioning	None

The decrease in the rate of heat loss because of the added wall insulation is calculated as follows:

$$\Delta q_h = 0.024\ \text{Btu/(°F·h·ft}^2\text{)} \times 1700\ \text{ft}^2 \times (70°\text{F} - 15°\text{F}) \tag{7-6}$$

$$= 2244\ \text{Btu/h}$$

By using the degree-day method, the thermal benefits of the Styrofoam may be calculated as follows:

$$B_h = \frac{\$1.55/\text{gal} \times 2244\ \text{Btu/h} \times 4811\ °\text{F·days} \times 24\ \text{h/day} \times 0.63}{55°\text{F} \times 0.55 \times 140{,}000\ \text{Btu/gal}}$$

$$= \$60\ \text{[See Equation (6-3).]}$$

Since there is no air-conditioning system in the house, the insulation will have no impact on energy savings during the summer cooling season. Also, since the reduction in the peak

(Cont. on p. 154)

TABLE 7-2 Thermal Resistances of Plane Air Spaces*

Position of air space	Direction of heat flow	Air space: Mean temperature, °F‡	Air space: Temperature difference, °F‡	0.5-in air space†: Value of E‡§					0.75-in air space*:		
				0.03	0.05	0.2	0.5	0.82	0.03	0.05	0.2
Horizontal	Up	90	10	2.13	2.03	1.51	0.99	0.73	2.34	2.22	1.61
		50	30	1.62	1.57	1.29	0.96	0.75	1.71	1.66	1.35
		50	10	2.13	2.05	1.60	1.11	0.84	2.30	2.21	1.70
		0	20	1.73	1.70	1.45	1.12	0.91	1.83	1.79	1.52
		0	10	2.10	2.04	1.70	1.27	1.00	2.23	2.16	1.78
		−50	20	1.69	1.66	1.49	1.23	1.04	1.77	1.74	1.55
		−50	10	2.04	2.00	1.75	1.40	1.16	2.16	2.11	1.84
45° slope	Up	90	10	2.44	2.31	1.65	1.06	0.76	2.96	2.78	1.88
		50	30	2.06	1.98	1.56	1.10	0.83	1.99	1.92	1.52
		50	10	2.55	2.44	1.83	1.22	0.90	2.90	2.75	2.00
		0	20	2.20	2.14	1.76	1.30	1.02	2.13	2.07	1.72
		0	10	2.63	2.54	2.03	1.44	1.10	2.72	2.62	2.08
		−50	20	2.08	2.04	1.78	1.42	1.17	2.05	2.01	1.76
		−50	10	2.62	2.56	2.17	1.66	1.33	2.53	2.47	2.10
Vertical	Horizontal	90	10	2.47	2.34	1.67	1.06	0.77	3.50	3.24	2.08
		50	30	2.57	2.46	1.84	1.23	0.90	2.91	2.77	2.01
		50	10	2.66	2.54	1.88	1.24	0.91	3.70	3.46	2.35
		0	20	2.82	2.72	2.14	1.50	1.13	3.14	3.02	2.32
		0	10	2.93	2.82	2.20	1.53	1.15	3.77	3.59	2.64
		−50	20	2.90	2.82	2.35	1.76	1.39	2.90	2.83	2.36
		−50	10	3.20	3.10	2.54	1.87	1.46	3.72	3.60	2.87
45° slope	Down	90	10	2.48	2.34	1.67	1.06	0.77	3.53	3.27	2.10
		50	30	2.64	2.52	1.87	1.24	0.91	3.43	3.23	2.24
		50	10	2.67	2.55	1.89	1.25	0.92	3.81	3.57	2.40
		0	20	2.91	2.80	2.19	1.52	1.15	3.75	3.57	2.63
		0	10	2.94	2.83	2.21	1.53	1.15	4.12	3.91	2.81
		−50	20	3.16	3.07	2.52	1.86	1.45	3.78	3.65	2.90
		−50	10	3.26	3.16	2.58	1.89	1.47	4.35	4.18	3.22
Horizontal	Down	90	10	2.48	2.34	1.67	1.06	0.77	3.55	3.29	2.10
		50	30	2.65	2.54	1.88	1.24	0.91	3.77	3.52	2.38
		50	10	2.67	2.55	1.89	1.25	0.92	3.84	3.59	2.41
		0	20	2.94	2.83	2.20	1.53	1.15	4.18	3.96	2.83
		0	10	2.96	2.85	2.22	1.53	1.16	4.25	4.02	2.87
		−50	20	3.25	3.15	2.58	1.89	1.47	4.60	4.41	3.36
		−50	10	3.28	3.18	2.60	1.90	1.47	4.71	4.51	3.42

*Resistances of horizontal spaces with heat flow downward are substantially independent of temperature differences.

†Credit for an air space resistance value cannot be taken more than once and only for the boundary conditions established.

‡Interpolation is permissible for other values of mean temperature, temperature differences, and effective emittance E. Interpolation and moderate extrapolation for air spaces greater than 3.5 in are also permissible.

§Effective emittance of the space E is given by $1/E = 1/e_1 + 1/e_2 - 1$, *where* e_1 and e_2 are the emittances of the surfaces of the air space.

NOTE: All resistance values expressed in (h·ft²·°F temperature differences)/Btu. Values apply only to air spaces of uniform thickness bounded by plane smooth parallel surfaces with no leakage of air to or from the space. Thermal resistance values for multiple air spaces must be based on careful estimates of mean temperature differences for each air space.

SOURCE: *ASHRAE Handbook and Product Directory—1977 Fundamentals Volume*, American Society of Heating, Refrigerating and Air-Conditioning Engineers, Inc., New York, 1977, p. 22.12. Reprinted by permission.

Value of E‡§		1.5-in air space*: Value of E‡§					3.5-in air space*: Value of E‡§				
0.5	0.82	0.03	0.05	0.2	0.5	0.82	0.03	0.05	0.2	0.5	0.82
1.04	0.75	2.55	2.41	1.71	1.08	0.77	2.84	2.66	1.83	1.13	0.80
0.99	0.77	1.87	1.81	1.45	1.04	0.80	2.09	2.01	1.58	1.10	0.84
1.16	0.87	2.50	2.40	1.81	1.21	0.89	2.80	2.66	1.95	1.28	0.93
1.16	0.93	2.01	1.95	1.63	1.23	0.97	2.25	2.18	1.79	1.32	1.03
1.31	1.02	2.43	2.35	1.90	1.38	1.06	2.71	2.62	2.07	1.47	1.12
1.27	1.07	1.94	1.91	1.68	1.36	1.13	2.19	2.14	1.86	1.47	1.20
1.46	1.20	2.37	2.31	1.99	1.55	1.26	2.65	2.58	2.18	1.67	1.33
1.15	0.81	2.92	2.73	1.86	1.14	0.80	3.18	2.96	1.97	1.18	0.82
1.08	0.82	2.14	2.06	1.61	1.12	0.84	2.26	2.17	1.67	1.15	0.86
1.29	0.94	2.88	2.74	1.99	1.29	0.94	3.12	2.95	2.10	1.34	0.96
1.28	1.00	2.30	2.23	1.82	1.34	1.04	2.42	2.35	1.90	1.38	1.06
1.47	1.12	2.79	2.69	2.12	1.49	1.13	2.98	2.87	2.23	1.54	1.16
1.41	1.16	2.22	2.17	1.88	1.49	1.21	2.34	2.29	1.97	1.54	1.25
1.62	1.30	2.71	2.64	2.23	1.69	1.35	2.87	2.79	2.33	1.75	1.39
1.22	0.84	3.99	3.66	2.25	1.27	0.87	3.69	3.40	2.15	1.24	0.85
1.30	0.94	2.58	2.46	1.84	1.23	0.90	2.67	2.55	1.89	1.25	0.91
1.43	1.01	3.79	3.55	2.39	1.45	1.02	3.63	3.40	2.32	1.42	1.01
1.58	1.18	2.76	2.66	2.10	1.48	1.12	2.88	2.78	2.17	1.51	1.14
1.73	1.26	3.51	3.35	2.51	1.67	1.23	3.49	3.33	2.50	1.67	1.23
1.77	1.39	2.64	2.58	2.18	1.66	1.33	2.82	2.75	2.30	1.73	1.37
2.04	1.56	3.31	3.21	2.62	1.91	1.48	3.40	3.30	2.67	1.94	1.50
1.22	0.84	5.07	4.55	2.56	1.36	0.91	4.81	4.33	2.49	1.34	0.90
1.39	0.99	3.58	3.36	2.31	1.42	1.00	3.51	3.30	2.28	1.40	1.00
1.45	1.02	5.10	4.66	2.85	1.60	1.09	4.74	4.36	2.73	1.57	1.08
1.72	1.26	3.85	3.66	2.68	1.74	1.27	3.81	3.63	2.66	1.74	1.27
1.80	1.30	4.92	4.62	3.16	1.94	1.37	4.59	4.32	3.02	1.88	1.34
2.05	1.57	3.62	3.50	2.80	2.01	1.54	3.77	3.64	2.90	2.05	1.57
2.21	1.66	4.67	4.47	3.40	2.29	1.70	4.50	4.32	3.31	2.25	1.68
1.22	0.85	6.09	5.35	2.79	1.43	0.94	10.07	8.19	3.41	1.57	1.00
1.44	1.02	6.27	5.63	3.18	1.70	1.14	9.60	8.17	3.68	1.88	1.22
1.45	1.02	6.61	5.90	3.27	1.73	1.15	11.15	9.27	4.09	1.93	1.24
1.81	1.30	7.03	6.43	3.91	2.19	1.49	10.90	9.52	4.87	2.47	1.62
1.82	1.31	7.31	6.66	4.00	2.22	1.51	11.97	10.32	5.08	2.52	1.64
2.28	1.69	7.73	7.20	4.77	2.85	1.99	11.64	10.49	6.02	3.25	2.18
2.30	1.71	8.09	7.52	4.91	2.89	2.01	12.98	11.56	6.36	3.34	2.22

TABLE 7-3 **Thermal Properties of Typical Building and Insulating Materials—(Design Values)**[a] [These constants are expressed in Btu/(h·ft²·°F temperature difference)]

Description		Density, lb/ft³	Conductivity, k	Conductance, C	Customary unit: resistance (R)[b] Per inch thickness, $1/k$	For thickness listed, $1/C$	Specific heat, Btu/(lb·°F)	SI unit: resistance (R)[b] $\frac{m \cdot K}{W}$	$\frac{m^2 \cdot K}{W}$
Building board:									
Boards, panels, subflooring, sheathing, and woodboard panel products									
Asbestos cement board		120	4.0	...	*0.25*	...	0.24	1.73	
Asbestos cement board	0.125 in	120	...	33.00	...	*0.03*			*0.005*
Asbestos cement board	0.25 in	120	...	16.50	...	*0.06*			*0.01*
Gypsum or plaster board	0.375 in	50	...	3.10	...	*0.32*	0.26		*0.06*
Gypsum or plaster board	0.5 in	50	...	2.22	...	*0.45*			*0.08*
Gypsum or plaster board	0.625 in	50	...	1.78	...	*0.56*			*0.10*
Plywood (douglas fir)		34	0.80	...	*1.25*	...	0.29	8.66	
Plywood (douglas fir)	0.25 in	34	...	3.20	...	*0.31*			*0.05*
Plywood (douglas fir)	0.375 in	34	...	2.13	...	*0.47*			*0.08*
Plywood (douglas fir)	0.5 in	34	...	1.60	...	*0.62*			*0.11*
Plywood (douglas fir)	0.625 in	34	...	1.29	...	*0.77*			*0.19*
Plywood or wood panels	0.75 in	34	...	1.07	...	*0.93*	0.29		*0.16*
Vegetable fiberboard									
Sheathing, regular density	0.5 in	18	...	0.76	...	*1.32*	0.31		*0.23*
	0.78125 in	18	...	0.49	...	*2.06*			*0.36*
Sheathing, intermediate density	0.5 in	22	...	0.82	...	*1.22*	0.31		*0.21*
Nail-base sheathing	0.5 in	25	...	0.88	...	*1.14*	0.31		*0.20*
Shingle backer	0.375 in	18	...	1.06	...	*0.94*	0.31		*0.17*
Shingle backer	0.3125 in	18	...	1.28	...	*0.78*			*0.14*
Sound-deadening board	0.5 in	15	...	0.74	...	*1.35*	0.30		*0.24*
Tile and lay-in panels, plain or acoustic		18	0.40	...	*2.50*	...	0.14	17.33	
	0.5 in	18	...	0.80	...	*1.25*			*0.22*
	0.75 in	18	...	0.53	...	*1.89*			*0.33*
Laminated paperboard		30	0.50	...	*2.00*	...	0.33	13.86	
Homogeneous board from repulped paper		30	0.50	...	*2.00*	...	0.28	13.86	
Hardboard									
Medium-density		50	0.73	...	*1.37*	...	0.31	9.49	
High-density, service tempered service underlay		55	0.82	...	*1.22*	...	0.32	8.46	
High-density, standard tempered		63	1.00	...	*1.00*	...	0.32	6.93	
Particle board									
Low-density		37	0.54	...	*1.85*	...	0.31	12.82	
Medium-density		50	0.94	...	*1.06*	...	0.31	7.35	
High-density		62.5	1.18	...	*0.85*	...	0.31	5.89	
Underlayment	0.625 in	40	...	1.22	...	*0.82*	0.29		*0.14*
Wood subfloor	0.75 in		...	1.06	...	*0.94*	0.33		*0.17*

Description		Density, lb/ft³	Conductivity, k	Conductance, C	Customary unit: resistance (R)[b] Per inch thickness, $1/k$	For thickness listed, $1/C$	Specific heat, Btu/(lb·°F)	SI unit: resistance (R)[b] $\frac{m \cdot K}{W}$	$\frac{m^2 \cdot K}{W}$
Building membrane:									
Vapor—permeable felt		...	...	16.70	...	*0.06*			*0.01*
Vapor—seal, two layers of mopped 15-lb felt		...	...	8.35	...	*0.12*			*0.02*
Vapor—seal, plastic film		...	...	...	...	Negligible			
Finish flooring materials:									
Carpet and fibrous pad		...	...	0.48	...	*2.08*	0.34		*0.37*
Carpet and rubber pad		...	...	0.81	...	*1.23*	0.33		*0.22*
Cork tile	0.125 in	...	...	3.60	...	*0.28*	0.48		*0.05*
Terrazzo	1 in	...	...	12.50	...	*0.08*	0.19		*0.01*
Tile—asphalt, linoleum, vinyl, and rubber vinyl asbestos		...	...	20.00	...	*0.05*	0.30 0.24		*0.01*
Tile—ceramic							0.19		
Wood, hardwood finish	0.75 in			1.47		*0.68*			0.12
Insulating materials:									
Blanket and batt									
Mineral fiber, fibrous form processed from rock, slag, or glass									
approximately[e] 2–2.75 in		0.3–2.0	...	0.143	...	7[d]	0.17–0.23		*1.23*
approximately[e] 3–3.5 in		0.3–2.0	...	0.091	...	11[d]			*1.94*
approximately[e] 5.50–6.5		0.3–2.0	...	0.053	...	19[d]			*3.35*
approximately[e] 6–7 in		0.3–2.0		0.045		22[d]			*3.87*
approximately[d] 8.5 in		0.3–2.0		0.033		30[d]			*5.28*
Board and slabs									
Cellular glass		8.5	0.38	...	*2.63*	...	0.24	*18.23*	
Glass fiber, organic bonded		4–9	0.25	...	*4.00*	...	0.23	*27.72*	
Expanded rubber (rigid)		4.5	0.22	...	*4.55*	...	0.40	*31.53*	
Expanded polystyrene extruded—cut cell surface		1.8	0.25	...	*4.00*	...	*0.29*	*27.72*	
Expanded polystyrene extruded—smooth skin surface		2.2	0.20	...	*5.00*	...	0.29	*34.65*	
Expanded polystyrene extruded—smooth skin surface		3.5	0.19	...	*5.26*	...		*36.45*	
Expanded polystyrene, molded beads		1.0	0.28	...	*3.57*	...	0.29	*24.74*	
Expanded polyurethane[f] (R-11 expanded)		1.5	0.16	...	*6.25*	...	0.38	*43.82*	
(thickness 1 in or greater)		2.5							

TABLE 7-3 Thermal Properties of Typical Building and Insulating Materials—(Design Values)[a] (*cont.*)

Description		Density, lb/ft³	Conductivity, k	Conductance, C	Customary unit: resistance (R)[b] Per inch thickness, $1/k$	Customary unit: resistance (R)[b] For thickness listed, $1/C$	Specific heat, Btu/(lb·°F)	SI unit: resistance (R)[b] $\frac{m \cdot K}{W}$	SI unit: resistance (R)[b] $\frac{m^2 \cdot K}{W}$
Mineral fiber with resin binder		15	0.29	. . .	3.45	. . .	0.17	23.91	
Mineral fiberboard, wet-felted									
Core or roof insulation		16–17	0.34	. . .	2.94	. . .		20.38	
Acoustical tile		18	0.35	. . .	2.86	. . .	0.19	19.82	
Acoustical tile		21	0.37	. . .	2.70	. . .		18.71	
Mineral fiberboard, wet-molded									
Acoustical tile[g]		23	0.42	. . .	2.38	. . .	0.14	16.49	
Wood or cane fiberboard									
Acoustical tile[g]	0.5 in	. . .	. . .	0.80	. . .	1.25	0.31		0.22
Acoustical tile[g]	0.75 in	. . .	. . .	0.53	. . .	1.89			0.33
Interior finish (plank, tile)		15	0.35	. . .	2.86	. . .	0.32	19.82	
Wood shredded (cemented in preformed slabs)		22	0.60	. . .	1.67	. . .	0.31	11.57	
Loose fill:									
Cellulosic insulation (milled paper or wood pulp)		2.3–3.2	0.27–0.32	. . .	3.13–3.70	. . .	0.33	21.69–25.64	
Sawdust or shavings		8.0–15.0	0.45	. . .	2.22	. . .	0.33	15.39	
Wood fiber, softwoods		2.0–3.5	0.30	. . .	3.33	. . .	0.33	23.08	
Perlite, expanded		5.0–8.0	0.37	. . .	2.70	. . .	0.26	18.71	
Mineral fiber (rock, slag or glass)									
approximately[e] 3.75–5 in		0.6–2.0	. . .	. . .		11	0.17		1.94
approximately[e] 6.5–8.75 in		0.6–2.0	. . .	. . .		19			3.35
approximately[e] 7.5–10 in		0.6–2.0	. . .	. . .		22			3.87
approximately[e] 10.25–13.75 in		0.6–2.0	. . .	. . .		30			5.28
Vermiculite, exfoliated		7.0–8.2	0.47	. . .	2.13	. . .	3.20	14.76	
		4.0–6.0	0.44	. . .	2.27	. . .		15.73	
Roof insulation:[h]									
Preformed, for use above deck									
Different roof insulations are available in different thicknesses to provide the design C values listed.[h] Consult individual manufacturers for actual thickness of their material				0.72 to 0.12		1.39 to 8.33		. . .	0.24 to 1.47

Description		Density, lb/ft³	Conductivity, k	Conductance, C	Customary unit: resistance $(R)^b$ Per inch thickness, $1/k$	For thickness listed, $1/C$	Specific heat, Btu/(lb·°F)	SI unit: resistance $(R)^b$ $\frac{m \cdot K}{W}$	$\frac{m^2 \cdot K}{W}$
Masonry materials:									
Concretes									
Cement mortar		116	5.0	...	*0.20*	...		*1.39*	
Gypsum-fiber concrete, 87.5 percent gypsum, 12.5 percent wood chips		51	1.66	...	*0.60*	...	0.21	*4.16*	
Lightweight aggregates		120	5.2	...	*0.19*	...		*1.32*	
including expanded		100	3.6	...	*0.28*	...		*1.94*	
shale, clay, or slate;		80	2.5	...	*0.40*	...		*2.77*	
expanded slags;		60	1.7	...	*0.59*	...		4.09	
cinders; pumice;		40	1.15	...	*0.86*	...		*5.96*	
vermiculite; also		30	0.90	...	*1.11*	...		*7.69*	
cellular concretes		20	0.70		*1.43*			*9.91*	
Perlite, expanded		40	0.93		*1.08*			*7.48*	
		30	0.71		*1.41*			*9.77*	
		20	0.50		*2.00*		0.32	*13.86*	
Sand and gravel or stone aggregate (oven-dried)		140	9.0	...	*0.11*		0.22	*0.76*	
Sand and gravel or stone aggregate (not dried)		140	12.0	...	*0.08*			*0.55*	
Stucco		116	5.0	...	*0.20*			*1.39*	
Masonry units:									
Brick, common[i]		120	5.0	...	*0.20*	...	0.19	*1.39*	
Brick, face[i]		130	9.0	...	*0.11*	...		*0.76*	
Clay tile, hollow:									
One cell deep	3 in	...	...	1.25	...	*0.80*	0.21		*0.14*
One cell deep	4 in	...	...	0.90	...	*1.11*			*0.20*
Two cells deep	6 in	...	...	0.66	...	*1.52*			*0.27*
Two cells deep	8 in	...	...	0.54	...	*1.85*			*0.33*
Two cells deep	10 in	...	...	0.45	...	*2.22*			*0.39*
Three cells deep	12 in	...	...	0.40	...	*2.50*			*0.44*
Concrete blocks, three-oval core									
Sand and gravel aggregate	4 in	...	...	1.40	...	*0.71*	0.22		*0.13*
	8 in	...	...	0.90	...	*1.11*			*0.20*
	12 in	...	...	0.78	...	*1.28*			*0.23*
Cinder aggregate	3 in	...	...	1.16	...	*1.86*	0.21		*0.15*
	4 in	...	...	0.90	...	*1.11*			*0.20*
	8 in	...	...	0.58	...	*1.72*			*0.30*
	12 in	...	...	0.53	...	*1.89*			*0.33*
Lightweight aggregate	3 in	...	...	0.79	...	*1.27*	0.21		*0.22*
(expanded shale, clay,	4 in	...	...	0.67	...	*1.50*			*0.26*
slate or slag; pumice)	8 in	...	...	0.50	...	*2.00*			*0.35*
	12 in	...	...	0.44	...	*2.27*			*0.40*
Concrete blocks, rectangular core[e,j]									
Sand and gravel aggregate									
Two-core, 8 in, 36 lb[k,e]		...	...	0.96	...	*1.04*	0.22		*0.18*
Same with filled cores[j,e]		...	...	0.52	...	*1.93*	0.22		*0.34*

TABLE 7-3 Thermal Properties of Typical Building and Insulating Materials—(Design Values)[a] (*cont.*)

Description		Density, lb/ft³	Conductivity, *k*	Conductance, *C*	Customary unit: resistance (*R*)[b] Per inch thickness, 1/*k*	For thickness listed, 1/*C*	Specific heat, Btu/(lb·°F)	SI unit: resistance (*R*)[b] m·K/W	m²·K/W
Lightweight aggregate (expanded shale, clay, slate or slag, pumice):									
Three-core, 6 in, 19 lb[k,o]		...	...	0.61	...	*1.65*	0.21		*0.29*
Same with filled cores[l,o]		...	...	0.33	...	*2.99*			*0.53*
Two-core, 8 in, 24 lb[k,o]		...	...	0.46	...	*2.18*			*0.38*
Same with filled cores[l,o]		...	...	0.20	...	*5.03*			*0.89*
Three-core, 12 in, 38 lb[k,o]		...	...	0.40	...	*2.48*			*0.44*
Same with filled cores[l,o]		...	...	0.17	...	*5.82*			*1.02*
Stone, lime or sand		...	12.50	...	*0.08*	...	0.19	*0.55*	
Gypsum partition tile:									
3 by 12 by 30 in solid		...	...	0.79	...	*1.26*	*0.19*		*0.22*
3 by 12 by 30 in four-cell		...	...	0.74	...	*1.35*			*0.24*
4 by 12 by 30 in three-cell		...	...	0.60	...	*1.67*			*0.29*
Plastering materials:									
Cement plaster, sand aggregate		116	5.0	...	*0.20*	...	0.20	*1.39*	
Sand aggregate	0.375 in	...	...	13.3	...	*0.08*	0.20		*0.01*
Sand aggregate	0.75 in	...	...	6.66	...	*0.15*	0.20		*0.03*
Gypsum plaster:									
Lightweight aggregate	0.5 in	45	...	3.12	...	*0.32*			*0.06*
Lightweight aggregate	0.625 in	45	...	2.67	...	*0.39*			*0.07*
Lightweight aggregate on metal lath	0.75 in	...	...	2.13	...	*0.47*			*0.08*
Perlite aggregate		45	1.5	...	*0.67*	...	0.32	*4.64*	
Sand aggregate		105	5.6	...	*0.18*	...	0.20	*1.25*	
Sand aggregate	0.5 in	105	...	11.10	...	*0.09*			*0.02*
Sand aggregate	0.625 in	105	...	9.10	...	*0.11*			*0.02*
Sand aggregate on metal lath	0.75 in	...	...	7.70	...	*0.13*			*0.02*
Vermiculite aggregate		45	1.7	...	*0.59*	...		*4.09*	
Roofing:									
Asbestos cement shingles		120	...	4.76	...	*0.21*	0.24		*0.04*
Asphalt roll roofing		70	...	6.50	...	*0.15*	0.36		*0.03*
Asphalt shingles		70	...	2.27	...	*0.44*	0.30		*0.08*
Built-up roofing	0.375 in	70	...	3.00	...	*0.33*	0.35		*0.06*
Slate	0.5 in	...	...	20.00	...	*0.05*	0.30		*0.01*
Wood shingles, plain and plastic-film-faced		...	...	1.06	...	*0.94*	0.31		*0.17*
Siding materials (on flat surface):									
Shingles									
Asbestos cement		120	...	4.75	...	*0.21*			*0.04*
Wood, 16 in, 7.5 exposure		...	...	1.15	...	*0.87*	0.31		*0.15*

Description		Density, lb/ft³	Conductivity, k	Conductance, C	Customary unit: resistance (R)[b]		Specific heat, Btu/(lb·°F)	SI unit: resistance (R)[b]	
					Per inch thickness, $1/k$	For thickness listed, $1/C$		$\frac{m \cdot K}{W}$	$\frac{m^2 \cdot K}{W}$
Wood, double, 16-in, 12-in exposure		. . .	. . .	0.84	. . .	*1.19*	0.28		*0.21*
Wood, plus insulated backer board, 0.3125 in		. . .	. . .	0.71	. . .	*1.40*	0.31		*0.25*
Siding									
Asbestos cement, 0.25 in, lapped		. . .	. . .	4.76	. . .	*0.21*	0.24		*0.04*
Asphalt roll siding		. . .	. . .	6.50	. . .	*0.15*	0.35		*0.03*
Asphalt insulating siding (0.5-in bed)		. . .	. . .	0.69	. . .	*1.46*	0.35		*0.26*
Hardboard siding, 0.4375 in		40	1.49	. . .	*0.67*		0.28	*4.65*	
Wood, drop, 1 by 8 in		. . .	. . .	1.27	. . .	*0.79*	0.28		*0.14*
Wood, bevel, 0.5 by 8 in, lapped		. . .	. . .	1.23	. . .	*0.81*	0.28		*0.14*
Wood, bevel, 0.75 by 10 in, lapped		. . .	. . .	0.95	. . .	*1.05*	0.28		*0.18*
Wood, plywood, 0.375 in, lapped		. . .	. . .	1.59	. . .	*0.59*	0.29		*0.10*
Aluminum or steel[m], over sheathing									
Hollow-backed		. . .	. . .	1.61	. . .	*0.61*	0.29		*0.11*
Insulating-board-backed nominal 0.375 in		. . .	. . .	0.55	. . .	*1.82*	0.32		*0.32*
Insulating-board-backed nominal 0.375 in, foil-backed				0.34		*2.96*			*0.52*
Architectural glass		. . .	. . .	10.00	. . .	*0.10*	0.20		*0.02*
Woods:									
Maple, oak, and similar hardwoods		45	1.10	. . .	*0.91*	. . .	0.30	*6.31*	
Fir, pine, and similar softwoods		32	0.80	. . .	*1.25*	. . .	0.33	*8.66*	
Fir, pine, and similar softwoods	0.75 in	32	. . .	1.06	. . .	*0.94*	0.33		*0.17*
	1.5 in		. . .	0.53	. . .	*1.89*			*0.33*
	2.5 in		. . .	0.32	. . .	*3.12*			*0.60*
	3.5 in		. . .	0.23	. . .	*4.35*			*0.75*

[a]Representative values for dry materials were selected by ASHRAE TC4.4, Insulation and Moisture Barriers. They are intended as design (not specification) values for materials in normal use. For properties of a particular product, use the value supplied by the manufacturer or by unbiased tests.

[b]Resistance values are the reciprocals of C before C is rounded off to two decimal places.

[c]Also see "Insulating Materials: Board and Slabs."

[d]Does not include paper backing and facing, if any.

[e]Conductivity varies with fiber diameter. Insulation is produced by different densities; therefore, there is a wide variation in thickness for the same R value among manufacturers. No effort should be made to relate any specific R value to any specific thickness. Commercial thicknesses generally available range from 2 to 8.5.

[f]Values are for aged board stock.

[g]Insulating values of acoustical tile vary, depending on density of the board and on type, size, and depth of perforations.

[h]The U.S. Department of Commerce, *Simplified Practice Recommendation for Thermal Conductance Factors for Preformed Above-Deck Roof Insulation*, No. R 257-55, recognizes the specification of roof insulation on the basis of the C values shown. Roof insulation is made in thicknesses to meet these values.

[i]Face brick and common brick do not always have these specific densities. When density is different from that shown, there will be a change in thermal conductivity.

[j]Data on rectangular-core concrete blocks differ from the above data on oval-core blocks owing to core configuration, different mean temperatures, and possibly differences in unit weights. Weight data on the oval-core blocks tested are not available.

[k]Weights of units approximately 7.625 in high and 15.75 in long. These weights are given as a means of describing the blocks tested, but conductance values are all for 1 ft^2 of area.

[l]Vermiculite, perlite, or mineral wool insulation. When insulation is used, vapor barriers or other precautions must be considered to keep insulation dry.

[m]Values for metal siding applied over flat surfaces vary widely, depending on amount of ventilation of air space beneath the siding; whether air space is reflective or nonreflective; and on thickness, type, and application of insulating backing board used. Values given are averages for use as design guides and were obtained from several guarded hotbox tests (ASTM C236) or calibrated hotbox (BSS 77) on hollow-backed types and types made using backing boards of wood fiber, foamed plastic, and glass fiber. Departures of ±50 percent or more from the values given may occur.

NOTE: Conductivities k are per inch thickness, and conductances C are for thickness or construction stated, not per inch thickness. All values are for a mean temperature of 75°F, except those noted by an asterisk (*), which have been reported at 45°F.

SOURCE: *ASHRAE Handbook and Product Directory—1977 Fundamentals Volume*, American Society of Heating, Refrigerating and Air-Conditioning Engineers, Inc., New York, 1977, p. 22.13. Reprinted by permission.

heat load is less than 10,000 Btus per hour, no size reduction and cost savings in heating equipment may be realized.

The added cost of the Styrofoam is calculated as follows:

$$\begin{aligned} \text{Styrofoam: } \$0.80/\text{ft} \times 1700\text{ ft} &= \$1360 \\ \text{Plywood: } \$0.60/\text{ft} \times 1700\text{ ft} &= \underline{(\$1020)} \\ C_0 &= \$340 \end{aligned}$$

A simple cost-benefit analysis yields the following:

$$\text{Simple payback period} = \frac{\$340}{\$60/\text{year}} = 5.7\text{ years}$$

$$\text{Simple return on investment} = \frac{\$60/\text{year}}{\$340} = 17.6\text{ percent/year}$$

The additional insulation is cost-effective.

CONVECTION: CHANGES IN WINTER HEAT LOSS BY INFILTRATION

Designs which reduce the amount of heat convected out of a building during the wintertime may be evaluated by using the methods described in this section. Such designs include weatherstripping, entry alcoves, storm windows, and storm doors. (The designer is referred to Chapter 4 for other convection-related design approaches.)

Infiltration occurs in winter when the insides of buildings contain higher temperatures and lower air pressures than the outside air. The result is the movement of higher-pressure outside air through cracks and openings in a building's exterior skin to the lower-pressure interior. If this air movement is basically uncontrolled by a building's residents, the process is called infiltration. Infiltration due simply to temperature-created pressure differences will be a function primarily of the location of the openings in a building's envelope.

For infiltration to occur, however, there must be a place for air to move out of the building as well (this is sometimes called exfiltration). In the heating season, infiltration will typically occur low in a building's form, and exfiltration will occur through openings nearer the top of the building.

TABLE 7-4 Effective Resistance of Ventilated Attics[*] (Summer condition)

Ventilation air temperature, °F	Sol-air temperature, °F§	No ventilation		Natural ventilation		Power ventilation†					
		Ventilation rate, $ft^3/(min \cdot ft^2)$									
		0		0.1		0.5		1.0		1.5	
		1/*U* Ceiling Resistance, *R*‡									
		10	20	10	20	10	20	10	20	10	20
Nonreflective surfaces											
80	120	1.9	1.9	2.8	3.4	6.3	9.3	9.6	16	11	20
	140	1.9	1.9	2.8	3.5	6.5	10	9.8	17	12	21
	160	1.9	1.9	2.8	3.6	6.7	11	10	18	13	22
90	120	1.9	1.9	2.5	2.8	4.6	6.7	6.1	10	6.9	13
	140	1.9	1.9	2.6	3.1	5.2	7.9	7.6	12	8.6	15
	160	1.9	1.9	2.7	3.4	5.8	9.0	8.5	14	10	17
100	120	1.9	1.9	2.2	2.3	3.3	4.4	4.0	6.0	4.1	6.9
	140	1.9	1.9	2.4	2.7	4.2	6.1	5.8	8.7	6.5	10
	160	1.9	1.9	2.6	3.2	5.0	7.6	7.2	11	8.3	13
Reflective surfaces											
80	120	6.5	6.5	8.1	8.8	13	17	17	25	19	30
	140	6.5	6.5	8.2	9.0	14	18	18	26	20	31
	160	6.5	6.5	8.3	9.2	15	18	19	27	21	32
90	120	6.5	6.5	7.5	8.0	10	13	12	17	13	19
	140	6.5	6.5	7.7	8.3	12	15	14	20	16	22
	160	6.5	6.5	7.9	8.6	13	16	16	22	18	25
100	120	6.5	6.5	7.0	7.4	8.0	10	8.5	12	8.8	12
	140	6.5	6.5	7.3	7.8	10	12	11	15	12	16
	160	6.5	6.5	7.6	8.2	11	14	13	18	15	20

[*]The term "effective resistance" is used when there is attic ventilation. A value for no ventilation is also included. The effective resistance of the attic may be added to the resistance (1/*U*) of the ceiling to obtain the effective resistance of the combination based on sol-air and room temperatures. These values apply to wood frame construction with a roof deck and roofing having a conductance of 1.0 $Btu/(h \cdot ft^2 \cdot F)$.

†Based on air discharging outward from attic.

‡*Resistance* is 1 $(h \cdot ft^2 \cdot F)/Btu$.

§Roof surface temperature rather than sol-air temperature may be used if 0.25 is subtracted from the attic resistance shown.

¶Surfaces with effective emittance *E* of 0.05 between ceiling joists facing the attic space.

SOURCE: *ASHRAE Handbook and Product Directory—1977 Fundamentals Volume,* American Society of Heating, Refrigerating and Air-Conditioning Engineers, Inc., New York, 1977, p. 22.23. Reprinted by permission.

TABLE 7-5 Coefficients of Transmission (*U*) of Windows, Skylights, and Light-Transmitting Partitions [Values for heat transfer from air to air, Btu/(h·ft^2·°F)]

Part A: Vertical panels (exterior windows, sliding patio doors, and partitions)—flat glass, glass block, and plastic sheet

Description	Exterior[a] Winter	Exterior[a] Summer	Interior
Flat glass[b]			
Single glass	1.10	1.04	0.73
Insulating glass—double[c]			
0.1875-in air space[d]	0.62	0.65	0.51
0.25-in air space[d]	0.58	0.61	0.49
0.5-in air space[e]	0.49	0.56	0.46
0.5-in air space, low-emittance coating[f]			
$e = 0.20$	0.32	0.38	0.32
$e = 0.40$	0.38	0.45	0.38
$e = 0.60$	0.43	0.51	0.42
Insulating glass—triple[c]			
0.25-in air spaces[d]	0.39	0.44	0.38
0.5-in air spaces[g]	0.31	0.39	0.30
Storm windows			
1- to 4-in air space[d]	0.50	0.50	0.44
Plastic sheet			
Single-glazed			
0.125 in thick	1.06	0.98	. . .
0.25 in thick	0.96	0.89	. . .
0.5 in thick	0.81	0.76	. . .
Insulating unit—double[c]			
0.25-in air space[d]	0.55	0.56	. . .
0.5-in air space[c]	0.43	0.45	. . .
Glass block[h]			
6 by 6 by 4 in thick	0.60	0.57	0.46
8 by 8 by 4 in thick	0.56	0.54	0.44
—with cavity divider	0.48	0.46	0.38
12 by 12 by 4 in thick	0.52	0.50	0.41
—with cavity divider	0.44	0.42	0.36
12 by 12 by 2 in thick	0.60	0.57	0.46

Part B: Horizontal panels (skylights)—flat glass, glass block, and plastic domes

Description	Exterior[a] Winter[i]	Exterior[a] Summer[j]	Interior[i]
Flat glass[e]			
Single glass	1.23	0.83	0.96
Insulating glass—double[c]			
0.1875-in air space[d]	0.70	0.57	0.62
0.25-in air space[d]	0.65	0.54	0.59
0.5-in air space[c]	0.59	0.49	0.56
0.5-in air space, low-emittance coating[f]			
$e = 0.20$	0.48	0.36	0.39
$e = 0.40$	0.52	0.42	0.45
$e = 0.60$	0.56	0.46	0.50
Glass block[h]			
11 by 11 by 3 in thick with cavity divider	0.53	0.35	0.44
12 by 12 by 4 in thick with cavity divider	0.51	0.34	0.42
Plastic domes[k]			
Single-walled	1.15	0.80	. . .
Double-walled	0.70	0.46	. . .

Part C: Adjustment factors for various window and sliding patio door types (multiply *U* values in parts A and B by these factors)

Description	Single glass	Double or triple glass	Storm windows
Windows			
All glass[l]	1.00	1.00	1.00
Wood sash—80 percent glass	0.90	0.95	0.90
Wood sash—60 percent glass	0.80	0.85	0.80
Metal sash—80 percent glass	1.00	1.20[m]	1.20[m]
Sliding patio doors			
Wood frame	0.95	1.00	. . .
Metal frame	1.00	1.10[m]	. . .

[a]See Part C for adjustment for various window and sliding patio door types.
[b]Emittance of uncooled glass surface = 0.84.
[c]Double and triple refer to the number of lights of glass.
[d]0.125-in glass.
[e]0.25-in glass.
[f]Coating on either glass surface facing air space; all other glass surfaces uncoated.
[g]Window design: 0.25-in glass—0.125-in glass—0.25-in glass.
[h]Dimensions are nominal.
[i]For heat flow up.
[j]For heat flow down.
[k]Based on area of opening, not total surface area.
[l]Refers to windows with negligible opaque area.
[m]Values will be less than these when metal sash and frame incorporate thermal breaks. In some thermal break designs, *U* values will be equal to or less than those for the glass. Window manufacturers should be consulted for specific data.

SOURCE: *ASHRAE Handbook and Product Directory—1977 Fundamentals Volume*, American Society of Heating, Refrigerating and Air-Conditioning Engineers, Inc., New York, 1977, p. 22.24. Reprinted by permission.

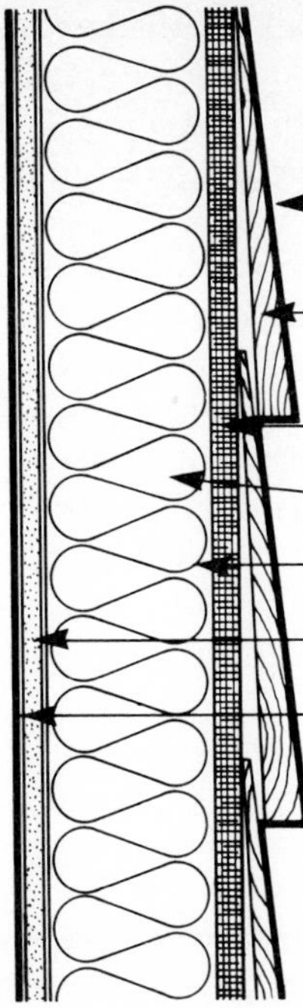

	R	
	At framing	Between framing
Outside surface film (15-mph wind)	0.17	0.17
Wood siding, 0.5 by 8 in, lapped	0.81	0.81
Plywood sheathing, 0.675 in	0.77	0.77
Wood studs, pine, 3.5 in	4.35	....
Fiberglass insulation, 3.5 in	....	11.00
Gypsum board, 0.5 in	0.45	0.45
Inside surface (still air)	0.68	0.68
R_{total}	7.23	13.88
U	0.138	0.072

Weighted-average U, assuming 20 percent of wall area used for framing

U average = (0.2 x 0.138) + (0.8 x 0.072) = 0.085 Btu/(°F · h · ft²)

A

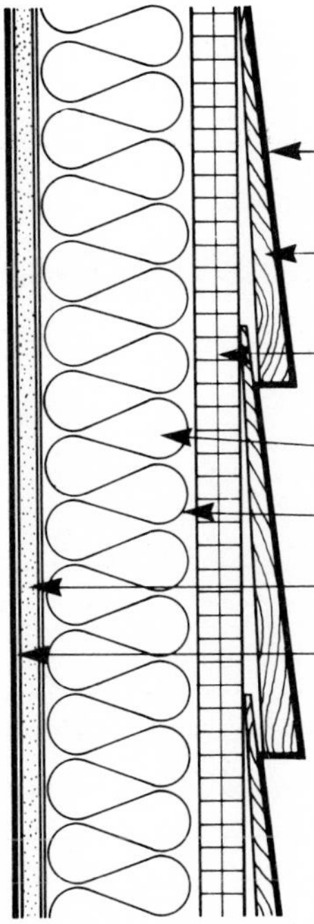

	R	
	At framing	Between framing
Outside surface film (15-mph wind)	0.17	0.17
Wood siding, 0.5 by 8.0 in, lapped	0.81	0.81
1-in expanded polystyrene, smooth skin	5.26	5.26
Wood studs, pine, 3.5 in	4.35	....
Fiberglass insulation, 3.5 in	....	11.00
Gypsum board, 0.5 in	0.45	0.45
Inside surface (still air)	0.68	0.68
R_{total}	11.72	18.22
U	0.085	0.055

Weighted-average U, assuming 20 percent wall area used for framing

U average = (0.2 x 0.085) + (0.8 x 0.055) = 0.061 Btu/(°F · h · ft²)

B

FIGURE 7-2 Wall section and U-value calculations for two different insulation conditions.

The pressure difference between inside and outside air may also be increased because of the impact of wind forces. In this case, infiltration will be primarily through openings on the windward side of the building, with exfiltration on the leeward side. In either case, heated air is lost from the building and replaced with unheated air.

The openings through which infiltration and exfiltration occur include doors, windows, cracks around door and window frames, and minor openings in walls and roofs. The challenge to the designer in terms of creating fuel savings is, of course, to reduce infiltration during the heating season by a more effective design of windows, doors, and skylights or, in the case of wind-induced infiltration, by a reduction in the number of possible openings on the windward side of the building.

The following method provides a means of estimating sensible infiltration heat losses, that is, heat losses affecting *air temperatures only,* not humidity levels.

The energy required to raise the temperature of infiltrating outdoor air to the indoor air temperature may be calculated by

$$\Delta q_{s,h} = c \times \Delta V \times d(t_i - t_o) \qquad (7\text{-}9)$$

in units,

$$\text{Btu/h} = \text{Btu/(lb}\cdot{}^\circ\text{F)} \times \text{ft}^3\text{/h} \times \text{lb/ft}^3 \times {}^\circ\text{F}$$

where $\Delta q_{s,h}$ = (given a design improvement) change in the peak rate of sensible heat flow for a given set of steady-state conditions; change in the heat required to raise the temperature of air leaking into a building, Btu/h.

c = specific heat of dry air, 0.24 Btu/(lb·°F)

ΔV = change in the volume of outdoor air entering a building, ft³/h

d = density of dry air at temperature t_o (assume 0.075 lb/ft³)

t = air temperature, °F

Therefore, given air as the infiltration mode,

$$\Delta q_{s,h} = 0.24 \times \Delta V \times 0.075(t_i - t_o)$$

$$\text{or} \quad \Delta q_{s,h} = 0.018\Delta V(t_i - t_o) \qquad (7\text{-}10)$$

in units,

$$\text{Btu} = \text{Btu/(ft}^3\cdot{}^\circ\text{F)} \times \text{ft}^3\text{/h} \times {}^\circ\text{F}$$

$$\text{or} \quad \Delta q_{s,h} = 1.08\,\Delta V(t_i - t_o) \qquad (7\text{-}11)$$

where ΔV = ft³/min

For calculating *annual* energy consumption savings due to a change in infiltration rates, particularly for nonresidential buildings, the following equations may be used:

$$\Delta Q_{s,h} = 0.018\,\Delta V \times \text{DH}_h \qquad (7\text{-}12)$$

in units,

$$\text{Btu/year} = \text{Btu/(ft}^3\cdot{}^\circ\text{F)} \times \text{ft}^3\text{/h} \times ({}^\circ\text{F}\cdot\text{h})\text{/year}$$

where $\Delta Q_{s,h}$ = change in annual rate of sensible heat flow, Btu/year
ΔV = change in volume of infiltrating outdoor air, ft³/h
DH_h = bin degree-hour data reflecting annual heating season outdoor climate and indoor temperature conditions (*excluding* the effect of sol-air temperatures), (°F·h)/year (See Tables 7-6 and 7-7.)

Equation (7-12), when ΔV is in units of cubic feet per minute, becomes, of course,

$$\Delta Q_{s,h} = 1.08\ \Delta V \times DH_h \tag{7-13}$$

The designer should note that bin degree-hour data for infiltration calculations need *not* be adjusted for sol-air temperatures. Tables 7-6 and 7-7 are in the same form as Tables 6-5 and 6-6 except that *no* adjustment has been made in outside temperature because of the sol-air phenomenon.

Calculation of ΔV may be made by one of two methods:

- Crack-length method
- Air-change method

The choice depends on the building component being analyzed, that is, windows, doors, or walls. Typically, construction-joint air leakage is analyzed by using

TABLE 7-6 Degree-Hours for a 70°F Indoor Temperature and Nonsleeping and Sleeping Periods in Residential Buildings, Mitchel Air Force Base, Nassau County, New York, Heating Season

Average bin temperature, °F	Difference from 70°F (A)	Hours of occurrence during nonsleeping periods (7 A.M.–11 P.M.) (B)	(°F·h)/year (A·B)	Hours of occurrence during sleeping periods (11 P.M.–7 A.M.) (C)	(°F·h)/year (A·C)
67	3	66	198	4	12
62	8	87	696	20	160
57	13	186	2,418	76	988
52	18	290	5,220	137	2,466
47	23	410	9,430	198	4,554
42	28	482	13,496	266	7,448
37	33	523	17,259	298	9,834
32	38	403	15,314	220	8,360
27	43	228	9,804	150	6,450
22	48	124	5,952	107	5,136
17	53	67	3,551	51	2,703
12	58	23	1,334	20	1,160
7	63	7	441	7	441
2	68	1	68	...	68
			85,181		49,780

SOURCE: Calculated by the author from data in Table 6-4.

TABLE 7-7 Degree-Hours for a 70°F Indoor Temperature during Occupied Periods and a 55°F Indoor Temperature during Unoccupied Periods in Nonresidential Buildings, Mitchel Air Force Base, Nassau County, New York, Heating Season

Average bin temperature (°F)	Difference from 70°F (A)	Occupied period: hours of occurrence (8 A.M.–6 P.M., Monday–Friday) (B)	(°F·h)/year (A·B)	Difference from 55°F (C)	Unoccupied period: hours of occurrence (6 P.M.–8 A.M., Monday–Friday; Saturday and Sunday) (D)	(°F·h)/year (C·D)
67	3	24	72	..	...	.....
62	8	50	400	..	...	.....
57	13	100	1,300	..	...	.....
52	18	139	2,502	3	270	810
47	23	196	4,508	8	380	3,040
42	28	211	5,908	13	458	5,954
37	33	216	7,128	18	545	9,810
32	38	165	6,270	23	437	10,051
27	43	90	3,870	28	265	7,420
22	48	50	2,400	33	150	4,950
17	53	26	1,378	38	86	3,268
12	58	8	464	43	33	1,419
7	63	2	126	48	11	528
2	68	0	0	53	1	53
			36,326			47,303

SOURCE: Calculated by the author from data in Table 6-4.

the crack-length method, and rooms and door openings are evaluated with the air-change method.

Walls actually leak a small amount of air into a building when there are pressure differences between the inside and the outside. Infiltration rates for wall construction are not well known. Tests have been conducted in laboratories to measure the infiltration rates of various wall assemblies. However, the difference between these laboratory tests and field experience has been substantial.[2] Current knowledge suggests the values for wall construction infiltration rates indicated in Table 7-8.

Crack-Length Method

A "crack" may be defined as the joints between operable windows and doors and the fixed building components to which they are attached. The manner in which the crack length in a building should be measured depends on the exposure of the rooms associated with the windows and/or doors in question. For a simple building

[2] *ASHRAE Handbook and Product Directory—1977 Fundamentals Volume,* American Society of Heating, Refrigerating and Air-Conditioning Engineers, Inc., New York, 1977, p. 21.7. Reprinted by permission.

TABLE 7-8 **Infiltration Rates for Various Wall Types** [Expressed in $ft^3/(h \cdot ft^2)$][a,b]

Type of wall		Pressure difference, in of water[c] 0.05	0.10	0.20	0.30	0.40
Brick wall[d]		12	25	50	75	100
8.5-in	Plain	5[a]	9[a]	16[a]	24[a]	28[a]
	Plastered[e]	0.05[a]	0.08[a]	0.14[a]	0.20[a]	0.27[a]
13-in	Plain	5[a]	8[a]	14[a]	20[a]	24[a]
	Plastered[e]	0.01[a]	0.04[a]	0.05[a]	0.09[a]	0.11[a]
	Plaster[f]	0.03[a]	0.24[a]	0.46[a]	0.66[a]	0.84[a]
Frame wall	Lath and plaster[g]	0.09[a]	0.15[a]	0.22[a]	0.29[a]	0.32[a]

[a]Multiply by 0.0258 for $L/(s \cdot m)$ of crack.
[b]For a 7.5-mph wind, use 0.05 in of water.
[c]1 in of water = 249.082 Pa.
[d]Constructed of porous brick and lime mortar (workmanship poor).
[e]Two coats of prepared gypsum plaster on brick.
[f]Furring, lath, and two coats of prepared gypsum plaster on brick.
[g]Wall construction: bevel siding painted or cedar shingles, sheathing, building paper, wood lath, and three coats of gypsum plaster.

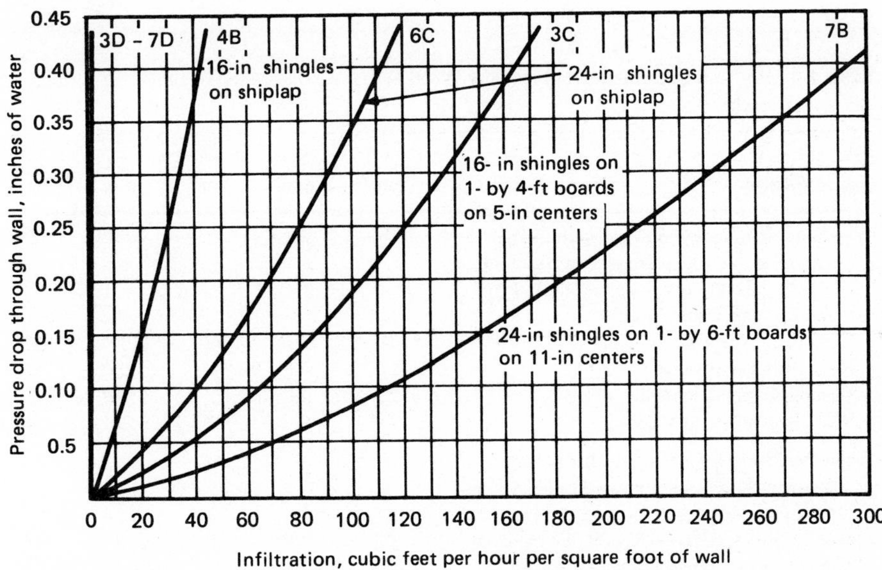

3D–7D: 3-D–16-in shingles on 1- by 4-in boards on 5-in centers with paper; 7-D–16-in shingles, shiplap, and paper.

SOURCE: *ASHRAE Handbook and Product Directory—1977 Fundamentals Volume*, American Society of Heating, Refrigerating and Air-Conditioning Engineers, Inc., New York, 1977, p. 21.6. Reprinted by permission.

with no interior walls, the cracks on the windward side are used for computing crack lengths; those on the leeward side are not.

The crack length for a building with partitions should be computed on a room-by-room basis.[3] Total crack length in a room with one exposed side equals the

[3]Ibid., p. 24.6. Reprinted by permission.

measured crack length. In a room with from two to four exposed walls, total crack length equals one of the following, whichever is greater:

- The crack length of the wall with the greatest crack length
- One-half of the sum of the crack length of all exposed walls

Table 7-9 lists infiltration rates for crack lengths in double-hung wood windows. Table 7-10 lists infiltration rates for crack lengths in other kinds of windows and also on doors.

Storm windows have the effect of reducing infiltration heat loss as well as transmission losses. In terms of conductive, that is, transmission losses, an air space which reduces conductivity and the chance of frosting is provided. One may assume that a storm window fitted onto an operable window reduces infiltration by the following amounts:

$$V_{\text{storm+prime}} = 0.65\,V_{\text{prime}} \text{ (for a well-constructed prime window)}$$

$$V_{\text{storm+prime}} = 0.50\,V_{\text{prime}} \text{ (for a poorly constructed prime window)}$$

TABLE 7-9 Infiltration through Double-Hung Wood Windows (Expressed in cubic feet per hour per foot of crack)°

	Pressure difference, in of water				
Type of window	**0.10**	**0.20**	**0.30**	**0.40**	**0.50**
Wood double-hung window (locked; leakage expressed as cubic feet per hour per foot of sash crack; only leakage around sash and through frame given)	25	50	25	100	125
Nonweatherstripped, loose fit†	77°	122°	150°	194°	225°
Nonweatherstripped, average fit‡	27°	43°	57°	69°	80°
Weatherstripped, loose fit	28°	44°	58°	70°	81°
Weatherstripped, average fit	14°	23°	30°	36°	42°
Frame wall leakage (leakage is that passing between the frame of a wood double-hung window and the wall)§					
Around frame in masonry wall, not caulked	17°	26°	34°	41°	48°
Around frame in masonry wall, caulked	3°	5°	6°	7°	8°
Around frame in wood frame wall	13°	21°	29°	35°	42°

°For a 15-mph wind, use 0.10 in of water pressure difference.

†A 0.094-in crack and clearance represent a poorly fitted window, much poorer than average.

‡The fit of the average double-hung wood window was determined as 0.0625-in crack and 0.047-in clearance by measurements on approximately 600 windows under heating season conditions.

§The values given for frame leakage are per foot of sash perimeter, as determined for double-hung wood windows. Some of the frame leakage in masonry walls originates in the brick wall itself and cannot be prevented by caulking. For the additional reason that caulking is not done perfectly and deteriorates with time, it is considered advisable to choose the masonry frame leakage values for caulked frames as the average determined by the caulked and noncaulked tests.

SOURCE: *ASHRAE Handbook and Product Directory—1977 Fundamentals Volume,* American Society of Heating, Refrigerating and Air-Conditioning Engineers, Inc., New York, 1977, p. 21.5. Reprinted by permission.

TABLE 7-10 Window and Door Specifications

Specification	Material	Type or class	Air leakage*
ANSI A134.1	Aluminum	A-B1 (awning)	0.75 $ft^3/(min \cdot ft)$ crack
		A-A2 (awning)	0.50 $ft^3/(min \cdot ft)$ crack
		C-B1 (casement)	0.50 $ft^3/(min \cdot ft)$ crack
		C-A2 (casement)	0.50 $ft^3/(min \cdot ft)$ crack
		C-A3 (casement)	0.50 $ft^3/(min \cdot ft)$ crack
		DH-B1 (hung)	0.75 $ft^3/(min \cdot ft)$ crack
		DH-A2 (hung)	0.50 $ft^3/(min \cdot ft)$ crack
		DH-A3 (hung)	0.50 $ft^3/(min \cdot ft)$ crack
		DH-A4 (hung)	0.50 $ft^3/(min \cdot ft)$ crack
		HS-B1 (sliding)	0.75 $ft^3/(min \cdot ft)$ crack
		HS-B2 (sliding)	0.75 $ft^3/(min \cdot ft)$ crack
		HS-A2 (sliding)	0.75 $ft^3/(min \cdot ft)$ crack
		HS-A3 (sliding)	0.50 $ft^3/(min \cdot ft)$ crack
		J-B1 (jalousie)	1.50 $ft^3/(min \cdot ft^2)$
		JA-B1 (jalousie-awning)	0.75 $ft^3/(min \cdot ft)$ crack
		P-B1 (projected)	0.50 $ft^3/(min \cdot ft)$ crack
		P-A2 (projected)	0.50 $ft^3/(min \cdot ft)$ crack
		P-A2.50 (projected)	0.375 $ft^3/(min \cdot ft)$ crack
		P-A3 (projected)	0.50 $ft^3/(min \cdot ft)$ crack†
		TH-A2 (inswinging)	0.375 $ft^3/(min \cdot ft)$ crack
		TH-A3 (inswinging)	0.50 $ft^3/(min \cdot ft)$ crack†
		VP-A2 (pivoted)	0.375 $ft^3/(min \cdot ft)$ crack
		VP-A3 (pivoted)	0.50 $ft^3/(min \cdot ft)$ crack†
		VS-B1 (vertical sliding)	0.75 $ft^3/(min \cdot ft)$ crack
ANSI A134.2	Aluminum	SGD-B1 (sliding glass door)	1.0 $ft^3/(min \cdot ft^2)$
		SGD-B2 (sliding glass door)	0.50 $ft^3/(min \cdot ft^2)$
		SGD-A2	0.50 $ft^3/(min \cdot ft^2)$
		SGD-A3 (sliding glass door)	0.50 $ft^3/(min \cdot ft^2)$†
ANSI A200.1	Wood	All types of windows	
		Class A	0.50 $ft^3/(min \cdot ft)$
		Class B	0.50 $ft^3/(min \cdot ft)$
ANSI A200.2	Wood	All types of sliding glass doors	0.50 $ft^3/(min \cdot ft^2)$
FMHC & SS‡ 280.403	All	Windows (all types); sliding glass doors	0.50 $ft^3/(min \cdot ft^2)$
FMHC & SS‡ 280.405	All	Vertical entrance	1.20 $ft^3/(min \cdot ft^2)$ (1976) 1.0 $ft^3/(min \cdot ft^2)$ (1977)

*At 1.56 lbf/ft^2 (75 Pa) equivalent to 25 mph (11.2 m/s) wind velocity pressure.

†At 6.24 lbf/ft^2 (300 Pa) equivalent to 50 mph (22.3 m/s) wind velocity pressure.

‡Federal Mobile Home Construction and Safety Standard.

SOURCE: *ASHRAE Handbook and Product Directory—1977 Fundamentals Volume,* American Society of Heating, Refrigerating and Air-Conditioning Engineers, Inc., New York, 1977, p. 21.5. Reprinted by permission.

In terms of doors (Table 7-10 and Figure 7-3), weatherstripping may reduce the leakage rate to 50 percent of the rate for a nonweatherstripped door. Infiltration rates through swinging-door cracks, when doors are used infrequently as in some residential entrances, are also shown in Figure 7-3.

EXAMPLE

If a designer changed the configuration and orientation of the rooms of a house so that no windows were required on the north side, where the prevailing winter winds occurred, what would the value of this change be in terms of fuel savings? The relevant statistics for answering this question are as follows:

Window type	3 by 5 ft
Number of north-facing windows	Five
Fuel cost	$1.40/gal
Location	New York City
Wall construction	Wood frame
Design outdoor winter temperature	15°F

The operable sash crack length is calculated as follows:

Window width	3 ft	
Number of cracks	×3	
		9 ft
Window height	5 ft	
Number of cracks	×2	
		10 ft
Total sash crack length		19 ft

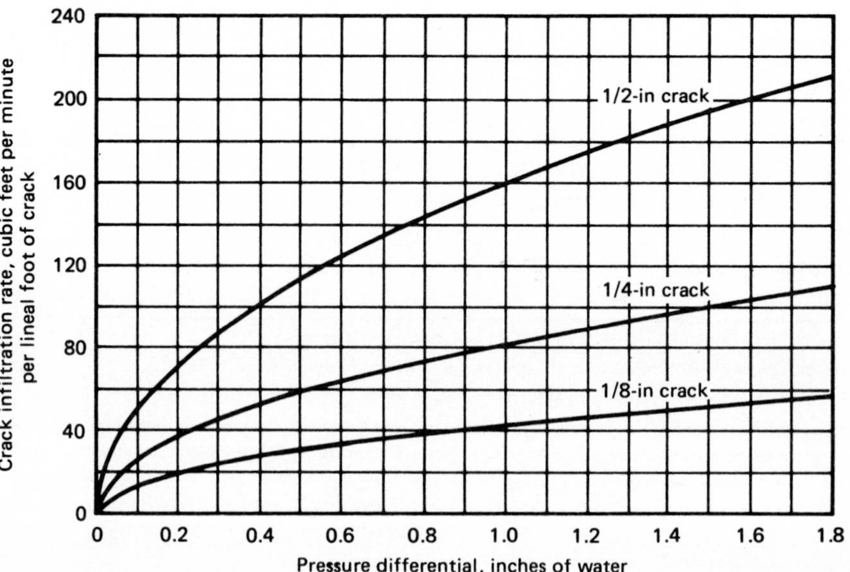

FIGURE 7-3 **Infiltration rates through swinging-door cracks.** [ASHRAE Handbook and Product Directory—1977 Fundamentals Volume, *American Society of Heating, Refrigerating and Air-Conditioning Engineers, Inc., New York, 1977, p. 21.9. Reprinted by permission.*]

The frame-to-wall crack length is calculated below:

Window width	3 ft	
Number of cracks	×2	
		6 ft
Window height	5 ft	
Number of cracks	×2	
		10 ft
Total frame-to-wall crack length		16 ft

If an average 7.5-mph wind is assumed, the following are infiltration rates from Table 7-9:

$$\text{Sash cracks: } V = 7\ \text{ft}^3/(\text{h}\cdot\text{ft}) \times 19\ \text{ft} = 133\ \text{ft}^3/\text{h}$$

$$\text{Frame wall cracks: } V = 3\ \text{ft}^3/(\text{h}\cdot\text{ft}) \times 16\ \text{ft} = 48\ \text{ft}^3/\text{h}$$

$$\text{Total infiltration} = 181\ \text{ft}^3/\text{h}$$

The thermal value of this infiltration may be calculated as follows:

$$\Delta q_{s,h} = 0.018\ \text{Btu}/(°\text{F}\cdot\text{ft}^3) \times 181\ \text{ft}^3/\text{h} \times (70°\text{F} - 15°\text{F}) \qquad (7\text{-}10)$$

$$= 179\ \text{Btu/h}$$

Using the degree-day method, the following is the monetary value of the thermal savings:

$$B_h = \frac{\$1.40/\text{gal} \times 179\ \text{Btu/h} \times 4811\ °\text{F}\cdot\text{day} \times 24\ \text{h/day} \times 0.63}{55°\text{F} \times 0.55 \times 140{,}000\ \text{Btu/gal}}$$

$$= \$4/\text{year}\ [\text{See Equation (6–3).}]$$

or for five windows,

$$B_h = \$4/\text{year} \times 5 = \$20/\text{year}$$

Since no cost is associated with simply repositioning windows in a design yet to be built, a cost-benefit analysis is not possible, but the design is clearly worth implementing.

Air-Change Method

The air-change method is generally considered inaccurate for nonresidential (commercial and industrial) buildings because of the wide range of different window designs used in these building types. The crack-length method, which relates directly to fenestration design, is recommended instead.[4] The only exception to this rule applies to door air-change rates, for which an air-change estimating method may be valid for both residential and commercial buildings.

"Air change" simply refers to the rate at which a volume of air, such as that contained in a room or a vestibule, is replaced. For normal residential construction, the designer may assume that air from the outside infiltrates to the inside in roughly the manner indicated in Table 7-11. For rooms with weatherstripped windows or with storm sashes, use two-thirds of the values in Table 7-11.

[4]Ibid., p. 21.6. Reprinted by permission.

TABLE 7-11 Infiltration Air-Change Rates for Various Types of Residential Rooms

Type of room	Number of air changes per hour
Room without windows or exterior doors	0.5
Rooms with windows or exterior doors on one side	1.0
Rooms with windows or exterior doors on two sides	1.5
Rooms with windows or exterior doors on three sides	2
Entrance halls	2

SOURCE: *ASHRAE Handbook and Product Directory—1977 Fundamentals Volume,* American Society of Heating, Refrigerating and Air-Conditioning Engineers, Inc., New York, 1977, p. 21.5. Reprinted by permission.

For doors, the overall infiltration rate is a combination of the leakage through the crack length around the intersection between the door and the frame when the door is closed and the amount of air which passes through the doorway when the door is open. The figures in Table 7-12 indicate the open-door infiltration rates for various types of doors. These may be used for both residential and commercial buildings. The door-opening rate will vary significantly from residential to commercial applications.

EXAMPLE

The designer of an office building may wish to assess the difference between the use of eight doors to create a double-door entrance vestibule and a single row of four revolving doors. The analysis for that design decision is presented below. The assumptions necessary for the analysis are as follows:

Location	New York City
Fuel cost	\$1.50/gal
Vestibule floor area	300 ft^2
Building cost	\$45/ft^2
Summer air conditioning	None
Swinging-door cost	\$200
Revolving-door cost	\$10,500
Electrical cost	\$0.13/kWh
Entry traffic flow	1000 people/h
Design outdoor temperature	15°F
Corporate income tax rate	45 percent

The infiltration rate difference between swinging doors in a double-bank vestibule design and revolving doors is as follows:

Two-door vestibule	550 ft^3/person
Revolving, manual	60 ft^3/person
	490 ft^3/person

Each revolving door or two-door vestibule will handle one-quarter of the traffic:

$$1000 \text{ people/h} \div 4 = 250 \text{ people/h}$$

The infiltration savings achieved by using revolving doors instead of swinging doors will be

$$490 \text{ ft}^3\text{/person} \times 250 \text{ persons/h} = 122{,}500 \text{ ft}^3\text{/h}$$

The thermal value of that amount is calculated as follows by using degree-hour data from Table 7-7:

$$\Delta Q_{s,h} = 0.018 \text{ Btu/(°F·h)} \times 122{,}500 \text{ ft}^3\text{/h} \times 36{,}326 \text{ (°F·h)/year} \qquad (7\text{-}12)$$

$$= 80{,}098{,}830 \text{ Btu/year}$$

The value of the heating savings may be estimated as follows:

$$B_h = \frac{\$1.50\text{/gal} \times 80{,}098{,}830 \text{ Btu/year}}{0.55 \times 140{,}000 \text{ Btu/gal}}$$

$$= \$1560\text{/year [See Equation (6-1).]}$$

The aftertax value of these savings is calculated as

$$B_h = \$1560\text{/year} \times (1 - 0.45)$$

$$= \$858\text{/year}$$

The reduction in heating system equipment size permitted by the decreased infiltration load is estimated as follows:

$$\Delta q_{s,h} = 0.018 \times 122{,}500 \text{ ft}^3\text{/h} \times (70°\text{F} - 15°\text{F}) \qquad (7\text{-}10)$$

$$= 121{,}272 \text{ Btu/h}$$

Using data from Table 5-8,

$$B_O = 121{,}275 \text{ Btu/h} \times \$8/1000 \text{ Btu/h}$$

$$= \$970$$

TABLE 7-12 Infiltration Rates for Various Types of Doors

Door type	Infiltration (ft^3/person) per instance of use
Single, swinging	900
Two-door, vestibule	550
Revolving, manual	60
Revolving, automatic	32

SOURCE: *ASHRAE Handbook and Product Directory—1977 Fundamentals Volume*, American Society of Heating, Refrigerating and Air-Conditioning Engineers, Inc., New York, 1977, p. 21.11. Reprinted by permission.

The additional cost of the revolving door over the double-bank vestibule is calculated as follows:

Revolving door		$10,500
Vestibule doors (two doors plus adjacent floor area):		
Two doors at $200 each	$ 400	
Floor area (300 ft^2 ÷ 4) × $45/ft^2	3375	
	$3775	
Additional cost for revolving door	$7125	
Less heating equipment cost reduction	970	
Net additional cost	$6155	

A simple cost-benefit analysis yields the following:

$$\text{Simple payback period} = \frac{\$6155}{\$858/\text{year}} = 7.2 \text{ years}$$

$$\text{Simple return on investment} = \frac{\$858/\text{year}}{\$6155} = 13.9 \text{ percent/year}$$

The revolving doors appear to be cost-effective and would be even more economical if the building were air-conditioned and cooling savings realized.

RADIATION: CHANGES IN SOLAR HEAT GAIN

In climates in which outdoor air temperatures during the winter are below the human comfort range, buildings need to provide heat. The sun provides a source for that heat if a building is designed to collect, absorb, and store the sun's heat. Designs which provide that ability have a number of key aspects in common.

First, they have a lot of south-facing glass. As described in Chapter 2, radiated electromagnetic energy is transmitted through glass and is absorbed by other materials, becoming heat energy. Because thermal energy, or heat, is not reradiated through glass, a room with south-facing glass will tend to collect and store solar energy as heat. The effectiveness of such a room depends on its ability to absorb, store, and distribute its heat within a temperature range compatible with human comfort.

Architectural designs which collect wintertime solar radiation are generally called "passive solar designs." They are passive in the sense that they typically do not require fans and pumps or other mechanical moving components to collect, store, and distribute solar heat gain.

Designs used by architects to provide passive solar heat gain in buildings have included concepts that in the late 1970s were given the following names: direct gain, indirect gain, and sun spaces (see Figure 7-4).

Direct-gain approaches involve designing a building with south-facing windows and skylights so that the sun *directly* penetrates the rooms adjacent to the windows. Typically, the surfaces of a room are designed so that solar radiation is effectively absorbed and turned into heat. The south-facing windows may be insulated at night so that the solar heat gained during the day is not lost at night by conduction back through the windows.

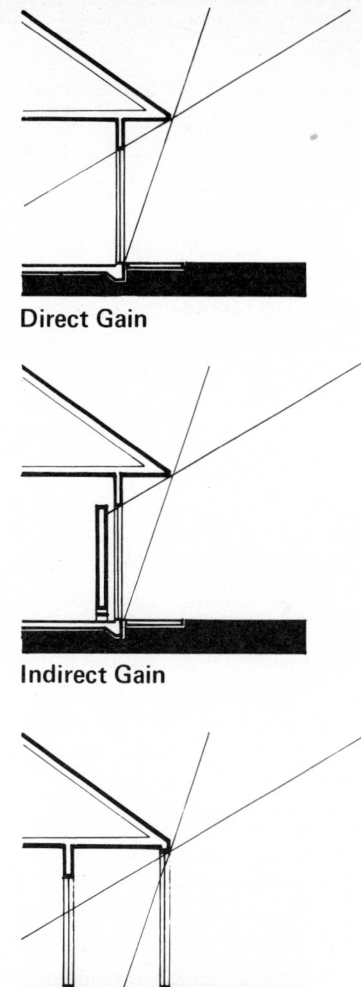

FIGURE 7-4 Direct-gain, indirect-gain, and sun-space passive solar designs.

Indirect-gain designs provide an intermediate stop for the solar heat before it enters the room. Typically, the sun passes through south-facing glass and is absorbed by a masonry or water-filled wall. The wall is often painted a dark color to increase its absorptive ability. The solar heat absorbed by the wall is transferred to the room by radiation from the wall to other surfaces in the room and by convection of air around the wall. Unwanted summertime gain by the wall may be prevented by shading the wall or, to some extent, by venting it at the top. An unshaded, vented wall will still absorb solar heat and radiate it to the inside during the summer. A Frenchman, Félix Trombe, devised one of the early applications of an indirect-gain design, and hence such designs are often called Trombe walls.

Sun-space, or greenhouse, designs are conceptually similar to indirect-gain designs except that the space between the wall and the glass is enlarged so that it can be used for certain kinds of human activity. Typically, a greenhouse will be quite hot on sunny, warm days (unless vented and/or shaded) and quite cold on winter nights (unless nocturnal insulation is used and/or heat is supplied). Sometimes the warm air at the top of a greenhouse is drawn off and directed to other locations in the attached building.

A designer needs to be familiar with some of the properties of sunlight as it falls on the surfaces of a building. (The reader is referred to Chapter 2 for the fundamentals of radiation.) Two primary characteristics of solar radiation influence the design of building components: intensity and profile angle.

The intensity of solar radiation is typically measured in Btus per square foot. Table 7-13 lists average solar intensities for horizontal surfaces and for various vertical surfaces. These data reflect cloud cover conditions.

The angle of the sun with respect to the earth varies throughout the day and the year. That angle is called the sun's altitude. The position of the sun with respect to due south, called the solar azimuth, also varies with the time of day and the day of the year. Neither angle, however, will help a designer design a horizontal shading device. The vertical angle of the sun relative to a wall of a particular azimuth is what is needed. This angle is called the profile angle. Table 7-14 lists the altitude, azimuth, and profile angle of various orientations of vertical walls.

Average profile angles may be used to determine the design of an overhang or a horizontal shading device which permits sun access to a window during the winter but shades it during the summer. For example, Table 7-15 shows average profile angles monthly and seasonally for a vertical wall facing due south in a 40° north latitude location. The seasonal average profile angle is 30° from the horizontal during the winter months and 71° during the summer months. In lieu of a computer simulation of hour-by-hour sun angles, the average seasonal profile angle data approximate the optimum angle for effective design of horizontal shading devices (see Figure 7-5).

A common conclusion, after examining seasonal profile angles in latitudes significantly above or below the equator, is that vertical surfaces are better for solar collection than are horizontal surfaces. They are closer to being perpendicular to the sun's rays in winter, when solar heat is needed, and quite oblique to solar radiation in summer, when heat is not required.

Estimating Winter Solar Heat Gain in High-Internal-Load Commercial Buildings

Estimating the value of wintertime solar radiation incoming to commercial, that is, nonresidential, buildings involves two main considerations:

- Availability of solar radiation
- Need for heat

The amount of solar radiation which makes its way into a building is a function of exterior insolation available on clear as well as on overcast days and of the transmissivity of the glass through which the sun's rays pass. Since the peak heat load in a building during the winter usually occurs at night or on cloudy days, there is

(*Cont. on p. 174*)

TABLE 7-13 Monthly Average Solar Radiation, Temperature, and Degree-Days for Selected Cities

	January	February	March	April	May	June	July	August	September	October	November	December	Year
Phoenix, Arizona (latitude, 33.4°N; elevation, 1112 ft)													
HS	1021	1374	1814	2355	2676	2739	2486	2293	2015	1576	1150	932	1869
VS	1472	1589	1552	1388	1211	1128	1059	1186	1482	1643	1561	1419	16692
TA	51.2	55.1	59.7	67.7	76.3	84.6	91.2	89.1	83.8	72.2	59.8	52.5	70.3
*D*50	78	29	9	1	0	0	0	0	0	0	9	60	187
*D*55	162	85	36	4	0	0	0	0	0	1	34	137	459
*D*60	285	168	100	16	0	0	0	0	0	5	96	250	919
*D*65	428	292	185	60	0	0	0	0	0	17	182	388	1552
*D*70	584	419	327	130	24	2	0	1	3	64	314	544	2411
Los Angeles, California (latitude, 33.9°N; elevation, 105 ft)													
HS	926	1214	1619	1951	2060	2119	2307	2079	1681	1317	1004	848	1594
VS	1353	1424	1405	1168	944	880	993	1091	1255	1392	1382	1309	14599
TA	54.5	55.6	56.5	58.8	61.9	64.5	68.5	69.5	68.7	65.2	60.5	56.9	61.7
*D*50	21	13	11	5	2	1	0	0	0	0	2	9	64
*D*55	83	59	53	26	9	4	1	1	1	3	15	47	299
*D*60	186	143	138	91	47	20	5	4	5	17	65	129	849
*D*65	331	270	267	195	114	71	19	15	23	77	158	279	1819
*D*70	481	404	419	338	257	180	99	83	93	168	289	407	3216
Denver, Colorado (latitude, 39.7°N; elevation, 5331 ft)													
HS	840	1127	1530	1879	2135	2351	2273	2044	1727	1300	883	732	1568
VS	1440	1551	1572	1344	1147	1114	1130	1277	1535	1616	1424	1327	16478
TA	29.9	32.8	37.0	47.5	57.0	66.0	73.0	71.6	62.8	52.0	39.4	32.6	50.1
*D*50	623	482	406	130	18	1	0	0	3	63	324	540	2592
*D*55	778	622	559	240	63	5	0	0	14	143	469	695	3588
*D*60	933	762	713	379	143	23	0	0	51	261	618	849	4733
*D*65	1088	902	868	525	253	80	0	0	120	408	768	1004	6016
*D*70	1243	1042	1023	675	406	158	50	69	232	559	918	1159	7535
Washington, D.C. (latitude, 38.9°N; elevation, 289 ft)													
HS	572	815	1125	1459	1718	1901	1817	1617	1340	1004	651	481	1208
VS	959	1097	1130	1019	902	882	884	986	1163	1221	1027	852	12123
TA	32.1	33.8	41.8	53.1	62.6	71.1	75.3	73.6	66.9	55.9	44.7	34.0	53.7
*D*50	555	454	262	38	2	0	0	0	0	17	179	497	2004
*D*55	710	594	411	109	10	1	0	0	2	68	313	651	2869
*D*60	865	734	564	219	45	3	0	0	12	156	460	806	3864
*D*65	1020	874	719	357	131	5	0	0	43	291	609	961	5010
*D*70	1175	1014	874	507	240	63	20	34	131	438	759	1116	6372
Miami, Florida (latitude, 25.8°N; elevation 7 ft)													
HS	1057	1314	1603	1859	1844	1708	1763	1630	1456	1303	1119	1019	1473
VS	1236	1224	1088	881	725	650	677	696	848	1088	1231	1260	11605
TA	67.2	67.8	71.3	75.0	78.0	81.0	82.3	82.9	81.7	77.8	72.2	68.3	75.5
*D*50	1	1	0	0	0	0	0	0	0	0	0	1	3
*D*55	4	3	1	0	0	0	0	0	0	0	1	3	14
*D*60	18	14	6	0	0	0	0	0	0	0	4	13	55
*D*65	53	67	17	0	0	0	0	0	0	0	13	56	206
*D*70	142	118	76	31	15	6	4	4	5	15	61	122	599
Atlanta, Georgia (latitude, 33.6°N; elevation, 1033 ft)													
HS	718	969	1304	1686	1854	1914	1812	1708	1422	1200	883	674	1345
VS	1041	1127	1122	1000	843	791	775	889	1052	1258	1205	1032	12136
TA	42.4	45.0	51.1	61.1	69.1	75.6	78.0	77.5	72.3	62.4	51.4	43.5	60.8
*D*50	246	161	67	3	0	0	0	0	0	2	61	217	758
*D*55	393	284	153	16	1	0	0	0	0	11	142	360	1362
*D*60	546	421	283	65	7	0	0	0	2	49	266	512	2150
*D*65	701	560	443	144	27	0	0	0	8	137	408	667	3095
*D*70	856	700	586	274	98	19	9	11	49	246	558	822	4228

TABLE 7-13 Monthly Average Solar Radiation, Temperature, and Degree-Days for Selected Cities (*cont.*)

	January	February	March	April	May	June	July	August	September	October	November	December	Year
Chicago, Illinois (latitude, 41.8°N; elevation, 623 ft)													
HS	507	759	1107	1459	1789	2007	1944	1719	1354	969	566	401	1215
VS	921	1106	1207	1113	1023	1006	1026	1146	1280	1276	967	771	12845
TA	24.3	27.4	36.8	49.9	60.0	70.5	74.7	73.7	65.9	55.4	40.4	28.5	50.6
D50	797	633	414	98	10	1	0	0	2	33	299	687	2954
D55	952	773	565	187	36	2	0	1	8	94	441	822	3881
D60	1107	913	719	313	99	9	0	4	28	183	589	977	4940
D65	1262	1053	874	453	208	26	0	8	57	316	738	1132	6127
D70	1417	1193	1029	604	320	90	39	49	167	456	888	1287	7537
San Francisco, California (latitude, 37.6°N; elevation, 16 ft)													
HS	708	1009	1455	1920	2226	2377	2392	2116	1742	1226	821	642	1553
VS	1145	1311	1408	1288	1126	1068	1124	1240	1455	1438	1250	1097	14951
TA	48.3	51.2	53.0	55.3	58.3	61.6	62.5	63.0	64.1	61.0	55.3	49.7	56.9
D50	82	32	17	5	1	0	0	0	0	0	5	58	202
D55	210	117	88	47	15	3	2	1	1	4	47	170	705
D60	363	247	219	148	82	30	21	17	10	39	148	320	1643
D65	518	386	372	291	210	120	93	84	66	137	291	474	3042
D70	673	526	527	441	363	253	234	219	181	280	441	629	4768
New Orleans, Louisiana (latitude, 30.0°N; elevation, 10 ft)													
HS	835	1112	1415	1780	1968	2004	1813	1717	1514	1335	973	779	1437
VS	1097	1169	1093	948	827	786	728	809	1003	1262	1203	1081	12005
TA	52.9	55.6	60.7	68.6	75.1	80.4	81.9	81.9	78.2	69.8	60.1	54.8	68.3
D50	73	39	14	2	0	0	0	0	0	2	16	51	197
D55	150	96	42	7	0	0	0	0	0	5	46	118	465
D60	252	173	105	22	0	0	0	0	0	17	110	208	887
D65	403	299	188	29	0	0	0	0	0	40	179	327	1465
D70	533	409	308	133	48	15	11	11	24	118	313	476	2399
Kansas City, Missouri (latitude, 39.3°N; elevation, 1033 ft)													
HS	648	895	1203	1575	1873	2080	2102	1862	1452	1092	737	561	1340
VS	1098	1218	1222	1113	994	975	1034	1149	1276	1343	1176	1005	13604
TA	27.1	32.3	40.7	54.2	64.1	73.0	77.5	76.5	68.0	57.6	42.3	31.3	53.7
D50	710	497	303	46	4	0	0	0	1	22	252	581	2417
D55	865	636	447	114	15	1	0	0	5	67	387	735	3273
D60	1020	776	599	206	49	5	0	0	19	144	533	890	4242
D65	1175	916	753	336	127	15	0	0	50	259	681	1045	5357
D70	1330	1056	908	477	216	60	22	28	133	391	831	1200	6651
Boston, Massachusetts (latitude, 42.4°N; elevation, 16 ft)													
HS	475	710	1016	1326	1620	1817	1749	1486	1260	890	503	403	1105
VS	878	1052	1127	1030	944	927	940	1009	1212	1192	874	788	11972
TA	29.2	30.4	38.1	48.6	58.6	68.0	73.3	71.3	64.5	55.4	45.2	33.0	51.3
D50	645	549	371	96	5	0	0	0	1	16	163	527	2374
D55	800	689	524	203	29	1	0	0	4	70	297	682	3300
D60	955	829	679	344	99	7	0	2	21	164	445	837	4381
D65	1110	969	834	492	218	27	0	8	76	301	594	992	5621
D70	1265	1109	989	642	355	106	32	57	180	453	744	1147	7080
New York (Central Park), New York (latitude, 40.8°N; elevation, 187 ft)													
HS	500	721	1037	1364	1636	1710	1688	1483	1214	895	533	404	1099
VS	884	1023	1100	1009	908	834	866	959	1115	1147	886	755	11485
TA	32.2	33.4	41.1	52.1	62.3	71.6	76.6	74.9	68.4	58.7	47.4	35.5	54.5
D50	552	465	282	50	2	0	0	0	0	7	122	451	1931
D55	707	605	432	127	11	0	0	0	1	33	238	605	2759
D60	862	745	586	246	49	0	0	0	7	103	380	760	3737
D65	1017	885	741	387	137	0	0	0	29	209	528	915	4848
D70	1172	1025	896	537	248	56	14	23	104	353	678	1070	6177

	January	February	March	April	May	June	July	August	September	October	November	December	Year
Minneapolis–St. Paul, Minnesota (latitude, 44.9°N; elevation, 837 ft)													
HS	464	764	1103	1442	1737	1927	1970	1687	1255	860	480	353	1170
VS	921	1212	1312	1208	1092	1057	1140	1237	1297	1233	895	742	13346
TA	12.2	16.5	28.3	45.1	57.1	66.9	71.9	70.2	60.0	50.0	32.4	18.6	44.1
D50	1172	938	673	178	18	1	0	0	8	93	529	973	4584
D55	1327	1078	828	305	63	4	1	2	30	186	678	1128	5631
D60	1482	1218	983	449	143	18	5	8	90	318	828	1283	6824
D65	1637	1358	1138	597	271	65	11	21	173	472	978	1438	8159
D70	1792	1498	1293	747	403	142	66	90	308	620	1128	1593	9680
Houston, Texas (latitude, 30.0°N; elevation, 108 ft)													
HS	772	1034	1297	1522	1775	1898	1828	1686	1471	1276	924	730	1351
VS	1014	1087	1002	810	746	744	734	795	975	1206	1142	1013	11267
TA	52.1	55.3	60.8	69.4	75.8	81.1	83.3	83.4	79.2	70.9	61.1	54.6	68.9
D50	71	31	9	1	0	0	0	0	0	1	8	41	161
D55	150	87	31	3	0	0	0	0	0	2	28	108	409
D60	263	168	89	12	0	0	0	0	0	8	82	201	825
D65	416	294	189	23	0	0	0	0	0	24	155	333	1434
D70	556	414	298	107	31	8	4	4	13	88	281	480	2285
Seattle–Tacoma, Washington (latitude, 47.4°N; elevation, 400 ft)													
HS	262	495	849	1293	1714	1802	2248	1616	1148	656	337	211	1053
VS	559	841	1082	1166	1164	1066	1405	1278	1273	1007	674	478	11994
TA	38.2	42.3	44.1	48.7	54.9	59.8	64.5	63.8	59.6	52.2	44.6	40.5	51.1
D50	367	220	192	85	13	2	0	0	2	36	173	297	1386
D55	521	356	339	197	68	14	2	3	15	116	313	450	2393
D60	676	496	493	340	171	67	16	20	71	246	462	605	3662
D65	831	636	648	489	313	167	80	82	170	397	612	760	5185
D70	986	776	803	639	468	308	181	200	313	552	762	915	6903
Edmonton, Alberta (latitude, 53.6°N; elevation, 2220 ft)													
HS	324	649	1080	1541	1931	1939	2005	1570	1109	719	376	236	1095
VS	836	1314	1631	1662	1584	1387	1516	1493	1461	1310	905	650	15748
TA	6.6	10.7	22.1	39.5	...	...	...	...	...	41.2	24.5	13.3	36.9
D65	1810	1520	1330	765	400	222	74	180	411	738	1215	1603	10268
Vancouver, British Columbia (latitude, 49.3°N; elevation, 310 ft)													
HS	265	383	686	1261	1721	1777	2005	1463	925	586	346	203	1025
VS	598	686	921	1202	1239	1114	1328	1225	1082	948	732	487	11563
TA	37.2	39.2	43.2	48.3	...	...	...	...	...	...	43.1	39.6	49.9
D65	862	723	676	501	310	156	81	87	219	456	657	787	5515
Winnipeg, Manitoba (latitude, 49.9°N; elevation, 820 ft)													
HS	468	840	1338	1596	1869	1961	2105	1780	1183	774	420	328	1216
VS	1076	1531	1826	1549	1370	1252	1421	1518	1407	1273	904	802	15928
TA	.2	3.6	17.7	37.9	...	...	...	...	...	43.0	23.3	8.5	35.7
D65	2008	1719	1465	813	405	147	38	71	322	683	1251	1751	10679
Dartmouth, Nova Scotia (latitude, 44.6°N; elevation, 136 ft)													
HS	417	715	1017	1309	1589	1570	1710	1423	1253	840	461	402	1076
VS	820	1125	1200	1087	990	853	981	1034	1284	1195	852	838	12258
TA	25.9	24.9	31.8	40.3	49.3	...	...	...	...	...	41.3	30.4	44.8
D65	1213	1122	1030	742	487	237	58	51	180	457	710	1074	7361
Toronto, Ontario (latitude, 43.7°N; elevation, 443 ft)													
HS	501	722	1109	1463	1847	1935	2005	1629	1301	829	453	365	1194
VS	961	1109	1276	1182	1119	1024	1119	1151	1299	1150	816	741	12949
TA	25.2	25.0	32.3	44.5	...	...	...	...	...	...	39.7	29.2	46.3
D65	1233	1119	1013	616	298	62	7	18	151	439	760	1111	6827

TABLE 7-13 Monthly Average Solar Radiation, Temperature, and Degree-Days for Selected Cities (*cont*)

	January	February	March	April	May	June	July	August	September	October	November	December	Year
						Normandin, Quebec (latitude, 48.8°N; elevation, 450 ft)							
HS	424	785	1294	1434	1762	1629	1640	1360	1073	601	372	328	1006
VS	943	1387	1714	1348	1249	1005	1070	1122	1238	959	775	775	13586
TA	4.4	7.2	19.6	35.3	48.2	...	...	...	...	43.0	29.2	11.5	36.2
D65	1879	1619	1407	891	521	231	102	136	327	682	1074	1659	10528

NOTES:

HS = normal daily value of total hemispheric solar radiation on a horizontal surface, Btu/(ft·day).

VS = normal daily value of total solar radiation on a vertical south-facing surface, Btu/(ft·day).

TA = $(T_{min} + T_{max})/2$, where T_{min} and T_{max} are monthly (or annual) normals of daily minimum and maximum ambient temperature, °F.

Dxx = monthly (or annual) normals of heating degree-days below the base temperature *xx*, °F·days.

SOURCE: J. Douglas Balcomb et al., *Passive Solar Design Handbook*, vol. II, U.S. Department of Energy, Washington, 1980, pp. A-1–A-18.

no need to calculate the change in peak load as influenced by solar heat gain. A designer may wish, however, to know the effect on overall heating energy consumption of a particular design improvement for a building. The following equation may be used for that purpose:

$$\Delta Q_h = I_h \times \Delta(A_g \times \tau) \times \text{SF} \times T_h \tag{7-14}$$

in units,

$$\text{Btu/year} = \text{Btu/(ft}^2\cdot\text{day)} \times \text{ft}^2 \times \text{days/year}$$

where ΔQ_h = change in annual heating energy consumption, Btu/year

I_h = average daily insolation (solar radiation) incident on a surface during the heating season, Btu/(ft²·day) (See Table 7-13.)

Δ = change in a quantity due to an architectural design change

A_g = glass area, ft²

τ = solar heat transmittance of glass, no units (See Table 7-16.)

SF = shading factor, no units (If no shading device were proposed, this factor would be 1.0. Specific shading factors, considering diffuse as well as direct solar radiation, must be calculated for each design proposal.)

T_h = time, days/year (This will be a function of the number of workdays during the heating season for commercial buildings.)

The designer should note that in preparing an estimate for a shading factor indirect light from the sky has a solar radiation component. Shading a window with an overhang will, for example, eliminate direct solar radiation from the sun but will not eliminate indirect solar radiation from the sky. Table 8-13 presents indirect solar radiation data. This must be considered when estimates of shading factors are being prepared.

EXAMPLE

Suppose that an architect of a simple one-story office building for a light-manufacturing facility proposes to enlarge the south-facing glass of the building above his client's stan-

(*Cont. on p. 182*)

TABLE 7·14 Solar Position and Profile Angles for Various Latitudes

Date	Solar time, A.M.	Solar position: Altitude	Solar position: Azimuth	N	NNE	NE	ENE	E	ESE	SE	SSE	S	SSW	SW	WSW
				Profile (shadow line) angle											
16° north latitude															
December	7	7	63			21	10	8	7	7	9	15	58		
	8	19	57			59	32	23	20	20	23	33	63		
	9	31	49			83	53	38	32	31	34	42	62		
	10	41	37				74	55	45	41	42	47	60	81	
	11	48	21					72	58	51	48	50	57	70	88
	12	51	0					90	73	60	53	51	53	60	73
January and November	7	8	66			21	11	9	8	9	11	19	83		
	8	21	61			55	32	24	21	22	26	38	73		
	9	33	52			79	52	39	34	33	37	47	68		
	10	43	40				72	56	47	44	45	51	64	85	
	11	51	23				90	73	60	53	51	53	60	73	
	12	54	0					90	74	63	56	54	56	63	74
February and October	7	11	75		56	21	14	11	11	13	18	38			
	8	25	70		85	48	32	26	25	27	34	53			
	9	38	62			70	51	42	38	39	45	59	83		
	10	50	50			86	69	57	51	50	53	62	76		
	11	59	30				86	74	65	60	60	63	70	81	
	12	63	0					90	79	70	65	63	65	70	79
March and September	7	14	86		39	21	16	14	15	19	30	74			
	8	29	81		67	43	33	29	29	34	46	74			
	9	43	75		82	62	50	44	43	47	56	74			
	10	56	64			77	66	59	56	58	64	74	88		
	11	68	44				82	74	70	68	70	74	81	90	
	12	74	0					90	84	79	75	74	75	79	84
April and August	6	3	101	16	6	4	3	3	4	6	16				
	7	17	97	68	32	22	18	18	20	27	50				
	8	32	94	84	54	39	33	32	35	43	63				
	9	46	90	90	70	56	48	46	48	56	70				
	10	61	85		80	70	63	61	62	67	76	87			
	11	75	75		88	82	78	75	75	77	81	86			
	12	86	0					90	88	87	86	86	86	87	88
May and July	6	5	109	16	8	6	5	6	7	12	59				
	7	19	106	51	29	22	19	20	24	36	72				
	8	33	104	70	48	37	33	34	39	51	77				
	9	47	102	72	62	52	48	48	53	63	81				
	10	61	103	83	73	65	62	62	66	74	85				
	11	75	108	85	80	77	75	76	79	83	89				
	12	86	180	86	86	87	88	90							
June	6	6	113	16	9	7	6	7	9	16					
	7	20	110	47	28	22	20	21	26	40	82				
	8	33	108	65	46	37	33	35	41	55	83				
	9	47	107	74	59	51	47	49	55	67	85				
	10	61	110	79	69	63	61	62	68	77	88				
	11	74	120	82	77	75	74	76	80	86					
	12	83	180	83	83	85	87	90							
				N	NNW	NW	WNW	W	WSW	SW	SSW	S	SSE	SE	ESE

TABLE 7-14 Solar Position and Profile Angles for Various Latitudes (*cont.*)

Date	Solar time, A.M.	Solar position: Altitude	Solar position: Azimuth	Profile (shadow line) angle: N	NNE	NE	ENE	E	ESE	SE	SSE	S	SSW	SW	WSW
							24° north latitude								
December	7	3	63			10	5	4	3	3	4	7	33		
	8	15	55			56	26	18	15	15	18	25	52		
	9	26	46			88	50	34	52						
		34	34				74	51	39	35	35	39	51	74	
	11	40	18					70	53	44	40	42	48	62	85
	12	43	0					90	67	52	45	43	45	52	67
January and November	7	5	66			13	7	5	5	5	7	11	69		
	8	17	58			53	27	20	17	17	20	30	62		
	9	28	49			83	50	35	29	28	31	39	59		
	10	37	36				73	52	42	38	38	43	56	79	
	11	44	20					71	55	47	44	45	52	66	87
	12	46	0					90	70	56	48	46	48	56	70
February and October	7	9	74		55	18	11	9	9	10	14	30			
	8	22	66			48	30	24	22	23	29	45	87		
	9	34	57			73	50	39	34	35	39	51	75		
	10	45	44				70	55	47	45	46	54	68	88	
	11	52	25				88	72	60	54	52	55	62	75	
	12	55	0					90	75	64	57	55	57	64	75
March and September	7	14	84		41	21	16	14	14	17	27	66			
	8	27	77		73	44	32	28	27	31	41	66			
	9	40	68		90	65	50	42	40	43	50	66			
	10	52	55			82	68	58	53	53	57	66	80		
	11	62	33				84	74	66	62	62	66	73	84	
	12	66	0					90	80	73	68	66	68	73	80
April and August	6	5	101	24	9	6	5	5	6	8	22				
	7	18	95	76	36	23	19	18	20	27	47				
	8	32	89		60	42	34	32	34	41	57	88			
	9	46	82		76	60	50	46	47	52	64	82			
	10	59	72		87	75	65	60	59	62	69	79			
	11	71	52			88	81	75	72	71	73	78	85		
	12	78	0					90	85	81	79	78	79	81	85
May and July	6	8	108	24	12	9	8	8	11	17	63				
	7	21	103	59	34	24	21	22	26	36	67				
	8	35	98	78	53	41	35	35	39	49	71				
	9	48	94	87	69	56	50	48	51	59	74				
	10	62	88		80	70	64	62	63	69	77	89			
	11	76	77		88	82	78	76	76	78	81	87			
	12	86	0					90	88	87	86	86	86	87	88
June	6	9	112	24	13	10	9	10	13	22	85				
	7	22	107	55	33	25	22	23	28	41	76				
	8	36	103	73	51	40	36	36	41	53	76				
	9	49	99	82	66	55	50	49	53	63	78				
	10	63	95	87	77	68	64	63	65	72	81				
	11	76	91	90	84	80	77	76	77	80	85				
	12	89	0					90	90	90	89	89	89	90	90
				N	NNW	NW	WNW	W	WSW	SW	SSW	S	SSE	SE	ESE

Date	Solar time, A.M.	Solar position		Profile (shadow line) angle											
		Altitude	Azimuth	N	NNE	NE	ENE	E	ESE	SE	SSE	S	SSW	SW	WSW
				32° north latitude											
December	8	10	54			50	19	13	11	10	12	17	37		
	9	20	44				45	28	22	20	21	26	42	86	
	10	28	31				74	45	33	28	28	31	41	65	
	11	33	16					66	46	36	33	34	40	53	81
	12	35	0					90	61	44	37	35	37	44	61
January and November	7	1	65			4	2	2	1	2	2	3	32		
	8	13	56			48	22	15	13	13	15	22	49		
	9	22	46			88	46	30	24	22	24	31	48		
	10	31	33				73	47	36	31	31	35	46	71	
	11	36	18					68	49	39	36	37	44	58	83
	12	38	0					90	64	48	40	38	40	48	64
February and October	7	7	73		52	14	9	7	7	8	10	22			
	8	18	64			46	27	20	19	19	24	37	79		
	9	29	53			76	48	35	30	30	33	43	66		
	10	38	39				70	52	42	39	40	46	59	82	
	11	45	21					70	55	47	45	47	54	68	89
	12	47	0					90	70	57	49	47	49	57	70
March and September	7	13	82		42	21	15	13	13	16	24	58			
	8	25	73		78	45	31	26	25	28	36	58			
	9	37	62			69	50	40	37	38	44	58	83		
	10	47	47			88	69	56	49	47	50	58	72		
	11	55	27				87	72	62	56	55	58	65	78	
	12	58	0					90	77	66	60	58	60	66	77
April and August	6	6	100	32	11	7	6	6	7	11	26				
	7	19	92	84	39	25	20	19	20	27	44				
	8	31	84		65	44	35	32	33	38	52	80			
	9	44	74		83	63	51	45	44	48	57	74			
	10	56	60			80	67	59	56	57	62	71	85		
	11	65	37				83	74	68	66	66	70	77	87	
	12	70	0					90	82	75	71	70	71	75	82
May and July	6	10	107	32	16	12	10	11	13	22	63				
	7	23	100	67	38	27	23	23	27	36	63				
	8	35	93	86	59	44	37	35	38	47	65				
	9	48	85		75	60	52	48	49	55	67	85			
	10	61	73		87	75	66	62	61	64	70	81			
	11	72	52			88	81	76	73	72	74	79	85		
	12	78	0					90	85	81	79	78	79	81	85
June	5	1	118	1	1	1	1	1	1	2					
	6	12	110	32	18	13	12	13	16	27	79				
	7	24	103	63	38	28	25	25	29	41	71				
	8	37	97	81	57	44	38	37	41	50	70				
	9	50	89		72	59	52	50	52	59	72	90			
	10	62	80		84	73	66	63	63	67	74	85			
	11	74	61			86	80	76	74	75	78	82	88		
	12	81	0					90	87	84	82	81	82	84	87
				N	**NNW**	**NW**	**WNW**	**W**	**WSW**	**SW**	**SSW**	**S**	**SSE**	**SE**	**ESE**

TABLE 7·14 Solar Position and Profile Angles for Various Latitudes (*cont.*)

Date	Solar time, A.M.	Solar position: Altitude	Solar position: Azimuth	Profile (shadow line) angle: N	NNE	NE	ENE	E	ESE	SE	SSE	S	SSW	SW	WSW
							40° north latitude								
December	8	5	53			35	11	7	6	6	6	9	21		
	9	14	42				37	20	15	14	15	18	30	78	
	10	21	29				72	38	26	21	21	23	31	54	
	11	25	15					61	37	28	25	26	31	43	75
	12	27	0					90	53	35	28	27	28	35	53
January and November	8	8	55			38	15	10	8	8	10	14	34		
	9	17	44				40	24	18	17	18	23	37	87	
	10	24	31				72	41	29	24	24	27	36	61	
	11	28	16					63	41	32	29	29	35	48	78
	12	30	6					90	56	39	32	30	32	39	56
February and October	7	4	72		43	9	6	4	4	5	7	14			
	8	15	62			43	23	17	15	15	19	29	69		
	9	24	50			80	45	31	25	24	27	35	56		
	10	32	35				70	47	36	32	33	38	50	75	
	11	37	19					67	49	40	37	39	45	60	85
	12	39	0					90	65	49	41	39	41	49	65
March and September	7	11	80		43	13	13	12	12	14	21	50			
	8	23	70		85	45	29	24	23	25	31	50			
	9	33	57			72	48	37	33	33	38	50	75		
	10	42	42				69	53	45	42	43	50	64	87	
	11	48	23				90	71	57	50	48	50	57	71	
	12	50	0					90	72	59	52	50	52	59	72
April and August	6	7	99	40	14	9	8	8	9	12	29				
	7	19	89		42	26	20	19	20	26	41	88			
	8	30	79		71	46	35	31	31	35	47	72			
	9	41	67			67	51	44	41	43	51	66	90		
	10	51	51			85	69	58	52	51	55	63	77		
	11	59	29				86	73	64	60	59	62	69	81	
	12	62	0					90	78	69	63	62	63	69	78
May and July	5	2	115	5	3	2	2	2	3	6					
	6	13	106	40	20	15	13	13	16	25	62				
	7	24	97	75	42	30	25	24	27	36	58				
	8	35	87		65	47	38	35	37	44	59	86			
	9	47	76		82	64	53	48	47	51	61	77			
	10	57	61			80	68	61	58	58	63	73	86		
	11	66	37				84	75	69	66	67	71	77	87	
	12	70	0					90	82	76	71	70	71	76	82
June	5	4	117	9	6	4	4	5	7	14					
	6	15	108	40	22	16	15	16	19	31	75				
	7	26	100	71	42	31	27	26	30	40	66				
	8	37	91	89	63	47	39	37	40	48	64				
	9	49	80		79	63	54	49	50	54	65	82			
	10	60	66			78	68	62	60	61	67	77	89		
	11	69	42				83	76	71	69	70	74	81	89	
	12	73	0					90	84	78	75	73	75	78	84
				N	**NNW**	**NW**	**WNW**	**W**	**WSW**	**SW**	**SSW**	**S**	**SSE**	**SE**	**ESE**

Date	Solar time, A.M.	Solar position		Profile (shadow line) angle											
		Altitude	Azimuth	N	NNE	NE	ENE	E	ESE	SE	SSE	S	SSW	SW	WSW
								48° north latitude							
December	8	1	53			5	1	1	1	1	1	1	2		
	9	8	41				24	12	9	8	8	10	17	63	
	10	14	28				68	27	17	14	14	15	21	40	
	11	17	14					51	27	20	17	18	21	31	66
	12	19	20					90	41	25	20	19	20	25	41
January and November	8	3	55			20	6	4	4	4	4	6	15		
	9	11	43				29	16	12	11	12	15	25	78	
	10	17	29				68	32	21	17	17	19	26	48	
	11	21	15					55	32	24	21	21	25	37	71
	12	22	0					90	47	30	24	22	24	30	47
February and October	7	2	72		23	4	2	2	2	2	3	6			
	8	11	60			37	18	13	11	11	14	21	56		
	9	19	47			83	39	25	20	19	21	27	45		
	10	25	33				69	41	30	26	26	30	40	66	
	11	30	17					63	42	33	30	31	36	51	81
	12	31	0					90	58	41	33	31	33	41	58
March and September	7	10	79		42	18	12	10	10	12	18	42			
	8	20	67			44	27	21	20	21	26	42	88		
	9	28	53			75	46	34	29	28	32	42	66		
	10	35	38				70	49	39	36	36	42	55	80	
	11	40	20					68	52	43	40	42	49	63	87
	12	42	0					90	67	52	44	42	44	52	67
April and August	6	9	98	48	17	11	9	9	10	14	31				
	7	19	87		46	27	20	19	20	24	38	80			
	8	29	75		77	47	34	29	29	32	42	64			
	9	38	61			70	51	42	38	39	45	58	82		
	10	46	45				70	56	48	46	48	55	69	90	
	11	51	24				89	72	60	53	52	54	61	74	
	12	54	0					90	74	62	56	54	56	62	74
May and July	5	5	114	13	7	6	5	6	8	15					
	6	15	104	48	24	17	15	15	18	27	60				
	7	25	93	83	47	32	26	25	27	34	54				
	8	35	82		71	49	39	35	35	41	53	78			
	9	44	68		89	68	54	46	44	47	54	69			
	10	53	51			85	70	60	54	53	57	65	78		
	11	59	29				86	74	65	61	60	63	70	81	
	12	62	0					90	78	69	64	62	64	69	78
June	5	8	117	17	10	8	8	9	12	24					
	6	17	106	48	26	19	17	18	22	33	70				
	7	27	96	79	47	33	28	27	30	39	61				
	8	37	85		69	50	41	37	38	44	58	83			
	9	47	72		86	67	55	48	47	50	58	74			
	10	56	55			83	70	61	56	56	60	69	81		
	11	63	31				86	75	67	63	63	66	73	83	
	12	65	0					90	80	72	67	65	67	72	80
				N	**NNW**	**NW**	**WNW**	**W**	**WSW**	**SW**	**SSW**	**S**	**SSE**	**SE**	**ESE**

TABLE 7·14 Solar Position and Profile Angles for Various Latitudes (*cont.*)

Date	Solar time, A.M.	Solar position		Profile (shadow line) angle											
		Altitude	Azimuth	N	NNE	NE	ENE	E	ESE	SE	SSE	S	SSW	SW	WSW
				56° north latitude											
December	9	2	40				6	3	2	2	2	2	4	23	
	10	7	27				53	14	9	7	7	7	10	21	
	11	10	14					35	16	11	10	10	12	18	48
	12	11	0					90	26	15	11	11	11	15	26
January and November	9	5	42				15	8	6	5	5	7	12	58	
	10	10	28				59	20	13	10	10	11	15	31	
	11	13	14					43	21	15	13	13	16	24	59
	12	14	0					90	33	19	15	14	15	19	33
February and October	8	7	59			26	11	8	7	7	8	13	39		
	9	13	46			88	31	19	14	13	15	19	33		
	10	19	31				66	33	23	19	19	22	30	55	
	11	22	16					56	33	25	22	23	27	40	74
	12	23	0					90	48	31	25	23	25	31	48
March and September	7	8	77		40	15	10	9	8	10	14	34			
	8	16	64			41	24	18	16	17	21	34	80		
	9	23	50			78	43	29	24	23	26	34	56		
	10	29	35				69	44	33	29	30	34	46	72	
	11	33	18					64	45	36	33	34	40	55	83
	12	34	0					90	60	44	36	34	36	44	60
April and August	5	1	109	4	2	2	1	2	2	3	21				
	6	10	97	56	19	12	10	10	11	15	32				
	7	18	84		49	27	20	18	19	23	34	72			
	8	26	71		83	48	33	27	26	29	36	56			
	9	34	56			74	50	39	34	34	39	50	74		
	10	40	40				71	53	43	40	41	47	61	84	
	11	44	21					70	55	47	44	46	53	67	88
	12	46	0					90	69	55	48	46	48	55	69
May and July	4	1	126	2	1	1	1	1	2	7					
	5	8	113	21	12	9	8	9	12	22					
	6	16	102	56	28	20	17	17	20	28	57				
	7	25	89		51	33	27	25	26	33	50	89			
	8	33	76		77	51	39	34	33	37	48	70			
	9	41	62			72	54	45	41	42	48	61	83		
	10	48	44				71	58	50	48	50	57	70	89	
	11	52	23				89	73	61	54	52	55	62	74	
	12	54	0					90	74	63	56	54	56	63	74
June	4	4	127	7	5	4	4	5	8	28					
	5	11	115	25	15	12	11	13	17	31					
	6	28	92	87	52	36	29	28	30	37	56				
	7	28	92	87	52	36	29	28	30	37	56				
	8	36	79		75	52	41	36	36	41	53	75			
	9	44	64			71	55	47	44	45	52	66	86		
	10	51	46			89	72	59	53	51	53	61	74		
	11	56	25				88	74	63	57	56	58	65	77	
	12	57	0					90	76	66	59	57	59	66	76
				N	NNW	NW	WNW	W	WSW	SW	SSW	S	SSE	SE	ESE

NOTE: Dates vary from year to year within plus or minus 3 days of the twenty-first day of the month.

SOURCE: *ASHRAE Handbook and Product Directory—1977 Fundamentals Volume*, American Society of Heating, Refrigerating and Air-Conditioning Engineers, Inc., New York, pp. 26.4–26.8. Reprinted by permission.

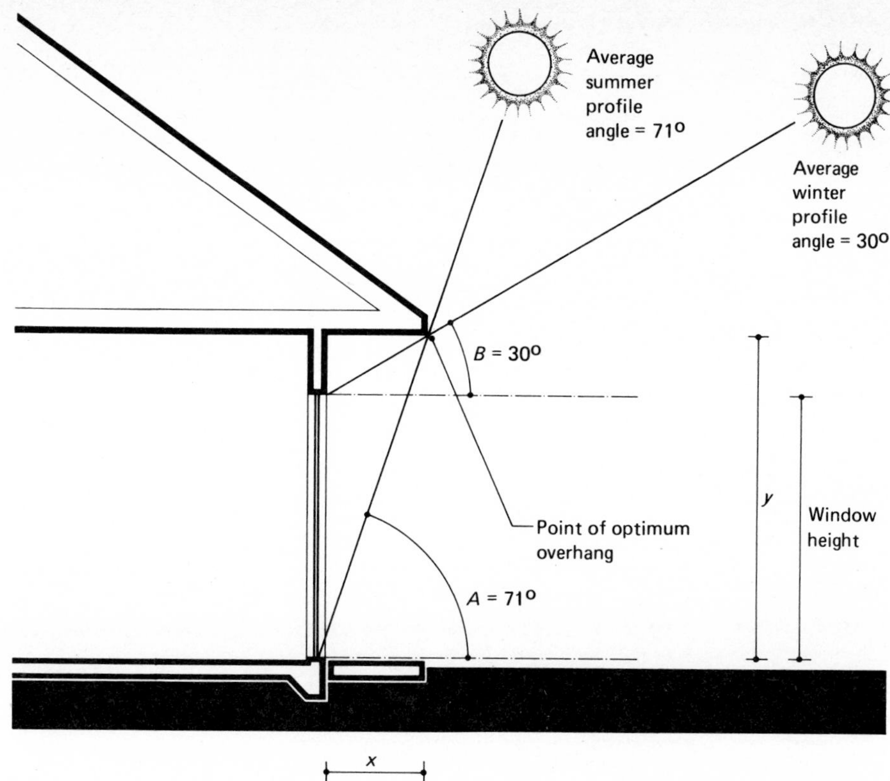

FIGURE 7·5 Use of average seasonal profile angles for the design of horizontal shading devices: latitude, 40° north; $x = \frac{\text{window height}}{\tan A - \tan B}$; $y = x (\tan A)$.

TABLE 7·15 Average Solar Profile (Shadow Line) Angles for a South-Facing Vertical Wall, 9 A.M.–5 P.M., 40° North Latitude

Month	Solar time 9	10	11	12	1	2	3	4	5	Monthly average	Seasonal average*	Season	Seasonal midpoint†
December	18	23	26	27	26	23	18	9	..	21			
January	23	27	29	30	29	27	23	14	..	25	27	Winter	30
February	35	38	39	39	39	38	35	29	14	34			
March	50	50	50	50	50	50	50	50	50	50			
April	66	63	62	62	62	63	66	72	80	66	64	Spring	71
May	77	73	71	70	71	73	77	86	..	75			
June	82	77	74	73	74	77	82	..	..	77			
July	77	73	71	70	71	73	77	86	..	75	73	Summer	71
August	66	63	62	62	62	63	66	72	80	66			
September	50	50	50	50	50	50	50	50	50	50			
October	35	38	39	39	39	38	35	29	14	34	36	Autumn	30
November	23	27	29	30	29	27	23	14	..	25			

*Seasonal averages are calculated by using the following monthly groupings: winter = December, January, and February; spring = March, April, and May; summer = June, July, and August; and autumn = September, October, and November.

†The "observed" seasonal midpoint is defined as the point halfway between the beginning of the season and the end of the season. For example, the winter seasonal midpoint would be halfway between December 21 and March 21 or, in the table, halfway between the months of January and February.

SOURCE: Calculated by the author by using data from Table 7-14.

TABLE 7-16 Solar and Daylight Transmittance of Various Glass Types*

Glass	Thickness, in	Transmittance daylight, percent	Solar percentage
	Monolithic		
Clear	⅛	89	80
	¼	87	75
	½	82	61
	¾	78	51
Clear with RC†	¼	14	16
Blue green	⅛	83	63
	¼	75	47
Blue green with RC	¼	50	35
Gray	⅛	61	63
	¼	44	46
	½	19	22
Gray with RC	¼	14	17
Bronze	⅛	68	65
	¼	52	49
	½	28	24
Bronze with RC	¼	34	31
	Insulating‡		
Clear	⅛	80	89
	¼	77	59
Clear with RC	1	13	12
Blue green	⅛	75	52
	¼	66	36
Blue green with RC	1	45	28
Gray	⅛	55	52
	¼	39	35
Gray with RC	1	30	29
Bronze	⅛	61	54
	¼	46	38
Bronze with RC	1	30	25

*These are typical values which will vary between manufacturers.

†RC = reflective coating.

‡The inside pane is clear in all cases.

SOURCE: *How to Predict Interior Daylight Illumination*, Libbey-Owens-Ford Company, Toledo, Ohio, 1976, p. 16.

dard 2-foot strip windows. The building is not air-conditioned in summer and has no daylighting controls. Along with the additional glass, the architect proposes to extend the overhangs that he ordinarily uses so that the additional glass will be shaded during the summer. Is the design cost-effective? The analysis presented below will provide the answer.

The following are additional details of the proposed building:

Location	New York City
Roof *U*	0.06 Btu/(h·ft²·°F)
Wall *U*	0.10
Window *U*	0.69
Floor-to-roof height	12 ft
Slab perimeter U_p	0.55 Btu/(h·°F·ft) [See Equation (9-3).]
Occupant load	200 ft²/person
Lighting load	2 W/ft²
Glass transmissivity	0.59

For a 10-foot strip of exterior wall, the following data apply:

Old glass area	20 ft²
New glass area	30 ft²
Heating system	Oil
Oil cost	$1.70/gal
Glass cost	$71/ft²
Wall cost	$5/ft²

The analysis will be made for the exterior zone of the building only, that is, for the 15-foot strip of space next to the exterior wall, for reasons explained in Chapter 6.

An analysis of internal and solar heat gain yields the following:

Lighting:

$$q = 2.0 \text{ W/ft}^2 \times 150 \text{ ft}^2 \times 3.413 \text{ Btu/Wh}$$
$$= 1024 \text{ Btu/h}$$

or, assuming 9 hours per day, a 5-day week, and a 6-month heating season,

$$Q = 1{,}198{,}080 \text{ Btu/year}$$

People:

$$q = 150 \text{ ft}^2 \div 150 \text{ ft}^2 \text{ person} \times 510 \text{ Btu/person}$$
$$= \text{Btu/h}$$

or $Q = 596{,}700$ Btu/year

Solar:[5]

$$\text{Old } q_h = 943 \text{ Btu/(day·ft}^2) \times 20 \text{ ft}^2 \times 0.59$$
$$= 11{,}127 \text{ Btu/day}$$

or $Q_h = 1{,}446{,}510$ Btu/year

$$\text{New } q_h = 943 \text{ Btu/(day·ft}^2) \times 30 \text{ ft}^2 \times 0.59$$
$$= 16{,}691 \text{ Btu/day}$$

or $Q_h = 2{,}169{,}830$ Btu/year

[5]The figures of 943 Btu/(day·ft²) is taken from Table 7-13, averaged for 6 months, November through April.

An analysis of heat loss through the walls, windows, ceiling, and slabs during the *daytime* yields the following:

Walls:[6]

$$\text{Old } Q_h = 0.10 \text{ Btu/(h}\cdot{}^\circ\text{F}\cdot\text{ft}^2) \times 19{,}102\ ({}^\circ\text{F}\cdot\text{h})/\text{year} \times 100 \text{ ft}^2 \quad (7\text{-}7)$$

$$= 191{,}020 \text{ Btu/year} \quad (7\text{-}7)$$

$$\text{New } Q_h = 0.10 \text{ Btu/(h}\cdot{}^\circ\text{F}\cdot\text{ft}^2) \times 19{,}102\ ({}^\circ\text{F}\cdot\text{h})/\text{year} \times 90 \text{ ft}^2$$

$$= 171{,}918 \text{ Btu/year}$$

Roof (see Table 7-17):

$$Q_h = 0.06 \text{ Btu/(h}\cdot{}^\circ\text{F}\cdot\text{ft}^2) \times 31{,}242\ ({}^\circ\text{F}\cdot\text{h})/\text{year} \times 150 \text{ ft}^2 \quad (7\text{-}7)$$

$$= 281{,}178 \text{ Btu/year}$$

Slab:

$$Q_h = 0.55 \text{ Btu/(h}\cdot{}^\circ\text{F}\cdot\text{ft}) \times 10 \text{ ft} \times 31{,}242\ ({}^\circ\text{F}\cdot\text{h})/\text{year} \quad (7\text{-}7)$$

$$= 171{,}831 \text{ Btu/year}$$

Infiltration:[7]

$$\text{Old } Q_h = 0.018 \text{ Btu/(}{}^\circ\text{F}\cdot\text{ft}^3) \times [3 \text{ ft}^3/(\text{h}\cdot\text{ft}) \times 24 \text{ ft}] \times 36{,}326\ ({}^\circ\text{F}\cdot\text{h})/\text{year} \quad (7\text{-}13)$$

$$= 47{,}078 \text{ Btu/year}$$

$$\text{New } Q_h = 0.018 \text{ Btu/(}{}^\circ\text{F}\cdot\text{ft}^3) \times [3 \text{ ft}^3/(\text{h}\cdot\text{ft}) \times 26 \text{ ft}] \times 36{,}326\ ({}^\circ\text{F}\cdot\text{h})/\text{year} \quad (7\text{-}12)$$

$$= 51{,}002 \text{ Btu/year}$$

Windows:

$$\text{Old } Q_h = 0.69 \text{ Btu/(h}\cdot\text{ft}^2\cdot{}^\circ\text{F}) \times 20 \text{ ft}^2 \times 36{,}326\ ({}^\circ\text{F}\cdot\text{h})/\text{year} \quad (7\text{-}7)$$

$$= 501{,}299 \text{ Btu/year}$$

$$\text{New } Q_h = 0.69 \text{ Btu/(h}\cdot\text{ft}^2\cdot{}^\circ\text{F}) \times 30 \text{ ft}^2 \times 36{,}326\ ({}^\circ\text{F}\cdot\text{h})/\text{year} \quad (7\text{-}7)$$

$$= 751{,}948 \text{ Btu/year}$$

Total heat gains (Btu/year):

	Old	New
Lighting	1,198,080	1,198,080
People	596,700	596,700
Solar	1,446,510	2,169,830
	3,241,240	3,964,610

Total heat loss (Btu/year):

	Old	New
Walls	191,020	171,918
Roof	281,178	281,178
Slab	171,831	171,831
Infiltration	47,078	51,002
Windows	501,299	751,948
	1,192,406	1,427,877

[6]The figure of 19,102 (°F·h)/year is taken from Table 6-6.

[7]The figure of 36,326 (°F·h)/year is taken from Table 7-7.

TABLE 7-17 Degree-Hours for Roofs, a 70°F Indoor Temperature during Occupied Periods, and a 55°F Indoor Temperature during Unoccupied Periods in Nonresidential Buildings, Mitchel Air Force Base, Nassau County, New York, Heating Season

Average bin temperature, °F	Difference from 70°F	Adjusted for sol-air temperature* (A)	Occupied period: hours of occurrence (8 A.M.–6 P.M., Monday–Friday) (B)	(°F·h)/year (A·B)	Difference from 55°F (C)	Adjusted for sol-air temperature* (D)	Nonoccupied period: hours of occurrence — Evenings (6 P.M.–8 A.M.)	Nonoccupied period: hours of occurrence — Weekend days (8 A.M.–6 P.M.)	Adjusted (°F·h)/year (C·E) + (D·F)
67	3	−1	24	....	..	..	...	..	....
62	8	4	50	200	..	..	...	..	....
57	13	9	100	900	..	..	...	..	....
52	18	14	139	1,949	3	−1	222	48	618
47	23	19	196	3,724	8	4	312	68	2,768
42	28	24	211	5,064	13	9	389	69	5,678
37	33	29	216	6,264	18	14	479	66	9,546
32	38	34	165	5,610	23	19	389	48	9,859
27	43	39	90	3,510	28	24	241	24	7,324
22	48	44	50	2,200	33	29	137	13	4,898
17	53	49	26	1,274	38	34	80	6	3,244
12	58	54	8	432	43	39	32	1	1,415
7	63	59	2	118	48	44	11	..	528
2	68	64	0	....	53	49	1	..	53
				31,242					45,931

*$t_{sa} = t_o + (71°F \times 0.15) - 7°F$
$= t_o + 4°F$

(Figure 8-1 with data from Table 7-13)

SOURCE: Calculated by the author from data in Table 6-4.

From the analysis thus far, it should be evident that increasing the window area to increase wintertime solar heat gain is of no value in reducing overall energy consumption in the proposed building. With 2-foot-high windows the building has more than enough solar gain. Increasing the window area will only increase both daytime and nighttime conducted heat loss, the nighttime loss being of real economic consequence. Unless the building is equipped to capitalize on the natural-light component of solar radiation, the building is better off with less window area, rather than more, in terms of energy use. (Chapter 10 will discuss the economic potential of natural light.)

The portion of building just analyzed, in fact, has an overheating condition in the exterior space even with 2-foot-high windows. Most new office and other commercial buildings are equipped with economizer-cycle ventilation systems which use outside winter air to cool overheated interior spaces. In any case, 0.2 to 0.25 $ft^3/(min \cdot ft^2)$ of fresh outside air is usually required for such buildings. This provides essentially "free" cooling, so changes in the overheating of exterior zones will create neither a cost nor a benefit in terms of fuel or electricity expenditures.

Estimating Solar Heat Gain in Residential Buildings

The method presented here for estimating the thermal value of passive solar heating designs for housing is the result of work performed by the staff at the Los Alamos Scientific Laboratory headed by J. Douglas Balcomb and sponsored by the U.S. Department of Energy. This method was developed on the basis of data gathered during experiments both with scaled test rooms and with actual buildings. It yields an estimate of the percentage of available solar radiation which becomes useful heat within a room.

Residential buildings and buildings of wood frame construction are perhaps most amenable to effective and accurate applications of this method. The exterior zones of *small* office buildings may also be compatible with the method, although the accuracy of this application has not as yet been measured. One of the key constraints, according to the developers of the method, is that it applies to buildings dominated by exterior heat loads, that is, by the sun and air temperatures. This is in contrast to buildings which have large internal heat loads such as heat from people, lights, and equipment.

The method is based on passive solar designs with the following general characteristics:[8]

- No winter shading of south-facing glazing
- 0.3 ground reflectance
- Vertical south-facing glazing
- 5.4 gal of water per square foot of glazing for water walls
- Backdraft dampers top and bottom (3 percent of wall area) on Trombe walls

[8]J. Douglas Balcomb et al., *Passive Solar Design Handbook*, vol. II, U.S. Department of Energy, Washington, 1980, p. 40.

- Double glazing (transmittance = 0.75; ¼-in spacing)
- Building interior temperature range, 65 to 75°F
- Night insulation, *R*9 when used
- Wall-to-room heat transfer coefficient, 1.0 Btu/(h·°F·ft²)
- Building mass negligible relative to the mass wall
- Thermal mass properties:

Thermal conductivity	1.0 Btu/(ft·h·°F)
Mass surface emittance	0.9
Mass surface absorbance	0.8 (direct gain)
	1.0 (Trombe water walls)
Density	150 lb/ft³
Specific heat	0.2 Btu/(lb·°F)
	225 lb/ft² of glazing
Thickness	6 in (direct gain)
	18 in (Trombe walls)
Storage capacity	45 Btu/(°F·ft²) of glazing
Mass-to-glass-surface-area ratio	3:1 (direct gain)
	1:1 (Trombe water walls)

The estimating method uses the following abbreviations:

WW	water wall
WWNI	water wall with night insulation
TW	Trombe wall
TWNI	Trombe wall with night insulation
DG	direct gain
DGNI	direct gain with night insulation

The developers of the method suggest that sun spaces, that is, greenhouse designs, be evaluated by using data developed for Trombe walls. In other words, the thermal performance of the two types is somewhat similar.

The method uses a measure of building thermal performance called a "building heat load coefficient," which is defined as follows:

$$\text{Building heat load coefficient (BHLC)} = \frac{24 \times q_h^\circ}{t_i - t_o} \qquad (7\text{-}15)$$

in units,

$$\text{Btu/(°F·day)} = \frac{\text{h/day} \times \text{Btu/h}}{\text{°F}}$$

where q_h° = "solar" design heat loss *exclusive* of the south-facing glazing, Btu/h
t_i = inside design temperature, normally 70°F in winter
t_o = outside design temperature, normally at the 97.5 percent percentile (See Table 6-3 for winter outdoor design temperature for various locations.)

The designer must estimate the BHLC *exclusive* of the south-facing glazing and divide it by the area of south glazing A_g to obtain another measure called the "load collector ratio" (LCR):

$$\text{LCR} = \frac{\text{BHLC}}{A_g} \tag{7-16}$$

Then, using Table 7-18, the designer may look up a solar savings fraction (abbreviated in the table as SSF). The SSF is defined as the fraction of a building's heating requirements provided by the sun's energy.

EXAMPLE

A designer decides to add a greenhouse to the south side of a house. The greenhouse is expected to reduce the heating requirements for the house as well as provide space for growing plants and vegetables. The designer's client wishes to know how cost-effective the greenhouse will be. The house and attached greenhouse have the following characteristics:

Solar design heat loss (q_h°)	25,000 Btu/h (excluding south-facing glazing)
Overall design heat loss (q_h)	26,000 Btu/h (including south-facing glazing)
Winter outdoor design temperature (t_o)	15°F
Greenhouse south-facing glass area	160 ft² (20 by 8 ft)
Greenhouse cost (C_0)	$3000
Auxiliary fuel	Oil
Fuel cost	$1.75/gal
Annual heating degree-days	4811 °F·days
Location	New York City
Income tax credit	40 percent
Night insulation	*R*9

The building heat load coefficient is calculated as follows:

$$\text{BHLC} = \frac{24\ \text{h/day} \times 25{,}000\ \text{Btu/h}}{70°\text{F} - 15°\text{F}} = 10{,}909\ \text{Btu/(°F·day)} \tag{7-15}$$

The LCR then is

$$\text{LCR} = \frac{10{,}909\ \text{Btu/(°F·day)}}{160\ \text{ft}^2} = 68 \tag{7-16}$$

By using the LCR calculated above and data in Table 7-18, the SSF for Trombe walls with night insulation (TWNI) by interpolation is

$$\text{SSF} = 0.21,\ \text{or 21 percent}$$

The cost of heating the house *without* the help of the greenhouse may be calculated by using the degree-day method [see Equation 6-2)]:

$$C_H = \frac{\$1.75/\text{gal} \times 26{,}000\ \text{Btu/h} \times 4811\ °\text{F·h} \times 24\ \text{h/day} \times 0.63}{55°\text{F} \times 0.55 \times 140{,}000\ \text{Btu/gal}}$$

$$= \$782/\text{year}$$

(Cont. on p. 192)

TABLE 7·18 Load Collector Ratio (LCR) and Solar Savings Fraction (SSF) Data

Design approach		Solar savings fraction								
		0.1	0.2	0.3	0.4	0.5	0.6	0.7	0.8	0.9
Phoenix, Arizona (33.4°N; 1552 degree-days; January temperature, 51°F)										
	WW	467	219	139	100	75	58	45	34	22
L	WWNI	620	293	188	136	104	82	65	51	36
C	TW	436	202	126	87	63	46	34	25	16
R	TWNI	583	275	176	126	95	73	56	42	28
	DG	555	256	157	107	75	53	37	24	12
	DGNI	673	316	201	143	107	82	62	45	29
Los Angeles, California (33.9°N; 1819 degree-days; January temperature, 54°F)										
	WW	563	259	161	115	87	68	54	41	27
L	WWNI	737	342	215	153	117	93	75	60	43
C	TW	513	238	147	101	73	54	40	29	20
R	TWNI	687	320	200	143	108	84	65	49	33
	DG	665	304	187	127	90	65	46	31	18
	DGNI	793	369	231	163	123	94	72	53	35
San Francisco, California (37.6°N; 3042 degree-days; January temperature, 48°N)										
	WW	332	163	103	72	53	40	31	22	13
L	WWNI	453	225	145	103	77	60	47	37	26
C	TW	313	149	92	63	45	33	23	16	10
R	TWNI	428	210	134	94	71	54	41	30	20
	DG	385	180	109	72	49	32	20	11	. .
	DGNI	491	239	151	106	79	59	44	42	20
Denver, Colorado (39.7°N; 6016 degree-days; January temperature, 30°F)										
	WW	136	63	39	27	20	15	11	7	. .
L	WWNI	218	105	67	48	37	29	24	19	13
C	TW	132	61	38	25	17	12	8	5	3
R	TWNI	207	99	63	45	34	27	21	15	10
	DG	127	54	28	13	. .	. .	. .	. .	. .
	DGNI	227	108	68	48	36	27	20	14	9
Washington, D.C. (38.9°N; 5010 degree-days; January temperature, 32°F)										
	WW	92	42	25	17	11	8	4	. .	. .
L	WWNI	169	80	51	36	27	21	17	13	9
C	TW	94	42	25	16	10	6	3	. .	. .
R	TWNI	160	76	48	34	25	19	15	11	7
	DG	69	19	. .	. .	. .	. .	. .	. .	. .
	DGNI	171	80	50	35	25	19	13	9	5
Miami, Florida (25.8°N; 206 degree-days; January temperature, 67°F)										
	WW	2285	1138	731	516	389	307	242	186	130
L	WWNI	2804	1401	906	641	483	382	307	242	174
C	TW	2102	1013	641	449	329	245	184	135	94
R	TWNI	2638	1304	832	589	446	344	265	198	133
	DG	2912	1403	886	620	452	336	249	181	121
	DGNI	3119	1534	975	692	520	398	303	224	151
Atlanta, Georgia (33.6°N; 3095 degree-days; January temperature, 42°F)										
	WW	172	79	48	33	25	19	14	9	4
L	WWNI	264	126	79	56	42	33	27	21	15

TABLE 7·18 Load Collector Ratio (LCR) and Solar Savings Fraction (SSF) Data (*cont.*)

Design approach	Solar savings fraction								
	0.1	0.2	0.3	0.4	0.5	0.6	0.7	0.8	0.9
C TW	166	75	46	31	21	15	10	7	4
R TWNI	249	118	74	52	39	30	23	17	11
DG	173	74	41	23	10	..	..	..	..
DGNI	276	129	80	56	42	32	23	17	10
Chicago, Illinois (41.8°N; 6127 degree-days; January temperature, 24°F)									
WW	73	31	17	11	6	..	..	..	..
L WWNI	149	69	43	30	22	17	14	10	7
C TW	78	33	18	11	6	..	..	..	..
R TWNI	141	65	40	28	21	16	12	9	5
DG	34	..	..	..	..	..	..	..	..
DGNI	148	67	41	28	20	14	10	7	3
New Orleans, Louisiana (30.0°N; 1465 degree-days; January temperature, 53°F)									
WW	374	169	104	74	56	44	34	25	16
L WWNI	506	235	146	105	80	64	51	40	29
C TW	342	158	97	66	47	35	25	18	12
R TWNI	474	219	137	98	74	57	44	33	22
DG	423	191	115	76	52	36	24	14	6
DGNI	542	249	156	110	83	63	48	35	23
Boston, Massachusetts (42.4°N; 5621 degree-days; January temperature, 29°F)									
WW	81	35	20	13	9	5	..	..	..
L WWNI	159	73	46	32	24	19	15	11	8
C TW	85	36	21	13	8	4	..	..	..
R TWNI	150	69	43	30	23	17	13	10	6
DG	49	..	..	..	..	..	..	..	..
DGNI	158	72	44	30	22	16	11	8	4
Minneapolis, Minnesota (44.9°N; 8159 degree-days; January temperature, 12°F)									
WW	54	21	10	..	..	..	..	..	..
L WWNI	126	58	36	25	18	14	11	8	5
C TW	59	24	12	5	..	..	..	..	..
R TWNI	120	55	34	23	17	13	9	7	4
DG	...	..	..	..	..	..	..	..	..
DGNI	122	54	32	22	15	10	7	4	..
Kansas City, Missouri (39.3°N; 5357 degree-days; January temperature, 27°F)									
WW	102	45	26	17	12	8	5	..	..
L WWNI	182	85	53	37	28	22	17	14	9
C TW	103	45	26	17	11	7	4	..	..
R TWNI	172	80	50	35	26	20	15	11	7
DG	79	25	..	..	..	..	..	..	..
DGNI	184	84	52	36	26	19	14	10	5
New York (Central Park), New York (40.8°N; 4848 degree-days; January temperature, 32°F)									
WW	85	37	22	14	10	6	..	..	..
L WWNI	159	76	48	34	25	20	16	12	8
C TW	87	38	22	14	8	5	2	..	..
R TWNI	151	72	45	32	24	18	14	10	6
DG	56	..	..	..	..	..	..	..	..
DGNI	161	74	46	32	23	17	12	8	4

	Design approach	Solar savings fraction								
		0.1	0.2	0.3	0.4	0.5	0.6	0.7	0.8	0.9
Houston, Texas (30.0°N; 1434 degree-days; January temperature, 52°F)										
	WW	336	148	93	66	50	39	30	22	14
L	WWNI	466	209	131	95	73	58	46	36	26
C	TW	309	140	86	59	42	31	22	16	10
R	TWNI	433	196	124	88	67	52	40	30	20
	DG	375	166	99	66	45	30	19	11	..
	DGNI	492	223	140	99	74	57	43	31	20
Seattle-Tacoma, Washington (47.4°N; 5185 degree-days; January temperature, 38°F)										
	WW	128	54	30	19	11	6	..	..	..
L	WWNI	213	98	59	41	30	22	16	11	7
C	TW	123	53	29	18	11	6	..	..	..
R	TWNI	199	91	55	38	27	20	14	10	6
	DG	108	33	..	..	..	..	..	..	..
	DGNI	217	97	58	38	27	19	13	8	3
Edmonton, Alberta (53.6°N; 10,268 degree-days; January temperature, 7°F)										
	WW	66	26	10	..	..	..	..	..	..
L	WWNI	139	65	39	27	19	13	10	7	4
C	TW	69	27	13	..	..	..	..	..	..
R	TWNI	132	61	37	25	17	12	9	6	3
	DG	...	..	..	..	..	..	..	..	..
	DGNI	136	61	35	23	15	10	6	3	..
Vancouver, British Columbia (49.3°N; 5515 degree-days; January temperature, 37°F)										
	WW	111	47	26	15	9	4	..	..	..
L	WWNI	193	89	54	37	27	20	15	11	7
C	TW	109	46	25	15	8	4	..	..	..
R	TWNI	181	83	50	34	24	18	13	9	6
	DG	86	..	..	..	..	..	..	..	..
	DGNI	195	88	52	34	24	17	11	7	3
Winnipeg, Manitoba (49.9°N; 10,679 degree-days; January temperature, —)										
	WW	53	21	9	..	..	..	..	..	..
L	WWNI	125	58	36	25	18	13	10	7	5
C	TW	59	23	11	4	..	..	..	..	..
R	TWNI	119	55	34	23	17	12	9	6	4
	DG	...	..	..	..	..	..	..	..	..
	DGNI	121	54	32	21	15	10	6	3	..
Dartmouth, Nova Scotia (44.6°N; 7361 degree-days; January temperature, 26°F)										
	WW	73	31	18	11	7	4	..	..	..
L	WWNI	148	68	43	30	23	18	14	11	7
C	TW	76	33	18	11	6	3	..	..	..
R	TWNI	140	64	40	28	21	16	12	9	6
	DG	34	..	..	..	..	..	..	..	..
	DGNI	146	66	41	28	20	15	11	7	3
Toronto, Ontario (43.7°N; 6827 degree-days; January temperature, 25°F)										
	WW	73	31	17	11	7	..	..	..	..
L	WWNI	148	68	43	30	22	17	14	11	7
C	TW	76	32	18	11	6	2	..	..	..

TABLE 7-18 Load Collector Ratio (LCR) and Solar Savings Fraction (SSF) Data (*cont.*)

Design approach	Solar savings fraction								
	0.1	0.2	0.3	0.4	0.5	0.6	0.7	0.8	0.9
R TWNI	140	65	40	28	21	16	12	9	6
DG	32	..	..	..	..	..	..	..	..
DGNI	146	66	40	28	20	14	10	7	3
Normandin, Quebec (48.8°N; 10,528 degree-days; January temperature, 4°N)									
WW	49	19	9	..	..	..	..	..	..
L WWNI	118	56	35	24	18	13	10	7	5
C TW	54	22	11	4	..	..	..	..	..
R TWNI	112	52	33	23	16	12	9	6	4
DG	...	..	..	..	..	..	..	..	..
DGNI	113	52	31	21	14	10	6	4	..

NOTE: Passive solar design approaches designated in this table are abbreviated as follows: WW = water wall; WWNI = water wall with night insulation (*R*9); TW = Trombe wall; TWNI = Trombe wall with night insulation (*R*9); DG = direct gain; DGNF = direct gain with night insulation (*R*9).

SOURCE: J. Douglas Balcomb et al., *Passive Solar Design Handbook*, vol. II, U.S. Department of Energy, Washington, 1980, pp. F1–F29, comp. by C. Dennis Barley.

Note that the overall peak heat load for the building, including the south glazing of 26,000 Btus per hour, is used instead of the "solar" design heat loss of 25,000 Btus per hour.

The saving in fuel provided by the greenhouse may be calculated by multiplying the SSF by the annual heating cost C_H:

$$B_h = \text{SSF} \times C_H$$
$$= 0.21 \times \$782/\text{year}$$
$$= \$164/\text{year}$$

The cost of the greenhouse less the investment tax credit is calculated below:

$$C_0 = (1 - 0.40) \times 3000$$
$$= \$1800$$

A simple cost-benefit analysis yields the following:

$$\text{Simple payback period} = \frac{\$1800}{\$164/\text{year}} = 11.0 \text{ years}$$

$$\text{Simple return on investment} = \frac{\$164/\text{year}}{\$1800} = 9.1 \text{ percent/year}$$

The investment based on measurable thermal benefits yields an average return for a homeowner. The more-difficult-to-quantify benefits of a greenhouse, however, such as its plant-growing potential and additional part-time living space, usually increase its cost-effectiveness.

Passive solar designs typically do not decrease the peak heating load of a dwelling, so no equipment savings can be realized with such designs. Simply adding more south-facing glass, for example, will *not* decrease the heat load on a dwelling after a series of cloudy days.

TABLE 7-19 Rules of Thumb for Sizing Passive Solar Interior Mass

Expected solar savings, percent	Thermal storage mass per square foot of solar glazing area	
	Water, lb	Masonry, lb
10	6	30
20	12	60
30	18	90
40	24	120
50	30	150
60	36	180
70	42	210
80	48	240
90	54	270

SOURCE: J. Douglas Balcomb et al., *Passive Solar Design Handbook*, vol. II, U.S. Department of Energy, Washington, 1980, p. 26.

A number of design guidelines which may help improve the thermal performance (SSF) of passive solar designs for residential buildings are offered in the following paragraphs.

Because most external-load-dominated buildings are of light construction, typically wood frame, additional mass for thermal storage can be an important aspect of a design for passive solar heating. The sun entering a room on a clear winter day may well carry the temperature above comfort levels, whereas the temperature in the evening in the same space may be below comfort levels unless heat is supplied by the building's mechanical system. The result is that not all the heat collected during the day may be used. If additional mass is added to the surfaces of the room, however, the temperature will rise less during the day because some of the heat will be absorbed by the mass. During the evening hours, the fuel needed to keep the space at adequate comfort levels will be reduced because the mass will release to the room some of the heat that it collected during the day.

No rigorous guidelines are yet available for determining the amount of mass needed for a space, although some rules of thumb which may be of assistance are presented below. The designer should make sure that some mass is provided in buildings of low structural mass if passive solar designs are to be effective.

If mass is placed so that the sun falls on it during the day, the values in Table 7-19 may be used to size passive solar storage mass. If the mass is not irradiated by the sun, these values should be increased by a factor of 4. Mass should also be about 4 to 6 inches thick and have 3 times as much exposed surface area as the south-facing glass area for the Table 7-19 values to be valid.[9]

To be effective, mass should be located in the same space which receives the solar heat gains unless a forced-air auxiliary heating system is used. In this case, the fan-powered air movement within the structure may suffice to distribute solar

[9]Ibid., pp. 25–26.

TABLE 7-20 Recommended Number of Glazings for Passive Solar Designs in Various Climates

Winter climate	Number of glazings in direct-gain designs	
	No night insulation	*R*9 night insulation
Mild	2	1
Moderate	2–3	1
	3–4*	2
Severe	4–5*	2

*For LCR = 10.

SOURCE: J. Douglas Balcomb et al., *Passive Solar Design Handbook*, vol. II, U.S. Department of Energy, Washington, 1980, p. 78.

gains from the space of origin to more remote spaces. Thermal mass located in walls is almost as effective as mass which is part of a floor. Four-inch thicknesses of masonry are more effective than greater thicknesses. Thicknesses of less than 4 inches may result in ineffective time lags between solar heat storage and release. Coverings such as carpets, wood flooring, and tapestries substantially reduce the effectiveness of thermal mass in a room.

The number of glazings recommended for south-facing glass areas in direct-gain designs is listed in Table 7-20. These recommendations are based on thermal performance optimums, *not* cost-effectiveness optimums.

For mass directly in sunlight in rooms adjacent to south-facing glass, it is generally recommended that high-density materials be dark in color and low-density materials light in color. Thus solar radiation is absorbed only on surfaces where the heat will be stored and is not emitted at high temperatures to the surrounding space, thus causing overheating.[10]

Some reflectance is recommended, however, to distribute solar heat gain more uniformly in direct-gain spaces. An absorptance of 0.8 is often suggested (see Table 7-21). At absorptances below 0.5, however, SSFs begin to decline significantly.

In Trombe wall designs, vents are usually placed at the bottom and the top of the wall to encourage convection around the wall as a means of transferring heat from the wall to the adjacent room. Too much convection during the day, however, can cause daytime overheating in the adjacent space and loss of effectiveness in the solar heat being collected. The vent areas presented in Table 7-22 are recommended.

Orientation of glass is another variable open to the designer. Some studies indicate that the optimum azimuth for vertical glass is 6° west of due south.[11] A tilt of about 55° from the horizontal is suggested, although this will vary from latitude to latitude. The "active" solar rule of thumb of 15° plus the latitude is also appropriate for passive solar designs. The amount of solar radiation per unit of glass surface is greatly increased when collector surfaces are perpendicular to the average profile angle of the sun. The designer should be aware, however, that tilted south-facing glass surfaces should also be shaded during the summer months.

[10]Ibid., p. 113.

[11]Ibid., p. 152.

The orientation of south-facing glass will affect the fuel savings potential of a passive solar design. Calculations prepared for the U.S. Department of Energy suggest that glass should not vary beyond 20° east of south or 32° west of south (see Table 7-23).

Insulation used behind solar glazing at night increases the SSF of passive solar direct-gain designs significantly, although such increases vary substantially according to climate (see Table 7-18). Designs which employ nocturnal insulation other than the *R*9 insulation on which Table 7-18 is based may be evaluated by using

TABLE 7-21 Solar Absorptance of Various Materials

Material	Absorptance	Material	Absorptance
Optical flat black paint	0.98	Red oil paint	0.74
Flat black paint	0.95	Red bricks	0.70
Black lacquer	0.92	Uncolored concrete	0.65
Dark-gray paint	0.91	Moderately light buff bricks	0.60
Black concrete	0.91	Medium-dull-green paint	0.59
Dark-blue lacquer	0.91	Medium-orange paint	0.58
Black oil paint	0.90	Medium-yellow paint	0.57
Stafford-blue bricks	0.89	Medium-blue paint	0.51
Dark-olive-drab paint	0.89	Medium-kelly-green paint	0.51
Dark-brown paint	0.88	Light-green paint	0.47
Dark-blue-gray paint	0.88	White semigloss paint	0.30
Azure-blue or dark-green lacquer	0.88	White gloss paint	0.25
Brown concrete	0.85	Silver paint	0.25
Medium-brown paint	0.84	White lacquer	0.21
Medium-light-brown paint	0.80	Polished-aluminum reflector sheet	0.12
Brown or green lacquer	0.79	Aluminized Mylar film	0.10
Medium-rust paint	0.78	Laboratory vapor-deposited coatings	0.02
Light-gray oil paint	0.75		

NOTE: This table is meant to serve as a guide only. Variations in texture, tone, overcoats, pigments, binders, etc., can alter these values.

SOURCE: J. Douglas Balcomb et al., *Passive Solar Design Handbook*, vol. II, U.S. Department of Energy, Washington, 1980, p. 75.

As presented in G. G. Gubareff et al., *Thermal Radiation Properties Survey*, 2d. ed., Minneapolis-Honeywell Regulator Company, Honeywell Research Center, Minneapolis, 1960; S. Moore, Los Alamos Scientific Laboratory, Solar Energy Group, unpublished data.

TABLE 7-22 Trombe Wall Vent Areas Relative to Various Solar Savings Fractions

Solar savings fraction, percent	Recommended vent areas relative to wall surface area, percent
25	3
50	1
75	½

SOURCE: J. Douglas Balcomb et al., *Passive Solar Design Handbook*, vol. II, U.S. Department of Energy, Washington, 1980, p. 132.

the following equation and factors drawn from Figure 7-6:

$$SSF_x = (SSF_9 - SSF_0)Y + SSF_0$$

where SSF_x = solar savings fraction of a passive solar design with night insulation other than $R9$

SSF_9 = solar savings fraction associated with $R9$ night insulation (See Table 7-18.)

SSF_0 = solar savings fraction associated with $R9$ night insulation (See Table 7-18.)

Y = fractional increase in performance compared with $R9$ night insulation (See Figure 7-6.)

TABLE 7-23 Decrease in Solar Savings Fraction as a Function of Orientation of Vertical Glazing for Direct-Gain Designs

Percentage decrease in solar savings fraction	Orientation of vertical glazing: Degrees east of south	Degrees west of south
5	10	30
10	20	40
20	42	54

SOURCE: J. Douglas Balcomb et al., *Passive Solar Design Handbook*, vol. II, U.S. Department of Energy, Washington, 1980, p. 28.

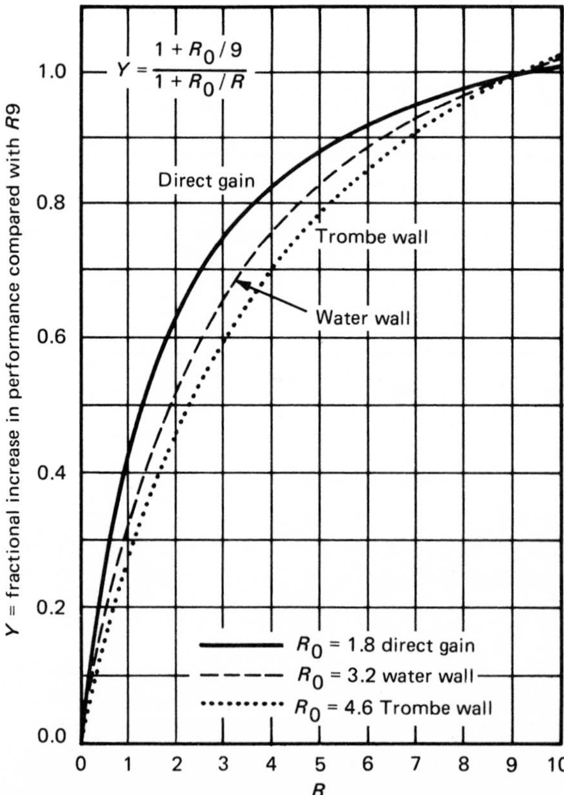

FIGURE 7-6 Effect of night insulation other than $R9$ on solar savings fraction improvements created by $R9$ insulation for direct-gain designs. [*J. Douglas Balcomb,* Passive Solar Design Handbook, *vol. II, U.S. Department of Energy, Washington, 1980, p. 54.*]

TABLE 7-24 Summary of Equations to Be Used for Estimating Winter Heating Savings

Equation	Description
Conduction	
$\Delta q_h = \Delta(U \times A)(t_i - t_o)$	7-6 Change in peak conductive heat loss rate, primarily in residential buildings
$\Delta Q_h = \Delta(U \times A) \times DH_h$	7-7 Change in winter season conductive heat loss, primarily in nonresidential buildings
Convection	
$\Delta q_{s,h} = 0.018\ \Delta V(t_i - t_o)$	7-10 Change in peak infiltration heat loss rate, primarily in residential buildings
$\Delta Q_{sh} = 0.018\ \Delta V \times DH_h$	7-12 Change in winter season infiltration heat loss, primarily in nonresidential buildings
Radiation	
$\Delta Q_h = I_h \times \Delta(A_g \times \tau) \times SF \times T_h$	7-14 Change in winter solar heat gain, primarily in nonresidential buildings
$SSF = f(LCR)$, where $LCR = \dfrac{BHLC}{A_g}$	7-16 Solar savings fraction (as a function of the load collector ratio), primarily in residential buildings

The size of the air gap between layers of insulating glass can affect the solar savings potential of passive direct-gain designs in cold climates. A minimum ½-inch gap is suggested for cold climates, while a ¼-inch gap is all right for more temperate areas.

Use of a selective surface on a mass surface that collects solar radiation will increase the effectiveness of the mass as a thermal storage medium. A selective surface such as black chromium reduces the reflection and reradiation of infrared energy back out through the glass through which it initially passed. Also, the use of a water-filled wall instead of masonry permits greater thermal storage capacity per unit of volume, thus reducing the space occupied by the wall within a building. However, leakage of water containers may be a problem.

Many more detailed and sophisticated aids for analyzing and evaluating passive solar designs are presented in the *Passive Solar Design Handbook*, and the reader is encouraged to obtain it as a basic addition to his or her architectural library.

Table 7-24 summarizes the principal equations presented in this chapter.

BIBLIOGRAPHY

ASHRAE Handbook and Product Directory—1977 Fundamentals Volume, American Society of Heating, Refrigerating and Air-Conditioning Engineers, Inc., New York, 1977.

ASHRAE Handbook and Product Directory—1980 Systems Volume, American Society of Heating, Refrigerating and Air-Conditioning Engineers, Inc., New York, 1980.

Balcomb, J. Douglas, et al.: *Passive Solar Design Handbook*, vol. II, U.S. Department of Energy, Washington, 1980.

EIGHT

COOLING SAVINGS

This chapter presents methods for estimating the thermal value of energy savings during the summer cooling season. Typically, these savings will be due to a reduction in either the peak cooling load q_c or the overall summer cooling energy consumption Q_c. As with winter heating savings, savings in q_c (Btus per hour) are typically calculated for residential buildings, whereas savings in Q_c (Btus per year) are usually calculated for nonresidential buildings. These answers will provide input to the methods for translating thermal savings into economic, that is, monetary savings presented in Chapter 6.

Cooling savings may be created by an architect or an interior designer by designs which improve the manner in which heat flows in and out of a building during the *summertime*. Designs which reduce the rate at which heat flows through walls and windows during the cooling season change the *conductive* qualities of the building. Designs which keep the sun from entering a building during the summer reduce cooling costs by changing the way in which solar *radiation* enters a building. And, finally, designs which increase internal air movement and cause evaporative cooling intervene with the *convective* qualities of a building's environment. These three modes of heat transfer and the methods for estimating their effects will be reviewed in the following sections.

CONDUCTION: CHANGES IN SUMMER HEAT GAIN

During the summer, exterior air temperatures are often higher than interior temperatures. Because heat flows in the conductive mode move from zones of high temperature to zones of lower temperature, conductive heat transfer during the summer will be from outdoor areas to the insides of buildings. In other words, buildings will *gain* heat by conduction during the summer whenever exterior temperatures are higher than indoor temperatures.

Designs which impede that inward heat flow are essentially the same as those which reduce winter heat loss by conduction. They include using greater amounts of insulation and more insulative materials. Other approaches such as reducing exterior surface area and using less glass or more insulating glass will also reduce summertime heat gain by conduction. (See Chapter 4, "Design Alternatives," for additional examples.)

Equation (7-6) from Chapter 7, therefore, is still conceptually valid for estimating conducted heat transfer during the summer:

$$\Delta q = \Delta(U \times A) \times (t_o - t_i)$$

As was briefly mentioned in Chapter 7, the impact of the sun on the exterior surfaces of walls and roofs has the effect of raising surface temperatures significantly above general outside air temperatures. Solar radiation strikes the surfaces of building materials and is partially absorbed by the materials, depending on their absorptive characteristics (see also Chapter 2).

Once radiation has been absorbed, it becomes heat. Higher exterior surface temperatures combine with air films next to the surface to create overall a higher exterior air temperature next to a building. This higher temperature is called a "sol-air temperature." Figure 8-1 provides a detailed description of sol-air temperatures.

Since the conductive heat transfer rate through a material is a function, among other things, of the difference between inside and outside temperatures on either side of the material, a higher outside temperature (given a constant indoor temperature) will cause a greater rate of heat movement toward the lower, inside temperature zone. In other words, heat gain in buildings is greater on sunny days, when the sun creates higher exterior surface air temperatures, than on cloudy days. Even on cloudy days, however, some solar radiation is moving its way through the atmosphere to buildings' surfaces. (Table 8-13 presents overcast solar diffuse radiation data for various locations.)

A method which simplifies accounting for sol-air temperatures in summer peak heat gain estimating has been developed. The general form of the conducted heat transfer equation [$\Delta q = \Delta(U \times A)(t_o - t_i)$] is used, but the temperature difference ($t_o - t_i$) is replaced by an adjusted factor called a "cooling load temperature difference" (CLTD).

The general form of the estimating method using this new variable is as follows:

$$\Delta q_c = \Delta(U \times A) \times \text{CLTD} \qquad (8\text{-}1)$$

in units,

$$\text{Btu/h} = \text{Btu/(°F·h·ft}^2) \times \text{ft}^2 \times \text{°F}$$

where Δq_c = change in peak heat flow rate during the cooling season, Btu/h
Δ = change in a quantity due to a change in architectural design
U = coefficient of conducted heat transfer, Btu/(°F·h·ft²)
A = mean cross-sectional area normal to heat flow, ft^2
CLTD = cooling load temperature difference, °F (See Tables 8-1, 8-3, and 8-4.)

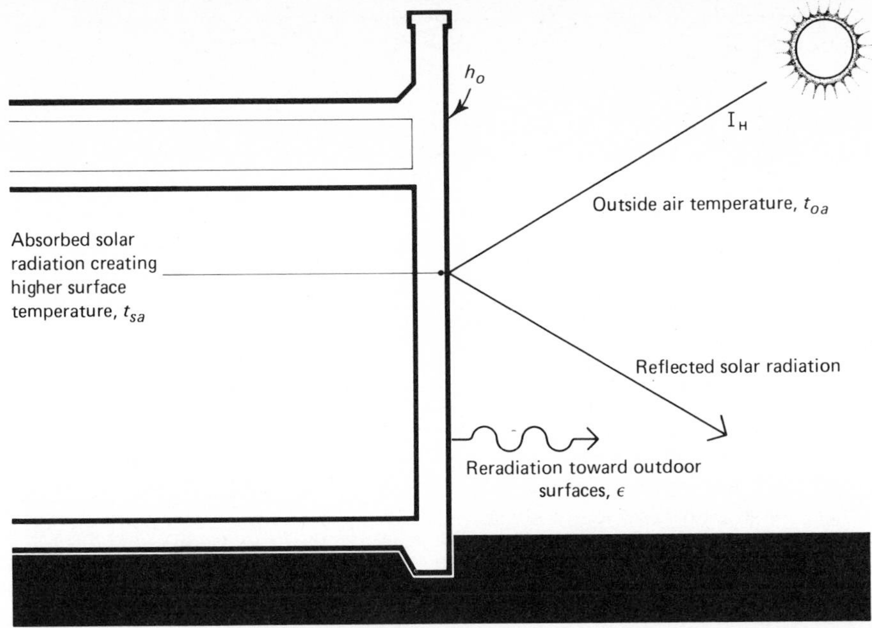

FIGURE 8-1 Explanation of sol-air temperature.

$$t_{sa} = t_{oa} + (\alpha/h_o \times I_H) - (\epsilon\Delta R/h_o)$$

in units,

$$°F = °F + \left(\frac{h \cdot ft^2 \cdot °F}{Btu} \times \frac{Btu}{ft^2 \cdot h}\right) - \left(\frac{Btu}{h \cdot ft^2} \div \frac{Btu}{h \cdot ft^2 \cdot °F}\right)$$

where t_{sa} = average sol-air temperature, °F
t_{oa} = temperature of outdoor air, °F
α = absorptance of surface for solar radiation, no units
h_o = Btu/(h·°F·ft²), surface conductance accounting also for convective heat transfer
I_H = hourly totals of solar radiation on surface in question, Btu/(ft²·h)
ϵ = hemispherical emittance of surface
R = difference between long-wave radiation incident on surface from outdoor surroundings and radiation emitted by a black body at outdoor air temperature, Btu/(h·ft²)

For horizontal surfaces, R is typically about 20 Btu/(h·ft²), $\epsilon = 1$, $h_o = 3.0$, and $\epsilon\Delta R/h_o$ = 7°F.

For vertical surfaces, it is common practice to assume that $\Delta R = 0$, so that $\epsilon\Delta R/h_o$ = 0°F.

For light-colored surfaces α/h_o = 0.15 (h·ft²·°F)/Btu.

For dark colored surfaces α/h_o = 0.30 (h·ft²·°F)/Btu. [ASHRAE Handbook and Product Directory—1977 Fundamentals Volume, *American Society of Heating, Refrigerating and Air-Conditioning Engineers, Inc., New York, 1977, p. 25.4. Reprinted by permission.*]

CLTD values in Table 8-1 are for flat roofs and those in Table 8-3 for sunlit walls. These values represent conditions for a specific latitude (40° north), date (July 21), average outdoor air temperature (85°F), and other typical conditions. Adjustments may be made to the numbers in these tables for other locations, climatic conditions, and construction materials according to the procedures described in the notes to the tables.

TABLE 8-1 Cooling Load Temperature Differences for Calculating Cooling Load from Flat Roofs (*cont.*)

Roof no.	Description of construction	Weight, lb/ft²	U-value, Btu/(h·ft²·°F)	Solar time, h 1	2	3	4	5	6	7	8	9	10
	Without suspended ceiling												
1	Steel sheet with 1-in (or 2-in) insulation	7 (8)	0.213 (0.124)	1	−2	−3	−3	−5	−3	6	19	34	49
2	1-in wood with 1-in insulation	8	0.170	6	3	0	−1	−3	−3	−2	4	14	27
3	4-in lightweight concrete	18	0.213	9	5	2	0	−2	−3	−3	1	9	20
4	2-in heavyweight concrete with 1-in (or 2-in) insulation	29	0.206 (0.122)	12	8	5	3	0	−1	−1	3	11	20
5	1-in wood with 2-in insulation	19	0.109	3	0	−3	−4	−5	−7	−6	−3	5	16
6	6-in lightweight concrete	24	0.158	22	17	13	9	6	3	1	1	3	7
7	2.5-in wood with 1-in insulation	13	0.130	29	24	20	16	13	10	7	6	6	9
8	8-in lightweight concrete	31	0.126	35	30	26	22	18	14	11	9	7	7
9	4-in heavyweight concrete with 1-in (or 2-in) insulation	52 (52)	0.200 (0.120)	25	22	18	15	12	9	8	8	10	14
10	2.5-in wood with 2-in insulation	13	0.093	30	26	23	19	16	13	10	9	8	9
11	Roof terrace system	75	0.106	34	21	28	25	22	19	16	14	13	13
12	6-in heavyweight concrete with 1-in (or 2-in) insulation	(75) 75	0.192 (0.117)	31	28	25	22	20	17	15	14	14	16
13	4-in wood with 1-in (or 2-in) insulation	17 (18)	0.106 (0.078)	38	36	33	30	28	25	22	20	18	17
	With suspended ceiling												
1	Steel sheet with 1-in (or 2-in) insulation	9 (10)	0.134 (0.092)	2	0	−2	−3	−4	−4	−1	9	23	37
2	1-in wood with 1-in insulation	10	0.115	20	15	11	8	5	3	2	3	7	13
3	4-in lightweight concrete	20	0.134	19	14	10	7	4	2	0	0	4	10
4	2-in heavyweight concrete with 1-in insulation	30	0.131	28	25	23	20	17	15	13	13	14	16
5	1-in wood with 2-in insulation	10	0.083	25	20	16	13	10	7	5	5	7	12
6	6-in lightweight concrete	26	0.109	32	28	23	19	16	13	10	8	7	8
7	2.5-in wood with 1-in insulation	15	0.096	34	31	29	26	23	21	18	16	15	15

1 *Application*. These values may be used for all normal air-conditioning estimates, usually without correction (except as noted below) in 0° to 50° north or south latitude when the load is calculated for the hottest weather.

2 *Corrections*. The values in the table were calculated for an inside temperature of 78°F and an outdoor maximum temperature of 95°F, with an outdoor daily range of 21°F. The table remains approximately correct for other outdoor maximums (93–102°F) and other outdoor daily ranges (16–34°F), provided the outdoor daily average temperature remains approximately 85°F. If the room air temperature is different from 78°F and/or the outdoor daily average temperature is different from 85°F, the following rules apply: (*a*) For room air temperature less than 78°F, add the difference between 78° and room air temperature; if greater than 78°F, subtract the difference. (*b*) For outdoor daily average temperature less than 85°F, subtract the difference between 85°F and the daily average temperature; if greater than 85°F, add the difference.

3 *Attics or other spaces between roof and ceiling*. If the ceiling is insulated and a fan is used for positive ventilation in the space between ceiling and roof, the total temperature difference for calculating the room load may be decreased by 25 percent. If the attic space contains a return duct or other air plenum, care should be taken in determining the portion of the heat gain that reaches the ceiling.

4 *Light colors*. Multiply the CLTDs in the table by 0.5. Credit should not be taken for light-colored roofs except when the permanence of light color is established by experience, as in rural areas or where there is little smoke.

11	12	13	14	15	16	17	18	19	20	21	22	23	24	Hour of maximum CLTD	Minimum CLTD	Maximum CLTD	Difference CLTD
61	71	78	79	77	70	59	45	30	18	12	8	5	3	14	−5	79	84
39	52	62	70	74	74	70	62	51	38	28	20	14	9	16	−3	74	77
32	44	55	64	70	73	71	66	57	45	34	25	18	13	16	−3	73	76
30	41	51	59	65	66	66	62	54	45	36	29	22	17	16	−1	67	68
27	39	49	57	63	64	62	57	48	37	26	18	11	7	16	−7	64	71
15	23	33	43	51	58	62	64	62	57	50	42	35	28	18	1	54	63
13	20	27	34	42	48	53	55	56	54	49	44	39	34	19	6	56	50
9	13	19	25	33	39	46	50	53	54	53	49	45	40	20	7	54	47
20	26	33	40	46	50	53	53	52	48	43	38	35	30	18	8	53	45
13	17	23	29	36	41	46	49	51	50	47	43	39	35	19	8	51	43
15	18	22	26	31	36	40	44	45	46	45	43	40	37	20	13	46	33
18	22	26	31	36	40	43	45	45	44	42	40	37	34	19	14	45	31
16	17	18	21	24	28	32	36	39	41	43	43	42	40	22	16	43	27
50	62	71	77	78	74	67	56	42	28	18	12	8	5	15	−4	78	82
21	30	40	48	55	60	62	61	58	51	44	37	30	25	17	2	62	60
19	29	39	48	56	62	65	64	61	54	46	38	30	24	17	0	65	65
20	25	30	35	39	43	46	47	46	44	41	38	35	32	18	13	47	34
18	25	33	41	48	53	57	57	56	52	46	40	34	29	18	5	57	52
11	16	22	29	36	42	48	52	54	54	51	47	42	37	20	7	54	47
16	18	21	25	30	34	38	41	43	44	44	42	40	37	21	15	44	29

5 *For solar transmission in other months.* The table values of temperature differences calculated for July 21 will be approximately correct for a roof in the following months:

Latitude	North latitude	South latitude
	Months	
0°	All months	All months
10°	All months	All months
20°	All months except November, December, and January	All months except May, June, and July
30°	March, April, May, June, July, August, and September	September, October, November, December, January, February, and March
40°	April, May, June, July, and August	October, November, December, January, and February
50°	May, June, and July	November, December, and January

6 For each 7 increase in R value owing to insulation added to the roof structures, use a CLTD for a roof whose weight is approximately the same but whose CLTD has a maximum value 2 h later. If this is not possible, owing to having already selected the roof with the longest time lag, use a Δt in the load calculation equal to the difference between the 24-h average sol-air temperature and the room air temperature.

SOURCE: *ASHRAE Handbook and Product Directory—1977 Fundamentals Volume,* American Society of Heating, Refrigerating and Air-Conditioning Engineers, Inc., New York, 1977, p. 25.7. Used by permission.

TABLE 8-1 Cooling Load Temperature Differences for Calculating Cooling Load from Flat Roofs (*cont.*)

Roof no.	Description of construction	Weight, lb/ft²	*U*-value, Btu/(h·ft²·°F)	Solar time, h 1	2	3	4	5	6	7	8	9	10
			Without suspended ceiling										
8	8-in lightweight concrete	33	0.093	39	36	33	29	26	23	20	18	15	14
9	4-in heavyweight concrete with 1-in (or 2-in) insulation	53 (54)	0.128 (0.090)	30	29	27	26	24	22	21	20	20	21
10	2.5-in wood with 2-in insulation	15	0.072	35	33	30	28	26	24	22	20	18	18
11	Roof terrace system	77	0.082	30	29	28	27	26	27	24	23	22	22
12	6-in heavyweight concrete with 1-in	77	0.125	29	28	27	26	25	24	23	22	21	21
13	4-in wood with 1-in (or 2-in) insulation	19 (20)	0.082 (0.064)	35	34	33	32	31	29	27	26	24	23

(Note that the explanation of wall groups for Table 8-3 is presented in Table 8-2.)

The calculation of a change in the annual heat gain conducted is made by using the same form as the analogous equation presented in Chapter 7.

$$\Delta Q_c = \Delta(U \times A) \times \mathrm{DH}_c \tag{8-2}$$

The degree-hours DH_c in Table 6-4 used for estimating cooling energy savings must, of course, be those which represent the cooling season. The example in the subsection "Bin Method" in Chapter 6 shows how changes in conducted heat flow during the summer may be used in calculating fuel savings. Table 6-10 presents DH_c for New York City area office buildings.

EXAMPLE

A designer decides to change his design of an apartment building from a dark-colored to a light-colored curtain wall, assuming that less radiation will be absorbed, sol-air temperatures reduced, and peak heat gain lowered. The client wishes to know the impact of such a change on the building's cooling costs. The information required for the analysis includes the following:

Location	New York City, near La Guardia Airport
Mean daily summer temperature range	16°F
Indoor room air temperature	80°F
Electrical cost	\$0.15/kWh, \$20/(kW·month) demand charge
Opaque wall area	11,200 ft²
Wall *U* value	0.091 Btu/(°F·ft²·h)
Cooling system type	30-ton central water-cooled system
Summer design peak outdoor temperature	89°F (2.5 percent)
Income tax bracket	40 percent

Note from Table 8-2 that a curtain wall is classified as a Group G wall.

11	12	13	14	15	16	17	18	19	20	21	22	23	24	Hour of maxi-mum CLTD	Mini-mum CLTD	Maxi-mum CLTD	Differ-ence CLTD
14	15	17	20	25	29	34	38	42	45	46	45	44	42	21	14	46	32
22	24	27	29	32	34	36	38	38	38	37	36	34	33	19	20	38	18
18	20	22	25	28	32	35	38	40	41	41	40	39	37	21	18	41	23
22	23	23	25	26	28	29	31	32	33	33	33	33	32	22	22	33	11
22	23	25	26	28	30	32	33	34	34	34	33	32	31	20	21	34	13
22	21	22	22	24	25	27	30	32	34	35	36	37	36	23	21	37	16

The air-conditioning system will be on from 8 A.M. to 5 P.M. each day. The peak sol-air temperature difference on all four facade orientations during that time occurs at 4 P.M. (see Table 8-3). The individual facade CLTDs at that time are as follows:

North	24°F
East	29°F
South	37°F
West	67°F
Average	39°F

Adjusting for an indoor air temperature higher than 78°F requires that (80 − 78), or 2°F, be subtracted from the CLTD (see notes at the bottom of Table 8-3).

Adjusting for the month of August when the peak cooling demand will occur,

$$\text{Adjustment factor} = (I_{DT}\ \text{August}/I_{DT}\ \text{July}) - 1(t_{sa} - t_{oa})$$

Using Table 8-4,

$$I_{DT}\ \text{August} = 474 + 474 = 948\ \text{Btu/(h}\cdot\text{ft}^2)$$

$$I_{DT}\ \text{July} = 352 + 352 = 704\ \text{Btu/(h}\cdot\text{ft}^2)$$

Summer outdoor design temperature = 89°F (See Table 6-3.)

$$t_{sa} = 89°\text{F} + [0.15\ (\text{h}\cdot\text{ft}^2\cdot°\text{F})/\text{Btu} \times 948\ \text{Btu/(ft}\cdot\text{h}) \div 13\ \text{h/day}]$$

$$= 100°\text{F}$$

$$\text{Adjustment factor} = (948/704) - 1\ (100 - 89) = 3.8°\text{F}$$

From bin data tables (Table 6-4) for the New York area, the median outdoor temperature during the hours of 10 A.M. to 5 P.M. may be observed. (The median temperature is that temperature which occurs most frequently.) The median daytime temperature for each month during the cooling season is presented below:

June	77°F
July	82°F
August	77°F
September	75°F
Average	78°F

TABLE 8-2 Wall Construction Group Description

Group number	Description of construction	Weight, lb/ft²	*U* value, Btu/(h·ft²·°F)	Code numbers of layers
4-in face brick + (brick)				
C	Air space + 4-in face brick	83	0.358	A0,A2,B1,A2,E0
D	4-in common brick	90	0.415	A0,A2,C4,E1,E0
C	1-in insulation or air space + 4-in common brick	90	0.174–0.301	A0,A2,C4,B1/B2,E1,E0
B	2-in insulation + 4-in common brick	88	0.111	A0,A2,B2,C4,E1,E0
B	8-in common brick	130	0.302	A0,A2,C9,E1,E0
A	Insulation or air space + 8-in common brick	130	0.154–0.243	A0,A2,C9,B1/B2,E1,E0
4-in face brick + (heavyweight concrete)				
C	Air space + 2-in concrete	94	0.350	A0,A2,B1,C5,E1,E0
B	2-in insulation + 4-in concrete	97	0.116	A0,A2,B3,C5,E1,E0
A	Air space or insulation + 8-in or more of concrete	143–190	0.110–0.112	A0,A2,B1,C10/11,E1,E0
4-in face brick + (lightweight or heavyweight concrete block)				
E	4-in block	62	0.319	A0,A2,C2,E1,E0
D	Air space or insulation + 4-in block	62	0.153–0.246	A0,A2,C2,B1/B2,E1,E0
D	8-in block	70	0.274	A0,A2,C7,A6,E0
C	Air space or 1-in insulation + 6-in or 8-in block	73–89	0.221–0.275	A0,A2,B1,C7/C8,E1,E0
B	2-in insulation + 8-in block	89	0.096–0.107	A0,A2,B3,C7/C8,E1,E0
4-in face brick + (clay tile)				
D	4-in tile	71	0.381	A0,A2,C1,E1,E0
D	Air space + 4-in tile	71	0.281	A0,A2,C1,B1,E1,E0
C	Insulation + 4-in tile	71	0.169	A0,A2,C1,B2,E1,E0
C	8-in tile	96	0.275	A0,A2,C6,E1,E0
B	Air space or 1-in insulation + 8-in tile	96	0.142–0.221	A0,A2,C6,B1/B2,E1,E0
A	2-in insulation + 8-in tile	97	0.097	A0,A2,B3,C6,E1,E0
Heavyweight concrete wall + (finish)				
E	4-in concrete	63	0.585	A0,A1,C5,E1,E0
D	4-in concrete + 1-in or 2-in insulation	63	0.119–0.200	A0,A1,C5,B2/B3,E1,E0
C	2-in insulation + 4-in concrete	63	0.119	A0,A1,B6,C5,E1,E0
C	8-in concrete	109	0.490	A0,A1,C10,E1,E0
B	8-in concrete + 1-in or 2-in insulation	110	0.115–0.187	A0,A1,C10,B5/B5,E1,E0
A	2-in insulation + 8-in concrete	110	0.115	A0,A1,B3,C10,E1,E0
B	12-in concrete	156	0.421	A0,A1,C11,E1,E0
A	12-in concrete + insulation	156	0.113	A0,C11,B6,A6,E0
Lightweight and heavyweight concrete block + (finish)				
F	4-in block + air space or insulation	29	0.161–0.263	A0,A1,C2,B1/B2,E1,E0
E	2-in insulation + 4-in block	29–37	0.105–0.114	A0,A1,B1,C2/C3,E1,E0
E	8-in block	47–51	0.294–0.402	A0,A1,C7/C8,E1,E0
D	8-in block + air space or insulation	41–57	0.149–0.173	A0,A1,C7/C8,B2,E1,E0
Clay tile + (finish)				
F	4-in tile	39	0.419	A0,A1,C1,E1,E0
F	4-in tile + air space	39	0.303	A0,A1,C1,B1,E1,E0
E	4-in tile + 1-in insulation	39	0.175	A0,A1,C1,B2,E1,E0
D	2-in insulation + 4-in tile	40	0.110	A0,A1,B1,C1,E1,E0
D	8-in tile	63	0.296	A0,A1,C6,E1,E0
C	8-in tile + air space or 1-in insulation	63	0.151–0.231	A0,A1,C6,B1/B2,E1,E0
B	2-in insulation + 8-in tile	63	0.099	A0,A1,B1,C6,E1,E0

Group number	Description of construction	Weight, lb/ft²	U value, Btu/(h·ft²·°F)	Code numbers of layers
Metal curtain wall				
G	With or without air space + 1-in, 2-in, or 3-in insulation	5–6	0.091–0.230	A0,A3,B5/B6/B12,A3,E0
Frame wall				
G	1-in to 3-in insulation	16	0.081–0.178	A0,A1,B1,B2/B3/B4,E1,E0

SOURCE: *ASHRAE Handbook and Product Directory—1977 Fundamentals Volume*, American Society of Heating, Refrigerating and Air-Conditioning Engineers, Inc., New York, 1977, p. 25.8. Reprinted by permission.

The difference between the average outdoor temperature on which the sol-air temperature differences in Table 8-3 are based and the average monthly median temperature during the cooling season is 85°F − 78°F = 7°F.

The revised peak CLTD for this example is then:

Average peak CLTD	39°F
Adjustment for:	
80°F inside temperature	− 2°F
August	+ 4°F
78°F average	− 7°F
	34°F

According to Note 3 of Table 8-3, if a light-colored surface is used, the CLTD value may be reduced by multiplying it by 0.65:

$$0.65 \times 34°F = 22°F$$

The use of a light-colored surface will result in a reduction of the following magnitude in the CLTD for a dark-colored wall:

$$34°F - 22°F = 12°F$$

The design heat gain reduction is then calculated as follows:

$$\Delta q_c = 0.091 \text{ Btu/(°F·h·ft}^2) \times 11{,}200 \text{ ft}^2 \times 12°F \quad (8\text{-}1)$$

$$= 12{,}230 \text{ Btu/h}$$

Using the method presented in Chapter 6, the value of these cooling savings is calculated below:

$$B_c = 0.94 \text{ kW/ton} \times \$0.15/\text{kWh} \times 500 \text{ h} \times [12{,}230 \text{ Btu/h} \div 12{,}000 \text{ Btu/(ton·h)}] = \$71$$ [See Equation (6-4).]

The reduction in demand charges is estimated below:

$$B_c = [12{,}230 \text{ Btu/h} \div 12{,}000 \text{ Btu/(ton·h)}] \times 0.94 \text{ kW/ton} \times \$20/(\text{kW·month}) \times 3 \text{ months} = \$57$$

The apartment building is operated as a business, so the aftertax value of these savings is

$$B_c = (\$71 + \$57) \times (1 - 0.40) = \$77$$

(Cont. on p. 211)

TABLE 8-3 Cooling Load Temperature Differences for Calculating Cooling Load from Sunlit Walls

North latitude, wall facing	Solar time, h													
	1	2	3	4	5	6	7	8	9	10	11	12	13	14
Group A walls														
North	14	14	14	13	13	13	12	12	11	11	10	10	10	10
Northeast	19	19	19	18	17	17	16	15	15	15	15	15	16	16
East	24	24	23	23	22	21	20	19	19	18	19	19	20	21
Southeast	24	23	23	22	21	20	20	19	18	18	18	18	18	19
South	20	20	19	19	18	18	17	16	16	15	14	14	14	14
Southwest	25	25	25	24	24	23	22	21	20	19	19	18	17	17
West	27	27	26	26	25	24	24	23	22	21	20	19	19	18
Northwest	21	21	21	20	20	19	19	18	17	16	16	15	15	14
Group B walls														
North	15	14	14	13	12	11	11	10	9	9	9	8	9	9
Northeast	19	18	17	16	15	14	13	12	12	13	14	15	16	17
East	23	22	21	20	18	17	16	15	15	15	17	19	21	22
Southeast	23	22	21	20	18	17	16	15	14	14	15	16	18	20
South	21	20	19	18	17	15	14	13	12	11	11	11	11	12
Southwest	27	26	25	24	22	21	19	18	16	15	14	14	13	13
West	29	28	27	26	24	23	21	19	18	17	16	15	14	14
Northwest	23	22	21	20	19	18	17	15	14	13	12	12	12	11
Group C walls														
North	15	14	13	12	11	10	9	8	8	7	7	8	8	9
Northeast	19	17	16	14	13	11	10	10	11	13	15	17	19	20
East	22	21	19	17	15	14	12	12	14	16	19	22	29	27
Southeast	22	21	19	17	15	14	12	12	12	13	16	19	22	24
South	21	19	18	16	15	13	12	10	9	9	9	10	11	14
Southwest	29	27	25	22	20	18	16	15	13	12	11	11	11	13
West	31	29	27	25	22	20	18	16	14	13	12	12	12	13
Northwest	25	23	21	20	18	16	14	13	11	10	10	10	10	11
Group D walls														
North	15	13	12	10	9	7	6	6	6	6	6	7	8	10
Northeast	17	15	13	11	10	8	7	8	10	14	17	20	22	23
East	19	17	15	13	11	9	8	9	12	17	22	27	30	32
Southeast	20	17	15	13	11	10	8	8	10	13	17	22	26	29
South	19	17	15	13	11	9	8	7	6	6	7	9	12	16
Southwest	28	25	22	19	16	14	12	10	9	8	8	8	10	12
West	31	27	24	21	18	15	13	11	10	9	9	9	10	11
Northwest	25	22	19	17	14	12	10	9	8	7	7	8	9	10
Group E walls														
North	12	10	8	7	5	4	3	4	5	6	7	9	11	13
Northeast	13	11	9	7	6	4	5	9	15	20	24	25	25	26
East	14	12	10	8	6	5	6	11	18	26	33	36	38	37
Southeast	15	12	10	8	7	5	5	8	12	19	25	31	35	37
South	15	12	10	8	7	5	4	3	4	5	9	13	19	24
Southwest	22	18	15	12	10	8	6	5	5	6	7	9	12	18
West	25	21	17	14	11	9	7	6	6	6	7	9	11	14
Northwest	20	17	14	11	9	7	6	5	5	5	6	8	10	13

15	16	17	18	19	20	21	22	23	24	Hours of maximum CLTD	Minimum CLTD	Maximum CLTD	Difference CLTD
10	10	11	11	12	12	13	13	14	14	2	10	14	4
17	18	18	18	19	19	20	20	20	20	22	15	20	5
22	23	24	24	25	25	25	25	25	25	22	18	25	7
20	21	22	23	23	24	24	24	24	24	22	18	24	6
14	15	16	17	18	19	19	20	20	20	23	14	20	6
17	17	18	19	20	22	23	24	25	25	24	17	25	8
18	18	18	19	20	22	23	25	26	26	1	18	27	9
14	14	15	15	16	17	18	19	20	21	1	14	21	7
9	10	11	12	13	14	14	15	15	15	24	8	15	7
18	19	19	20	20	21	21	21	20	20	21	12	21	9
24	25	26	26	27	27	26	26	25	24	20	15	27	12
21	23	24	25	26	26	26	26	25	24	21	14	26	12
14	15	17	19	20	21	22	22	22	21	23	11	22	11
14	15	17	20	22	25	27	28	28	28	24	13	28	15
14	15	17	19	22	25	27	29	29	30	24	14	30	16
12	12	13	15	17	19	21	22	23	23	24	11	23	9
10	12	13	14	15	16	17	17	17	16	22	7	17	10
21	22	22	23	23	23	23	22	21	20	20	10	23	13
29	29	30	30	30	29	28	27	26	24	18	12	30	18
26	28	29	29	29	29	28	27	26	24	19	12	29	17
17	20	22	24	25	26	25	25	24	22	20	9	26	17
15	18	22	26	29	32	33	33	32	31	22	11	33	22
14	16	20	24	29	32	35	35	35	33	22	12	35	23
12	13	15	18	22	25	27	27	27	26	22	10	27	17
12	13	15	17	18	19	19	19	18	16	21	6	19	13
23	24	24	25	25	24	23	22	20	18	19	7	25	18
33	33	32	32	31	30	28	26	24	22	16	8	33	25
31	32	32	32	31	30	28	26	24	22	17	8	32	24
20	24	27	29	29	29	27	26	24	22	19	6	29	23
16	21	27	32	36	38	38	37	34	31	21	8	38	30
14	18	24	30	36	40	41	40	38	34	21	9	41	32
12	14	18	22	27	31	32	32	30	27	22	7	32	25
15	17	19	20	21	23	20	18	16	14	20	3	22	19
26	26	26	26	25	24	22	19	17	15	16	4	26	22
36	34	33	32	30	28	25	22	20	17	13	5	38	33
37	36	34	33	31	28	26	23	20	17	15	5	37	32
29	32	34	33	31	29	26	23	20	17	17	3	34	31
24	32	38	43	45	44	40	35	30	26	19	5	45	40
20	27	36	43	49	49	45	40	34	29	20	6	49	43
16	20	26	32	37	38	36	32	28	24	20	5	38	33

TABLE 8-3 Cooling Load Temperature Differences for Calculating Cooling Load from Sunlit Walls (*cont.*)

North latitude, wall facing	Solar time, h													
	1	2	3	4	5	6	7	8	9	10	11	12	13	14
Group F walls														
North	8	6	5	3	2	1	2	4	6	7	9	11	14	17
Northeast	9	7	5	3	2	1	5	14	23	28	30	29	28	27
East	10	7	6	4	3	2	6	17	28	38	44	45	43	39
Southeast	10	7	6	4	3	2	4	10	19	28	36	41	43	42
South	10	8	6	4	3	2	1	1	3	7	13	20	27	34
Southwest	15	11	9	6	5	3	2	2	4	5	8	11	17	26
West	17	13	10	7	5	4	3	3	4	6	8	11	14	20
Northwest	14	10	8	6	4	3	2	2	3	5	8	10	13	15
Group G walls														
North	3	2	1	0	−1	2	7	8	9	12	15	18	21	23
Northeast	3	2	1	0	−1	9	27	36	39	35	30	26	26	27
East	4	2	1	0	−1	11	31	47	54	55	50	40	33	31
Southeast	4	2	1	0	−1	5	18	32	42	49	51	48	42	36
South	4	2	1	0	−1	0	1	5	12	22	31	39	45	46
Southwest	5	4	3	1	0	0	2	5	8	12	16	26	38	50
West	6	5	3	2	1	1	2	5	8	11	15	19	27	41
Northwest	5	3	2	1	0	0	2	5	8	11	15	18	21	27

NOTES:

1 *Application.* These values may be used for all normal air-conditioning estimates, usually without correction (except as noted below) when the load is calculated for the hottest weather.

2 *Corrections.* The values in the table were calculated for an inside temperature of 78°F and an outdoor daily range of 21°F. The table remains approximately correct for other outdoor maximums (93–102°F) and other outdoor daily ranges (16–34°F), provided the outdoor daily average temperature remains approximately 85°F. If the room temperature is different from 78°F and/or the outdoor daily average temperature is different from 85°F, the following rules apply: (*a*) For room air temperature less than 78°F, add the difference between 78°F and room air temperature; if greater than 78°F, subtract the difference. (*b*) For outdoor daily average temperature more than 85°F, subtract the difference between 85°F and the daily average temperature; if lower than 85°F, add the difference. The table values will be approximately correct for the east or west wall in any latitude (0 to 50° north or south) during the hottest weather.

3 *Color of exterior surface of wall.* For light colors, multiply the wall cooling load temperature difference in the table by 0.65. Use temperature differences for light walls only when the permanence of the light wall is estab-

TABLE 8-4 Cooling Load Temperature Differences for Conduction through Glass

Hour	2	4	6	8	10	12	14	16	18	20	22	24
CLTD, °F	0	−2	−2	0	4	9	13	14	12	8	4	2

CORRECTIONS: The values in the table were calculated for an inside temperature of 78°F and an outdoor maximum temperature of 95°F with an outdoor daily range of 21°F. The table remains approximately correct for other outdoor maximums (93–102°F) and other outdoor daily ranges (16–34°F), provided the outdoor daily average temperature remains approximately 85°F. If the room air temperature is different from 78°F and/or the outdoor daily average temperature is different from 85°F, the following rules apply: (1) For room air temperature less than 78°F, add the difference between 78°F and room air temperature; if greater than 78°F, subtract the difference. (2) For outdoor daily average temperature less than 85°F, subtract the difference between 85°F and the daily average temperature; if greater than 85°F, add the difference.

SOURCE: *ASHRAE Handbook and Product Directory—1977 Fundamentals Volume,* American Society of Heating, Refrigerating and Air-Conditioning Engineers, Inc., New York, 1977, p. 25.11. Reprinted by permission.

15	16	17	18	19	20	21	22	23	24	Hours of maximum CLTD	Minimum CLTD	Maximum CLTD	Difference CLTD
19	21	22	23	24	23	20	16	13	11	19	1	23	23
27	27	27	26	24	22	19	16	13	11	11	1	30	29
36	34	32	30	27	24	21	17	15	12	12	2	45	43
39	36	34	31	28	25	21	18	15	12	13	2	43	41
38	39	38	35	31	26	22	18	15	12	16	1	39	38
35	44	50	53	52	45	37	28	23	18	18	2	53	48
28	39	49	57	60	54	43	34	27	21	19	3	60	57
21	27	35	42	46	43	35	28	22	18	19	2	46	44
24	24	25	26	22	15	11	9	7	5	18	−1	26	27
27	26	25	22	18	14	11	9	7	5	9	−1	39	40
30	29	27	24	19	15	12	10	8	6	10	−1	55	56
32	30	27	24	19	15	12	10	8	6	11	−1	51	52
43	37	31	25	20	15	12	10	8	5	14	−1	46	47
59	63	61	52	37	24	17	13	10	8	16	0	63	63
56	67	72	67	48	29	20	15	11	8	17	1	72	71
37	47	55	55	41	25	17	13	10	7	18	0	55	55

lished by experience. For cream colors, use the light wall values. For medium colors, interpolate halfway between the dark and light values. Medium colors are medium blue and green, bright red, light brown, unpainted wood, and natural-color concrete. Dark blue, red, brown, and green are considered dark colors.

4 For each 7 increase in R value due to insulation added to the wall structures, use the CLTD for the wall group with the next higher letter in the alphabet. When the insulation is added to the exterior of the construction rather than the interior, use the CLTD for the wall group two letters higher. If this is not possible, owing to having already selected a wall in Group A, use a Δt for the load calculation equal to the difference between the 24-hour average sol-air temperature and the room air temperature.

SOURCE: *ASHRAE Handbook and Product Directory—1977 Fundamentals Volume*, American Society of Heating, Refrigerating and Air-Conditioning Engineers, Inc., New York, 1977, p. 25.9. Reprinted by permission.

The reduction in peak cooling load is slightly more than 1 ton [12,230 Btu/h ÷ 12,000 Btu/(ton·h) = 1.02 ton], so there are no cooling equipment installation cost savings.

The change in color from dark to light for the curtain wall does not cost anything extra, so the building owner simply saves money each year if the color change is made. Winter fuel costs will not be significantly affected by the change in color because cold air temperatures dominate, resulting in insignificant changes in average sol-air temperatures and no change in the peak heating load, which usually occurs at night or on cloudy days.

RADIATION: CHANGES IN SUMMER SOLAR HEAT GAIN

Designs which reduce solar heat gains include exterior shading devices, interior shading devices, designs reducing glass area, and those increasing the reflective and/or heat-absorbing qualities of glass in a building. Changing the transmission qualities of glass simply to reduce summertime solar heat gains often has negative implications at other times of the year or on other energy-consuming systems. In residential buildings, for example, such a strategy for south-facing windows will also reduce valuable wintertime solar heat gain. For office buildings, reducing solar heat gain with tinted or reflective glass will also reduce valuable natural-light inputs.

Interior shading devices are not as effective as exterior shades in reducing summertime solar heat gain. With their use solar radiation has a chance to reach the inside of a building and be partially converted into heat as well as partially reflected back out.

Exterior shading devices are perhaps the best approach to reducing summer solar heat gain. They can be sized so that winter sun is admitted to a building and summer sun is kept out.

The range of horizontal shade designs is large. The general rule, however, is that south-facing facades should have horizontal shades, while east- and west-facing facades should have either horizontal shades or a combination of vertical and horizontal shades.

As in the method for estimating winter solar heat gain, summer heat gain calculation methods account for direct solar radiation, the shading and transmission characteristics of the materials and components making up the glazing system, and the thermal storage effects of interior construction.

The general form of the estimating method for change in *peak* solar heat gain is presented below:

$$\Delta q_c = \Delta(A \times SC) \times SHGF \times CLF \qquad (8\text{-}3)$$

in units,

$$\text{Btu/h} = \text{ft}^2 \times \text{Btu/(h}\cdot\text{ft}^2)$$

where Δq_c = change in peak solar heat gain rate, Btu/h
Δ = change in a quantity due to an architectural design change
A = area of glazing, ft^2
SC = shading coefficient, no units, where SC = 1.00 represents clear ⅛-in-thick glass (See Tables 8-8 to 8-12.)
SHGF = maximum solar heat gain factor $Btu/(h\cdot ft^2)$ (See Table 8-5.)
CLF = Cooling load factor, which accounts for the time lag between the time at which radiant solar energy enters a space and the time and efficiency with which it becomes part of a building's thermal load, no units (See Tables 8-6 and 8-7. The maximum factor which meets the conditions of the problem being analyzed should be selected from these tables.)

The designer should note that the shading coefficient SC used above is based on clear ⅛-inch-thick glass as a reference point. For other calculations not involving the above equation, the actual transmittance τ of glass may have to be used to account for transmission losses through glass. Figure 8-2 shows shading coefficients and transmittances for a number of glass types.

For nonresidential buildings, a designer should calculate a change in seasonal cooling energy use ΔQ. The equation to be used for this purpose takes the same

TABLE 8-5 Maximum Solar Heat Gain Factors, Btu/(h · ft²)

Month	N	NE or NW	E or W	SE or SW	S	Horizontal	N	NE or NW	E or W	SE or SW	S	Horizontal
	16° north latitude						24° north latitude					
January	30	55	210	251	199	248	27	41	190	253	227	214
February	33	96	231	233	154	275	30	80	220	243	192	249
March	35	140	239	197	93	291	34	124	234	214	137	275
April	39	172	227	150	45	289	37	159	228	169	75	283
May	52	189	215	115	41	282	43	178	218	132	46	282
June	66	194	207	99	41	277	56	184	212	117	43	279
July	55	187	210	111	42	277	45	176	213	129	46	278
August	41	168	219	143	46	282	38	156	220	162	72	277
September	36	134	227	191	93	282	35	119	222	206	134	266
October	33	95	223	225	150	270	31	79	211	235	187	244
November	30	55	206	247	196	246	27	42	187	249	224	213
December	29	41	198	254	213	234	25	29	179	252	237	199
	32° north latitude						40° north latitude					
January	24	29	175	249	246	176	20	20	154	241	254	133
February	27	65	205	248	221	217	24	50	186	246	241	180
March	32	107	227	227	176	252	29	93	218	236	206	223
April	36	146	227	187	115	271	34	140	224	203	154	252
May	38	170	220	155	74	277	37	165	220	175	113	265
June	47	176	214	139	60	276	48	172	215	161	95	268
July	40	167	215	150	72	273	38	163	216	170	109	262
August	37	141	219	181	111	265	35	135	216	196	149	247
September	33	103	215	218	171	244	30	87	205	226	200	215
October	28	63	195	239	215	213	25	49	180	238	234	177
November	24	29	173	245	243	175	18	20	151	237	250	132
December	22	22	162	246	252	158	18	18	135	232	253	112
	48° north latitude						56° north latitude					
January	15	15	118	216	245	85	10	10	74	169	205	40
February	20	36	168	242	250	138	16	21	139	223	244	91
March	26	80	204	239	228	188	22	65	185	238	241	149
April	31	132	219	215	186	226	28	123	211	223	210	195
May	35	158	218	192	150	247	36	149	215	206	181	222
June	47	165	215	180	134	252	53	161	213	195	167	231
July	37	156	214	187	146	244	37	147	211	201	177	221
August	33	128	211	208	180	223	30	119	203	215	203	193
September	27	72	191	228	220	182	23	58	171	227	231	144
October	21	35	161	233	242	136	16	20	132	213	234	91
November	15	15	115	212	240	85	10	10	72	165	200	40
December	13	13	91	195	233	64	7	7	46	135	170	23

SOURCE: *ASHRAE Handbook and Product Directory—1977 Fundamentals Volume*, American Society of Heating, Refrigerating and Air-Conditioning Engineers, Inc., New York, 1977, p. 25.12. Reprinted by permission.

form as the heating season radiation equation [Equation (7-14)], except that data reflecting the cooling season must be used for the appropriate variables:

$$\Delta Q_c = \Delta(I_c \times A_g \times \tau \times \mathrm{SF} \times T_c) \tag{8-4}$$

in units,

$$\text{Btu/year} = \text{Btu/(ft}^2\cdot\text{day)} \times \text{ft}^2 \times \text{days/year}$$

where ΔQ_c = change in annual cooling energy consumption, Btu/year
Δ = change in a quantity due to a change in architectural design

TABLE 8-6 Cooling Load Factors for Glass without Interior Shading (Including Reflective and Heat-Absorbing Glass)

North latitude fenestration facing	Room construction	1	2	3	4	5	6	7	8	9
North	L	0.17	0.14	0.11	0.09	0.08	0.33	0.42	0.48	0.56
	M	0.23	0.20	0.18	0.16	0.14	0.34	0.41	0.46	0.52
	H	0.25	0.23	0.21	0.20	0.19	0.38	0.45	0.50	0.55
Northeast	L	0.04	0.04	0.03	0.02	0.02	0.23	0.41	0.51	0.51
	M	0.07	0.06	0.05	0.05	0.04	0.21	0.36	0.44	0.45
	H	0.09	0.08	0.08	0.07	0.07	0.23	0.37	0.44	0.44
East	L	0.04	0.04	0.03	0.02	0.02	0.19	0.37	0.51	0.57
	M	0.07	0.06	0.06	0.05	0.04	0.18	0.33	0.44	0.50
	H	0.09	0.09	0.08	0.08	0.07	0.21	0.34	0.45	0.50
Southeast	L	0.05	0.04	0.04	0.03	0.02	0.13	0.28	0.43	0.55
	M	0.09	0.08	0.07	0.06	0.05	0.14	0.26	0.38	0.48
	H	0.11	0.10	0.10	0.09	0.08	0.17	0.28	0.40	0.49
South	L	0.08	0.07	0.05	0.04	0.04	0.06	0.09	0.14	0.22
	M	0.12	0.11	0.09	0.08	0.07	0.08	0.11	0.14	0.21
	H	0.13	0.12	0.12	0.11	0.10	0.12	0.14	0.17	0.24
Southwest	L	0.12	0.10	0.08	0.06	0.05	0.06	0.08	0.10	0.12
	M	0.15	0.13	0.12	0.10	0.09	0.09	0.10	0.12	0.13
	H	0.15	0.14	0.13	0.12	0.11	0.12	0.13	0.14	0.16
West	L	0.12	0.10	0.08	0.07	0.05	0.06	0.07	0.08	0.10
	M	0.15	0.13	0.11	0.10	0.09	0.09	0.09	0.10	0.11
	H	0.14	0.13	0.12	0.11	0.10	0.11	0.12	0.13	0.13
Northwest	L	0.11	0.09	0.08	0.06	0.05	0.06	0.08	0.10	0.12
	M	0.14	0.12	0.11	0.09	0.08	0.09	0.10	0.11	0.13
	H	0.14	0.12	0.11	0.11	0.10	0.11	0.12	0.13	0.15
Horizontal	L	0.11	0.09	0.07	0.06	0.05	0.07	0.14	0.24	0.36
	M	0.16	0.14	0.12	0.11	0.09	0.11	0.16	0.24	0.33
	H	0.17	0.16	0.15	0.14	0.13	0.15	0.20	0.27	0.36

NOTES:
L = Light construction: frame exterior wall, 2-in concrete floor slab, approximately 30 lb of material per square foot of floor area.
M = Medium construction: 4-in concrete exterior wall, 4-in concrete floor slab, approximately 70 lb of building material per square foot of floor area.
H = Heavy construction: 6-in concrete exterior wall, 6-in concrete floor slab, approximately 130 lb of building materials per square foot of floor area.

SOURCE: *ASHRAE Handbook and Product Directory—1977 Fundamentals Volume,* American Society of Heating, Refrigerating and Air-Conditioning Engineers, Inc., New York, p. 25.13. Reprinted by permission.

I_c = *average* daily insolation (solar radiation) incident on a surface during the cooling season, Btu/(ft^2·day) (See Table 7-13.)
A_g = glass area, ft^2
τ = solar heat transmittance of glass, no units (See Table 7-16.)
SF = shading factor, no units (If no shading device is proposed, this factor would be 1.0. Specific shading factors must be calculated for each design proposal by considering diffuse as well as direct solar radiation.)
T_c = time, days/year, reflecting the number of workdays during the cooling season for commercial buildings

Solar time, h														
10	11	12	13	14	15	16	17	18	19	20	21	22	23	24
0.63	0.71	0.76	0.80	0.82	0.82	0.79	0.80	0.84	0.61	0.48	0.38	0.31	0.25	0.20
0.59	0.65	0.70	0.73	0.75	0.76	0.74	0.75	0.79	0.61	0.50	0.42	0.36	0.31	0.27
0.60	0.65	0.69	0.72	0.73	0.72	0.70	0.70	0.74	0.57	0.46	0.39	0.34	0.31	0.28
0.45	0.39	0.36	0.33	0.31	0.28	0.26	0.23	0.19	0.15	0.12	0.10	0.08	0.06	0.05
0.40	0.36	0.33	0.31	0.30	0.28	0.26	0.23	0.21	0.17	0.15	0.13	0.11	0.09	0.08
0.39	0.34	0.31	0.29	0.27	0.26	0.24	0.22	0.20	0.16	0.14	0.13	0.12	0.11	0.10
0.57	0.51	0.42	0.36	0.32	0.29	0.25	0.22	0.19	0.14	0.12	0.09	0.08	0.06	0.05
0.51	0.45	0.39	0.35	0.32	0.29	0.26	0.23	0.21	0.17	0.15	0.13	0.11	0.10	0.08
0.49	0.43	0.36	0.32	0.29	0.26	0.24	0.22	0.19	0.17	0.15	0.13	0.12	0.11	0.10
0.62	0.63	0.57	0.48	0.42	0.37	0.33	0.28	0.24	0.19	0.15	0.12	0.10	0.08	0.07
0.54	0.55	0.51	0.45	0.40	0.36	0.33	0.29	0.25	0.21	0.18	0.16	0.14	0.12	0.10
0.53	0.53	0.48	0.41	0.36	0.33	0.30	0.27	0.24	0.20	0.18	0.16	0.14	0.13	0.12
0.34	0.48	0.59	0.65	0.65	0.59	0.50	0.43	0.36	0.28	0.22	0.18	0.15	0.12	0.10
0.31	0.42	0.52	0.57	0.58	0.53	0.47	0.41	0.36	0.29	0.25	0.21	0.18	0.16	0.14
0.33	0.43	0.51	0.56	0.55	0.50	0.43	0.38	0.32	0.26	0.22	0.20	0.18	0.16	0.15
0.14	0.16	0.24	0.36	0.49	0.60	0.66	0.66	0.58	0.43	0.33	0.27	0.22	0.18	0.14
0.15	0.17	0.23	0.33	0.44	0.53	0.58	0.59	0.53	0.41	0.33	0.28	0.24	0.21	0.18
0.17	0.19	0.25	0.34	0.44	0.52	0.56	0.56	0.49	0.37	0.30	0.25	0.21	0.19	0.17
0.11	0.13	0.14	0.20	0.32	0.45	0.57	0.64	0.61	0.44	0.34	0.27	0.22	0.18	0.14
0.12	0.13	0.14	0.19	0.29	0.40	0.50	0.56	0.55	0.41	0.33	0.27	0.23	0.20	0.17
0.14	0.15	0.16	0.21	0.30	0.40	0.49	0.54	0.52	0.38	0.30	0.24	0.21	0.18	0.16
0.14	0.16	0.17	0.19	0.23	0.33	0.47	0.59	0.60	0.43	0.33	0.26	0.21	0.17	0.14
0.14	0.16	0.17	0.18	0.21	0.30	0.42	0.51	0.53	0.39	0.32	0.26	0.22	0.19	0.16
0.16	0.18	0.19	0.19	0.22	0.30	0.41	0.50	0.51	0.36	0.29	0.23	0.20	0.17	0.15
0.48	0.58	0.66	0.72	0.74	0.73	0.67	0.59	0.47	0.37	0.30	0.24	0.19	0.16	0.13
0.43	0.52	0.59	0.64	0.67	0.66	0.62	0.55	0.47	0.38	0.32	0.28	0.24	0.21	0.18
0.45	0.52	0.59	0.62	0.64	0.62	0.58	0.51	0.42	0.35	0.29	0.26	0.23	0.21	0.19

EXAMPLE

An architect decides to add balconies to the south facade of the apartment building she is designing. The balconies will cost $1000 each to install but will provide shade during the summer to the windows of the apartment below. She decides to analyze the impact of the balconies on the air-conditioning requirements of a two-bedroom apartment. The data required for the analysis are presented below and in Figure 8-3.

Cost	Two balconies at $1000 each = $2000
Number of south-facing apartments	20
Glass area	160 ft² (6 ft 8 in x 24 ft)
Location	New York City

TABLE 8-7 Cooling Load Factors for Glass with Interior Shading (Including Reflective and Heat-Absorbing Glass)

North latitude fenestration facing	Room construction	1	2	3	4	5	6	7	8	9
North	L	0.07	0.05	0.04	0.04	0.05	0.70	0.65	0.65	0.74
	M	0.08	0.07	0.06	0.06	0.07	0.73	0.66	0.65	0.73
	H	0.09	0.09	0.08	0.07	0.09	0.75	0.67	0.66	0.74
Northeast	L	0.02	0.01	0.01	0.01	0.02	0.55	0.76	0.75	0.60
	M	0.03	0.02	0.02	0.02	0.02	0.56	0.76	0.74	0.58
	H	0.03	0.03	0.03	0.03	0.04	0.57	0.77	0.74	0.58
East	L	0.02	0.01	0.01	0.01	0.01	0.45	0.71	0.80	0.77
	M	0.03	0.02	0.02	0.02	0.02	0.47	0.72	0.80	0.76
	H	0.04	0.03	0.03	0.03	0.03	0.48	0.72	0.80	0.75
Southeast	L	0.02	0.02	0.01	0.01	0.01	0.29	0.56	0.74	0.82
	M	0.03	0.03	0.02	0.02	0.02	0.30	0.56	0.74	0.81
	H	0.04	0.04	0.04	0.03	0.04	0.31	0.57	0.74	0.81
South	L	0.03	0.03	0.02	0.02	0.02	0.08	0.15	0.22	0.37
	M	0.04	0.04	0.03	0.03	0.03	0.09	0.16	0.22	0.38
	H	0.05	0.05	0.04	0.04	0.04	0.11	0.17	0.24	0.39
Southwest	L	0.05	0.04	0.03	0.02	0.02	0.06	0.10	0.13	0.16
	M	0.06	0.05	0.04	0.04	0.03	0.07	0.11	0.14	0.16
	H	0.06	0.05	0.05	0.04	0.04	0.08	0.12	0.15	0.18
West	L	0.05	0.04	0.03	0.02	0.02	0.05	0.08	0.11	0.13
	M	0.05	0.05	0.04	0.04	0.03	0.06	0.09	0.11	0.13
	H	0.05	0.05	0.04	0.04	0.04	0.07	0.10	0.12	0.14
Northwest	L	0.04	0.04	0.03	0.02	0.02	0.06	0.10	0.13	0.16
	M	0.05	0.04	0.04	0.03	0.03	0.07	0.11	0.14	0.17
	H	0.05	0.04	0.04	0.04	0.04	0.08	0.12	0.15	0.18
Horizontal	L	0.04	0.03	0.03	0.02	0.02	0.10	0.26	0.43	0.59
	M	0.06	0.05	0.04	0.04	0.03	0.12	0.27	0.44	0.59
	H	0.06	0.06	0.06	0.05	0.05	0.13	0.29	0.45	0.60

NOTES:

L = Light construction: frame exterior wall, 2-in concrete floor slab, approximately 30 lb of material per square foot of floor area.

M = Medium construction: 4-in concrete exterior wall, 4-in concrete floor slab, approximately 70 lb of building material per square foot of floor area.

H = Heavy construction: 6-in concrete exterior wall, 6-in concrete floor slab, approximately 130 lb of building materials per square foot of floor area.

SOURCE: *ASHRAE Handbook and Product Directory—1977 Fundamentals Volume*, American Society of Heating, Refrigerating and Air-Conditioning Engineers, Inc., New York, 1977, p. 25.13. Reprinted by permission.

Latitude	40° north
Air-conditioning season	June, July, and August
Electricity cost	\$0.16/kWh, \$20/(kW·month) demand charge
Air-conditioning system	Central, 100 tons, air-cooled
Glass	Double glazing, insulated, clear, ¼ in, $h_o = 4.0$, $\tau = 0.59$
Construction	Medium
Opaque wall	42 linear ft, 176 ft^2
Color	Dark
Inside temperature	80°F
Income tax bracket	40 percent

Solar time, h														
10	11	12	13	14	15	16	17	18	19	20	21	22	23	24
0.81	0.87	0.91	0.91	0.88	0.84	0.77	0.80	0.92	0.27	0.19	0.15	0.12	0.10	0.08
0.80	0.86	0.89	0.89	0.86	0.82	0.75	0.78	0.91	0.24	0.18	0.15	0.13	0.11	0.09
0.80	0.86	0.89	0.88	0.85	0.80	0.73	0.76	0.88	0.23	0.17	0.14	0.13	0.11	0.10
0.39	0.31	0.28	0.27	0.25	0.23	0.20	0.16	0.12	0.06	0.05	0.04	0.03	0.02	0.02
0.37	0.29	0.27	0.26	0.24	0.22	0.20	0.16	0.12	0.06	0.05	0.04	0.04	0.03	0.03
0.36	0.28	0.26	0.25	0.23	0.21	0.19	0.16	0.11	0.06	0.05	0.05	0.04	0.04	0.04
0.64	0.43	0.29	0.25	0.23	0.20	0.17	0.14	0.10	0.06	0.05	0.04	0.03	0.02	0.02
0.62	0.41	0.27	0.24	0.22	0.20	0.17	0.14	0.11	0.06	0.05	0.04	0.04	0.03	0.03
0.61	0.40	0.25	0.22	0.21	0.19	0.16	0.14	0.10	0.06	0.05	0.05	0.04	0.04	0.04
0.81	0.70	0.52	0.35	0.30	0.26	0.22	0.18	0.13	0.08	0.06	0.05	0.04	0.03	0.03
0.79	0.68	0.49	0.33	0.28	0.25	0.22	0.18	0.13	0.08	0.07	0.06	0.05	0.04	0.04
0.79	0.67	0.48	0.31	0.27	0.23	0.20	0.17	0.13	0.07	0.07	0.06	0.05	0.05	0.05
0.58	0.75	0.84	0.82	0.71	0.53	0.37	0.29	0.20	0.11	0.09	0.07	0.06	0.05	0.04
0.58	0.75	0.83	0.80	0.68	0.50	0.35	0.27	0.19	0.11	0.09	0.08	0.07	0.06	0.05
0.59	0.75	0.82	0.79	0.67	0.49	0.33	0.26	0.18	0.10	0.08	0.07	0.06	0.06	0.05
0.18	0.22	0.38	0.59	0.76	0.84	0.83	0.72	0.48	0.18	0.13	0.11	0.08	0.07	0.06
0.19	0.22	0.38	0.59	0.75	0.83	0.81	0.69	0.45	0.15	0.12	0.10	0.08	0.07	0.06
0.20	0.23	0.39	0.59	0.75	0.82	0.80	0.68	0.43	0.14	0.11	0.08	0.08	0.07	0.06
0.14	0.15	0.17	0.30	0.53	0.72	0.83	0.83	0.63	0.19	0.14	0.11	0.08	0.07	0.06
0.15	0.16	0.17	0.31	0.53	0.72	0.82	0.81	0.61	0.16	0.12	0.10	0.08	0.07	0.06
0.16	0.17	0.18	0.31	0.54	0.71	0.81	0.80	0.59	0.15	0.11	0.09	0.07	0.06	0.06
0.19	0.20	0.21	0.22	0.30	0.52	0.73	0.83	0.71	0.19	0.13	0.10	0.08	0.07	0.05
0.19	0.20	0.21	0.22	0.30	0.52	0.73	0.82	0.69	0.15	0.12	0.09	0.08	0.07	0.06
0.20	0.21	0.22	0.23	0.30	0.52	0.73	0.81	0.67	0.15	0.11	0.08	0.07	0.06	0.05
0.72	0.81	0.87	0.87	0.83	0.74	0.60	0.44	0.27	0.15	0.12	0.09	0.08	0.06	0.05
0.72	0.81	0.85	0.85	0.81	0.71	0.58	0.42	0.25	0.14	0.12	0.10	0.08	0.07	0.06
0.72	0.81	0.85	0.84	0.79	0.70	0.56	0.40	0.23	0.13	0.11	0.09	0.08	0.08	0.07

TABLE 8-8 Shading Coefficients for Single Glass and Insulating Glass*

Type of glass	Nominal thickness, in†	Solar transmittance†	Shading coefficient	
			$h_o = 4.0$	$h_o = 3.0$
Single glass				
Clear	⅛	0.84	1.00	1.00
	¼	0.78	0.94	0.95
	⅜	0.72	0.90	0.92
	½	0.67	0.87	0.88
Heat-absorbing	⅛	0.64	0.83	0.85
	¼	0.46	0.69	0.73
	⅜	0.33	0.60	0.64
	½	0.24	0.53	0.58
Insulating glass				
Clear out, clear in	⅛‡	0.71§	0.88	0.88
Clear out, clear in	¼	0.61	0.81	0.82
Heat-absorbing¶ out, clear in	¼	0.36	0.55	0.58

*Factory-fabricated units with 3/16-, ¼-, or ½-in air space or prime windows plus storm sash.

†Refer to manufacturer's literature for values.

‡Thickness of each pane of glass, not thickness of assembled unit.

§Combined transmittance for assembled unit.

¶Gray, bronze, and green tinted heat-absorbing float glass.

SOURCE: *ASHRAE Handbook and Product Directory—1977 Fundamentals Volume*, American Society of Heating, Refrigerating and Air-Conditioning Engineers, Inc., New York, 1977, p. 26.27. Reprinted by permission.

The profile angles for a south-facing 40° north latitude wall are presented in Table 7-15. An examination of the shadow angle created by the balcony indicates that whenever the profile angle is greater than 66°, the windows below the balconies will be completely shaded. An examination of Table 7-15 shows that in both June and July the windows will be completely shaded, provided the balconies extend horizontally beyond the edge of the windows below to furnish shading during early-morning and later-afternoon hours.

The month of August will have some exposure to the sun. The hours 11 A.M., 12 N., and 1:00 P.M. have the lowest profile angle, 62°. During those hours the amount of glass area that is exposed to the sun is calculated as follows:

$$\tan 62° = x/3.5 \text{ ft}$$

$$x = 6.58$$

$$\text{Exposed glass height} = 8 \text{ ft} - 6.58 \text{ ft} = 1.42 \text{ ft}$$

$$\text{Area of exposed glass} = 24 \text{ ft} \times 1.42 \text{ ft} = 34 \text{ ft}^2$$

$$\text{Fraction of exposed area} = 34 \text{ ft}^2 \div 160 \text{ ft}^2 = 0.21$$

$$\text{Area of shaded glass} = 160 \text{ ft}^2 - 34 \text{ ft}^2 = 126 \text{ ft}^2$$

Because air-conditioning savings for residential buildings depend on the reduction of peak cooling loads (see Chapter 6), the month of peak solar load must be determined. This will be August both before the shading balconies are installed and after they have been installed.

(Cont. on p. 222)

TABLE 8·9 Shading Coefficients for Single Glass with Indoor Shading by Venetian Blinds or Roller Shades

			Type of shading				
			Venetian blinds		Roller shade		
					Opaque		Translucent
	Nominal thickness, in*	Solar transmittance†	Medium	Light	Dark	White	Light
Clear	3/32–1/4	0.87–0.80					
Clear	1/4–1/2	0.80–0.71					
Clear pattern	1/8–1/2	0.87–0.79	0.64	0.55	0.59	0.25	0.39
Heat-absorbing pattern	1/8	. . .					
Tinted	3/16, 7/32	0.74, 0.71					
Heat-absorbing‡	3/16, 1/4	0.46					
Heat-absorbing pattern	3/16, 1/4	. . .	0.57	0.53	0.45	0.30	0.36
Tinted	1/8, 7/32	0.59, 0.45					
Heat-absorbing or pattern	. . .	0.44–0.30	0.54	0.52	0.40	0.28	0.32
Heat-absorbing or pattern	. . .	0.29–0.15 0.24	0.42	0.40	0.36	0.28	0.31
Reflective coated glass:							
SC§ = 0.30			0.25	0.23			
0.40			0.33	0.29			
0.50			0.42	0.38			
0.60			0.50	0.44			

*Refer to manufacturer's literature for values.

†For vertical blinds with opaque white and beige louvers in the tightly closed position, SC is 0.25 and 0.29 when used with glass of 0.71 to 0.80 transmittance.

‡Gray, bronze, and green tinted heat-absorbing glass.

§SC for glass with no shading device.

SOURCE: *ASHRAE Handbook and Product Directory—1977 Fundamentals Volume*, American Society of Heating, Refrigerating and Air-Conditioning Engineers, Inc., New York, 1977, p. 26.30. Reprinted by permission.

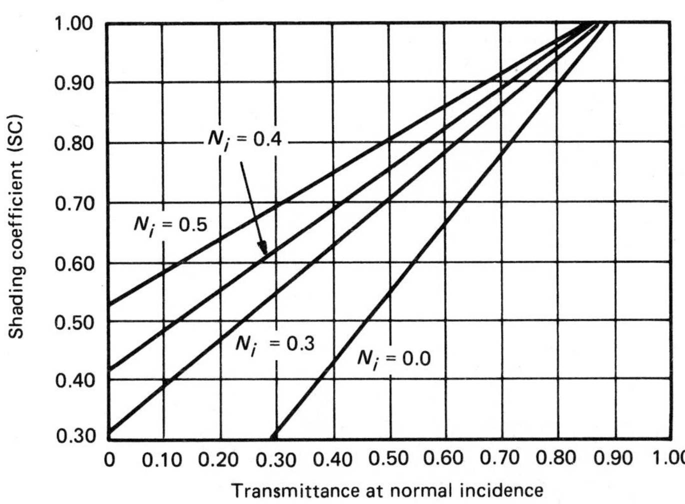

FIGURE 8·2 Shading coefficient versus transmittance for single glass. [ASHRAE Handbook and Product Directory—1977 Fundamentals Volume, *American Society of Heating, Refrigerating and Air-Conditioning Engineers, Inc., New York, 1977, p. 26.27. Reprinted by permission.*]

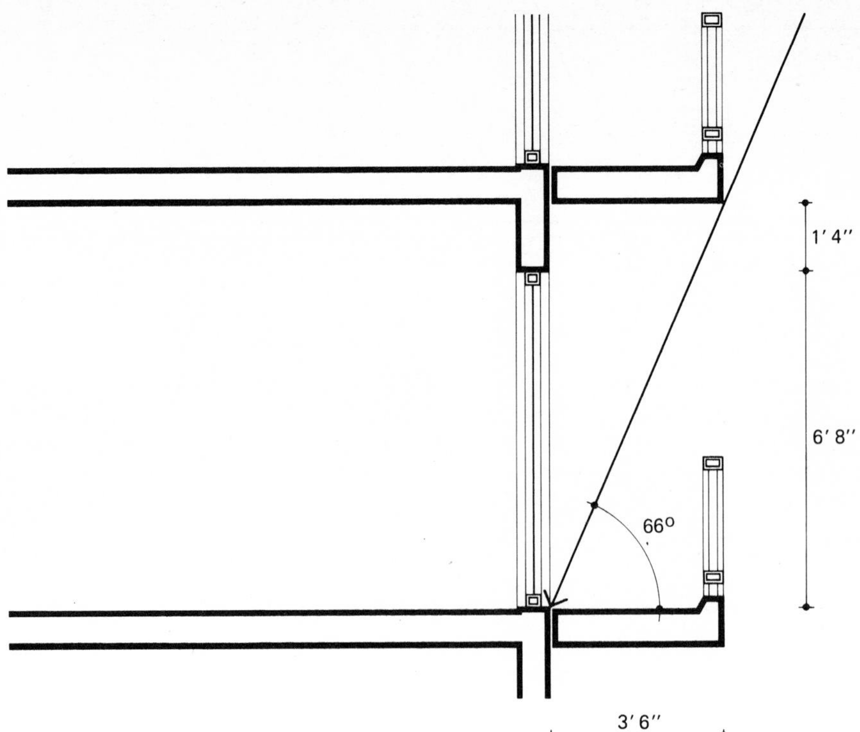

FIGURE 8·3 Section through an apartment building exterior wall and balcony.

TABLE 8·10 Shading Coefficients (SC) for Insulating Glass* with Indoor Shading by Venetian Blinds or Roller Shades

Type of glass	Nominal thickness, in, each light	Solar transmittance† Outer pane	Solar transmittance† Inner pane	Type of shading: Venetian blinds‡ Medium	Venetian blinds‡ Light	Roller shade Opaque Dark	Roller shade Opaque White	Roller shade Translucent Light
Clear out	3/32, 1/8	0.87	0.87					
Clear in				0.57	0.51	0.60	0.25	0.37
Clear out								
Clear in	1/4	0.80	0.80					
Heat-absorbing§ out, clear in	1/4	0.46	0.80	0.39	0.36	0.40	0.22	0.30
Reflective coated glass:								
SC = 0.20				0.19	0.18			
SC = 0.30				0.27	0.26			
SC = 0.40				0.34	0.33			

*Refers to factory-fabricated units with 3/16-, 1/4-, or 1/2-in air space or to prime windows plus storm windows.

†Consult manufacturer's literature for exact values.

‡For vertical blinds with opaque white or beige louvers, tightly closed, SC is approximately the same as for opaque white roller shades.

§Refers to bronze- or green-tinted heat-absorbing glass.

SOURCE: *ASHRAE Handbook and Product Directory—1977 Fundamentals Volume*, American Society of Heating, Refrigerating and Air-Conditioning Engineers, Inc., New York, 1977, p. 26.31. Reprinted by permission.

TABLE 8·11 Shading Coefficients for Louvered Horizontal Sun Screens

Profile angle,°	Transmittance	SC	Transmittance	SC
	Group 1		Group 2	
10	0.23	0.35	0.25	0.33
20	0.06	0.17	0.14	0.23
30	0.04	0.15	0.12	0.21
40 and above	0.04	0.15	0.11	0.20
	Group 3		Group 4	
10	0.40	0.51	0.48	0.59
20	0.32	0.42	0.39	0.50
30	0.21	0.31	0.28	0.38
40 and above	0.07	0.18	0.20	0.30
	Group 5		Group 6	
10	0.15	0.27	0.26	0.45
20	0.04	0.11	0.20	0.35
30	0.03	0.10	0.13	0.26
40	0.03	0.10	0.04	0.13

NOTE:

Group 1: Black; width-over-spacing ratio, 1.15:1; 23 louvers per inch.

Group 2: Light color; high reflectance; otherwise same as Group 1.

Group 3: Black or dark color; width-over-spacing ratio, 0.85:1; 17 louvers per inch.

Group 4: Light color or unpainted aluminum; high reflectance; otherwise same as Group 3.

Group 5: Same as Group 1 except for two lights of 0.25-in clear glass with 0.5-in air space.

Group 6: Same as Group 3 except for two lights of 0.25-in clear glass with 0.5-in air space.

U value = 0.85 Btu/(h·ft^2·°F) for all groups when used with single glazing.

SOURCE: *ASHRAE Handbook and Product Directory—1977 Fundamentals Volume,* American Society of Heating, Refrigerating and Air-Conditioning Engineers, Inc., New York, 1977, p. 26.36. Reprinted by permission.

TABLE 8·12 Shading Coefficients for Domed Skylights

Dome	Light diffuser (translucent)	Height, in	Width-to-height ratio	Shading coefficient	U factor
Clear	Yes	0	∞	0.61	0.46
(τ = 0.86)	(τ = 0.58)	9	5	0.58	0.43
		18	2.5	0.50	0.40
Clear		0	∞	0.99	0.80
(τ = 0.86)	None	9	5	0.88	0.75
		18	2.5	0.80	0.70
Translucent	None	0	∞	0.57	0.80
(τ = 0.52)		18	2.5	0.46	0.70
Translucent	None	0	∞	0.34	0.80
(τ = 0.27)		9	5	0.30	0.75
		18	2.5	0.28	0.70

SOURCE: *ASHRAE Handbook and Product Directory—1977 Fundamentals Volume,* American Society of Heating, Refrigerating and Air-Conditioning Engineers, Inc., New York, 1977, p. 26.37. Reprinted by permission.

The value of shading the incoming peak solar radiation will be a function of determining the direct but not the diffuse value of solar radiation. From Table 8-13, the following characteristics of diffuse radiation for the month of August may be found:

$$H_o = 3197 \text{ Btu/(day}\cdot\text{ft}^2)$$

$$K_D = 0.187 \text{ (no units)}$$

where H_o = daily total extraterrestial radiation on a horizontal surface
K_D = average daily diffuse radiation on a horizontal surface (or a vertical surface)

The diffuse component of solar radiation at the building site may be calculated as follows:

$$\text{Daily diffuse} = H_o \times K_D$$
$$= 3197 \text{ Btu/(day}\cdot\text{ft}^2) \times 0.187$$
$$= 598 \text{ Btu/(day}\cdot\text{ft}^2)$$

From Table 7-14 it may be inferred that the number of hours of sunlight in August is 13. The hourly diffuse solar radiation rate therefore is

$$\text{Hourly diffuse} = 598 \text{ Btu/(day}\cdot\text{ft}^2) - 13 = 46 \text{ Btu/(h}\cdot\text{ft}^2)$$

The adjusted maximum solar heat gain factor (SHGF), that is, the amount of peak solar heat gain that would be saved by the shading effect of the balcony, is calculated as follows:[1]

$$\text{SHGF} = \text{maximum solar heat gain—(diffuse} \times \text{transmissivity of } \tfrac{1}{8}\text{-in clear glass)}$$
$$= 149 \text{ Btu/(h}\cdot\text{ft}^2)\text{—[46 Btu/(h}\cdot\text{ft}^2) \times 0.80]$$
$$= 112 \text{ Btu/(h}\cdot\text{ft}^2)$$

[1]The figure of 0.80 is taken from Table 7-16.

TABLE 8-13 Diffuse Solar Radiation for Various Cities [Btu/(day·ft²)]

City	Month											
	1	2	3	4	5	6	7	8	9	10	11	12
Bethel, Alaska	59	160	248	411	630	690	624	475	309	159	58	29
Tucson, Arizona	301	386	516	441	650	558	609	547	414	364	299	254
Davis City, California	278	386	468	555	577	564	544	492	421	353	280	238
Los Angeles, California	321	406	493	594	647	646	577	537	459	397	315	277
Grand Junction, Colorado	257	338	433	540	591	553	551	523	388	323	257	213
Washington, D.C.	276	382	501	609	675	680	670	602	490	377	275	238
Miami, Florida	378	448	525	596	636	663	649	615	564	476	391	351
Atlanta, Georgia	334	432	526	605	650	668	660	597	526	412	329	293
Lemont, Illinois	657	572	461	599	669	685	657	572	461	351	245	209
Lake Charles, Louisiana	366	461	546	616	641	644	662	605	531	421	360	330
Boston, Massachusetts	237	345	468	589	679	708	675	591	471	343	234	198
St. Cloud, Minnesota	196	286	410	569	660	689	638	550	438	314	206	169
Columbia, Missouri	276	385	492	605	653	673	638	569	458	360	276	237
New York, New York	254	362	485	599	677	692	665	598	485	360	252	214
San Antonio, Texas	363	449	541	638	648	624	585	556	510	430	370	330
Seattle, Washington	182	292	431	573	653	703	632	557	435	290	182	144

SOURCE: Calculated by the author, using data from T. Kusuda and K. Ishii, *Hourly Solar Radiation Data for Vertical and Horizontal Surfaces on Average Days*, U.S. Dept. of Commerce, Washington, 1977.

The *reduction* in peak heat load may be calculated as follows:[2]

$$q_c = 126\ \text{ft}^2 \times 0.58 \times 112\ \text{Btu/(h·ft}^2) \times 0.81 \qquad (8\text{-}3)$$
$$= 6630\ \text{Btu/h}$$

The cooling savings accomplished by this reduction in cooling load demand may then be estimated:

$$B_c = 1.18\ \text{kW/ton} \times \$0.16/\text{kWh} \times 1000\ \text{h/year}$$
$$\times [6630\ \text{Btu/h} \div 12{,}000\ \text{Btu/(ton·h)}] = \$104/\text{year}$$ [See Equation (6-4).]

Reduction in demand charges is estimated below:

$$B_c = [6630\ \text{Btu/h} \div 12{,}000\ \text{Btu/(ton·h)}] \times 1.18\ \text{kW/ton} \times \$20/(\text{kW·month}) \times 3\ \text{months} = \$39$$

or on an aftertax basis,

$$B_c = (\$104 + \$39)/\text{year} \times (1 - 0.40) = \$86/\text{year}$$

The reduction in peak heat load for the entire building is calculated below:

$$\Delta q_c = 6436\ \text{Btu/h} \times 20\ \text{apartments}$$
$$= 132{,}600\ \text{Btu/h}$$

In terms of cooling tons,

$$\Delta q_c = 132{,}600\ \text{Btu/h} \div 12{,}000\ \text{Btu/(ton·h)} = 11.1\ \text{T.}$$

The savings in cooling equipment costs which will result are estimated below:

$$\Delta C_o = 11.1\ \text{T} \times \$520/\text{ton} = \$5772$$

or for each apartment,

$$\Delta C_o = \$5772 \div 20\ \text{apartments} = \$287/\text{apartment}$$

The adjusted construction cost is

$$C_o = (\$2000 - \$287) = \$1713$$

The $86 savings clearly will not justify the cost of the balcony even with equipment savings. Simple return on investment is $86/year ÷ $1713, or 5.0 percent. The added amenity of the balcony as an outdoor living space, however, may more than compensate for the relatively low fuel savings.

CONVECTION: CHANGES IN SUMMER HEAT GAIN AND EFFECTIVE INDOOR TEMPERATURES

Air movement out of and into a building during the summer can have a number of different effects. Heat gain by infiltration can occur, and cooling by natural ventilation and skin moisture evaporation can also occur.

In a tall air-conditioned building, the cooled indoor air will be slightly higher in pressure than the outdoor air because of mechanical-system-induced pressures

[2]The figure of 0.58 is taken from Table 8-6; that of 0.81, from Table 8-8.

and because of lower temperatures. As a result, cool indoor air will move through openings near the bottom stories of the building's envelope to the exterior, causing exfiltration. Infiltration will occur in the upper stories to replace the air which has fallen to the lower part of the building, and heat from the higher-temperature outdoor air will enter the building.

Air movements within a building, caused by exterior breezes passing through the building or by pressure differences caused by stack-effect designs (see Chapter 2), will, when moving across the skin of a human being, cause evaporation and cooling to occur. The result is that the presence of a breeze will allow people to tolerate higher indoor air temperatures while maintaining comfort levels. Economic savings will occur by increases in tolerable indoor air temperature limits and reductions in the number of hours when the air-conditioning system need be on.

Heat Gain by Exfiltration and Infiltration

Infiltration during the summer cooling season will cause warmer air to displace and/or mix with cooler air and increase air-conditioning requirements. Exfiltration results in the escape of cooled air and an increase in the fresh air required to replace the conditioned air which has escaped. In either case, additional heat must be taken out of the air to maintain adequate comfort conditions during the summer. The estimating methods presented in Chapter 7 for winter conditions can be used with some modification for summer cooling conditions.

The principal difference is that to condition air during the summer one must not only reduce the temperature of the air but also condense the water vapor in the air, that is, reduce its humidity level. This reduction may be accomplished by changing the vapor to a liquid state. Change of state requires the extraction of additional heat: the *latent* heat of evaporation-condensation. An air-conditioning system requires additional electricity to reduce humidity levels of infiltrating air quite apart from the heat required to reduce temperature levels. Simply lowering the temperature of air without condensing water vapor requires the removal of *sensible* heat only, not latent heat.

The general form of the equation which should be used for estimating changes in the *peak* sensible cooling load is the following:

$$\Delta q_{s,c} = [C_d + (C_v \times W)] \times \Delta V \times d \times (t_o - t_i) \tag{8-5}$$

in units,

$$\text{Btu/h} = \{\text{Btu/(lb}\cdot{}^\circ\text{F)} + [\text{Btu/(lb}\cdot{}^\circ\text{F)} \times \text{lb/lb}]\} \times \text{ft}^3\text{/h} - \text{lb/(ft}^3\cdot{}^\circ\text{F)}$$

where $\Delta q_{s,c}$ = change in the rate of *sensible* heat flow for a given set of steady-state conditions required to lower the temperature of air leaking into a building during the cooling season, Btu/h

C_d = specific heat of dry air [assume 0.24 Btu/(lb·°F)]

C_v = specific heat of water vapor [assume 0.45 Btu/(lb·°F)]

W = humidity ratio, pounds of water per pound of dry air (assume 0.01 lb/lb unless other data are available)

ΔV = change in the volume of outdoor air entering a building, ft^3/h
d = density of dry air (assume 0.075 lb/ft^3)
t = air temperature, °F

Substituting the values shown, the above equation becomes

$$\Delta q_{s,c} = 0.018\ \Delta V\ (t_o - t_i) \qquad (8\text{-}6)$$

in units,

$$\text{Btu/h} = \text{Btu/(ft}^3 \cdot {}^\circ\text{F)} \times \text{ft}^3\text{/h} \times {}^\circ\text{F}$$

or when ΔV is in units of ft^3/min,

$$\Delta q_{s,c} = 1.08\ \Delta V\ (t_o - t_i)$$

in units,

$$\text{Btu/h} = \text{Btu min/(ft}^3 \cdot \text{h} \cdot {}^\circ\text{F)} \times \text{ft}^3\text{/min} \times {}^\circ\text{F}$$

As in previous sections and chapters, the form of the above equation becomes the following when needed for estimating overall seasonal energy consumption, particularly for nonresidential buildings:

$$\Delta Q_{s,c} = 0.018\ \Delta V \times \text{DH}_c \qquad (8\text{-}7)$$

in units,

$$\text{Btu/year} = \text{Btu/(ft}^3 \cdot {}^\circ\text{F)} \times \text{ft}^3\text{/h} \times ({}^\circ\text{F} \cdot \text{h})\text{/year}$$

where all variables are as defined above except

$\Delta Q_{s,c}$ = change in the annual rate of sensible heat flow required to lower the temperature of air leaking into a building, Btu/year
ΔV = change in volume of infiltrating air, ft^3/h
DH_c = bin degree-hour data reflecting annual *cooling* season outdoor and indoor temperature conditions, (°F·h)/year (See Table 8-14.)

Equation (8-7), when ΔV is in units of cubic feet per minute, becomes, of course,

$$\Delta Q_{s,c} = 1.08\ \Delta V \times \text{DH}_c$$

As described in Chapter 7 for the heating season, degree-hour data for *infiltration* calculations need not be analyzed for sol-air temperatures. Table 8-14 is in the same form as Table 6-10, except that no adjustment has been made in outside temperature to account for sol-air surface heat.

The change in *latent* heat gain which results when more humid air enters a building than is maintained by the cooling system may be estimated by using the following form:[3]

$$\Delta q_{l,c} = \Delta V \times d(C_{v75} - C_{W50}) \times (W_o - W_i) \qquad (8\text{-}8)$$

[3] *ASHRAE Handbook and Product Directory—1977 Fundamentals Volume*, American Society of Heating, Refrigerating and Air-Conditioning Engineers, Inc., New York, 1977, p. 25.23. Reprinted by permission.

TABLE 8-14 **Degree-Hours for an 80°F Indoor Temperature and 65°F Cooling System Activation Temperature, Weekdays in Nonresidential Buildings, Mitchel Air Force Base, Nassau County, New York, Cooling Season**

Average bin temperature	Difference from 80°F (A)	Total hours of occurrence (adjusted for 5-day week) (B)	(°F·h)/year (A·B)
102	22	1	22
97	17	6	102
92	12	24	288
87	7	79	553
82	2	156	312
77	−3	207	− 621
72	−8	174	−1392
67	−13	119	−1547
			−2283*

*A negative number means that, in terms of *sensible* heat, outside air during the day is on average a benefit, not a cost, in the cooling season. (Latent heat is considered in Table 8-15.)

NOTE: This table represents the New York area climate. The designer should assemble his or her own table by using bin degree-hour data for the climate in which he or she is working.

SOURCE: Calculated by the author from data in Table 6-10.

in units,

$$\text{Btu/h} = \text{ft}^3\text{/h} \times \text{lb/ft}^3(\text{Btu/lb} - \text{Btu/lb}) \times (\text{lb/lb} - \text{lb/lb})$$

where $\Delta q_{l,c}$ = change in the *peak* rate of *latent* heat flow required to lower the humidity of air leaking into a building, Btu/h

ΔV = change in volume of outdoor air entering a building, ft³/h

d = density of dry air (assume 0.075 lb/ft³)

C_{v75} = heat content of 50 percent relative humidity vapor at 75°F, a common design condition assumption, Btu/lb

C_{W50} = energy content of water at 50°F, the normal condensate temperature coming from dehumidifying and cooling coils, Btu/lb

$(C_{v75} - C_{W50})$ = 1076 Btu/lb

W_o = humidity ratio of outside air, lb/lb (in lieu of outdoor humidity data, assume 0.016 lb/lb)

W_i = humidity ratio of inside air (assume 0.010 lb/lb)

Substituting the values shown above, the equation becomes

$$\Delta q_{l,c} = 80.7\,\Delta V(W_o - W_i) \qquad (8\text{-}9)$$

in units,

$$\text{Btu/h} = \text{Btu/ft}^3 \times \text{ft}^3\text{/h} \times \text{lb/lb}$$

or when ΔV is in units of ft³/min,

$$q_{l,c} = 4842\ \Delta V \times (W_o - W_i)$$

in units,

$$\text{Btu/h} = \text{Btu/(min·ft}^3\text{·h)} \times \text{ft}^3\text{/min} \times \text{lb/lb}$$

Peak humidity ratios used for calculating peak cooling loads may be determined by using the chart in Figure 8-4 and dry-bulb–wet-bulb temperature data from Table 6-3. These two temperatures will intersect one another on Figure 8-4. The intersection point will indicate the humidity ratio on the vertical right-hand scale. For example, from Table 6-3 the summer design dry-bulb and wet-bulb temperatures at the 2.5 percent level for the New York City–La Guardia area are 89°F and 73°F, respectively. The intersection of these two temperatures in Figure 8-4 yields a humidity ratio of 0.0142.

For estimating change in overall *seasonal* latent heat infiltration, the following equation may be used:

$$\Delta Q_{l,c} = 80.7\ \Delta V \times \text{HRH} \tag{8-10}$$

in units,

$$\text{Btu/year} = \text{Btu/ft}^3 \times \text{ft}^3\text{/h} \times (\text{lb/lb} \times \text{h/year})$$

where $\Delta Q_{l,c}$ = change in the overall summer daytime rate of latent heat flow required to lower the humidity of air leaking into a building, Btu/year

ΔV = change in the volume of infiltrating air, ft³/h

HRH = humidity ratio hours, lb/lb × h/year, as obtained from bin data assembled in a form such as that presented in Table 8-15

TABLE 8-15 Humidity Ratio Hours for a 0.010 lb/lb Interior Humidity Ratio, a 65°F Cooling System Activation Temperature, Weekdays in Nonresidential Buildings, Mitchel Air Force Base, Nassau County, New York, Cooling Season

Average bin temperature (dry-bulb)	6-month average coincident wet-bulb	Outside humidity ratio, W_o*	Difference from W_i = 0.010 lb/lb (A)	Hours of occurrence (B)	$(W_o - W_i)$ hr/year (A·B)
102	79	0.017	0.007	1	0.007
97	76	0.015	0.005	6	0.030
92	74	0.014	0.004	24	0.096
87	72	0.013	0.003	79	0.237
82	70	0.013	0.003	156	0.468
77	67	0.013	0.003	207	0.621
72	66	0.012	0.002	174	0.348
67	61	0.010	. . .	119	. . .
					1.807

*From Figure 8-4.

SOURCE: Calculated by the author from data in Table 6-4.

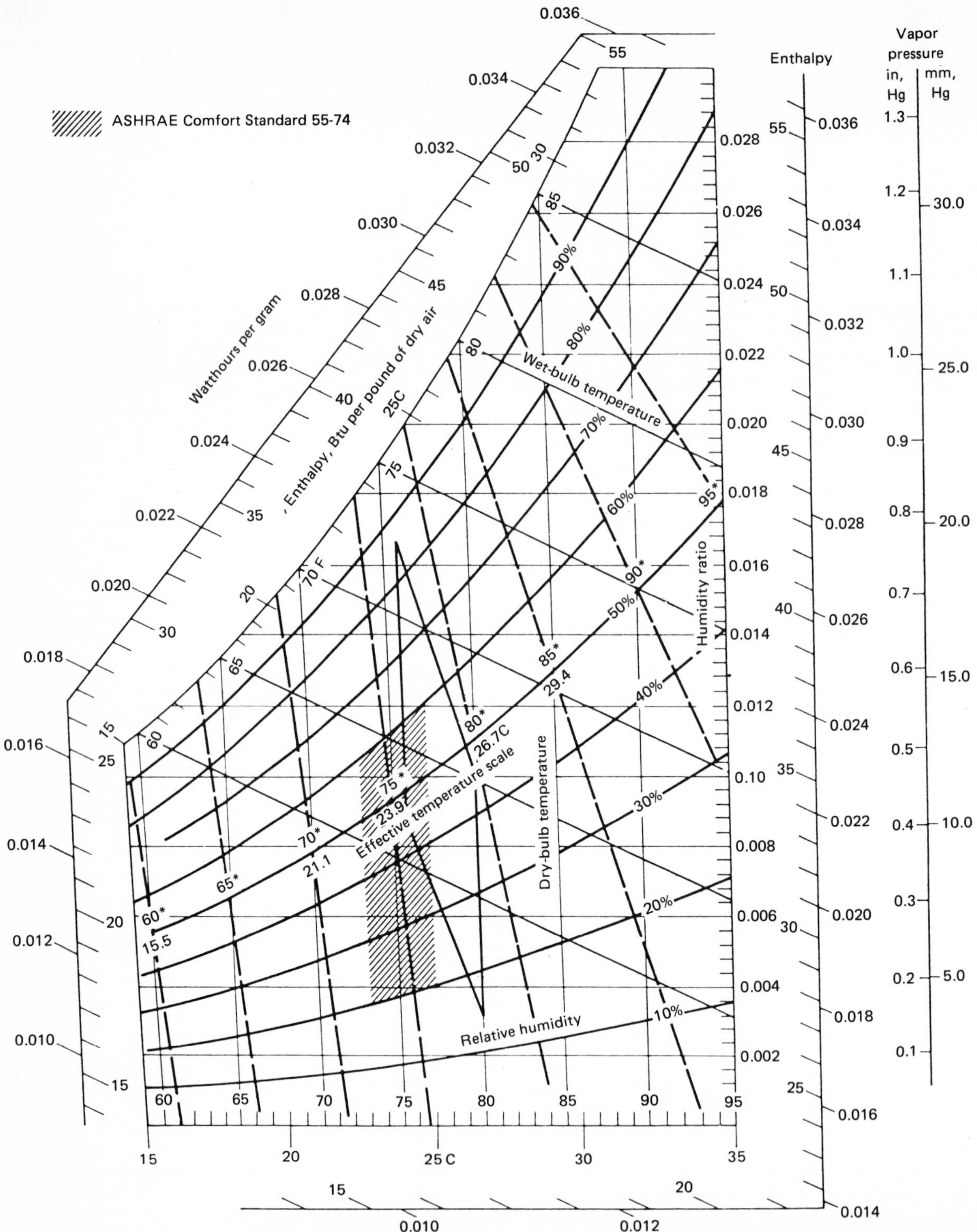

FIGURE 8-4 New effective temperature scale. The envelope applies for lightly clothed, sedentary individuals in spaces with low air movement, where the mean radiant temperature equals air temperature. [ASHRAE Handbook and Product Directory—1977 Fundamentals Volume, *American Society of Heating, Refrigerating and Air-Conditioning Engineers, Inc., New York, 1977, p. 8.21. Reprinted by permission.*]

EXAMPLE

The use of these equations and charts for estimating energy consumption is illustrated in the following example. An architect is renovating an apartment building and decides to replace double-hung windows with casement windows of the same size in order to obtain a less obstructed view and at the same time reduce infiltration. There are eight double-hung windows per apartment. An estimate of the value of a reduction in summer (and winter) infiltration heat gains (and losses) needs to be made.

The information necessary for the analysis is as follows:

Apartments per building	25
Wall construction	Masonry wall, caulked
Double-hung window	3 by 5 ft; crack length = 19 ft; loose fit, weatherstripped
Casement window	Wood, 3 by 5 ft; crack length[4] = 16 ft
Cooling equipment	Through-the-wall units
Electrical cost	\$0.15/kWh, \$20/(kW·month) demand charge
Heating fuel	Oil at \$1.40/gal
Casement window cost	\$200 each
Wind speed	15 mph (0.10 in of water pressure)
Location	New York City–La Guardia
Design dry-bulb	Summer, 2.5 percent: Exterior, 89°F Interior, 80°F
Design wet-bulb	75°F
Interior relative humidity	50 percent
Design dry-bulb	Winter, 97.5 percent = 15°F
Income tax bracket	40 percent

The difference in crack length is 3 feet per window; with 8 windows per apartment, 24 feet per dwelling.

From Table 7-6, the following infiltration rates may be found for double-hung windows:

Window: 28 $ft^3/(h \cdot ft)$

Frame wall: 3 $ft^3/(h \cdot ft)$

From Table 7-10, the following infiltration rates may be selected for wood casement windows:

Window: 0.50 $ft^3/(min \cdot ft)$, or 30 $ft^3/(h \cdot ft)$

The difference in infiltration rates per window is calculated below:

$$\text{Double-hung: } 19\ \text{ft}^3 \times 28\ \text{ft}^3/(\text{h}\cdot\text{ft}) = 532\ \text{ft}^3/\text{h}$$

$$16\ \text{ft} \times 3\ \text{ft}^3/(\text{h}\cdot\text{ft}) = \frac{48}{580}$$

$$\text{Casement: } 16\ \text{ft} \times 30\ \text{ft}^3/(\text{h}\cdot\text{ft}) = 480$$

$$\text{Difference} = 100\ \text{ft}^3/\text{h}$$

[4]The horizontal break between the upper and lower panes of a double-hung window accounts for the additional crack length when compared with that of a casement window.

Summer peak heat gain reductions are estimated as follows:

Sensible (dry-bulb) heat gain:

$$\Delta q_{s,c} = 0.018 \times 100\ \text{ft}^3/\text{h} \times (89°\text{F} - 80°\text{F}) \tag{8-6}$$
$$= 16\ \text{Btu/h}$$

The intersection of an interior dry-bulb temperature of 80°F and 50 percent relative humidity yields an interior humidity ratio of 0.0112.

Latent (wet-bulb) heat gain:

$$\Delta q_{l,c} = 80.7 \times 100\ \text{ft}^3/\text{h} \times (0.0142\ \text{lb/lb} - 0.0112\ \text{lb/lb}) \tag{8-9}$$
$$= 24\ \text{Btu/h}$$

Total sensible and latent infiltration heat gain change:

$$\Delta q_{s,c} + \Delta q_{l,c} = 16 + 24 = 40\ \text{Btu/h}$$

The value of the savings is calculated below:

$$B_c = P \times C_C \times T \times (\Delta q_c \div 12{,}000)\ \text{[See Equation (6-4).]}$$
$$= 1.64\ \text{kW/ton} \times \$0.15/\text{kWh} \times 1000\ \text{h/year}$$
$$\times\ [40\ \text{Btu/h} \div 12{,}000\ \text{Btu/(ton}\cdot\text{h)}]$$
$$= \$0.82/\text{year, or with 8 windows per apartment, } \$7/\text{year}$$

Reduction in demand charges is estimated below:

$$B_c = [40\ \text{Btu/h} \div 12{,}000\ \text{Btu/(ton}\cdot\text{h)}] \times 1.64\ \text{kW/ton} \times \$20/(\text{kW}\cdot\text{month})$$
$$\times\ 3\ \text{months/year}$$
$$= 0.33/\text{year, or with 8 windows per apartment, } \$3/\text{year}$$

The winter infiltration heat loss may be estimated as follows:

$$\Delta q_{s,h} = 0.018\ \text{Btu/(°F}\cdot\text{ft}^3) \times 100\ \text{ft}^3/\text{h} \times (70°\text{F} - 15°\text{F})$$
$$= 99\ \text{Btu/h [See Equation (7-10).]}$$

The value of these thermal savings is estimated below:

$$B_h = \frac{\$1.40/\text{gal} \times 99\ \text{Btu/h} \times 4811°\text{F}\cdot\text{days} \times 24\ \text{h/day} \times 0.63}{55°\text{F} \times 0.55 \times 140{,}000\ \text{Btu/gal}}$$
$$= \$2.38/\text{year, or with 8 windows per apartment, } \$19/\text{year [See Equation (6-2).]}$$

Since the building already exists along with its heating and cooling equipment, it is not possible to achieve any savings in terms of reduced heating and cooling equipment size requirements.

The total summer and winter savings of \$29 per year before tax or \$16 per year after tax, at a cost of 8 windows × \$200 = \$1600, does not provide a sufficient return on investment to justify complete replacement of the windows. The designer should perhaps examine the cost-effectiveness of adding storm windows, using better weatherstripping, or adopting other options with a lower first cost.

Effective Cooling by Increased Natural Ventilation

Cooling cost savings may be achieved during the summer months within certain temperature ranges by causing air movement through the rooms of a building. Air movement will cause some evaporation on the skin of the occupants of a room, making them feel cooler. In effect, the existence of air movement in a room increases the tolerance of a human being for ambient (that is, dry-bulb) temperature. A person will feel an equivalent level of comfort at higher ambient temperatures if air movement exists in a room. Air movement within buildings, as mentioned earlier, may be caused either by wind or by pressure differences.

Cooling by Breezes

The accuracy of estimating the value of designs which capture summer breezes is limited by the accuracy of available data describing wind conditions. Many of the data currently available are very generalized. The maps in Figure 8-5 indicate the prevailing wind direction and average speed for four months. These data may not be accurate because local conditions may substantially alter the prevailing direction and speed of the wind. Such conditions include adjacent buildings, trees, hills, and bodies of water, all of which may change wind characteristics. Designers should obtain and use data describing local wind conditions for each specific site on which they are working in order to make any design analysis of wind benefits as accurate as possible. In lieu of such data, the maps in Figure 8-5 may be used to calculate approximations of the economic value of designs for capturing summer breezes.

There are some general guidelines that should be followed in the placement of wall openings such as operable windows relative to the prevailing wind direction. The effect of wind-induced air movement within a space is accommodated by inlet openings and outlet openings. Both types must be present in a room. Inlets and outlets are most effective per unit area if their areas are equal. If the areas are unequal, the increase in equivalent inlet-outlet area above the area of the smaller of the two types of openings is approximated by using the curve in Figure 8-6.

For example, if a room in a house has an inlet window opening of 12 square feet and an outlet window opening of 8 square feet, the effective opening for purposes of calculating energy savings is determined as follows:

$$\frac{12 \text{ ft}^2}{8 \text{ ft}^2} = 1.5$$

$$\text{Increase (Figure 8-6)} = 17 \text{ percent}$$

$$\text{Effective opening} = 1.17 \times 8 \text{ ft}^2 = 9.4 \text{ ft}^2$$

Inlets should face the prevailing wind direction and preferably be low on a wall. Outlets should be on the leeward side of a building and high in the room being ventilated. The inlet and outlet openings should not be opposite each other in the direction of the wind, however, because short-circuiting of air movement within the room may then occur. If short-circuiting does occur, only that portion of the

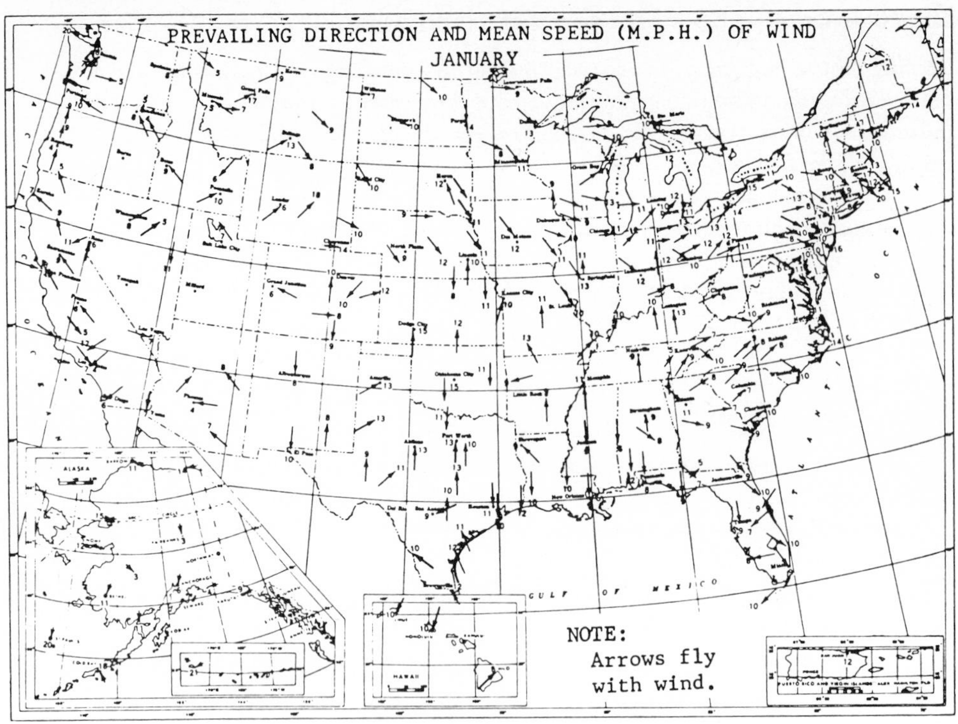

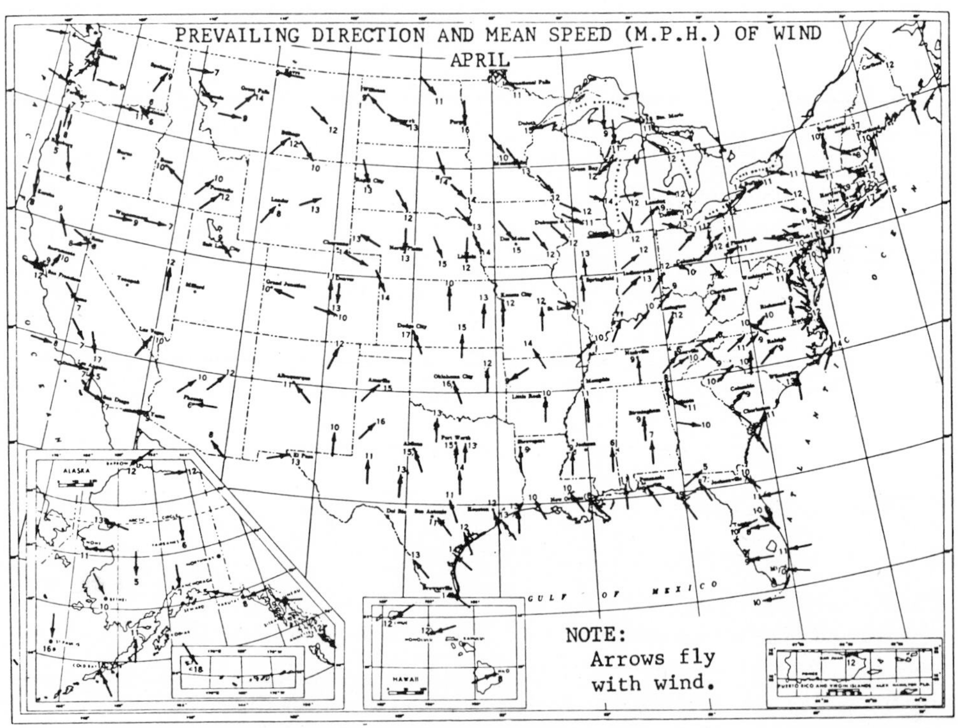

FIGURE 8-5 **Prevailing direction and mean speed of wind for four months.** [Climatic Atlas of the United States, *U.S. Department of Commerce, National Climatic Center, Asheville, N.C., 1968, p. 73.*]

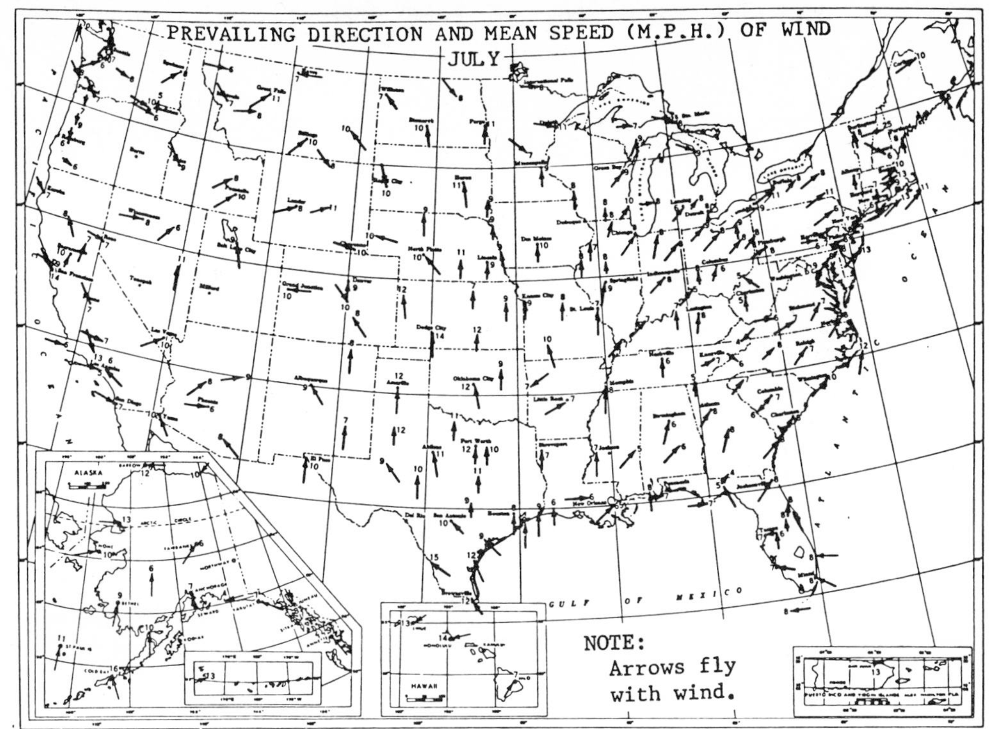
PREVAILING DIRECTION AND MEAN SPEED (M.P.H.) OF WIND
JULY
NOTE:
Arrows fly with wind.
GULF OF MEXICO
ALASKA
HAWAII

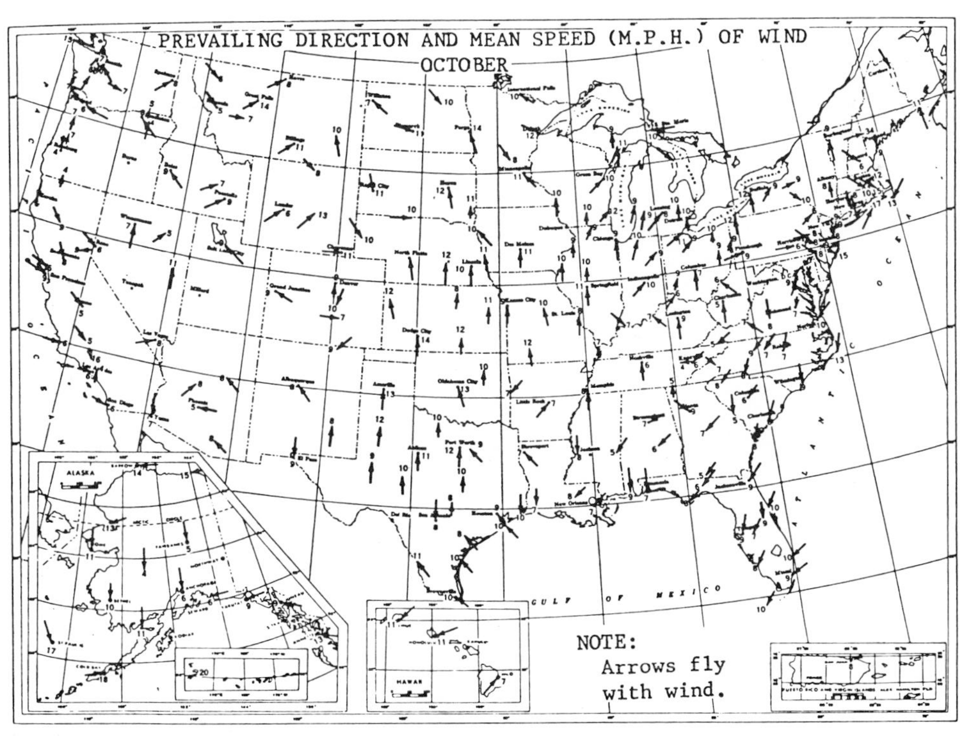
PREVAILING DIRECTION AND MEAN SPEED (M.P.H.) OF WIND
OCTOBER
NOTE:
Arrows fly with wind.
GULF OF MEXICO
ALASKA
HAWAII

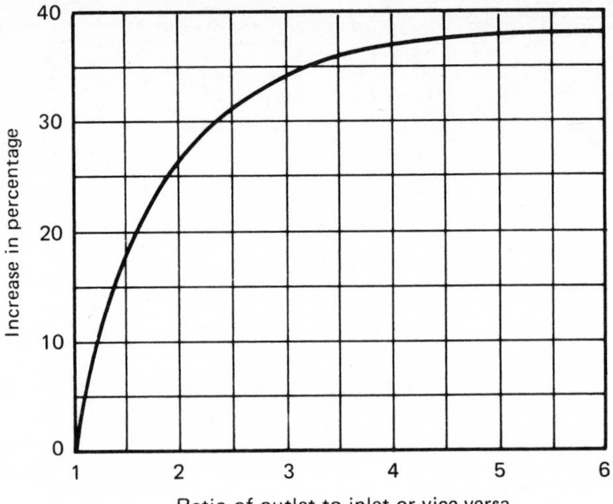

FIGURE 8-6 **Increase in flow caused by the excess of one opening over another.** [ASHRAE Handbook and Product Directory—1977 Fundamentals Volume, *American Society of Heating, Refrigerating and Air-Conditioning Engineers, Inc., New York, 1977, p. 21.12. Reprinted by permission.*]

room directly in the path between the inlet opening and the outlet opening will experience any significant air movement.

Velocity of air movement within a room may be calculated in the following manner:

$$VE_r = \frac{A_o \times VE_w}{A_r} \times E \tag{8-11}$$

in units,

$$\text{mi/h} = \frac{\text{ft}^2 \times \text{mi/h}}{\text{ft}^2}$$

where VE_r = velocity of air movement within a room, mi/h

A_o = effective area of the inlet opening adjusted as necessary by using Figure 8-6, ft^2

A_r = cross-sectional area of the room, ft^2

VE_w = average velocity of the wind, mi/h

E = effectiveness of the inlet opening (Assume 0.55 if the prevailing wind direction is perpendicular to the inlet opening and 0.35 if the prevailing wind direction is at a diagonal to the inlet opening.)[5]

For example, from Figure 8-5 the prevailing wind direction and average speed for the New York area during the summer months is

July 8 mi/h, southwest

If a window of 42 square feet is facing south and is in the wall of a room with a 112-square-foot cross-sectional area and an operable window of 35 square feet

[5] *ASHRAE Handbook and Product Directory—1977 Fundamentals Volume,* American Society of Heating, Refrigerating and Air-Conditioning Engineers, Inc., New York, 1977, p. 21.11. Reprinted by permission.

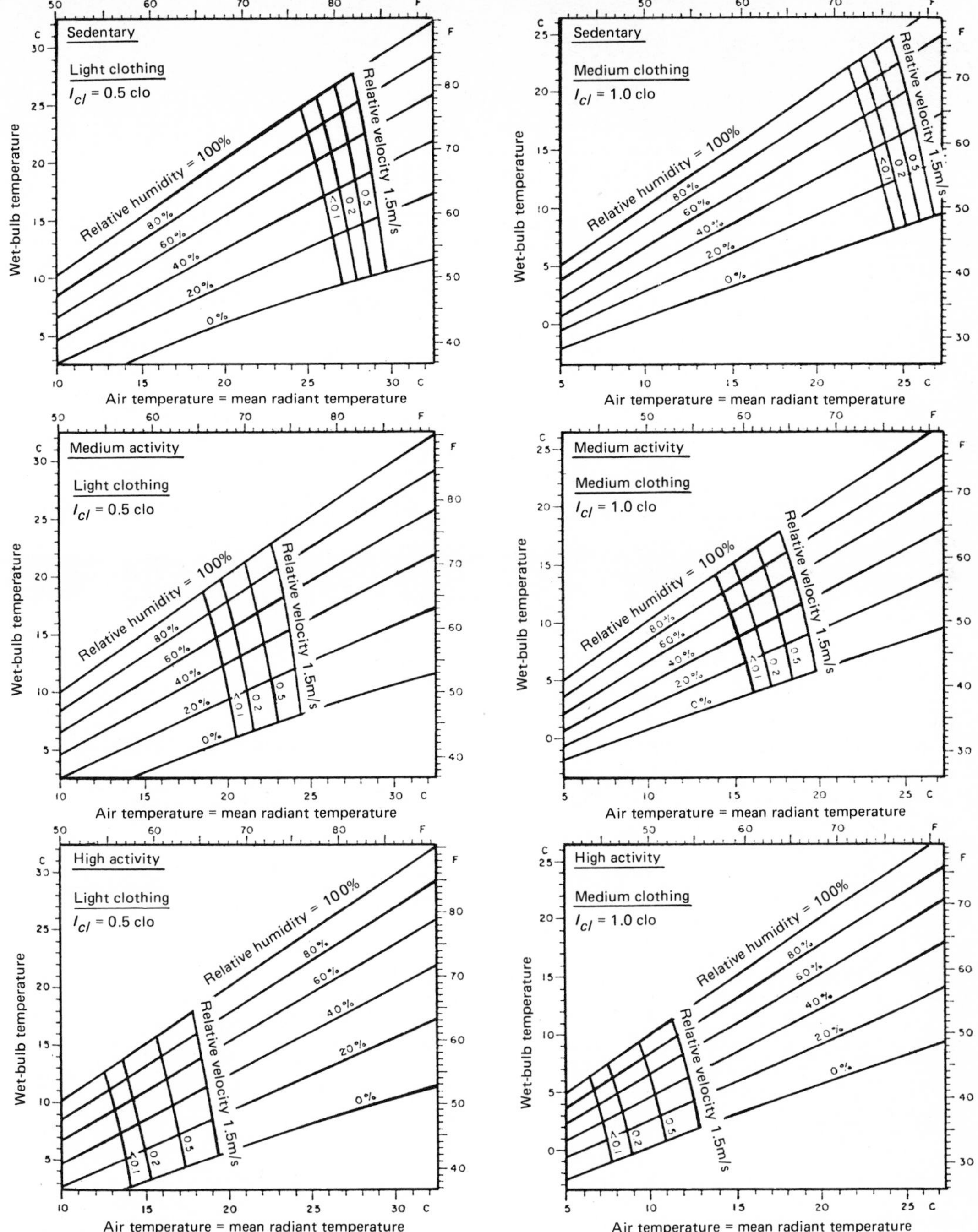

FIGURE 8-7 Combined influence of humidity, air velocity, and ambient temperature. The comfort lines are curves through different combinations of ambient temperature and humidity which provide thermal comfort. The six diagrams apply to six different combinations of activity and clothing where air temperature equals mean radiant temperature. [ASHRAE Handbook and Product Directory—1977 Fundamentals Volume, *American Society of Heating, Refrigerating and Air-Conditioning Engineers, Inc., New York, 1977, p. 8.25. Reprinted by permission.*]

on the northwest corner of the room, the average velocity of air movement within the room is calculated as follows:

$$\frac{42\ \text{ft}^2}{35\ \text{ft}^2} = 1.2$$

Increase (Figure 8-7) = 8 percent

$$\text{Effective opening} = 1.08 \times 35\ \text{ft}^2 = 37.8\ \text{ft}^2$$

$$VE_r = \frac{37.8\ \text{ft}^2 \times 8\ \text{mi/h}}{112\ \text{ft}^2} \times 0.35 = 0.945\ \text{mi/h}$$

Estimating the comfort, and ultimately the economic value, of breezes flowing through a room during the cooling season requires an understanding of additional concepts. First, the comfort of people during the cooling season and the amount of cooling required to maintain that comfort depend on the amount and type clothing they wear. Obviously, people who wear bathing suits indoors all summer will require less mechanical cooling than people who wear sweaters. A measure of clothing insulation whose unit is designated the "clo" has been developed. The data in Table 8-16 indicate relative clothing insulation (I_{cl}) values for various clothing ensembles.

Also, as mentioned in previous sections, comfort levels indoors during the cooling season depend on the level of humidity in the air. The combined effect of dry-bulb air temperature and relative humidity yields an "effective temperature." From Figure 8-5 it may be shown, for example, that an indoor dry-bulb temperature of 80°F with a 20 percent relative humidity has an effective temperature of 78°F, barely within the comfort zone. An 80°F dry-bulb temperature at an 80 percent relative humidity has an effective temperature of about 84°F, which is outside the comfort zone.

Summer indoor comfort is also a function of activity level. People in sedentary jobs require less cooling than people in high-activity jobs.

TABLE 8-16 Typical Data for Ensembles of Men and Women (While Sedentary)

Clothing ensemble	I_{cl} (basic clo)
Men	
Woven shirt, cool trousers	0.42
Woven shirt, warm trousers	0.45
Woven shirt, warm jacket, warm trousers	0.77
Women	
Cool dress	0.21
Cool sweater, cool dress	0.30
Cool sweater, cool slacks	0.36
Warm dress	0.49
Warm sweater, warm skirt	0.56
Warm sweater, warm skirt, warm blouse	0.64
Warm sweater, warm slacks, warm blouse	0.77

SOURCE: *ASHRAE Handbook and Product Directory—1977 Fundamentals Volume,* American Society of Heating, Refrigerating and Air-Conditioning Engineers, Inc., New York, 1977, p. 8.7. Reprinted by permission.

The speed of air movement, finally, will also affect comfort and the effective temperature of a space. The sensitivity of these variables is indicated in Figure 8-7. These diagrams along with degree-day data will allow a designer to conduct a cost-benefit analysis of designs for natural ventilation in residential buildings.

EXAMPLE

A designer decides to change the fixed glass windows on the south side of a house in the New York area to an operable design in order to capture summertime breezes and reduce air-conditioning costs. The added cost of operable windows over fixed glass is $3 per square foot of window.

The other relevant data required for analyzing the design are as follows:

South-facing glass area	210 ft^2
Amount converted to operable status	105 ft^2
Crack length of new operable south window	100 ft
West- and east-facing existing operable window area	120 ft^2
Average wind speed	8 mi/h
Prevailing wind direction during cooling period	Southwest
Electricity cost	$0.15 kWh
Oil cost	$1.50/gal
Cooling system	Central air
Relative humidity	60 percent
Activity level	Sedentary
Clothing	Light (I_{cl} = 0.5 clo)
Room cross section	432 ft^2
Average cooling load[6]	3.5 tons

The value of the operable windows for summer cooling is calculated as follows:

$$\text{Outlet} = 120 \text{ ft}^2$$

$$\text{Inlet} = 105 \text{ ft}^2$$

$$\text{Increase (Figure 8-7)} = 5 \text{ percent}$$

$$\text{Effective opening} = 1.05 \times 105 \text{ ft}^2 = 110 \text{ ft}^2$$

$$VE_r = \frac{110 \text{ ft}^2}{432 \text{ ft}^2} \times 8 \text{ mi/h} \times 0.35$$

$$= 0.713 \text{ mi/h} \tag{8-11}$$

or in terms of meters per second,

$$VE_r = 0.713 \text{ mi/h} \times \frac{1609 \text{ m/mi}}{3600 \text{ s/h}}$$

$$= 0.32 \text{ m/s}$$

From Figure 8-7 the change from no air movement (less than 0.1 meter per second) to above 0.2 meter per second suggests a change in air temperature from 76 to 79°F at a

[6]The *average*, not peak, cooling load is used in this particular estimating method.

constant 60 percent relative humidity. In other words, 79°F is a comfortable temperature with the air movement provided by the operable windows, whereas 76°F was the highest temperature in the comfort zone without the operable windows. The air conditioner, which normally might come on at 76°F, may remain inactive until a 79°F outside temperature is reached. This assumes, of course, that under conditions of natural ventilation in residential buildings the indoor and outdoor temperatures are equal.

An examination of bin-hour data for the New York area cooling season (Table 6-4) indicates that the temperature bin of 75 to 79°F has 456 hours. Adjusted for 3° instead of 5°, the result is 274 hours.

The value of this figure in monetary terms is calculated as follows:[7]

$$B_c = 1.49 \text{ kWh/(ton}\cdot\text{h)} \times \$0.15/\text{kWh} \times 274 \times 3.5 \text{ T}$$
$$= \$214/\text{year [See Equation (6-14).]}$$

The cost of additional winter heat loss due to the additional crack length is calculated as follows:

$$\Delta q_{s,h} = 1.08\,\Delta V(t_i - t_o) \text{ [See Equation (7-11).]}$$
$$= 1.08\,[0.375 \text{ ft}^3/(\text{min}\cdot\text{ft}) \times 100 \text{ ft}]\,(70°\text{F} - 15°\text{F})$$
$$= 2228 \text{ Btu/h}$$
$$C_h = \frac{\$1.50/\text{gal} \times 2228 \text{ Btu/h} \times 4811°\text{F}\cdot\text{days} \times 24 \text{ h/day} \times 0.63}{55°\text{F} \times 0.55 \times 140{,}000 \text{ Btu/gal}}$$
$$= \$57/\text{year [See Equation (6-2).]}$$

The air-conditioning savings of $214 per year are offset to some extent by the additional heating costs of $57 per year, yielding a net benefit of $157.

The use of operable windows does not reduce the peak cooling load since breezes may not always coincide with peak cooling load occurrences. Additional summer infiltration when the windows are closed has been ignored in this example.

The cost of using operable windows instead of fixed glass on the south side is

$$C_0 = \$3/\text{ft}^2 \times 105 \text{ ft}^2 = \$315$$

A cost-benefit analysis yields the following:

$$\text{Simple payback period} = \frac{\$315}{\$157/\text{year}} = 2.0 \text{ years}$$

$$\text{Simple return on investment} = \frac{\$157}{\$315} = 49.8 \text{ percent}$$

The operable windows appear to be highly cost-effective.

Cooling by Temperature-Induced Air Movement

Air movement can also be created in a building when no wind is available. This may be accomplished by heating air at a high point in the building and allowing

[7]This equation uses the average cooling load (3.5 tons in this case) to represent the need for cooling in the 76–79°F range. This is probably an overestimate. The analyst should estimate the specific cooling load for the particular temperature range, using bin data (Table 6-4) for greater accuracy.

the warm air to rise up and exhaust out. The rising warmed air creates a lower-pressure area at the top of the building. Higher-pressure air from lower zones then moves into the lower-pressure area, setting up air currents. If the sun is the heat source for this process, the air motion is caused without need for auxiliary electricity or fuel. This is often called a solar stack effect. (See also Chapters 3 and 4.)

Figure 3-12 in Chapter 3 shows a townhouse design which uses this approach to natural cooling. During the summer the sun shines through the south-facing glass at the top of the building, heating the surface on the interior of the structure. Air passes over this surface, is heated, and moves up and out of the louvers opposite the glass. The device that facilitates this phenomenon has historically been called a monitor, a lantern, or a cupola. (Additional discussion of this subject is presented in Chapter 3.)

The process of estimating the value of fuel-saving benefits that might be caused by such a design includes the following steps:

- Calculate the average daytime temperature during the cooling season by using degree-hour data (see Table 6-4).
- Calculate an interior sol-air temperature by using the equation in Figure 8-1.
- Identify the air movement's effect on interior comfort by using Figure 8-7.
- Identify the number of hours of reduced air-conditioning time by using degree-hour data (see Table 6-4).

The average outdoor daytime temperature for the New York area is calculated in Table 8-17.

TABLE 8-17 **Calculation of Average Daytime Temperature for June, July, and August from 10:00 A.M. to 5:00 P.M. in the New York City Area**

Temperature range, °F	(A) Middle temperature, °F	(B) Hours observed (10–17) June	July	August	(A) × (B)
100–104	102	0	1	0	102
95–99	97	2	4	3	873
90–94	92	7	16	8	2,852
85–89	87	22	45	35	8,874
80–84	82	41	74	66	14,842
75–79	77	58	73	73	15,708
70–74	72	51	28	44	8,856
65–69	67	36	5	16	3,819
60–64	62	17	1	3	1,302
55–59	57	6	1	0	399
		240	248	248	57,627°F·h
					÷ 736 h
					78.3°F

SOURCE: Calculated by the author by using data from Table 6-4.

The temperature of the air that is heated by the solar-heated absorbing surface is essentially a sol-air temperature, which is explained in detail in Figure 8-1. The sol-air temperature concept was initially developed for outdoor surfaces, but it is applicable to indoor surfaces as well when outside air is moving through the interior of a building.

The equation which may be used to estimate the velocity of stack-effect air movement is presented below:[8]

$$VE_r = \frac{9.4\ A_o\sqrt{h(t_{sa} - t_o)}}{A_r} \tag{8-12}$$

where VE_r = velocity of air movement within a room, ft/min
A_o = effective area of inlet opening adjusted by using Figure 8-7, ft^2
h = height from inlet to outlet, ft
t_{sa} = indoor sol-air temperature at height h, °F (See Figure 8-1.)
t_o = average outdoor daytime temperature, °F
A_r = cross-sectional area of room, ft^2
9.4 = proportionality constant, assuming a 65 percent effectiveness of inlet and outlet openings (50 percent would yield a 7.2 constant), no units

EXAMPLE

Using the house described in the subsection "Cooling by Breezes," calculate the value of a roof monitor 25 feet above the first-floor level, assuming the inlet and outlet openings are both 105 ft^2.

The average monthly sol-air temperature for a wall in the New York area is calculated as follows:

$$\alpha/h_o = 0.30\ (\text{ft}^2\cdot\text{h}\cdot°\text{F})/\text{Btu}$$

$$t_{oa} = 78.3°\text{F (See Table 8-17.)}$$

$$I = 886\ \text{Btu}/(\text{ft}^2\cdot\text{day})\ \text{(from Table 7-13, average of June, July, and August)}$$

$$t_{sa} = 78.3°\text{F} + 0.30\ (\text{ft}^2\cdot\text{h}\cdot°\text{F})/\text{Btu} \times [886\ \text{Btu}/(\text{ft}^2\cdot\text{day}) \div 15\ \text{h/day}]$$

The velocity of the solar-induced air movement is estimated as follows:

$$\begin{aligned} VE_r &= \frac{9.4 \times 105\ \text{ft}^2\sqrt{23\ \text{ft} \times (96°\text{F} - 78.3°\text{F})}}{432\ \text{ft}^2} \\ &= 46\ \text{ft/min} \times \frac{0.3048\ \text{m/ft}}{60\ \text{s/min}} \\ &= 0.234\ \text{m/s} \end{aligned} \tag{8-13}$$

From Figure 8-7, at 60 percent relative humidity a change from less than 0.1 meter per second to 0.97 meter per second implies a change from a 76°F comfort threshold temperature to a 78°F comfort threshold temperature.

Bin-hour data for the New York area cooling season during the daylight hours of 10 A.M. to 5 P.M. (see Table 6-4) indicate that there are 271 hours per year in which the temper-

[8] SOURCE: *ASHRAE Handbook and Product Directory—1977 Fundamentals Volume,* American Society of Heating, Refrigerating and Air-Conditioning Engineers, Inc., New York, 1977, p. 21.11.

ature ranges from 75 to 79°F. Since this analysis is concerned with the reduction in the need for air conditioning from 76 to 78°F, or 40 percent of the 5°F range, the number of hours in which air movement has made indoor conditions more comfortable is 271 hours × 0.4, or 108 hours.

The economic value of this reduction in cooling time is calculated below (the same energy cost and cooling system type as in the earlier example are assumed):[9]

$$B_c = 1.49 \text{ kWh/(ton} \cdot \text{h)} \times \$0.15/\text{kWh} \times 108 \text{ h/year} \times 3.5 \text{ tons}$$

$$= \$84/\text{year [See Equation (6-4).]}$$

The roof monitor is insulated during the winter, so additional heat loss is minimal. However, the winter solar heat gain by the glass as well as the summer conducted heat gain should be estimated to complete a comprehensive cost-benefit analysis of this option.

The estimating method presented here is rudimentary. The answers it yields are approximate, and for highly rigorous analysis they should be verified by more sophisticated computer analysis or by physical modeling.

Table 8-18 is a summary of the principal equations presented in this chapter.

[9]3.5 tons is the average, not peak, cooling load.

TABLE 8-18 Summary of Equations to Be Used for Estimating Summer Cooling Savings

Equation	Description
Conduction	
$\Delta q_c = \Delta(U \times A) \times \text{CLTD}$	8-1 Change in peak conducted heat gain using cooling load temperature differences (residential buildings)
$\Delta Q_c = \Delta(U \times A) \times \text{DH}_c$	8-2 Change in summer season conducted heat gain (nonresidential buildings)
Radiation	
$\Delta q_c = \Delta(A \times \text{SC}) \times \text{SHGF} \times \text{CLF}$	8-3 Change in peak solar heat gain rate (residential buildings)
$\Delta Q_c = \Delta(I_c \times A_g \times \tau \times \text{SF} \times T_c)$	8-4 Change in summer season solar heat gain (nonresidential buildings)
Convection	
$\Delta q_{s,c} = 0.018\, \Delta V(t_o - t_i)$	8-6 Change in peak summer heat gain by sensible heat infiltration (residential buildings)
$\Delta Q_{s,c} = 0.018\, \Delta V \times \text{DH}_c$	8-7 Change in overall cooling season heat gain by sensible heat infiltration (nonresidential buildings)
$\Delta q_{l,c} = 80.7\, \Delta V(W_o - W_i)$	8-9 Change in peak summer heat gain by latent heat infiltration (residential buildings)
$\Delta Q_{l,c} = 80.7\, \Delta V \times \text{HRH}$	8-10 Change in overall cooling season heat gain by latent heat infiltration (nonresidential buildings)
$VE_r = \dfrac{A_o \times VE_w}{A_r} \times E$	8-11 Velocity of air in a room as a function of breezes (residential buildings)
$VE_r = \dfrac{9.4\, A_o \sqrt{h(t_{sa} - t_o)}}{A_r}$	8-12 Velocity of air in a room as a function of temperature-induced air movement (residential buildings)

BIBLIOGRAPHY

ASHRAE Handbook and Product Directory—1977 Fundamentals Volume, American Society of Heating, Refrigerating and Air-Conditioning Engineers, Inc., New York, 1977.

Kusuda, T., and K. Ishii: *Hourly Solar Radiation Data for Vertical and Horizontal Surfaces on Average Days*, U.S. Department of Commerce, Washington, 1977.

NINE

HEATING AND COOLING SAVINGS WITH THERMAL MASS

Methods for estimating yearly savings when massive material is employed as part of a design approach are presented in this chapter. More specifically, the following design options are discussed:

- Earth-covered buildings
- Enclosure materials with thermal inertia

The common element in these approaches, of course, is the employment of massive materials to store heat for use at a later time. This storage effect takes the form of a time lag from the moment when heat enters a material until it is dissipated. In underground buildings, the heat of summer is lagged into winter, and the heat of winter is lagged into summer. For walls and roofs, massive materials such as masonry have the impact of lagging the heat of the day into the evening and the "cool" of the evening into the day.

The ultimate impact on energy use, as will be shown, is to decrease the range of temperature extremes to which the interior of a building is subjected. This will reduce not only peak loads but also overall fuel consumption.

The use of *additional* mass as an energy-saving design approach is usually more cost-effective in residential buildings than in commercial buildings. This is true because commercial buildings are normally designed with massive materials and additional mass often is not needed. Also, covering commercial buildings with earth, for example, reduces access to valuable natural light. There are, of course, notable exceptions to these generalizations.

EARTH-COVERED BUILDINGS

A design approach which conserves energy by reducing not only conductive heat transfer but convective transfers as well involves either burying a building partially or completely underground or covering it with earth. The following discussion presents a method for estimating the energy consumption reduction which such a design approach may provide.

In buildings surrounded by earth there is essentially no air infiltration through walls and roofs. This reduces not only winter heat loss and summer heat gain but the intake of fresh air as well. As a result, humidity, ventilation, and odor control may need special consideration in such design approaches.

Earth-covered buildings see substantially higher outside temperatures during the heating season in cold climates and lower outside temperatures during the cooling season. In the United States the temperature of the earth in the temperate climatic areas remains at a constant 50°F at 15 feet or more below the earth's surface. Above that level, the temperature begins to rise to about 60°F during the summer and to fall to about 40°F in the winter.

The effect of earth sheltering on each of the surfaces of a building should be analyzed separately. The sections below present the factors that should be considered for each surface and examples of how energy savings may be estimated.

Increased construction costs often occur as a result of placing buildings underground. These are due primarily to increased structural and waterproofing requirements. However, some construction cost savings may be realized as well. These include reduced exterior finishing costs and some reductions in insulation and wind loads.

Underground walls and footings must resist lateral loads due to earth and underground water pressures as well as increased dead loads due to earth cover. Moreover, roof planes must be stronger to resist dead loads related to earth cover.

The presence of water pressure and/or damp earth must be alleviated by waterproofing and dampproofing and sometimes by special drainage techniques. The cost of waterproofing, however, may be offset by savings in the cost of finish materials for the exterior of walls.

Roofs

The addition of earth to roofs will often result in lower energy consumption than occurs with the use of lower-mass roofs. High-mass roof structures respond more slowly to short-term exterior temperature fluctuations than do low-mass roof structures. As a result, peak load temperature conditions are reduced. Another thermal effect of grass-covered roofs is the reduction of surface sol-air temperatures, thus helping to reduce summer heat gain by conduction. Grass surfaces absorb significantly less radiation than do hard smooth white surfaces. This advantage is due mainly to the moisture released by the grass, which produces an evaporative cooling effect called transpiration.

According to a rough rule of thumb, an earth-covered roof structure will lose or gain about 8 percent less heat at peak conditions[1] than an above-grade roof structure of equal thermal resistance. In other words, for earth-covered roofs in temperate climates

$$\Delta q = 0.08\, q \qquad (9\text{-}1)$$

[1]SOURCE: Underground Space Center, *Earth Sheltered Housing Design*, Van Nostrand Reinhold Company, New York, 1979.

in units,

$$\text{Btu/h} = \text{Btu/h}$$

where Δq = reduction in peak heat loss through the roof of an earth-covered roof in comparison with an above-grade house, Btu/h

q = peak conducted heat loss rate through the roof of an above-grade house, Btu/h

Walls

A thermal analysis of heat gain or loss through the walls of an underground building depends on the depth of the building below grade. The designer should assume 10 feet as the line below which earth temperature is constant.

Table 9-1 gives peak temperature conditions in summer and winter for various depths of soil.

A bermed treatment of a wall will result in a slight increase (approximately 5 percent) in heat loss through the wall in comparison with a fully buried wall.[2]

Floors

The variation in the temperature of the earth under floor slabs at depths below 10 feet ranges from 40 to 60°F. The winter heat loss rate through an uninsulated floor slab has been calculated at 0.38 Btu per hour per square foot of floor area.[3]

Adding insulation below a floor slab is not recommended because it impedes the cooling effect of the earth under the floor during the summer. If 0.1 inch of polystyrene insulation is installed, however, the winter heat loss rate becomes slightly smaller: approximately 0.36 Btu per hour per square foot of floor area with little change in summer cooling effect.

One of the problems with an uninsulated concrete slab is a lack of comfort: the slab is cold to the touch. Adding carpeting or other insulative floor covering will

[2]Ibid., p. 66.

[3]Ibid., p. 61.

TABLE 9-1 Peak Temperatures of the Earth at Various Depths in Summer and Winter in Minnesota

	Peak temperature, °F	
Depth, ft	Summer	Winter
0.33	70	25
2.60	65	30
10.50	60	40

SOURCE: Extrapolated by the author from curves presented in Underground Space Center, *Earth Sheltered Housing Design*, Van Nostrand Reinhold Company, New York, 1979, p. 53.

help alleviate the cold feeling, however, without impairing the cooling effect of the slab during the summer.

EXAMPLE

The use of the above information to evaluate the cost-effectiveness on any earth-sheltered house design is illustrated in the example presented here. A designer of a simple south-facing single-family house is asked by her client to estimate the cost-benefit impact of covering the nonglass portions of the house with earth. The roof will have 1 foot of earth, and the walls will be buried up to the roof. The house design has the following characteristics (see Figure 9-1):

East or west wall area	180 ft^2, not including window
North wall area	416 ft^2, not including entry
Floor area or roof area	1400 ft^2
Heating fuel	Oil at $1.50/gal
Electricity	$0.15/kWh
U of roof	0.026 Btu/(°F·ft^2·h)
U of walls	0.069 Btu/(°F·ft^2·h)
Cost increases due to:	
Added roof load on walls	$0.30/ft of wall
Added roof load on roofs	$0.70/ft of roof
Added lateral load on walls	$0.50/ft of wall
Excavation costs	$500
Location	New York City

The analysis which follows will examine impacts first on conduction and then on convection (infiltration) created by the design change. There is no direct change in solar radiation heat gain because of the design. Seasonal changes in conduction through the roof, walls, and stairs will be analyzed separately.

The peak *winter* heat loss through the roof *without* earth on it will be

$$q_h = 0.026 \text{ Btu/(h}\cdot\text{°F}\cdot\text{ft}^2) \times 1400 \text{ ft}^2 \times (70\text{°F} - 15\text{°F})$$

$$= 2002 \text{ Btu/h [See Equation (7-6).]}$$

The peak *summer* heat gain through the roof *without* the earth will be[4]

$$q_c = 0.026 \text{ Btu/h} \times 1400 \text{ ft}^2 \times 17\text{°F}$$

$$= 619 \text{ Btu/h [See Equation (8-1).]}$$

When using the 8 percent rule of thumb, the peak heat transfer reductions through a roof with earth cover will be as follows:

$$\Delta q_{h\ \text{winter}} = 2002 \text{ Btu/h} \times 0.08 = 160 \text{ Btu/h} \qquad (9\text{-}1)$$

$$\Delta q_{c\ \text{summer}} = 619 \text{ Btu/h} \times 0.08 = 50 \text{ Btu/h} \qquad (9\text{-}1)$$

The reductions in winter peak heat loss through the walls will be estimated by using the difference between the outside air and earth temperatures which will affect the heat transfer. The outside air temperature for purposes of estimating the peak heat load (97.5 percentile) in the New York area is 15°F. (See Table 6-3.)

[4]From Table 8-1.

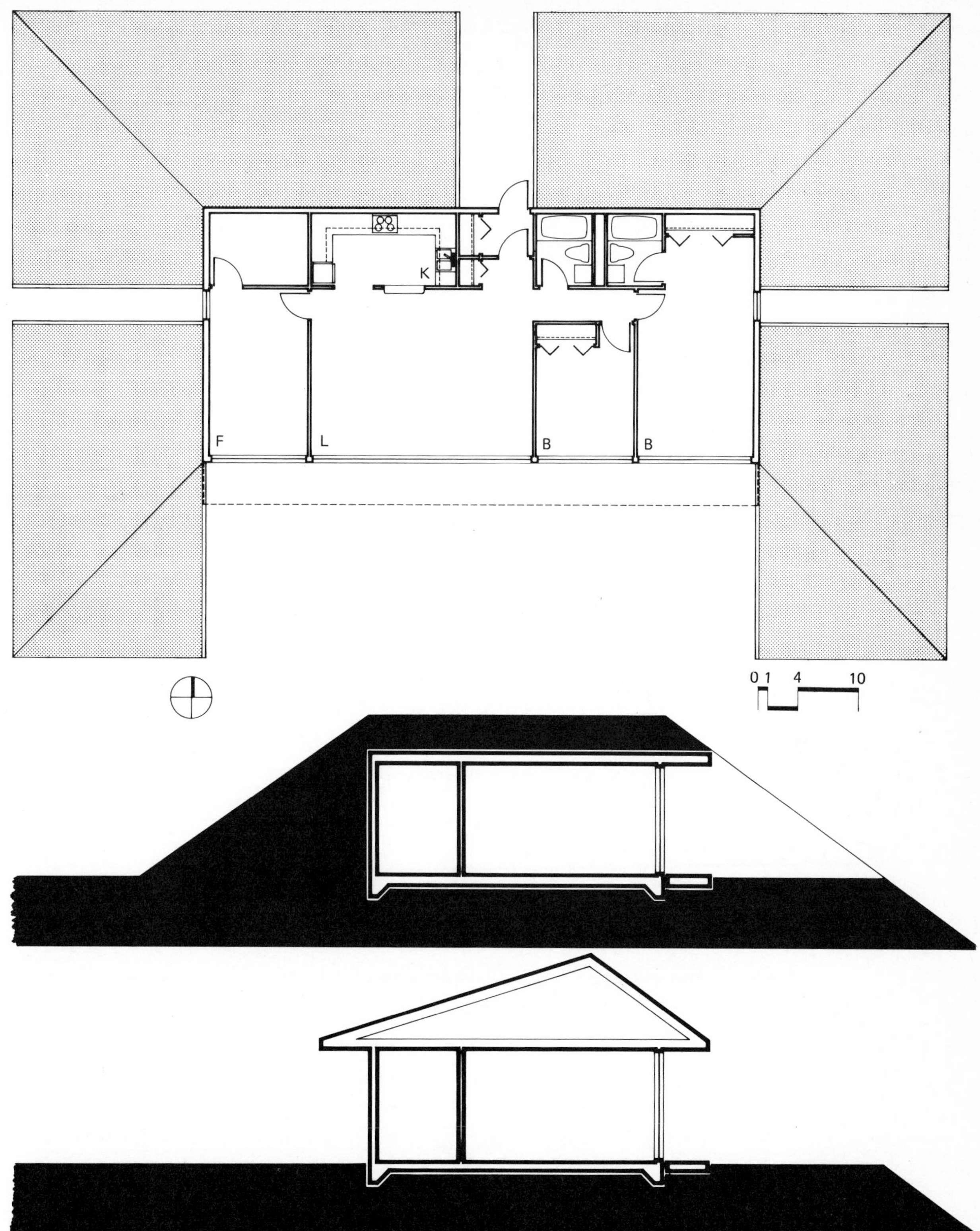

FIGURE 9·1 Plan and section of a house redesigned for a below-grade condition.

The ground temperature at 9 feet below the earth's surface is about 38° during the winter. The temperature at the surface is assumed to be the peak load temperature of 15°F. The peak outside temperature that the underground portions of the wall will experience during the winter therefore will be as follows:

$$\text{Average peak underground temperature } t_o = (15°\text{F} + 38°\text{F}) \div 2 = 26.5°\text{F}$$

$$\text{Outside peak temperature increase} = 26.5°\text{F} - 15°\text{F} = 11.5°\text{F}$$

The winter peak heat loss *reduction* due to the underground position may be estimated as follows:

$$\Delta q_h = 0.069 \text{ Btu/(°F·ft}^2\text{·h)} \times 776 \text{ ft}^2 \times 11.5°\text{F}$$

$$= 616 \text{ Btu/h [See Equation (7-6).]}$$

The underground house will not have any heat gain through the walls during the summer because of the stable ±67°F temperature of the earth cover during the cooling season. The savings between the two houses therefore will be the total heat gain through the walls of the *aboveground* house:

The following calculations of heat gain for the aboveground design are based on the approach presented in Chapter 8:

	North	East	West
Maximum CLTD	26°F	55°F	72°F
80°F inside temperature	− 2°F	− 2°F	− 2°F
August	+ 4°F	+ 4°F	+ 4°F
78°F August outside temperature	− 7°F	− 7°F	− 7°F
	21°F	50°F	67°F

$$\text{North wall: } q_c = 0.069 \text{ Btu/(°F·h·ft}^2) \times 416 \text{ ft}^2 \times 21°\text{F}$$

$$= 603 \text{ Btu/h [See Equation (8-1).]}$$

$$\text{East wall: } q_c = 0.069 \text{ Btu/(°F·h·ft}^2) \times 180 \text{ ft}^2 \times 50°\text{F}$$

$$= 621 \text{ Btu/h [See Equation (8-1).]}$$

$$\text{West wall: } q_c = 0.069 \text{ Btu/(°F·h·ft}^2) \times 180 \text{ ft}^2 \times 67°\text{F}$$

$$= 832 \text{ Btu/h [See Equation (8-1).]}$$

$$\text{Total: } q_c = 2056 \text{ Btu/h}$$

Wintertime peak heat loss through the floor slab of the underground house will be:

$$q_h = 0.38 \text{ Btu/(h·ft}^2) \times 1400 \text{ ft}^2$$

$$= 532 \text{ Btu/h}$$

Peak heat loss through the slab of an above-grade house may be estimated as follows (see subsection "Basement Floors and Slabs at Grade" for an explanation):

$$q_h = U_{p,s} \times P_s \times (t_i - t_o)$$

$$= 0.55 \text{ Btu/(ft·°F)} \times 162 \text{ ft} \times (70°\text{F} - 15°\text{F}) \qquad (9\text{-}5)$$

$$= 4901 \text{ Btu/h}$$

Floor slab peak heat loss reductions because of the underground design therefore are

$$\Delta q_h = 4901 \text{ Btu/h} - 532 \text{ Btu/h} = 4369 \text{ Btu/h}$$

The total reductions in the *conducted* winter peak heating load are summed below:

Roof	160 Btu/h
Walls	616 Btu/h
Floor	4369 Btu/h
Total	5145 Btu/h

Total reductions in summer *conducted* peak heat gain are

Roof	50 Btu/h
Walls	2056 Btu/h
Total	2106 Btu/h

Infiltration savings are estimated next. There will be no infiltration through the walls of the underground house during either winter or summer. Infiltration through windows, which are not earth-covered, will remain the same as in the aboveground design.

Winter infiltration through the walls of the above-grade house is estimated below:

$$q_h = 0.018 \text{ Btu/(ft}^3\cdot{}^\circ\text{F)} \times [10 \text{ ft}^3\text{/(h}\cdot\text{ft}^2) \times 776 \text{ ft}^2] \times (70^\circ\text{F} - 15^\circ\text{F})$$

$$= 7682 \text{ Btu/h [See Equation (7-10).]}$$

Summer infiltration is estimated as follows:

$$q_{c,s} = 0.018 \text{ Btu/(}^\circ\text{F}\cdot\text{ft}^3) \times [10 \text{ ft}^3\text{/(h}\cdot\text{ft}^2) \times 776 \text{ ft}^2] \times (89^\circ\text{F} - 80^\circ\text{F})$$

$$= 1257 \text{ Btu/h [See Equation (8-6).]}$$

$$q_{s,l} = 80.7 \text{ Btu/ft}^3 \times [10 \text{ ft}^3\text{/(h}\cdot\text{ft}^2) \times 776 \text{ ft}^2] \times (0.0142 \text{ lb/lb} - 0.0112 \text{ lb/lb})$$

$$= 1879 \text{ Btu/h [See Equation (8-9).]}$$

The economic value of the thermal benefits is estimated below:

Conduction and infiltration winter peak heat load *reductions* created by the below-grade designs are the following:

Conduction	5,145 Btu/h
Infiltration	7,682 Btu/h
Total	12,827 Btu/h

The value of annual heating savings is estimated below:

$$B_h = \frac{\$1.50\text{/gal} \times 12{,}827 \text{ Btu/h} \times 4811 \text{ (}^\circ\text{F}\cdot\text{days)/year} \times 24 \text{ h/day} \times 0.63}{55^\circ\text{F} \times 0.55 \times 140{,}000 \text{ Btu/gal}}$$

$$= \$330\text{/year}$$

The reductions in peak cooling load are summarized below:

Conduction	2106 Btu/h
Infiltration:	
Sensible	1257 Btu/h
Latent	1879 Btu/h
Total	5242 Btu/h

The value of the reductions in annual cooling load is calculated below:

$$B_c = 1.49 \text{ kW/ton} \times \$0.15/\text{kWh} \times 1000 \text{ h/year} \times [5242 \text{ Btu/h} \div 12{,}000 \text{ Btu/(ton}\cdot\text{h)}]$$

$$= \$98/\text{year [See Equation (6-4).]}$$

Total annual fuel-related savings are summarized below:

Heating savings, B_h	\$330/year
Cooling savings, B_c	\$ 98/year
	\$428/year

The added cost of the underground house is estimated below:

Excavation	\$1500
Roof load on east-west walls, \$0.30/ft² × 360 ft²	108
Roof load on roof, \$0.70/ft² × 1400 ft²	980
Lateral load on walls, \$0.50/ft² × 776 ft²	388
Total	\$2976

Note that no cost increase has been included for waterproofing because the requirement for exterior finish has been eliminated and the two costs are approximately the same.

A simple cost-benefit analysis yields the following:

$$\text{Simple payback period} = \frac{\$2976}{\$428/\text{year}} = 7.0 \text{ years}$$

$$\text{Simple return on investment} = \frac{\$428/\text{year}}{\$2976} = 14.4 \text{ percent/year}$$

The design is cost-effective.

A separate analysis of the cost-effectiveness of the earth cover on the roof alone is presented below.

The peak heat load reduction caused by the roof covering is 160 Btus per hour. The annual heating value of this amount is estimated below:

$$B_h = \frac{\$1.50/\text{gal} \times 160 \text{ Btu/h} \times 4811 \text{ (°F}\cdot\text{days)/year} \times 24 \text{ h/day} \times 0.63}{55\text{°F} \times 0.55 \times 150{,}000 \text{ Btu/gal}}$$

$$= \$4/\text{year [See Equation (6-2).]}$$

The peak cooling load reduction attributable to the roof is 50 Btus per hour. The annual value of this reduction is estimated below:

$$B_c = 1.49 \text{ kW/ton} \times \$0.15/\text{kWh} \times 1000 \text{ h} [50 \text{ Btu/h} \div 12{,}000 \text{ Btu/(ton}\cdot\text{h)}]$$

$$= \$1/\text{year [See Equation (6-4).]}$$

Total savings due to the earth-covered roof are

B_h	\$4/year
B_c	\$1/year
Total	\$5/year

The cost of the earth-covered roof is estimated below:

Roof load on east-west walls	\$ 108
Roof load on roof	980
Total	\$1088

The cost-effectiveness of the roof cover is:

$$\text{Simple payback period} = \frac{\$1088}{\$5/\text{year}} = 218 \text{ years}$$

$$\text{Simple return on investment} = \frac{\$5}{\$1088} = 0.05 \text{ percent/year}$$

Clearly the earth cover on the roof is not worth the investment. Removing this aspect from the design will improve overall cost-effectiveness. The costs and benefits of the house without an earth-covered roof are presented below:

$$\text{Cost} = \$2976 - \$1088 = \$1888$$

$$\text{Savings} = \$428 - \$5 = \$423$$

$$\text{Simple payback period} = \frac{\$1888}{\$423/\text{year}} = 4.5 \text{ years}$$

$$\text{Simple return on investment} = \frac{\$423/\text{year}}{\$1888} = 22.4 \text{ percent/year}$$

The simple payback period has improved from 7.0 years to 4.5 years, and the return on investment from 14.4 percent per year to 22.4 percent per year.

OTHER ESTIMATING METHODS FOR EARTH-COVERED BUILDINGS

Basement Walls

Another approach to estimating peak heat loss from below-grade walls has been developed by the American Society of Heating, Refrigerating and Air-Conditioning Engineers (ASHRAE). Data from experiments conducted by ASHRAE have been compiled and are presented in Table 9-2. When using this method, the designer must select a different perimeter heat loss rate U_p for each foot of depth of basement below grade. The outside temperature that should be used in calculating heat loss from basement walls when using this method is the following:

$$t_{o,w} = t_a - A \tag{9-2}$$

TABLE 9-2 Heat Loss below Grade in Basement Walls*

Depth ft	Path length through soil, ft	Heat loss ($U_{p,w}$), Btu/(h·ft·°F) Uninsulated	Insulation 1 in	Insulation 2 in	Insulation 3 in
0–1 (first)	0.68	0.410	0.152	0.093	0.067
1–2 (second)	2.27	0.222	0.116	0.079	0.059
2–3 (third)	3.88	0.155	0.094	0.068	0.053
3–4 (fourth)	5.52	0.119	0.079	0.060	0.048
4–5 (fifth)	7.05	0.096	0.069	0.053	0.044
5–6 (sixth)	8.65	0.079	0.060	0.048	0.040
6–7 (seventh)	10.28	0.069	0.054	0.044	0.037

* k_{soil} = 9.6 (Btu·h·in)/(ft²·°F); $k_{insulation}$ = 0.24 (Btu·h·in)/ft²·°F).

SOURCE: *ASHRAE Handbook and Product Directory—1977 Fundamentals Volume,* American Society of Heating, Refrigerating and Air-Conditioning Engineers, Inc., New York, 1977, p. 24.4. Reprinted by permission

in units,

$$°\text{F} = °\text{F} - °\text{F}$$

where $t_{o,w}$ = temperature outside basement walls, °F
t_a = average *annual* air temperature, °F
A = amplitude of ground surface temperature fluctuations, °F (This varies with geographic location and may be obtained from Figure 9-2.)

By using this temperature, the heat loss rate of a basement wall may be estimated by means of the following

$$q_h = U_{p,w} \times P_w \times (t_{o,w} - t_i) \tag{9-3}$$

in units,

$$\text{Btu/h} = \text{Btu/(h·ft·°F)} \times \text{ft} \times °\text{F}$$

where q_h = peak basement wall heat loss rate, Btu/h
$U_{p,w}$ = basement wall perimeter heat loss coefficient, Btu/(h·ft·°F) (See Table 9-2 and add the $U_{p,w}$ for each foot of depth below grade.)
P_w = perimeter of basement wall, ft
$t_{o,w}$ = temperature outside a basement wall as calculated by using Equation (9-2), °F
t_i = inside air temperature, °F

EXAMPLE

For the example described in the section "Earth-Covered Buildings," the difference in heat loss through the walls by using this method may be recalculated as presented below:

Peak load heat loss from above-grade walls:

$$q_h = 0.069 \text{ Btu/(°F·h·ft}^2) \times 776 \text{ ft}^2 \times (70°\text{F} - 15°\text{F})$$
$$= 2945 \text{ Btu/h [See Equation (7-6).]}$$

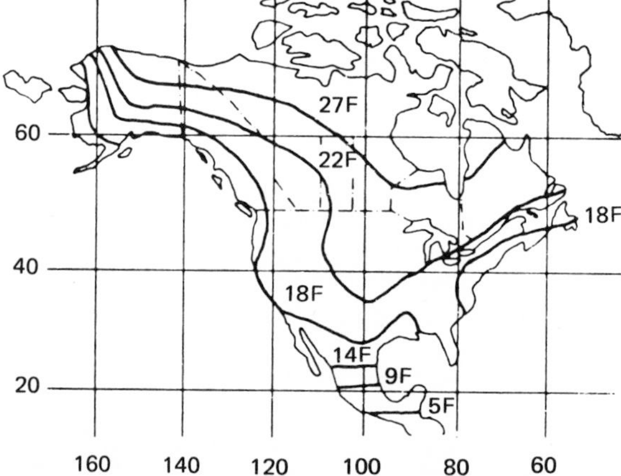

FIGURE 9-2 Lines of constant temperature and amplitude. [ASHRAE Handbook and Product Directory—1977 Fundamentals Volume, *American Society of Heating, Refrigerating and Air-Conditioning Engineers, Inc., New York, 1977, p. 24.5. Reprinted by permission.*]

Peak load heat loss from below-grade walls:

Depth, ft	$U_{p,w}$ 3-in insulation (Table 9-2)
0–1	0.067
1–2	0.059
2–3	0.053
3–4	0.048
4–5	0.044
5–6	0.040
6–7	0.037
7–8	0.037
Total $U_{p,w}$	0.385 Btu/(h·ft·°F)

$$\text{Base perimeter} = 106 \text{ feet}$$

$$t_{o,w} = 54.3°\text{F}^{5} - 18°\text{F}$$

$$= 36.3°\text{F} \qquad (9\text{-}2)$$

$$q_h = 0.385 \text{ Btu/(h·ft·°F)} \times 106 \text{ ft} \times (70°\text{F} - 36.3°\text{F})$$

$$= 1375 \text{ Btu/h} \qquad (9\text{-}3)$$

The saving in heat loss because of the underground location of the walls is

Aboveground	2945 Btu/h
Below grade	1375 Btu/h
	1570 Btu/h

This method yields a higher estimate of heat loss reduction through basement walls than does the method used in the preceding example (1570 Btu/h compared with 616 Btu/h).

Basement Floors and Slabs at Grade

Heat loss from basement floors by using an ASHRAE method may be estimated with the data in Table 9-3:

$$q_h = U_b \times A_b \times (t_i - t_o) \qquad (9\text{-}4)$$

in units,

$$\text{Btu/h} = \text{Btu/(h·ft}^2\text{·°F)} \times \text{ft}^2 \times (°\text{F} - °\text{F})$$

where q_h = peak heat loss rate, Btu/h
U_b = heat loss coefficient of basement floors, Btu/(°F·h·ft²) (See Table 9-3 for U_b as a function of depth below grade.)
A_b = area of basement floor, ft²
t_o = temperature of earth at basement floor depth, °F

Calculate by using Table 9-1 or Equation (9-2).

[5]Median annual air temperature from Table 6-4.

TABLE 9-3 **Heat Loss through Uninsulated Basement Floors** [(Btu/(h·ft²·°F)]

Depth of foundation wall below grade, ft	Width of house, ft			
	20	24	28	32
5	0.032	0.029	0.026	0.023
6	0.030	0.027	0.025	0.022
7	0.029	0.026	0.023	0.021

SOURCE: *ASHRAE Handbook and Product Directory—1977 Fundamentals Volume*, American Society of Heating, Refrigerating and Air-Conditioning Engineers, Inc., New York, 1977, p. 24.5. Reprinted by permission.

The heat loss from a slab on grade may be estimated as follows:

$$q_h = U_{p,s} \times P_s \times (t_i - t_o) \tag{9-5}$$

in units,

$$\text{Btu/h} = \text{Btu/(h·ft·°F)} \times \text{ft} \times \text{°F}$$

where q_h = peak slab heat loss rate, Btu/h
$U_{p,s}$ = slab perimeter heat loss coefficient, Btu/(h·ft·°F) ($U_{p,s}$ = 0.81 for a slab with no edge insulation and and 0.55 for a slab with 1 in of insulation.[6])
P_s = perimeter of slab edge, ft
t_o = outside air temperature, °F
t_i = inside air temperature, °F

Heat loss from a slab-on-grade structure may also be estimated by using the data in Table 9-4, also compiled by ASHRAE.

EXAMPLE

As in the example presented earlier, the difference in peak heat loss between a slab on grade and a basement floor by using the ASHRAE method is presented below.

The slab-on-grade heat loss, assuming 2-inch-edge insulation and using data from Table 9-4, is calculated below:

$$q_h = 40 \text{ Btu/(h·ft)} \times 162 \text{ ft} = 6480 \text{ Btu/h}$$

This incidentally is larger than the 4901 Btu/h calculated with Equation (9-5).

The basement floor peak heat loss, assuming a 24-foot-wide house 7 feet below grade, is

$$q_h = 0.026 \text{ Btu/(h·°F·ft}^2) \times 1400 \text{ ft}^2 \times (70\text{°F} - 36.3\text{°F}) \tag{9-4}$$

$$= 1227 \text{ Btu/h}$$

This is a larger heat loss than that estimated by using the earlier method: 1227 Btu/h compared with 532 Btu/h.

[6] *ASHRAE Handbook and Product Directory—1977 Fundamentals Volume*, American Society of Heating, Refrigerating and Air-Conditioning Engineers, Inc., New York, 1977, p. 24.5. Reprinted by permission.

The choice of estimating method must be made by the designer. As shown here, ASHRAE-based methods sometimes yield more conservative results and sometimes more liberal results. These methods have, however, been subjected to an extensive peer review process and, in that manner, are perhaps better tested.

ENCLOSURE MATERIALS WITH THERMAL INERTIA

In many types of low-rise buildings, an architect often has the choice of using either lightweight materials such as wood framing and sheet materials or heavier-weight materials such as masonry for the walls and roof of a building. Both types often meet code requirements, and the choice typically depends on issues of aesthetics and economics. The economic issues include, of course, the impact on a building's need for energy. Typically, a building enclosed with low-mass materials will cost less to construct but more to heat and cool when compared with a building enclosed with high-mass materials. The choice involves comparing construction costs with fuel-saving benefits.

All materials have a property of "thermal inertia," which means basically that they take some time to heat up or cool down. This time lag effect varies with the materials and the environment around them.

Building materials with high thermal inertia have high mass. Such materials place smaller thermal loads on heating and cooling systems than low-mass materials. This is true because, in effect, the outside surface temperature of a material which has high thermal inertia and a long thermal lag time will usually not be as cold as the outside air in the heating season or as warm as the outside air in the cooling season. Because of the rate at which outside air temperatures change in most climates, a high-mass–long-thermal-lag material will be, for example, just beginning to cool down when the outside air temperature has reached a low point and has begun cycling up again. The temperature of the outer surface of such a material doesn't react as quickly as does the outside air temperature. The material's relatively slow temperature decline never reaches the low point in the outside air temperature cycle because it's forced to reverse its direction when the more rapidly changing air temperature begins its upward path: it attempts to follow the air temperature cycle but usually never catches up.

TABLE 9-4 Heat Loss of Concrete Floors at or Near Grade Level per Foot of Exposed Edge

Outdoor design temperature, °F	Heat loss per foot of exposed edge, Btu/(h · ft)		
	Recommended 2-in edge insulation	1-in edge insulation	No edge insulation
−20 to −30	50	55	75
−10 to −20	45	50	65
0 to −10	40	45	40

SOURCE: *ASHRAE Handbook and Product Directory—1977 Fundamentals Volume*, American Society of Heating, Refrigerating and Air-Conditioning Engineers, Inc., New York 1977, p. 24.5. Reprinted by permission.

Heat flow rates through materials under *static* temperature conditions are measured in terms of U values and R values (see Chapter 7). These rates are reasonably accurate for low-mass–short-thermal-lag materials under *dynamic* temperature conditions but are less accurate for materials with high thermal inertia under such conditions.

Thermal inertia may be described by an index called gamma (γ), which has no units. In physical terms, it represents the ratio of wall or roof thickness to the "thermal" thickness of a material.

$$\gamma = \sqrt{\frac{2 \cdot \rho \cdot c}{24 \cdot 2 \cdot k}} \times L = \sqrt{\frac{0.1309 \cdot \rho \cdot c}{k}} \times L \tag{9-6}$$

in units,

$$\frac{\text{lb/ft}^3 \times \text{Btu/(lb}\cdot{}^\circ\text{F)}}{\text{h} \times \text{Btu/(h}\cdot\text{ft}\cdot{}^\circ\text{F)}} \times \text{ft}$$

where γ = gamma, or the thermal inertia index, no units
ρ = mass density, lb/ft^3
c = specific heat, Btu/(lb·°F)
k = conductivity, Btu/(h·°F·ft)
L = length (thickness), ft

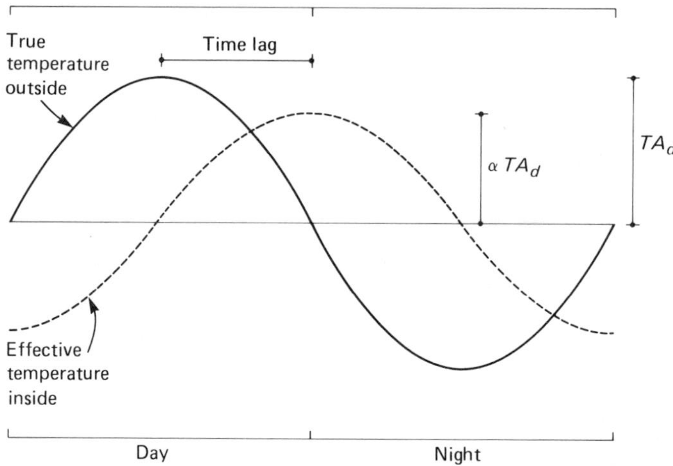

FIGURE 9·3 Difference between true outside temperature and effective inside temperature as caused by the thermal inertia of the enclosing conductive material.

TA_d = daily temperature amplitude
Time lag (T_L) = time between peaks of two different waves of heating flowing through a material
α = attenuation factor, the amount of reduction in the temperature savings (amplitude) experienced

[*Francisco Arumi,* Thermal Inertia in Architectural Walls, *Northeast Solar Energy Center, Cambridge, Mass., 1979, p. II-13.*]

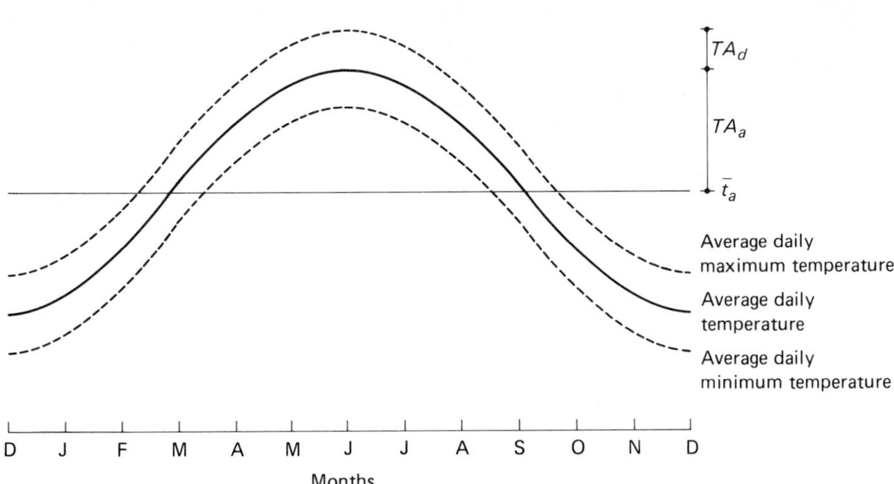

FIGURE 9-4 Outdoor dry-bulb temperature oscillations annually and daily.

TA = **temperature amplitude**
TA_d = **daily temperature amplitude**
TA_a = **annual temperature amplitude**
$\bar{t}_a$ = **mean (average) annual temperature**

[*Francisco Arumi,* Thermal Inertia in Architectural Walls, *Northeast Solar Energy Center, Cambridge, Mass., 1979, p. II-17.*]

Building materials with low insulation qualities but high thermal inertia values may still provide for lower energy consumption than materials with high insulative properties and low thermal inertia.

To prepare energy consumption estimates which acknowledge thermal inertia, the following concepts must be defined. As shown in Figure 9-3, temperature changes throughout a typical day may be described by a sinusoidal oscillating curve. Typically, temperatures are highest during the day and lowest during the night. As shown by the solid line in the diagram, the temperature in a room enclosed and protected from outdoor temperatures will be less extreme and will oscillate with some delay when compared with outside temperature oscillations. (This is indicated on a dotted line in Figure 9-3.) The smaller extremes in oscillation are described as changes in temperature amplitude. The amount of amplitude change may be quantified as an "attenuation factor" called alpha (α). The delay in the timing of the temperature oscillation is described as a "time lag" (T_L). The thermal inertia of an enclosing material affects both the attenuation factor and the time lag.

The characteristics of a climate must be described in terms of temperature oscillations to determine the effectiveness of the thermal inertia of a wall or roof on building energy consumption. Both daily and annual temperature fluctuations are described diagrammatically in Figure 9-4.

TABLE 9-5 Annual Weather Data (1964 data unless noted otherwise)

	$\bar{t}_a$, °F	TA_d, °F	TA_a, °F
Fairbanks, Alaska	25.8	11.4	35.4
Phoenix, Arizona	69.0	15.7	20.1
Los Angeles, California	61.9	7.9	7.4
San Francisco, California	56.8	6.0	5.7
Denver, Colorado	49.5	14.5	17.3
Washington, D.C.	57.0	8.8	20.7
Miami, Florida	75.5	7.6	7.9
Atlanta, Georgia	61.6	10.3	17.4
Honolulu, Hawaii	75.9	6.1	3.5
Chicago, Illinois	50.8	8.0	24.8
New Orleans, Louisiana	68.3	9.4	14.5
Boston, Massachusetts	51.4	7.7	21.9
Minneapolis–St. Paul, Minnesota	43.7	10.9	30.0
Kansas City, Missouri	56.8	9.8	24.9
Newark, New Jersey	54.6	9.0	22.0
Houston, Texas	68.9	10.9	15.7
Seattle, Washington	53.2	6.8	12.2

NOTE: If weather data are available for the particular location of interest, annual weather can be easily calculated:

t_a: From the table of normals, means, and extremes the annual mean temperature ($\bar{t}_a$) can be read directly (see Figure 9-3).

TA_d: The daily temperature amplitude is calculated by taking half of the difference between the maximum and minimum daily temperatures (see Figure 9-3).

TA_a: The annual amplitude of the mean daily temperature is calculated by taking half of the difference between the mean maximum and minimum monthly values (see Figure 9-3).

SOURCE: Francisco Arumi, *Thermal Inertia in Architectural Walls*, Northeast Solar Energy Center, Cambridge, Mass., 1979, pp. III-26–III-35. Reprinted by permission.

Aggregate measures which relate outside temperature oscillations to desired inside temperature comfort levels and the attenuation properties of enclosing materials are presented below. These measures will be used in an analysis procedure which will yield estimates of both peak load and annual energy consumption as a function of thermal inertia effects.

Annual Temperature Ratio (A_t)

Cooling season:

$$A_t = \frac{\bar{t}_a - t_{i,c}}{\alpha(t_o - t_{i,c})} = \frac{\bar{t}_a - t_{i,c}}{\alpha TA_d} \qquad (9\text{-}7)$$

Heating season:

$$A_t = \frac{t_{i,h} - \bar{t}_a}{\alpha(t_{i,h} - t_o)} = \frac{\bar{t}_a - t_{i,h}}{\alpha TA_d} \qquad (9\text{-}8)$$

where A_t = annual temperature ratio, no units
$\bar{t}_a$ = mean annual temperature, °F (See Table 9-5.)
$t_{i,c}$ = thermostat temperature during the cooling season
$t_{i,h}$ = thermostat setting during the heating season
α = attenuation factor, no units (See Table 9-6.)
t_o = peak design outside dry-bulb temperature, °F
TA_d = average amplitude of daily temperature swings, °F (This figure is tabulated in Table 9-5 on an annual, not a seasonal, basis. For most climate areas, it varies little between winter and summer.)

Amplitude Ratio (B)

$$B = \frac{TA_a}{\alpha TA_d} \tag{9-9}$$

where B = amplitude ratio, no units
TA_a = annual amplitude of the mean daily temperature, °F (See Table 9-5.)
α = attenuation factor, no units (See Table 9-10.)
TA_d = average amplitude of daily temperature swings, °F (See Table 9-5.)

The overall static thermal conductance U of a material, its temperature amplitude attenuation factor α, and the climate surrounding it may be used to estimate the heat flow rate through the material and, finally, the energy consumption implied by that rate. The equations in the following subsections show the relationship between these variables.

Heat Flow Factor

$$J = U \times \alpha \times TA_d \tag{9-10}$$

in units,

$$\text{Btu/(h·ft}^2) = \text{Btu/(h·ft}^2\text{·°F)} \times \text{°F}$$

TABLE 9-6 Dynamic Attenuation Factors (Alpha)

	Conductance, Btu/(h·ft²·°F)									
Gamma	0.04	0.20	0.36	0.52	0.68	0.84	1.00	1.16	1.32	1.48
0.50	1.00	1.00	1.00	1.00	1.00	1.00	1.00	0.99	0.99	0.99
1.00	0.98	0.97	0.96	0.95	0.95	0.94	0.93	0.92	0.92	0.91
1.50	0.90	0.87	0.84	0.81	0.79	0.76	0.74	0.73	0.71	0.70
2.00	0.74	0.69	0.64	0.60	0.57	0.54	0.52	0.50	0.48	0.47
2.50	0.56	0.50	0.45	0.41	0.38	0.36	0.34	0.32	0.31	0.30
3.00	0.41	0.35	0.31	0.27	0.25	0.23	0.22	0.21	0.20	0.19
3.50	0.28	0.24	0.20	0.18	0.16	0.15	0.14	0.13	0.12	0.12
4.00	0.20	0.16	0.13	0.11	0.10	0.09	0.09	0.08	0.08	0.07
4.50	0.13	0.10	0.08	0.07	0.06	0.06	0.05	0.05	0.05	0.05
5.00	0.09	0.07	0.05	0.05	0.04	0.04	0.03	0.03	0.03	0.03

SOURCE: Francisco Arumi, *Thermal Inertia in Architectural Walls*, Northeast Solar Energy Center, Cambridge, Mass., 1979, pp. III-15–III-19. Reprinted by permission.

where J = heat flow factor, Btu/(h·ft²)
U = heat transfer coefficient, Btu/(h·ft·°F)
α = attenuation factor, no units (See Table 9-6.)
TA_d = average amplitude of daily temperature swings, °F (See Table 9-5.)

Annual Energy Demand (Q)

$$Q = J \times \text{annual factor} \times A \tag{9-11}$$

in units,

$$\text{Btu/year} = \text{Btu/(h·ft}^2) \times \text{h/year} \times \text{ft}^2$$

where Q = annual energy consumption, Btu/year
J = heat flow factor, Btu/(h·ft²)
Annual factor = factor dependent on the annual temperature ratio A_t and the amplitude ratio B, h/year. (See Table 9-7.)
A = area of wall or roof, ft²

The steps to be followed in estimating energy consumption in a manner which acknowledges thermal inertia are listed below:

1 Identify the conductivity k, density ρ, specific heat c, resistance R, and thermal inertia γ of the material being analyzed (see Tables 9-8, 9-9, and 9-10).

2 Calculate the conductance $1/R$ and the U value $l/\Sigma R$.

3 Identify the following temperature measures from Table 9-5:

$\bar{t}_a$ = mean annual temperature
TA_a = annual temperature amplitude
TA_d = daily temperature amplitude

4 Calculate the heat flow factor J for the heating season and the cooling season.

TABLE 9-7 Annual Energy Consumption Factor (Entry from Table Multiplied by 10,000 h/year)

	Relative annual amplitude, B								
A	**0.00**	**1.00**	**2.00**	**3.00**	**4.00**	**5.00**	**6.00**	**7.00**	**8.00**
−8.00	0.00	0.00	0.00	0.00	0.00	0.00	0.00	0.00	0.03
−6.00	0.00	0.00	0.00	0.00	0.00	0.00	0.03	0.12	0.28
−4.00	0.00	0.00	0.00	0.00	0.04	0.14	0.32	0.54	0.78
−2.00	0.00	0.00	0.05	0.19	0.40	0.65	0.90	1.17	1.43
0.00	0.28	0.36	0.59	0.86	1.13	1.41	1.68	1.96	2.24
2.00	1.75	1.75	1.80	1.94	2.15	2.40	2.66	2.92	3.19
4.00	3.50	3.50	3.50	3.50	3.54	3.65	3.83	4.04	4.28
6.00	5.26	5.26	5.26	5.26	5.26	5.26	5.29	5.38	5.54
8.00	7.01	7.01	7.01	7.01	7.01	7.01	7.01	7.01	7.03

SOURCE: Francisco Arumi, *Thermal Inertia in Architectural Walls,* Northeast Solar Energy Center, Cambridge, Mass., 1979, p. III-36–III-41. Reprinted by permission.

TABLE 9-8 Thermal Characteristics of Wall and Roof Components

Description	L	k	ρ	c	R	Gamma (γ)
1-in insulation (glass, fiber)	0.0833	0.025	5.7	0.20	3.33	0.20
2-in insulation (perlite, vermiculite)	0.1670	0.025	5.7	0.20	6.68	0.41
1-in wood	0.0833	0.070	37.0	0.60	1.19	0.54
4-in wood	0.333	0.70	37.0	0.60	4.76	2.15
2-in wood	0.1670	0.70	37.0	0.60	3.39	1.08
4-in clay tile	0.3330	0.330	70.0	0.20	1.01	0.78
4-in lightweight concrete block	0.3330	0.220	38.0	0.20	1.51	0.71
4-in heavyweight concrete block	0.333	0.470	61.0	0.20	0.71	0.61
4-in common brick	0.333	0.42	120.0	0.20	0.79	0.91
4-in heavyweight concrete	0.333	1.0	140.0	0.20	0.33	0.64
8-in clay tile	0.667	0.330	70.0	0.20	2.02	1.57
8-in lightweight concrete block	0.667	0.330	38.0	0.20	2.02	1.16
8-in heavyweight concrete block	0.667	0.60	61.0	0.20	1.11	1.09
8-in common brick	0.667	0.420	120.0	0.20	1.59	1.82
8-in heavyweight concrete	0.6670	1.00	140.0	0.20	0.67	1.28
12-in heavyweight concrete	1.00	1.00	140.0	0.20	1.00	1.91
2-in heavyweight concrete	0.1670	1.00	140.0	0.20	0.17	0.32
8-in lightweight concrete	0.6670	0.100	40.0	0.20	6.67	2.16
Inside surface resistance					0.685	
¾-in plaster or gypsum	0.0625	0.420	100.0	0.20	0.15	0.16
½-in slag or stone	0.0417	0.830	55.0	0.40	0.05	0.08
⅜-in felt and membrane	0.0313	0.110	70.0	0.40	0.28	0.18
Ceiling air space					1.0	
Acoustical tile	0.0625	0.035	30.0	0.20	1.79	0.30
1-in stucco (asbestos cement, wood siding, plaster, etc.)	0.0833	0.400	116.0	0.20	0.21	0.23
4-in face brick (dense concrete)	0.3330	0.770	125.0	0.22	0.43	0.72
Steel siding (aluminum or other lightweight cladding)	0.005	26.0	480.0	0.10	0.00	0.00
½-in slag, membrane, and ⅜-in felt	0.0417	0.830	55.0	0.40	0.05	0.08
Outside surface resistance					0.333	
Finish	0.0417	0.240	78.0	0.26	0.17	0.14
Air space resistance					0.910	
2-in insulation or polyurethane	0.1670	0.025	2.0	0.20	6.68	0.24
3-in insulation or polystyrene	0.25	0.025	2.0	0.20	10.00	0.36

NOTE: The walls in this table are taken from the list given in the *ASHRAE Handbook and Product Directory—1977 Fundamentals Volume*, p. 25.30. The thermal resistance [(h·°F·ft²)/Btu] does not include the air film resistances. The conductance [Btu/(h·ft²·°F)] does not include the air film contribution. The thermal inertia index is the overall gamma value of the wall valid for sinusoidal diurnal thermal variations. The time lag (hours) is the time lapse between the time when the maximum external surface temperature occurs and the time when the maximum internal surface temperature occurs. The attenuation factor α is the fraction of the heat delivered by the time-dependent component of the heat transfer when compared with the same component in the static calculation.

L = thickness, ft
k = conductivity, Btu/(h·ft·°F)
ρ = density, lb/ft³
c = specific heat, Btu/(lb·°F)
R = resistance, (h·ft·°F)/Btu
Gamma = diurnal thermal inertia index, dimensionless

SOURCE: Francisco Arumi, *Thermal Inertia in Architectural Walls*, Northeast Solar Energy Center, Cambridge, Mass., 1979, p. III-1.; *ASHRAE Handbook and Product Directory—1977 Fundamentals Volume*, American Society of Heating, Refrigerating and Air-Conditioning Engineers,Inc., New York, 1977, p. 25.10. Reprinted by permission.

TABLE 9-9 Thermal Characteristics of Wall Assemblies

Description	Resistance, R	Conductance, C	Thermal inertia, γ	Time lag	Attenuation factor, α
4-in face brick, 2-in insulation, 4-in lightweight concrete block, ¾-in gypsum	8.77	0.11	1.95	5.2	0.74
4-in face brick, air space, 4-in common brick, ¾-in gypsum	2.18	0.46	2.04	6.0	0.60
4-in face brick, air space, 4-in heavyweight concrete block, ¾-in gypsum	2.1	0.48	1.59	4.4	0.78
1-in stucco, 8-in heavyweight concrete, 2-in insulation, ¾-in gypsum	7.70	0.13	2.84	6.9	0.42
1-in stucco, 8-in heavyweight concrete, ¾-in gypsum	1.02	0.98	1.82	5.3	0.60
4-in face brick, air space, 4-in lightweight concrete block	4.57	0.22	1.65	4.4	0.81
4-in face brick, 1-in insulation, 4-in face brick	1.67	0.60	1.82	5.1	0.66
Metal curtain wall with 1-in insulation	3.33	0.30	0.35	0.2	1.0
Steel siding, 2-in insulation, 12-in heavyweight concrete block, stucco	7.85	0.13	4.43	9.6	0.13
Steel siding, 2-in insulation, 4-in heavyweight concrete block, stucco	7.19	0.14	2.62	4.9	0.48
8-in heavyweight concrete block, 2-in insulation, stucco	7.52	0.13	2.26	5.3	0.61
4-in heavyweight concrete, 2-in insulation, stucco	7.19	0.14	1.21	2.2	0.94
1-in stucco, air space, 3-in insulation, ¾-in gypsum	11.17	0.09	0.90	1.1	0.98
1-in stucco, 2-in insulation, 8-in heavyweight concrete block, ¾-in gypsum	7.70	0.13	3.58	7.4	0.24
1-in stucco, air space, 4-in heavyweight concrete, ¾-in gypsum	1.50	0.67	1.8	4.1	0.66
4-in face brick, 2-in insulation, 8-in heavyweight concrete block, ¾-in gypsum	8.37	0.12	2.89	7.7	0.41
4-in face brick, 2-in insulation, 8-in lightweight concrete block, ¾-in gypsum	9.28	0.11	2.63	7.4	0.49
4-in face brick, 2-in insulation, 4-in heavyweight concrete, ¾-in gypsum	7.59	0.13	2.74	6.6	0.45

TABLE 9-9 Thermal Characteristics of Wall Assemblies (*cont.*)

Description	Resistance, R	Conductance, C	Thermal inertia, γ	Time lag	Attenuation factor, α
1-in stucco, 8-in heavyweight concrete block, 1-in insulation, ¾-in gypsum	4.79	0.21	2.07	5.0	0.66
1-in stucco, 8-in lightweight concrete block, 1-in insulation, ¾-in gypsum	5.7	0.18	1.98	4.8	0.70
1-in stucco, 4-in heavyweight concrete, 2-in insulation, ¾-in gypsum	7.37	0.14	1.82	3.8	0.78
4-in face brick, 4-in common brick, 1-in insulation, ¾-in gypsum	4.69	0.21	2.36	6.2	0.55
Sheet metal, 3-in insulation, air space, sheet metal	10.81	0.09	0.46	0.30	1.0

NOTE: The walls in this table are taken from the list given in the *ASHRAE Handbook and Product Directory—1977 Fundamentals Volume*, p. 25.30. The thermal resistance [(h · °F · ft²)/Btu] does not include the air film resistances. The conductance [Btu/(h · ft² · °F] does not include the air film contribution. The thermal inertia index is the overall gamma value of the wall valid for sinusoidal diurnal thermal variations. The time lag (hours) is the time lapse between the time when the maximum external surface temperature occurs and the time when the maximum internal surface temperature occurs. The attenuation factor α is the fraction of the heat delivered by the time-dependent component of the heat transfer when compared with the same component in the static calculation.

SOURCE: Francisco Arumi, *Thermal Inertia in Architectural Walls*, Northeast Solar Energy Center, Cambridge, Mass., 1979, p. III-2.

5 Calculate the annual temperature ratio A_t and the amplitude ratio B.

6 Using factors A_t and B from Step 5, identify the annual energy consumption factor from Table 9-7.

7 Calculate the annual energy demand Q.

8 Calculate the annual fuel consumption and dollar expenditures by using the methods presented in Chapter 6.

EXAMPLE

An architect has designed a layout for a low-rise apartment building in a New York suburb. The building code allows the outside wall of the building to be constructed of either wood frame or masonry. Masonry will cost more, but the architect suspects that its mass will help to reduce energy consumption.

The wood frame construction being considered is composed of two-by-four studs covered with wood siding on plywood backed by 3 inches of fiberglass bat insulation and ¾-inch gypsum-board interior finish, costing $4 per square foot. The masonry construction desired is 4-inch face brick, 2-inch insulation, 4-inch lightweight concrete block, and ¾-inch gypsum, costing $7 per square foot.

The building is 60 by 150 feet and three stories (27 feet) high. It will be heated by oil at $1.50 per gallon and cooled by through-the-wall units at 15 cents per kilowatthours and $25 per kilowatt-month for demand charges.

From Table 9-8, the thermal characteristics of the wood-frame wall are as follows:

	Length	Conductivity, k	Density, ρ	Specific heat, c	Resistance, R	Thermal inertia, γ
Wood siding	0.063	0.40	116.0	0.20	0.21	0.23
1-inch wood	0.083	0.07	37.0	0.60	1.19	0.54
3-inch insulation	0.25	0.025	5.7	0.20	10.00	0.61
¾-inch gypsum	0.063	0.43	100.00	0.20	0.15	0.16
					11.55	1.54

From Table 9-6, the attenuation factor $\alpha = 0.89$.

$$C = 1/R = 0.087 \text{ Btu/(h·ft}^2\text{·°F)}$$

The following accounts for interior and exterior film resistances:

$$U_{\text{summer}} = \frac{1}{11.55 + 0.25 + 0.68} = 0.080 \text{ Btu/(h·°F·ft}^2\text{)}$$

$$U_{\text{winter}} = \frac{1}{11.55 + 0.17 + 0.68} = 0.81 \text{ Btu/(h·°F·ft}^2\text{)}$$

From Table 9-9, the thermal characteristics of the *brick* wall are as follows:

Resistance	8.77 (°F·h·ft²)/Btu
Conductance	0.11 Btu/(°F·h·ft²)
Thermal inertia	1.95
Attenuation factor α	0.74

$$U_{\text{summer}} = \frac{1}{8.77 + 0.25 + 0.68} = 0.103 \text{ Btu/(h·°F·ft}^2\text{)}$$

This accounts for interior and exterior air film resistances.

$$U_{\text{winter}} = \frac{1}{8.77 + 0.17 + 0.68} = 0.104 \text{ Btu/(h·°F·ft}^2\text{)}$$

Cooling season energy consumption is estimated as follows for a frame wall:

Heat flow factor:

$$J = 0.080 \text{ Btu/(h·°F·ft}^2\text{)} \times 0.89 \times 9\text{°F} = 0.64 \text{ Btu/(h·ft}^2\text{)} \tag{9-10}$$

Annual temperature ratio:

$$A_t = \frac{54.6\text{°F} - 80\text{°F}}{0.89 \times 9.0\text{°F}} = -3.17 \tag{9-7}$$

$$= -3.17$$

Amplitude ratio:

$$B = \frac{22.0\text{°F}}{0.89 \times 9.0\text{°F}} = 2.75 \tag{9-9}$$

Annual energy consumption (Table 9-7):

Annual factor = 0.02 × 10,000 = 200 h/year

Annual energy demand:

$$Q = 0.64 \text{ Btu/(h·ft}^2\text{)} \times 200 \text{ h/year} \tag{9-11}$$

$$= 128 \text{ Btu/(ft}^2\text{·year)}$$

TABLE 9-10 Thermal Characteristics of Roof Assemblies

Description	Resistance, R	Conductance, C	Thermal inertia, γ	Time lag	Attenuation factor, α
½-in slag or stone, ⅜-in felt and membrane, 8-in lightweight concrete, ceiling air space, acoustical tile	9.60	0.1	2.86	7.9	0.42
½-in slag or stone, ⅜-in felt and membrane, 4-in lightweight concrete, ceiling air space, acoustical tile	10.11	0.10	4.5	7.4	0.12
½-in slag or stone, ⅜-in felt and membrane, 2-in insulation, 4-in heavyweight concrete, ceiling air space, acoustical tile	9.94	0.10	3.99	6.5	0.18
½-in slag or stone, ⅜-in felt and membrane, 2-in insulation, 2-in heavyweight concrete, ceiling air space, acoustical tile	9.78	0.10	3.15	5.5	0.34
½-in slag or stone, ⅜-in felt and membrane, 2-in insulation, sheet steel, ceiling air space, acoustical tile	9.61	0.10	1.03	1.5	0.97
½-in slag or stone, ⅜-in felt and membrane, 4-in lightweight concrete	5.33	0.19	0.73	4.2	0.79
½-in slag or stone, ⅜-in felt and membrane, 2-in insulation, sheet metal	7.01	0.14	0.54	0.6	1.0

NOTE: The roofs in this table are taken from the list given in the *ASHRAE Handbook and Product Directory—1977 Fundamentals Volume*, p. 25–28. The thermal resistance [(h·°F·ft²)/Btu] does not include the air film resistances. The conductance [Btu/(h·ft²·°F)] does not include the air film contribution. The thermal inertia index is the overall gamma value of the wall valid for sinusoidal diurnal thermal variations. The time lag (hours) is the lapse between the time when the maximum external surface temperature occurs and the time when the maximum internal surface temperature occurs. The attenuation factor α is the fraction of the heat delivered by the time-dependent component of the heat transfer when compared with the same component in the static calculation.

SOURCE: Francisco Arumi, *Thermal Inertia in Architectural Walls*, Northeast Solar Energy Center, Cambridge, Mass., 1979, p. III-9. Reprinted by permission.

Cooling energy season consumption is estimated as follows for a brick wall:

Heat flow factor:

$$J = 0.103 \times 0.74 \times 9.0°\text{F} = 0.69 \text{ Btu/(h·ft}^2) \qquad (9\text{-}10)$$

Annual temperature ratio:

$$A = \frac{54.6°\text{F} - 80°\text{F}}{0.74 \times 9.0°\text{F}} = 3.81 \qquad (9\text{-}7)$$

Amplitude ratio:

$$B = \frac{22.0°\text{F}}{0.74 \times 9.0°\text{F}} = -3.30 \qquad (9\text{-}9)$$

Annual energy consumption:

$$\text{Annual factor} = 0.01 \times 10{,}000 = 100 \text{ h/year}$$

Annual energy demand:

$$Q = 0.69 \text{ Btu/(h}\cdot\text{ft}^2) \times 100 \text{ h/year} = 69 \text{ Btu/(ft}^2\cdot\text{year)} \quad (9\text{-}11)$$

Heating season energy consumption for each wall is estimated as follows:

	Frame wall	Brick wall
Heat flow factor [Equation (9-10)]	$0.081 \times 0.89 \times 9.0 = 0.65$	$0.104 \times 0.74 \times 9.0 = 0.69$
Annual temperature ratio [Equation (9-8)]	$\frac{54.6 - 70}{0.89 \times 9.0} = -1.92$	$\frac{54.6 - 70}{0.74 \times 9.0} = -2.31$
Amplitude ratio [Equation (9-9)]	$\frac{22.0}{0.89 \times 9.0} = 2.75$	$\frac{22.0}{0.74 \times 9.0} = 3.30$
Annual factor (Table 9-7)	$0.22 \times 10{,}000 = 2200$	$0.17 \times 10{,}000 = 1700$
Annual energy demand [Equation (9-11)]	$0.65 \times 2200 = 1430$	$0.69 \times 1700 = 1173$

The savings in annual energy consumption created by using the brick wall instead of the frame wall are as follows:

	Cooling season	Heating season
Frame wall	128 Btu/(ft²·year)	1430 Btu/(ft²·year)
Brick wall	[69 Btu/(ft²·year)]	[1173 Btu/(ft²·year)]
Savings	59 Btu/(ft²·year)	257 Btu/(ft²·year)

The value of these savings is estimated below. The wall area of the building is 60 × 150 × 27 ft = 243,000 ft².

Summer cooling savings:

$$\begin{aligned} B_c &= 1.64 \text{ kW/ton} \times \$0.15/\text{kWh} \\ &\quad \times \{[59 \text{ Btu/(ft}^2\cdot\text{year)} \times 243{,}000 \text{ ft}^2] \div 12{,}000 \text{ Btu/(ton}\cdot\text{h)}\} \\ &= \$294/\text{year [See Equation (6-5).]} \end{aligned}$$

Winter heating savings:

$$\begin{aligned} B_h &= \frac{\$1.50/\text{gal} \times 257 \text{ Btu/(ft}^2\cdot\text{year)} \times 243{,}000 \text{ ft}^2}{0.55 \times 140{,}000 \text{ Btu/gal}} \\ &= \$1217 \text{ [See Equation (6-1).]} \end{aligned}$$

The reduction in peak load due to a change in the heat flow factor J is presented below:

	Cooling season	Heating season
Frame wall	0.64 Btu/(h·ft²)	0.65 Btu/(h·ft²)
Brick wall	[0.69 Btu/(h·ft²)]	[0.69 Btu/(h·ft²)]
Reduction	0.05 Btu/(h·ft²)	0.04 Btu/(h·ft²)

Reduction in demand charges is estimated below:

$$B_e = 1.64 \text{ kW/ton} \times \$25/(\text{kW}\cdot\text{month}) \times 3 \text{ months} \times \{[0.05 \text{ Btu/(h}\cdot\text{ft}^2) \times 243{,}000 \text{ ft}^2] \div 12{,}000 \text{ Btu/(ton}\cdot\text{h)}\} = \$125$$

Reductions in equipment costs cannot be acknowledged because peak load reductions are not large enough.

Total annual benefits are summarized below:

Summer cooling savings	$ 294/year
Demand charge reductions	125/year
Winter heating savings	1217/year
Total	$1636/year

The additional cost of providing a brick exterior wall in place of a frame wall is estimated below:

Masonry wall cost	7.00/ft²
Frame wall cost	−$4.00/ft²
Increased cost	$3.00/ft²
Wall area	× 243,000 ft²
Total cost	$729,000

A simple cost-benefit analysis yields the following result:

$$\text{Simple payback period} = \frac{\$729{,}000}{\$1636/\text{year}} = 446 \text{ years}$$

$$\text{Simple return on investment} = \frac{\$1636/\text{year}}{\$729{,}000} = 0.2 \text{ percent/year}$$

The designer will have to develop a much less expensive method of high-mass wall construction for the thermal inertia fuel savings to justify the added cost of construction. Other factors apart from energy conservation may, of course, help to justify masonry construction.

The main equations presented in this chapter are summarized in Table 9-11.

TABLE 9-11 Summary of Equations to Be Used for Mass-Related Energy Consumption Analysis

Equation	Description
$\Delta q = 0.08q$	9-1 Conducted peak heat loss and gain savings of earth-covered residential roofs when compared with exposed roofs
$t_{o,w} = \bar{t}_a - A$	9-2 Temperature outside below-grade basement walls
$q_h = U_{p,w} \times P_w \times (t_{o,w} - t_i)$	9-3 Peak heat loss rate of a below-grade basement wall
$q_h = U_b \times A_b \times (t_i - t_o)$	9-4 Peak heat loss rate of basement floors
$q_h = U_{p,s} \times P_s \times (t_i - t_o)$	9-5 Peak heat loss rate of slabs on grade
$J = U \times \alpha \times TA_d$	9-10 Heat flow factor as a function of thermal inertia
$Q = J \times \text{annual factor} \times A$	9-11 Annual energy demand as a function of thermal inertia.

BIBLIOGRAPHY

Arumi, Francisco: *Thermal Inertia in Architectural Walls,* Northeast Solar Energy Center, Cambridge, Mass., 1979.

ASHRAE Handbook and Product Directory—1977 Fundamentals Volume, American Society of Heating, Refrigerating and Air-Conditioning Engineers, Inc., 1977, New York.

Underground Space Center: *Earth Sheltered Housing Design,* Van Nostrand Reinhold Company, New York, 1979.

TEN

LIGHTING BENEFITS

The primary energy conservation issue of concern in this chapter is the impact of daylighting, or natural lighting, on the reduction of electrical consumption required for artificial lighting. The effect of architectural designs for natural lighting on other building qualities such as thermal performance, acoustics, and ventilation will also be addressed.

The process described here for evaluating a design for natural lighting will involve the following steps:

- Determining the interior light levels needed
- Estimating the amount of natural light provided by the design proposal
- Estimating the amount of artificial light saved
- Estimating the economic value of the electricity and fuel saved
- Estimating the cost of constructing the proposed design
- Calculating the life-cycle cost-benefit of the proposed design

This process is described in general in Chapter 1 (see Figure 1-1). The use of natural lighting to supplement and sometimes to substitute for electrically powered artificial lighting and thereby to reduce energy costs is accomplished by designs which permit the windows and skylights of a building to admit light from the sun and sky more effectively. It is an approach which is best employed in building types in which electrical lighting is a major consumer of energy. Office buildings are perhaps the main building type which falls into this category. Lighting-related electrical consumption for large office buildings in the northeast in the late 1970s amounted to almost one-half of their annual energy expenditures. Table 10-1, a classification of energy costs calculated for a hypothetical five-story, 85,625-square-foot office building in New York City, illustrates this statistic.

TYPES OF NATURAL LIGHT

Natural light may be classified into three categories as a function of the direction of the light: diffuse, direct, and ground-reflected light (see Figure 10-1). Diffuse light is light from the sky. It takes the form of sunlight which is scattered by particles in the earth's atmosphere and by clouds. The important aspect of diffuse

TABLE 10-1 Energy Costs for a New York City Office Building

Items	BTUs × 10^9	Gallons	Kilowatthours	Dollars	Percent
Heating	1.184	8,457		3,806	7.9
Cooling	0.568		166,422	8,321	17.2
Lighting	1.503		433,420	21,371	44.3
Fans and pumps	0.406		118,957	5,948	12.3
Domestic hot water	0.286	2,044		920	1.9
Office equipment	0.404		113,438	5,975	12.4
Elevators	0.133		38,969	1,948	4.0
Total	4.484	10,501	871,206	48,289	100.0

SOURCE: "Cost Benefit Analysis of Passive Solar Design Alternatives," unpublished draft, The Ehrenkrantz Group, New York, 1978.

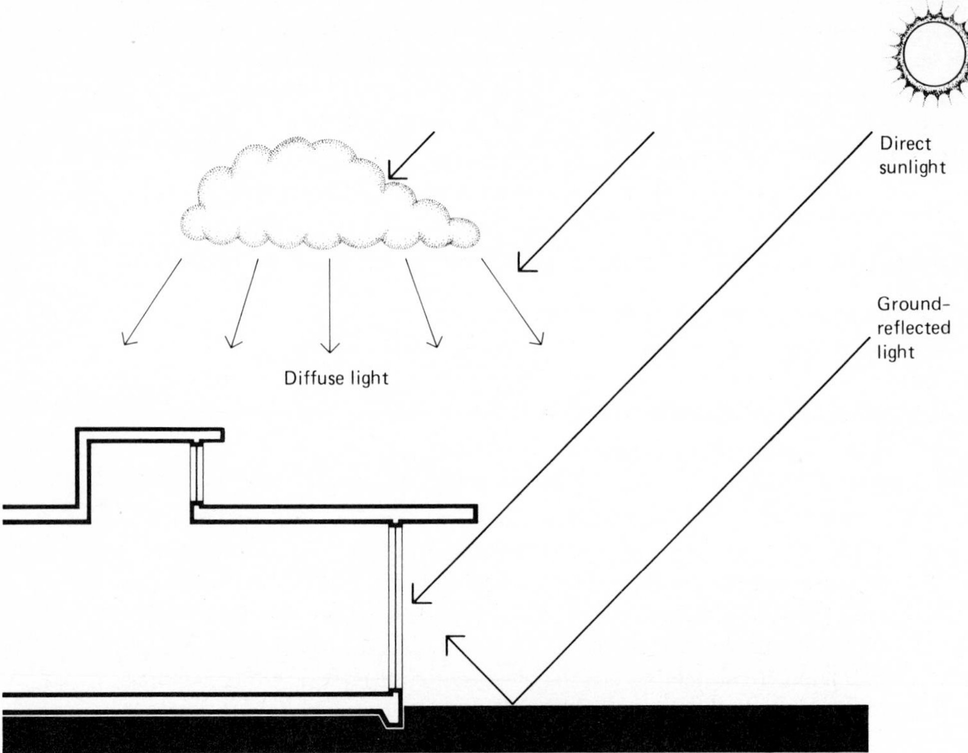

FIGURE 10-1 Daylight sources.

skylight for designers to remember is that it arrives at a building's envelope from all directions and that its intensity varies from 100 to 3000 footcandles, depending on the overcast quality of the sky and the altitude of the sun.

Skylight intensity varies with sky location and overcast conditions. To simplify calculations, the estimating methods presented here ignore these differences. In reality, however, an overcast sky is approximately 3 times brighter overhead than at the horizon, whereas the reverse is true on a clear day (see Table 10-2).

Direct natural light comes from the sun. It is different from diffuse light in that it is highly directional. The sun's direction is measured by its altitude (angle with respect to the horizontal) and its azimuth (angle with respect to due south). It varies from hour to hour and from day to day. (See Chapter 2 for further discussion of solar radiation and its characteristics.) The intensity of light received from the sun may be as high as 9000 footcandles, depending on its altitude, the season, and the angle of incidence with which it strikes a surface.

Both direct sunlight and diffuse light strike the ground and other objects outside a building as well as passing directly through windows and skylights. Some of this light will be reflected into a building's interior, however, adding to the illumination level created from diffuse and direct sources.

Building designs using natural lighting should minimize the undesirable features of the source as well as maximize its desirable qualities. In general terms, this means that daylight intensity inside a building should be distributed as evenly as possible and that interior spaces should be organized to minimize undesirable shadows and glare.

The intensity of natural light outside may be many times the level required inside. Typically an interior of a building may need an illumination level of around 50 footcandles, whereas the intensity of exterior light may often be 20 times that level (1000 footcandles) on a cloudy day or 100 times higher (5000 footcandles) on a sunny day. As a result, natural-light levels from a window, for example, will be more than adequate immediately adjacent to the window but will decrease rapidly farther from the window. A designer should develop designs for window walls which distribute natural-light intensities more evenly throughout a space. Various techniques, including inverted blinds and light shelves, have been developed for this purpose (see Figure 10-2). Most of these techniques rely on deflecting direct sunlight up to the ceiling, thereby reflecting it more deeply into the room adjacent to the window.

A designer must also make sure that a work surface is not subject to shadows, glare, or reflections. The position of a desk and a person at the desk is critical when most of the light is coming horizontally from a source such as a window (see Figure 10-3). In general, a desk should face parallel to the window and perpendicular to the light direction in order to make use of natural light from a window without also receiving glare, reflections, or shadows.

To maximize the usefulness of daylight from windows, it should be obstructed as little as possible. This limits the use of opaque full-height partitions to positions perpendicular to the window plane (see Figure 10-4). Low-height partitions or glass partitions are, of course, more acceptable for parallel-to-window positions.

TABLE 10-2 **Relative Brightness of Skylight as a Function of Location and Cloud Cover**

Cloud cover condition	Sky location	
	Horizon	Overhead
Overcast	1	3
Clear	3	1

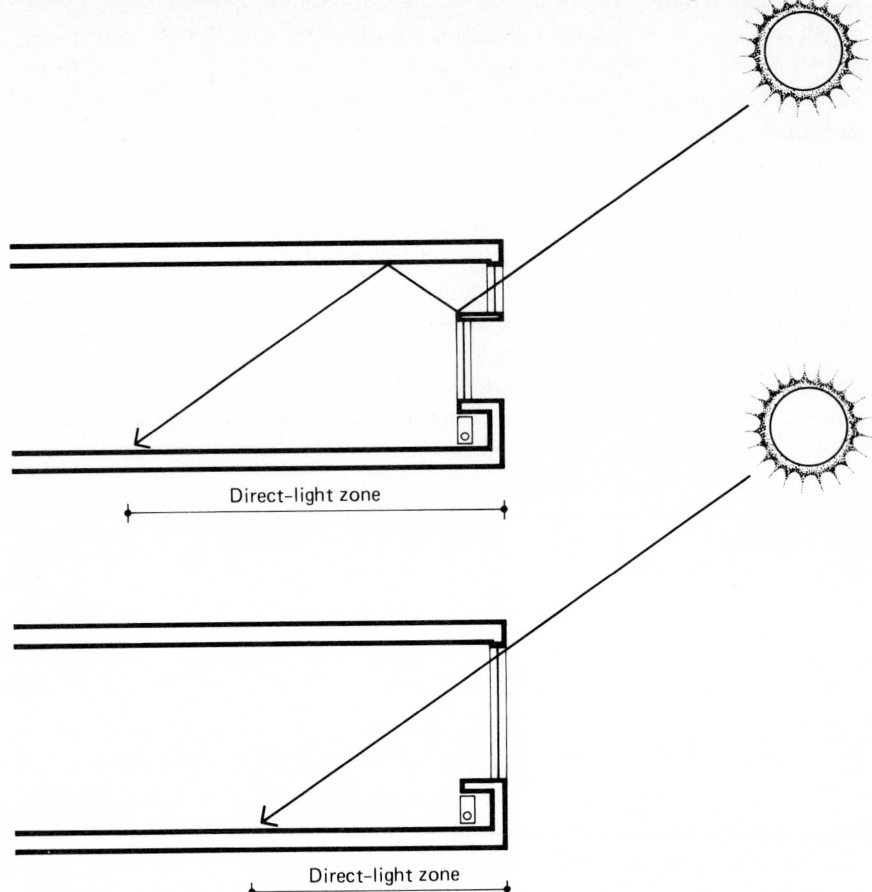

FIGURE 10-2 Building sections showing how a light shelf distributes natural light away from windows into rooms.

In terms of skylights, a designer should be cautioned that overhead lighting from skylights may sometimes create more reflections than does sidelighting from windows (see Figure 10-5). Desks should be positioned so that distracting reflections from skylights are eliminated. Typically, this means that desks should not be placed directly under skylights but rather off to the side though still within the range of natural light coming from the skylights. Alternatively, diffusers may be added to the inside of skylights to reduce reflections and glare on work surfaces below.

LIGHTING NEEDS

The proper use of natural light and lighting in general is important so that human comfort and quality of life are not sacrificed in an effort to achieve fuel savings.

First, lighting levels may not have to be as high as those we have been used to. There is, and probably will be for some time, debate among professionals about what light levels are necessary for human health, comfort, and productivity. The designer must make the choice because professional responsibility for client satisfaction is finally his or hers.

The debate about adequate lighting levels for the interiors of buildings is related to a relatively new measure of lighting, one that measures quality as well as quantity. This measure is called equivalent-sphere illumination (ESI). This concept rests on the proposition that visibility is the ultimate objective of any lighting design and that visibility is a function of, among other characteristics, lighting intensity, absence of reflections (veiling reflections and reflective glare), and absence of glare. A lighting design with low intensity and low reflections may well be equivalent in terms of task area visibility to a design which has high intensity and high levels of reflection. The former, of course, will have lower electrical consumption. ESI, as a method of measuring visibility, is a level of illumination that is reflection-free and glare-free, such as one might have on a task if surrounded by a diffusely lighted luminous *sphere*.

It is also important to remember that the electricity consumed by lighting may or may not be a scarce energy resource. In most cases it is, and in all cases it costs money. When electricity is generated by renewable sources such as hydroelectric

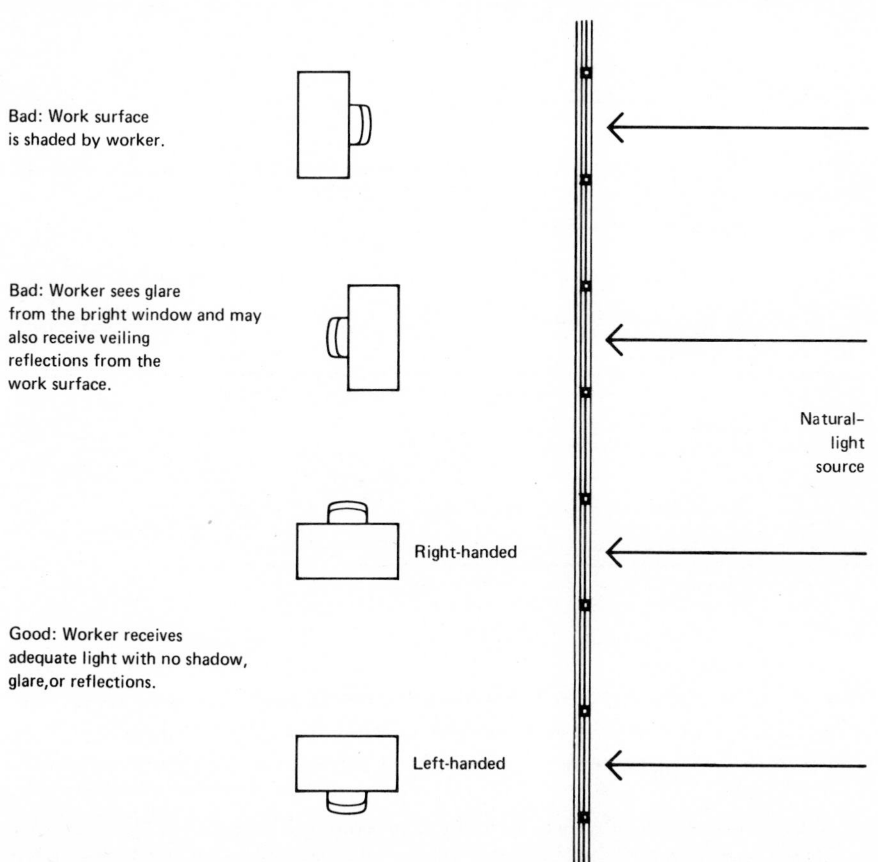

FIGURE 10-3 Position of office furniture to avoid glare from windows.

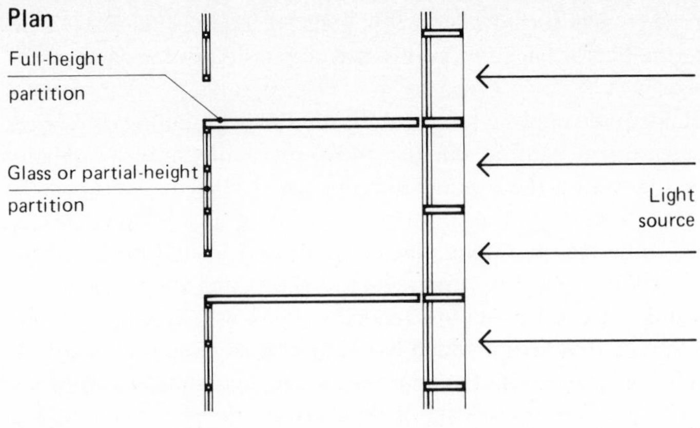

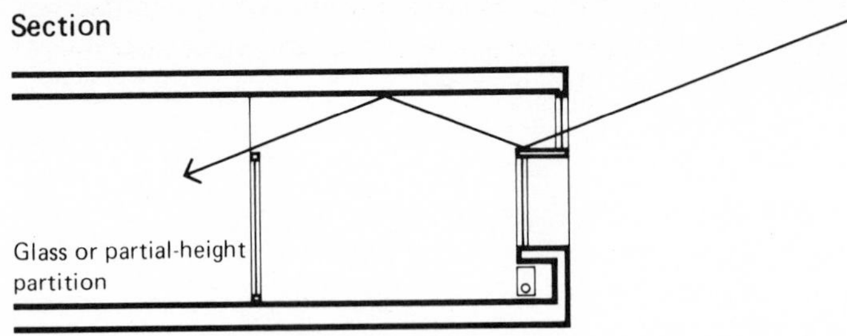

FIGURE 10·4 Impact of natural light from windows on partition design.

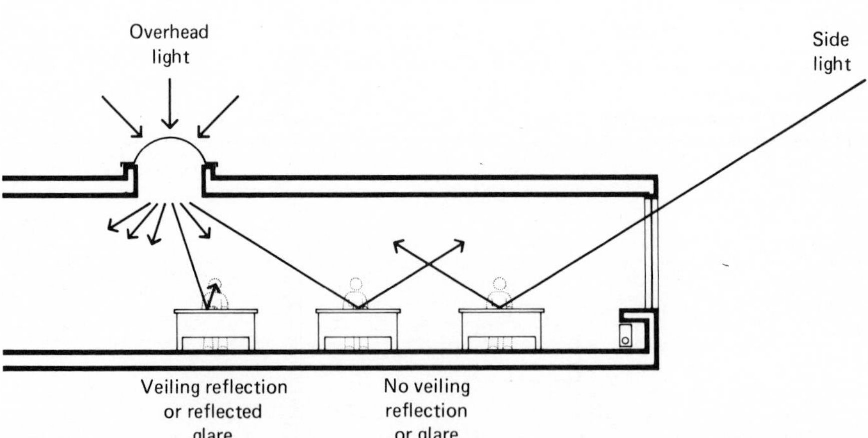

FIGURE 10·5 Comparison of skylight and window sources of natural light.

power or solar radiation, it will not be as important for a designer to provide designs which reduce electrical consumption as it will be in areas where electricity is generated by depletable sources such as coal, oil, or uranium.[1]

[1]Reduction of *peak* electrical demand may still be an important consideration with hydroelectric- or solar-generated electricity because of the high cost of electrical generators required with these energy sources.

Daylight has some qualitative benefits that are, perhaps, more valuable than its quantifiable assets. First, it changes in direction, intensity, and color throughout the day. This variety gives the occupant of a building a constant contact with nature. This constantly changing quality, however, makes daylight somewhat more difficult to quantify and control in terms of providing minimum light levels for tasks.

The technology of artificial-lighting controls, along with various design strategies, provides appropriate responses to this condition without interfering with the natural beauty of the source. For example, control technology which allows fluorescent lighting to be dimmed automatically in response to changing levels of natural light coming from windows or skylights is now available (see Figure 10-6). In some hours of the day, when natural lighting is high enough, artificial lights may be turned completely off. During other parts of the day, artificial lights may need to be on at low levels to make up for insufficient natural lighting.

In general, there are a variety of approaches to switching artificial-lighting levels off or down when natural lighting is available. All will save electrical energy.

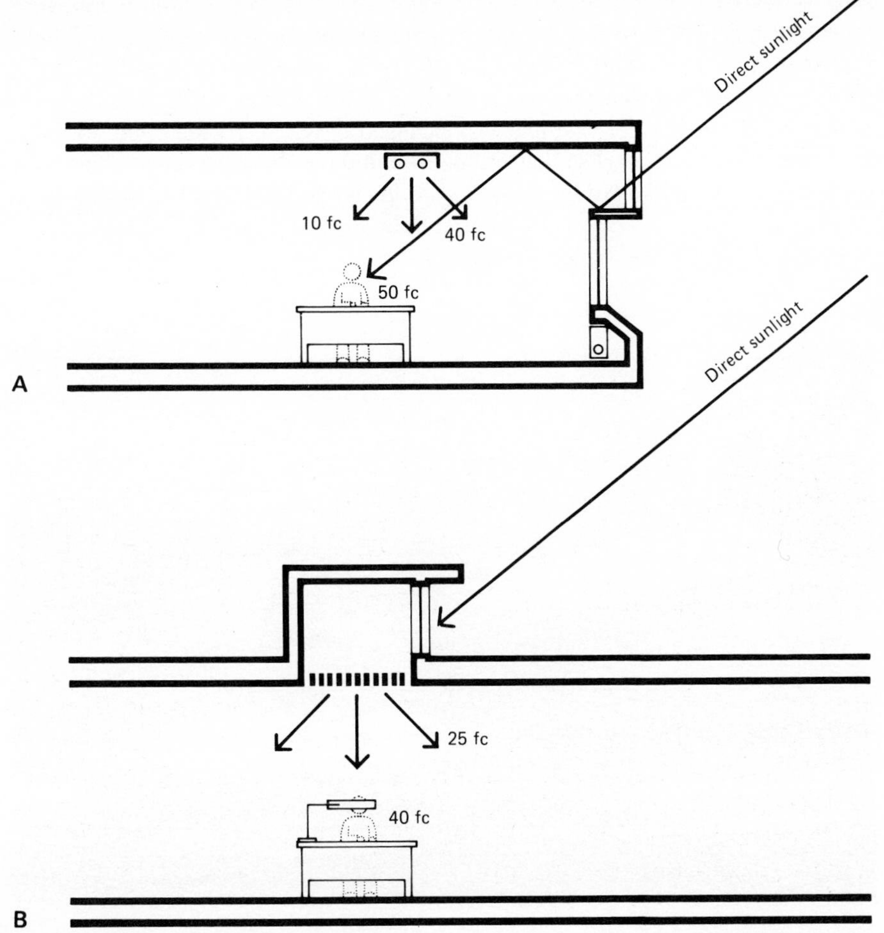

FIGURE 10-6 Approaches to using natural light in combination with artificial light.

A Using artificial light to balance fluctuating natural light levels. A photoelectric dimmer senses that the natural light load is 40 footcandles and adjusts the artificial light level to provide an additional 10 footcandles to bring the overall task light level to the desired 50 footcandles.

B Using natural light for general illumination only. The task light provides 40 footcandles, which is adequate for working, and the natural light provides general diffuse lighting between 10 and 25 footcandles, thereby eliminating the need for overhead lights during the daytime.

Some are more expensive than others, and some have an impact on the quality of lighting provided to users of the space. They are important because without such technology the designer of skylights and windows for transmitting natural light would not be able to create any energy savings for his or her client.

The following types of switching approaches are available:

1 Automatic switching

a. Stepped switching

(1) One-step (on-off)

(2) Two-step (high-low-off)

(3) Three-step (high-medium-low-off)

b. Dimming

2 Manual switching

All automatic switching controls that may be used in conjunction with natural lighting presently rely on photoelectric controls which sense light levels on surfaces such as desktops and adjust overhead fluorescent lights until desired illumination levels are reached. If, owing to the presence of both artificial and natural light, desk illumination is too high, a photoelectric cell can turn down the artificial lights until the desired overall light level is reached. When natural-light levels decrease, at the end of the day for example, a photoelectric switch can sense this and raise the artificial-lighting level so that the desired desktop illumination is maintained. Photoelectric controls may be connected to fluorescent lights either to shut them off or to dim them in response to natural-light levels. Figure 10-7 shows a photoelectric cell attached to a fluorescent fixture.

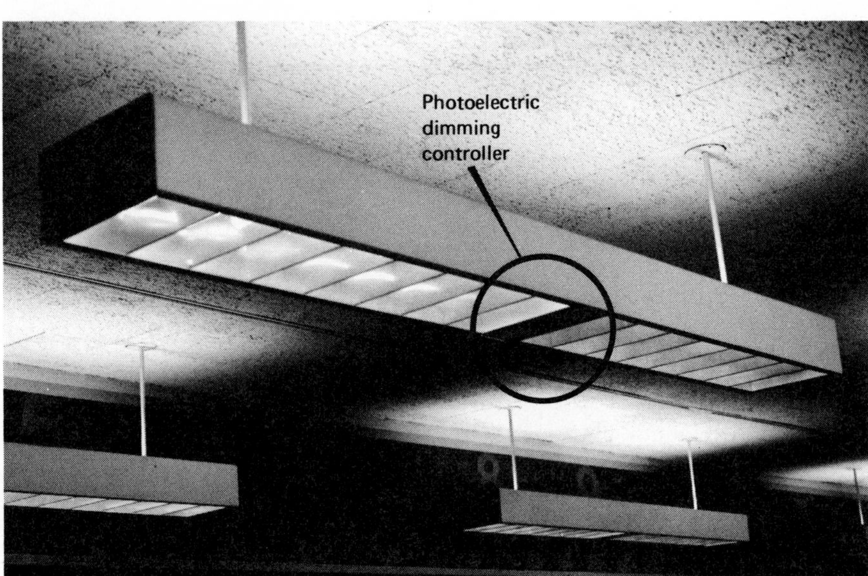

FIGURE 10-7 A photoelectric dimming controller installed in a fluorescent lighting fixture.

Stepped switching controls are the simplest form of automatic lighting control. In this case, electric lights may be turned off or on by photoelectric switching controls but not dimmed. This technology is available although not widely used as yet. Switches may turn lights off when natural-lighting levels are adequate, thus saving electricity costs. A problem that has been encountered with this technology is the effect on the people using the space when the switchover is made from artificial lighting to natural sources. For example, let us assume that the artificial-lighting system for an office building is designed to provide 50 footcandles of lighting. When a source of natural light such as a skylight also provides 50 footcandles, the sum of the two sources is 100 footcandles. As the natural-light intensity increases above the 50-footcandle threshold, a photoelectric switch may be designed to turn off the electric light, thus dropping the illumination level from 100 footcandles back to the normal 50-footcandle level. This drop in light intensity is sometimes distracting to people working during the changeover. Adjusting the switching system to operate at some predetermined time when natural-light levels are expected to be adequate and when disruptions may be minimized, such as lunchtime, may help to alleviate this problem.

Another control technique is called "two-step switching." By using this approach, fluorescent lights may be reduced to a fraction of their intensity when natural lighting provides the remainder of the desired level. In a two-step design, for example, if the desired lighting level is 50 footcandles and the natural light coming from a window or skylight is 25 footcandles (75 footcandles total), the first step of the switching control will switch off enough lamps to reduce the artificial light to 25 footcandles so that the combined level of natural and artificial lighting is maintained at 50 footcandles.

In a three-step design, the switching simply provides an opportunity to follow more closely changing natural-light levels. If 50 footcandles is desired, the artificial lighting may be reduced by one-third when natural lighting reaches 16.7 footcandles, by another third when natural lighting reaches 33.3 footcandles, and off when natural lighting reaches 50 footcandles. In effect, photoelectric controls may cause the switching to occur when the aggregate of natural and artificial lighting reaches unnecessarily high levels. Stepped switching designs, however, still provide noticeable changes in light intensity in a room and are often distracting to users of the space below.

Another system which minimizes distractions and yet allows a designer to capitalize on the fuel-saving benefits of natural lighting is a photocell-controlled dimming approach (see Figure 10-8). In this case, the switching system is designed to deliver whatever electric light that the natural light does not provide up to the level required. For example, if the desired lighting level is 50 footcandles and natural lighting from a skylight is only 15 footcandles, a dimming control can adjust the electric lighting system to provide the 35 footcandles necessary to reach the desired 50-footcandle level. The artificial-lighting system is dimmed lower and lower until the natural-light level reaches the desired level. At that time, the artificial-lighting system is turned completely off. In this way, electrical savings may be achieved for *any* level of natural lighting, no matter how low. The advantage of this approach is that people using the space below will not be subject to the switchover conditions and rapid change in light intensity caused by the simpler on-off control. With dimming controls, occupants are subjected to a constant lighting level which changes only in its mix of natural and artificial lighting. The dimming of the fluorescent lighting can be so gradual that viewers cannot perceive the change.

The only problem with use of dimming controls is that calculation of the savings due to using such a system is not possible with simple manual methods unless days are spent with a calculator. Computer programs have been developed for this purpose and should be used.

The estimating method that is presented in this chapter is useful only for estimating electrical savings when on-off photoelectric switching is employed. The method will always present an *underestimate* of the savings which might accrue when compared with a dimming approach. If cost-effectiveness can be achieved, of course, given an underestimate of benefits, the decision to build the system will still be valid.

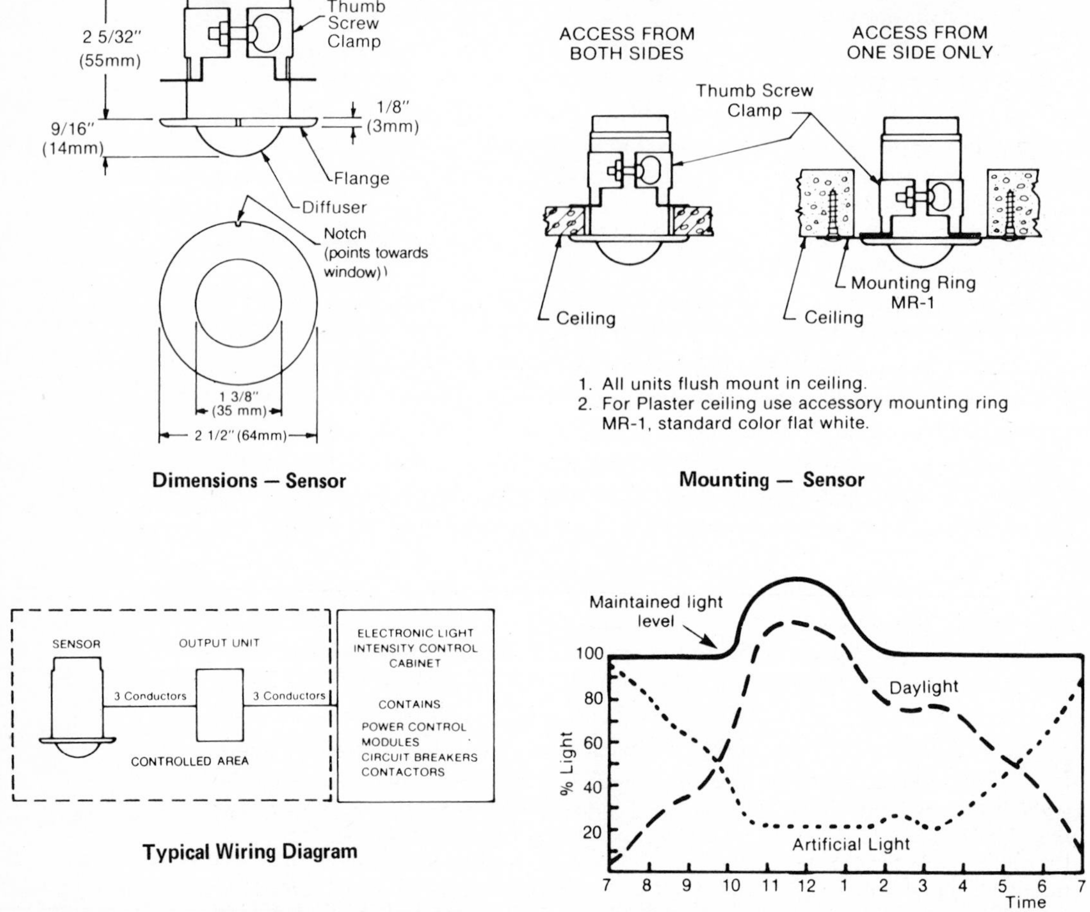

FIGURE 10-8 **Diagrams and details of a daylight-sensing photocell controller.** [*Manufactured by Lutron Electronics Co., Inc., Coopersburg, Pa. Reprinted by permission.*]

The methods for estimating lighting levels that will be presented in this chapter permit a designer to determine the number of hours during the day when interior light levels provided by natural sources are sufficient. From this information, the designer may determine the electricity which is saved and the value of such savings.

The impact of turning artificial lights off or down has a number of consequences:

- Electrical consumption for lighting may be reduced.
- Fuel consumption for heating during the winter may be increased because of lowered lighting-related heat loads.
- Electrical consumption for cooling during the summer may be decreased because of lowered lighting-related heat loads.
- Demand charges for electrical use during the cooling season may be reduced because of peak load cooling reductions.

The general form for estimating savings in electrical consumption for lighting is presented below:

$$B_L = C_e \times t \times P_L \times A_r \div 1000 \tag{10-1}$$

in units,

$$\$/\text{year} = \$/\text{kWh} \times \text{h/year} \times \text{W/ft}^2 \times \text{ft}^2 \div \text{Wh/kWh}$$

where B_L = annual benefits due to decreased artificial-lighting use, \$/year
C_e = cost of electrical power, \$/kWh
t = time when artificial lights are off or turned down, h/year
P_L = power required to provide artificial lighting, W/ft^2 (This figure may vary from about 1.8 W/ft^2 to 5 W/ft^2 or more, depending on the efficiency of the artificial-lighting design. The estimate of this level may be obtained from lighting consultants. In lieu of that, a conservative figure may be selected: 2.0 W/ft^2 is suggested for office lighting systems.)
A_r = area of the room being analyzed, ft^2

EXAMPLE

Suppose that a designer has developed an interior reflector system for use next to south-facing windows of a floor in an office building which increases interior light levels during the day so that, when equipped with photoelectric switches, the artificial lights may be turned off for an average of 2 hours per day on cloudy days and 5 hours on clear-sunny days. The designer's client wants to know whether or not the lighting savings are worth the cost of the switches and the reflectors.

The following information describes the characteristics of the space in question:

Hours of operation	9 h/day
Room floor area	150 ft² (1/100 of total floor area)
Building floor area	15,000 ft²
Exterior wall	10 ft
Lighting system power consumption	2.5 W/ft²
Cost of photoelectric switches	$0.75/ft² of floor area
Cost of reflectors	$10/ft of wall
Cost of electricity	$0.14/kWh
Cost of fuel oil	$1.20/gal
Cooling system type	Central, water-cooled, 75 tons
Heating system efficiency	0.55

Assume also that the general building construction, internal heat loads, and operating schedule are the same as in the second example in the section "Bin-Hour Methods" in Chapter 6.

One must first determine the average number of hours each day (or the total hours each year) during which the lights will be off. This involves, first of all, an assessment of the frequency of clear versus overcast conditions. Table 10-3 contains the results of such an assessment. In this table, mean sky cover fractions are used to calculate a weighted average for each month of overcast hours and clear-sunny hours when the electric lighting system may be turned off. Given the calculations in the table, electrical savings may be estimated as follows:

$$B_L = \$0.14/\text{kWh} \times (3.3\ \text{h/day} \times 5\ \text{days/week} \times 52\ \text{weeks/year}) \times 2.5\ \text{W/ft}^2 \times 150\ \text{ft}^2 \div 1000\ \text{W/kWh} \tag{10-1}$$

$$B_L = \$45$$

The impact of reduced electric light use on the heating and cooling systems must also be analyzed. All the electricity that goes into an artificial-lighting system eventually becomes

TABLE 10-3 Example Clear-Sky and Overcast-Sky Weighted-Average Calculations

Month	Clear sky [(Fraction · h)/day]		+	Overcast [(Fraction · h)/day]*		=	Weighted average (h/day)
November	0.42	5		0.58	2		3.3
December	0.40	5		0.60	2		3.2
January	0.38	5		0.62	2		3.1
February	0.42	5		0.58	2		3.3
March	0.41	5		0.59	2		3.3
April	0.48	5		0.52	2		3.4
May	0.42	5		0.58	2		3.3
June	0.43	5		0.57	2		3.3
July	0.44	5		0.56	2		3.3
August	0.48	5		0.52	2		3.4
September	0.50	5		0.50	2		3.5
October	0.50	5		0.50	2		3.5
Annual average							3.3 h/day

*The fraction data are taken from Table 10-8.

heat.[2] Initially some of it is transformed into light, but the light soon becomes heat as it is absorbed by the solid materials in the room. The conversion of electricity into heat involves following calculations:

$$3.413 \text{ Btu} = 1 \text{ Wh}$$

The general form for estimating the heat savings created by reduced artificial lighting use is the following:

$$\Delta q_L = P_L \times A_r \times 3.413 \qquad (10\text{-}2)$$

in units,

$$\text{Btu/h} = \text{W/ft}^2 \times \text{ft}^2 \times \text{Btu/Wh}$$

where Δq_L = hourly internal heat reduction due to reduced lighting load, Btu/h
P_L = power required for artificial lighting, W/ft²
A_r = area of room, ft²

In the example described above, the thermal impact of the reduced artificial-lighting usage is estimated as follows:

$$\Delta q_L = 2.5 \text{ W/ft}^2 \times 150 \text{ ft}^2 \times 3.413 \text{ Btu/Wh}$$
$$= 1280 \text{ Btu/h}$$

An examination of monthly daytime heat loss and heat gain data for this building will indicate whether or not the lower internal heat gain due to the lights' being turned off will necessitate additional fuel expenditures for heating. Data from Tables 10-4 and 10-5 yield the following thermal balance, given the lights' being turned off 3.3 hours per day:

	Btu/day			
	Clear day		Cloudy day	
Month	**Heat loss**	**Heat gain**	**Heat loss**	**Heat gain**
November	−1,008	47,971	6,318	21,792
December	2,835	47,405	9,828	20,895
January	6,012	48,609	13,338	21,792
February	5,256	48,207	11,583	22,854
March	4,500	42,496	9,828	25,191
April	4,743	37,415	8,073	25,615

From this comparison, it is evident that daytime heat losses never exceed daytime heat gains even when the lights are turned off according to the schedule permitted by natural lighting. The reduction, therefore, in the lighting heat gain because of the use of natural lighting does not require any additional fuel expenditures during the winter.

The savings due to a reduced cooling load from lights may be estimated as follows:

Hours during the cooling season (June, July, and August) when lights are off:[3]

$$3 \text{ months} \times 21.67 \text{ days/month} \times 3.3 \text{ h/day} = 215 \text{ h}$$

[2]If a light is near a window, however, not all the light will become heat internal to the building; some of it will radiate to surfaces outside the building. A factor of 0.8 to 0.85 is often used to account for this phenomenon.

[3]The figure of 3.3 h/day is taken from Table 10-3, averaged for June, July, and August.

The cooling ton equivalent of the lighting heat load is

$$1280 \text{ Btu/h} \div 12{,}000 \text{ Btu/(ton·h)} = 0.11 \text{ tons}$$

$$B_c = 0.94 \text{ kWh/ton} \times \$0.14\text{/kWh} \times 0.11 \text{ tons} \times 215 \text{ h/year}$$

$$= \$3.11\text{/year [See Equation (6-4).]}$$

The reduction in peak cooling load will reduce demand charges:

$$B_e = 0.11 \text{ tons} \times 0.94 \text{ kW/ton} \times \$20\text{/(kW·month)} \times 3 \text{ months/year}$$

$$= \$6.20\text{/year}$$

The summary of the annual costs and benefits created by being able to turn the lights off because of increased natural lighting is presented below:

Reduced lighting power consumption	\$45/year
Increased winter heating fuel consumption	. . .
Reduced summer cooling electrical consumption	3/year
Reduced demand charges	6/year
Net savings, B_e	\$54/year

TABLE 10-4 Winter Daytime Heat Loss from a South-Facing Office Building Wall, New York City

Month	Median daytime temperature*	Difference from 70°F†: Clear day (with sol-air temperature) (A)	Difference from 70°F†: Cloudy day (B)	UA [Btu/(h·°F)] (C)	0.018 V‡ [Btu/(h·°F)] (D)	Average daily heat loss, Btu/day: Clear day 9 [(A × C) + (B × D)]	Average daily heat loss, Btu/day: Cloudy day 9 [(B × C) + (B × D)]
November	52	−4	18	37	2	−1,008	6,318
December	42	7	28	37	2	2,835	9,828
January	32	16	38	37	2	6,012	13,338
February	37	14	33	37	2	5,256	11,583
March	42	12	28	37	2	4,500	9,828
April	47	13	23	37	2	4,743	8,073

*Median temperature between the hours of 10 A.M. and 5 P.M. from Table 6-4, Mitchel Air Force Base, Nassau County, New York.

†Calculated by using Figure 8-1 and clear-day insolation data from Table 10-6. The sol-air temperature should reflect the proportion of glass and wall used in the building being analyzed, or a separate sol-air temperature should be calculated for each material.

‡UA wall = 14 Btu/(h·°F); UA window = 23 Btu/(h·°F); 0.018 V (infiltration) = 2 Btu/(h·°F).

TABLE 10-5 Winter Daytime Heat Gain Behind a South-Facing Office Building Wall, New York City

Month	Solar radiation, Btu/(day·ft²)*: Clear sky (9 A.M.–6 P.M.)	Solar radiation, Btu/(day·ft²)*: Cloudy sky	Glazing transmittance	Glazing area, ft²	Solar heat gain, Btu/day: Clear sky (A)	Solar heat gain, Btu/day: Cloudy sky (B)	Lighting gains, Btu/day†: Clear sky (C)	Lighting gains, Btu/day†: Cloudy sky (D)	People, Btu/day‡ (E)	Total, Btu/day: Clear sky (A + C + E)	Total, Btu/day: Cloudy sky (B + D + E)
November	1,524	252	0.59	40	35,966	5,947	5,120	8,960	6,885	47,971	21,792
December	1,500	214	0.59	40	35,400	5,050	5,120	8,960	6,885	47,405	20,895
January	1,551	252	0.59	40	36,604	5,947	5,120	8,960	6,885	48,609	21,792
February	1,534	297	0.59	40	36,202	7,009	5,120	8,960	6,885	48,207	22,854
March	1,292	396	0.59	40	30,491	9,346	5,120	8,960	6,885	42,496	25,191
April	914	414	0.59	40	21,570	9,770	5,120	8,960	6,885	37,415	25,615

*From Table 10-6, less solar radiation before 9 A.M. or after 6 P.M.

†Lighting heat gains = 2.5 W/ft² × 150 ft² × 3.413 Btu/Wh × h/day when lights are on.

‡People heat gains = 510 Btu/(h·person) × (150 ft² ÷ 100 ft²/person) × 9 h/day.

TABLE 10-6 **Average Solar Radiation for South-Facing Walls, 40° North Latitude, New York City** (Btu/ft²)

	Clear day°		Cloudy day†	
	Daily	Hourly	Daily	Hourly
January	1626	148	254	28
February	1642	126	362	33
March	1388	107	485	44
April	976	65	599	46
May	716	48	677	44
June	630	37	692	41
July	704	47	665	44
August	948	63	598	46
September	1344	103	485	44
October	1582	122	360	33
November	1596	145	252	28
December	1550	141	214	24

°SOURCE: JCalculated by the author, using data from ASHRAE, *Handbook and Product Directory—1977 Fundamentals Volume*, American Society of Heating, Refrigerating and Air-Conditioning Engineers, Inc., New York, 1977, p. 26.22.

†SOURCE: Calculated by the author, using data from Table 8-13.

When this saving is adjusted to an aftertax basis, a 45 percent corporate income tax bracket will yield the following:

$$B_e = \$54/\text{year} \times (1 - 0.45) = \$30/\text{year}$$

If the designer is confident that the lights will always be off when the peak cooling load occurs, that is, between 9:30 A.M. and 2:30 P.M. on sunny days and between 11:00 A.M. and 1:00 P.M. on overcast days, a saving in cooling equipment may be assessed. The peak load reduction for the *entire* building[4] may be calculated as follows:

$$\Delta q = 0.11 \text{ tons} \times 100 = 11 \text{ tons}$$

This translates, using Table 5-8, into the following cooling system equipment cost savings:

$$B_0 = 11 \text{ tons} \times \$450/\text{ton} = \$4950$$

or for the portion of the building being analyzed,

$$B_0 = \$4950 \div 100 = \$49.50$$

The added cost of installing the photoelectric switches and the reflectors is calculated below:

Reflectors, $C_0 = \$10/\text{ft} \times 10 \text{ ft}$	\$100
Switches, $C_0 = 150 \text{ ft}^2 \times \$0.75/\text{ft}^2$	113
Total construction cost, C_0	\$213
Less cooling equipment cost reduction	(\$ 50)
Net cost	\$163

[4]The room being analyzed is one-hundredth of the building in terms of floor area.

Cost-benefit estimates are calculated below:

$$\text{Simple payback period} = \frac{\$163}{\$30/\text{year}} = 5.4 \text{ years}$$

$$\text{Simple return on investment} = \frac{\$30/\text{year}}{\$163} = 18.4 \text{ percent/year}$$

The designer may tell the client that the proposed energy-saving design is cost-effective, since 18 percent is higher than the client's required return on investment.

ESTIMATING LIGHTING LEVELS FROM NATURAL LIGHT

The designer should be cautioned that the estimating methods presented here are limited in the designs that they can analyze. Only certain types of skylights and a limited range of window designs may be analyzed. Also, in no case may a dimming control system be assumed. The methods are limited to an assumption of on-off switches and stepped switching. For analyzing specific designs beyond the range of these estimating approaches, the designer is encouraged to consider computer simulation programs or to construct scale models of a typical floor of his or her design. Physical models, if they are oriented in a manner similar to the actual building orientation and if interior reflectances and furnishings are accurate, will yield interior lighting conditions that are reasonably close to actual building interior natural-lighting levels. Measurements of interior lighting levels in a model may be made with light meters which measure light levels in a three-dimensional mode.

The designer should also be aware, before reading the following text, that lighting levels resulting from two light sources, such as windows *and* skylights, are additive. That is, one may simply calculate the lighting levels expected from each source separately and then add the two together to estimate the light level created by both sources.

The following pages describe two natural-lighting estimating methods:

- Lighting from skylights
- Lighting from windows

The results obtained from these methods will be estimates of the number of hours of each day for various months when natural-light sources provide illumination on interior work surfaces adequate to permit switching lights down or off. This result may then be used in the method described earlier for estimating electrical savings.

NATURAL LIGHTING FROM SKYLIGHTS

The following method has been developed for translucent or transparent *dome* skylights. It does not apply to skylight designs significantly different from dome designs, but clerestory designs may be analyzed by using this method for overcast-sky conditions only. A modification of the method presented for estimating daylight levels from windows may also be used to evaluate clerestory designs.

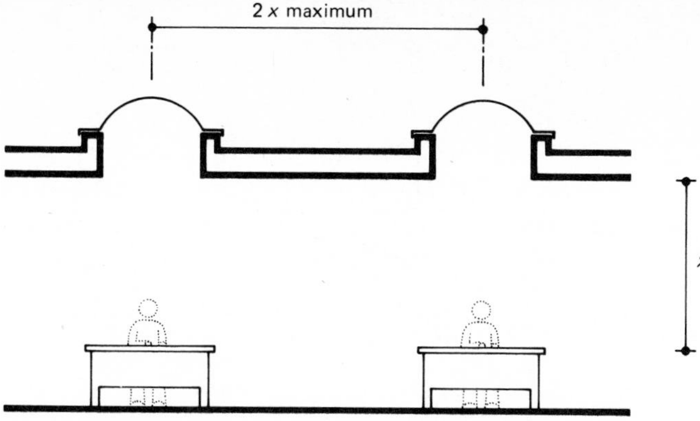

FIGURE 10-9 Maximum spacing of skylights to achieve good natural-lighting distribution.

As a general guide for designing dome skylights so that light levels below a skylight and between skylights are reasonably uniform, the width between skylights should be no more than twice the vertical distance between the work plane and the ceiling (Figure 10-9). It should be noted that other designs for skylights may well be more energy-effective than a dome design. Figure 10-10 shows, for example, a clerestory skylight which admits south light during the winter and excludes it during the summer. External shading devices may also help to exclude the unwanted summer heat gain that is otherwise present in a conventional unshaded dome design.

The general method for estimating natural lighting from skylights is presented below. As mentioned before, this procedure is based on the assumption that when natural-light levels reach an acceptable level of illumination, electric lights will be turned off automatically by a photoelectric switching control.

The outside illumination required for a given interior illumination level must first be estimated. This answer will then allow the designer to determine the minimum solar altitude of both clear-sunny-sky and overcast-sky conditions when exterior illumination on horizontal surfaces meets the required level (see Figure 10-11). The designer may then read from Table 10-7 the time intervals during each typical day in a month when the altitude is greater than the minimum required. These will be the times when the interior lighting levels created by the skylight meet or exceed the minimum levels required and when artificial lighting may be switched off, thus saving electricity. The hours of time determined for clear-sunny-sky and overcast-sky conditions may be combined by a weighted-averaging process, based on percentage overcast data from Table 10-8. This process is diagramed on Figure 10-12.

The general formula for estimating required exterior illumination to provide for adequate interior illumination from skylights is presented below:[5]

$$E_o = \frac{E_i \times A_r}{A_s \times C_u \times C_L} \qquad (10\text{-}3)$$

[5]Illuminating Engineering Society of North America, *Recommended Practice of Daylighting*, Anchor Press, Doubleday & Company, Inc., Garden City, N.Y., 1977, pp. 30–33.

in units,

$$\text{fc} = \frac{\text{fc} \times \text{ft}^2}{\text{ft}^2}$$

where E_o = outside illumination, fc or lm/ft^2

E_i = inside illumination level desired on the task surface, fc or lm/ft^2 (Current standards of practice are: hallways, 10 fc; normal office work, 50 fc; prolonged office work, 75 fc; and industrial tasks, 100 fc.)

A_r = area of room, ft^2

A_s = area of skylight, ft^2

C_L = coefficient of light loss, no units (ranging typically from 0.70 to 0.85)

C_u = coefficient of utilization, no units (See Figure 10-13, Tables 10-9 and 10-10, and the procedure below.)

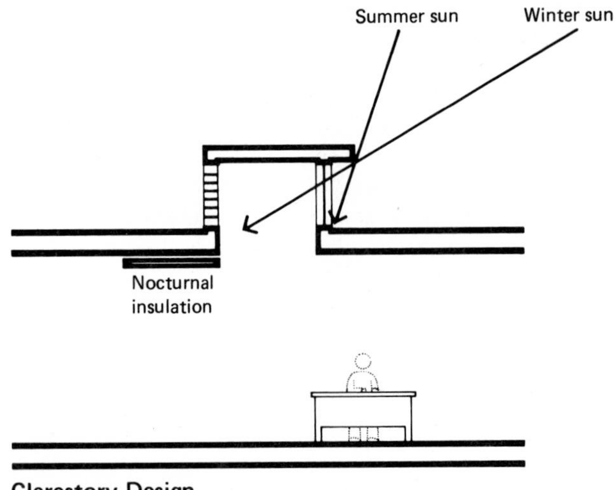

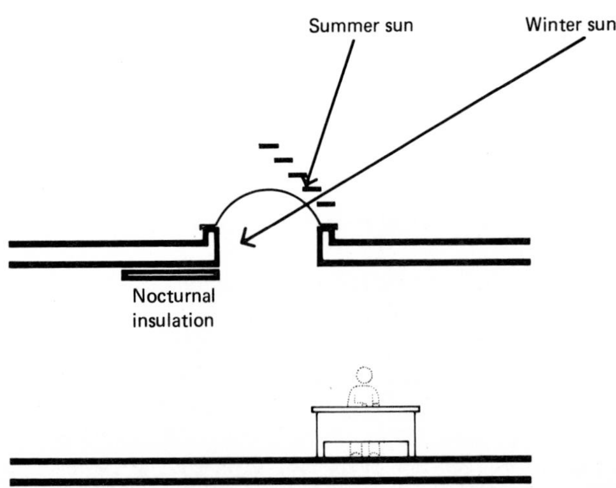

FIGURE 10-10 Examples of energy-conscious skylight designs.

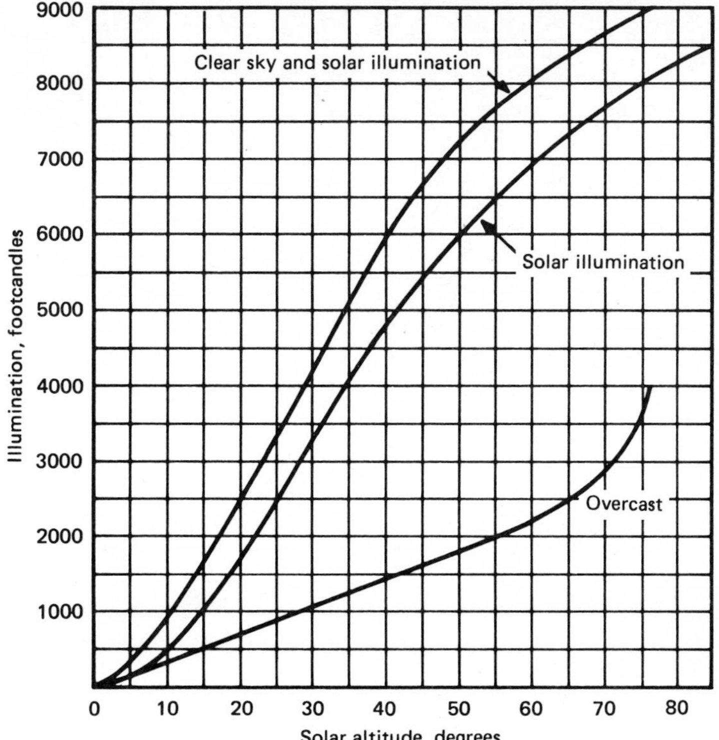

FIGURE 10·11 Clear-sunny-sky and overcast-sky solar illumination on a horizontal surface. [How to Predict Interior Daylight Illumination, *Libbey-Owens-Ford Company, Toledo, Ohio, 1976, p. 37.*]

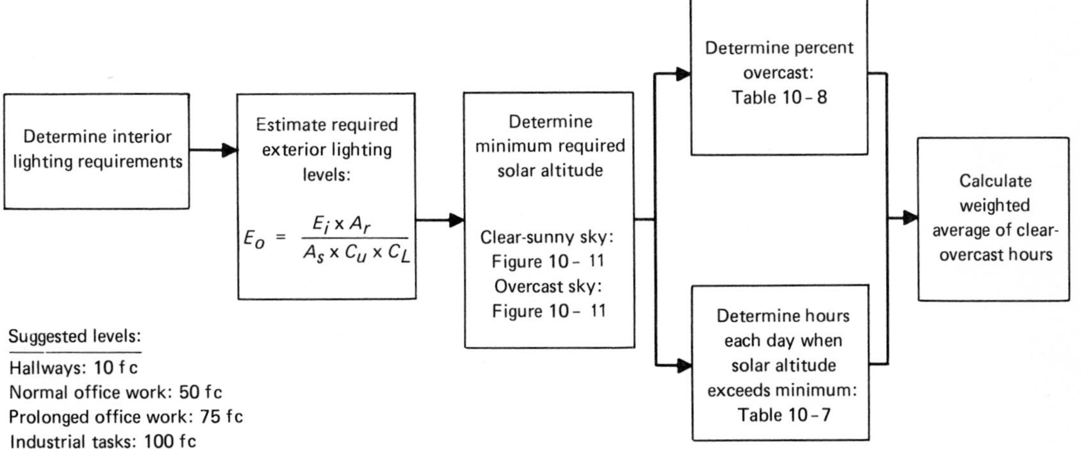

FIGURE 10·12 General process for estimating times of adequate interior natural lighting from skylights.

The coefficient of utilization C_u may be calculated by using the following steps:

1 Calculate the net toplight transmittance of the skylight by using the following equation:

$$T_n = \text{NG} \times L_e \times \tau_g \times \tau_c$$

where T_n = net toplight transmittance of skylight

(*Cont. on p. 295*)

TABLE 10-7 Solar Position and Angles of Incidence for Various Latitudes

Date	Solar time, A.M.	Solar position		Angles of incidence: vertical surfaces													Solar time, P.M.
		Altitude	Azimuth	N	NNE	NE	ENE	E	ESE	SE	SSE	S	SSW	SW	WSW	Hori-zontal	
16° north latitude																	
December	7	7	63			72	50	28	8	19	41	63	86			83	5
	8	19	57			78	57	37	22	23	39	59	80			71	4
	9	31	49			86	67	50	35	31	40	56	74			59	3
	10	41	37				79	63	49	41	43	53	68	84		49	2
	11	48	21					76	63	52	48	51	61	74	89	42	1
	12	51	0					90	76	63	54	51	54	63	76	39	12
January and November	7	8	66			69	47	25	8	23	45	67	89			82	5
	8	21	61			75	55	36	22	26	43	63	84			69	4
	9	33	52			84	65	48	36	34	43	59	77			57	3
	10	43	40				77	62	50	44	46	56	71	87		47	2
	11	51	23				90	76	63	54	51	55	64	76		39	1
	12	54	0					90	77	65	57	54	57	65	77	36	12
February and October	7	11	75		82	60	39	18	14	32	54	76				79	5
	8	25	70		88	68	48	32	25	34	52	72				65	4
	9	38	62			77	60	46	38	41	52	68	86			52	3
	10	50	50			87	73	61	52	50	55	66	79			40	2
	11	59	30				86	75	66	61	60	64	72	82		31	1
	12	63	0					90	80	71	65	63	65	71	80	27	12
March and September	7	14	86		72	51	30	15	23	43	64	86				76	5
	8	29	81		78	59	42	30	31	45	63	82				61	4
	9	43	75		85	69	55	45	43	50	63	79				47	3
	10	56	64			79	68	60	56	59	66	76	88			34	2
	11	68	44				82	75	70	68	70	75	82	90		22	1
	12	74	0					90	84	79	75	74	75	79	84	16	12
April and August	6	3	101	79	56	34	12	12	34	56	79					87	6
	7	17	97	83	62	41	23	19	34	54	76					73	5
	8	32	94	87	68	50	36	32	40	56	74					58	4
	9	46	90	90	74	61	50	46	50	61	75					44	3
	10	61	85		81	71	64	61	62	68	77	88				29	2
	11	75	75		88	82	78	75	75	77	81	86				15	1
	12	86	0					90	88	87	86	86	86	87	88	4	12
May and July	6	5	109	71	48	26	6	20	42	64	87					85	6
	7	19	106	75	54	34	20	25	42	63	84					71	5
	8	33	104	79	60	44	34	36	47	64	83					57	4
	9	47	102	82	67	55	48	48	56	68	83					43	3
	10	61	103	84	74	66	62	62	67	75	85					29	2
	11	75	108	85	80	77	75	76	79	83	89					15	1
	12	86	180	86	86	87	88	90								4	12
June	6	6	113	68	45	23	6	23	45	68						84	6
	7	20	110	72	51	32	20	28	46	66	87					70	5
	8	33	108	75	57	42	34	37	51	68	86					57	4
	9	47	107	78	64	53	47	50	59	72	87					43	3
	10	61	110	81	71	64	61	63	69	78	89					29	2
	11	74	120	82	77	75	74	76	80	86						16	1
	12	83	180	83	83	85	87	90								7	12

24° north latitude																	
December	7	3	63			72	50	28	6	18	40	63	85			87	5
	8	15	55			80	58	37	19	18	36	57	78			75	4
	9	26	46			89	69	50	33	26	34	51	71			64	3
	10	34	34				81	63	47	36	36	47	63	81		56	2
	11	40	18					76	60	47	41	44	55	70	87	50	1
	12	43	0					90	74	59	47	43	47	59	74	47	12
January and November	7	5	66			69	47	25	5	21	43	66	88			85	5
	8	17	58			77	56	36	19	21	39	60	81			73	4
	9	28	49			87	67	48	33	28	38	54	73			62	3
	10	37	36				79	62	47	38	39	50	66	83		53	2
	11	44	20					76	61	49	44	47	58	72	88	46	1
	12	46	0					90	75	61	50	46	50	61	75	44	12
February and October	7	9	74		84	62	40	18	11	30	52	74				81	5
	8	22	66			70	50	32	22	30	48	68	89			68	4
	9	34	57			80	62	46	35	36	47	63	81			56	3
	10	45	44				75	61	49	45	48	59	73	89		45	2
	11	52	25				89	75	63	55	52	56	65	78		38	1
	12	55	0					90	77	66	58	55	58	66	77	35	12
March and September	7	14	84		74	53	32	15	21	41	62	84				76	5
	8	27	77		82	62	44	30	29	41	59	78				63	4
	9	40	68		90	73	57	45	40	45	58	73				50	3
	10	52	55			84	71	60	53	53	59	69	82			38	2
	11	62	33				85	75	67	63	62	67	75	85		28	1
	12	66	0					90	81	73	68	66	68	73	81	24	12
April and August	6	5	101	79	57	35	13	12	33	56	78					85	6
	7	18	95	85	64	43	25	19	33	52	73					72	5
	8	32	89		72	54	39	32	38	52	70	89				58	4
	9	46	82		80	65	53	46	47	56	69	84				44	3
	10	59	72		88	77	67	61	59	63	70	81				31	2
	11	71	52			88	81	75	72	71	74	78	85			19	1
	12	78	0					90	85	81	79	78	79	81	85	12	12
May and July	6	8	108	72	50	28	9	20	42	64	86					82	6
	7	21	103	78	57	38	23	25	41	61	81					69	5
	8	35	98	83	65	49	37	36	45	61	79					55	4
	9	48	94	88	73	60	51	48	53	64	78					42	3
	10	62	88		81	71	65	62	64	70	79	89				28	2
	11	76	77		88	82	78	76	76	78	82	87				14	1
	12	86	0					90	88	87	86	86	86	87	88	4	12
June	6	9	112	69	47	25	9	23	45	67	89					81	6
	7	22	107	75	54	35	23	28	44	64	85					68	5
	8	36	103	80	62	47	37	37	48	64	82					54	4
	9	49	99	84	70	58	50	50	56	67	81					41	3
	10	63	95	88	78	69	64	63	66	73	82					27	2
	11	76	91	90	85	80	77	76	77	80	85					14	1
	12	89	0					90	90	90	89	89	89	90	90	1	12
32° north latitude																	
December	8	10	54			81	59	37	17	14	33	55	77			80	4
	9	20	44				70	50	31	20	29	47	68	89		70	3
	10	28	31				82	63	44	31	29	41	58	78		62	2
	11	33	16					76	58	42	33	36	49	66	85	57	1
	12	35	0					90	72	54	40	35	40	54	72	55	12

TABLE 10·7 Solar Position and Angles of Incidence for Various Latitudes (*cont.*)

Date	Solar time, A.M.	Solar position		Angles of incidence: vertical surfaces												Hori-zontal	Solar time, P.M.
		Altitude	Azimuth	N	NNE	NE	ENE	E	ESE	SE	SSE	S	SSW	SW	WSW		
								32° north latitude									
January	7	1	65			70	47	25	3	20	43	65	88			89	5
and	8	13	56			79	57	36	17	17	36	57	79			77	4
November	9	22	46			89	68	48	31	22	32	50	70			68	3
	10	31	33				81	62	45	33	32	44	61	80		59	2
	11	36	18					76	59	44	36	40	52	68	86	54	1
	12	38	0					90	72	56	43	38	43	56	72	52	12
February	7	7	73		85	62	40	18	9	29	51	73				83	5
and	8	18	64			72	51	32	19	26	45	65	86			72	4
October	9	29	53			83	64	46	33	30	41	58	77			61	3
	10	38	39				77	61	47	39	41	52	68	85		52	2
	11	45	21					75	61	50	45	49	59	73	89	45	1
	12	47	0					90	75	61	51	47	61	61	75	43	12
March	7	13	82		76	54	33	15	19	39	60	82				77	5
and	8	25	73		85	65	46	30	26	37	55	75				65	4
September	9	37	62			76	59	45	37	40	52	68	86			53	3
	10	47	47			88	73	60	50	47	52	63	77			43	2
	11	55	27				88	75	64	57	55	59	68	80		35	1
	12	58	0					90	78	68	61	58	61	68	78	32	12
April	6	6	100	80	58	36	14	12	33	55	77					84	6
and	7	19	92	88	67	46	27	19	31	50	71					71	5
August	8	31	84		76	58	41	32	35	48	66	85				59	4
	9	44	74		85	69	56	46	44	51	63	79				46	3
	10	56	60			81	70	61	56	57	64	74	86			34	2
	11	65	37				84	75	69	66	66	71	78	87		25	1
	12	70	0					90	82	76	71	70	71	76	82	20	12
May	6	10	107	73	51	30	12	20	41	63	85					80	6
and	7	23	100	81	60	41	26	25	39	58	79					67	5
July	8	35	93	88	70	53	40	36	43	57	74					55	4
	9	48	85		79	65	54	48	50	59	72	86				42	3
	10	61	73		87	77	68	62	61	64	72	82				29	2
	11	72	52			88	81	76	73	72	74	79	85			18	1
	12	78	0					90	85	82	79	78	79	82	85	12	12
June	5	1	118	62	40	17	5	28	50	73						89	7
	6	12	110	70	48	27	12	23	44	66	88					78	6
	7	24	103	78	58	39	26	28	42	62	82					66	5
	8	37	97	85	67	51	40	37	46	60	77					53	4
	9	50	89		76	63	53	50	53	62	75	90				40	3
	10	62	80		84	75	67	63	63	67	75	85				28	2
	11	74	61			86	80	76	74	75	78	82	88			16	1
	12	81	0					90	87	84	82	81	82	84	87	9	12

40° north latitude																	
December	8	5	53			82	60	37	16	10	31	53	76			85	4
	9	14	42				71	50	29	14	24	44	65	87		76	3
	10	21	29				84	63	43	26	22	35	55	75		69	2
	11	25	15					76	56	38	26	29	44	63	83	65	1
	12	27	0					90	70	51	34	27	34	51	70	63	12
January and November	8	8	55			80	58	36	15	13	34	56	78			82	4
	9	17	44				70	48	29	17	27	46	68	89		73	3
	10	24	31				82	62	43	27	25	38	57	77		66	2
	11	28	16					76	57	40	29	32	47	65	84	62	1
	12	30	0					90	71	52	37	30	37	52	71	60	12
February and October	7	4	72		85	63	41	18	6	27	50	72				86	5
	8	15	62			74	52	32	16	22	41	63	84			75	4
	9	24	50			86	65	46	30	25	36	54	74			66	3
	10	32	35				79	61	44	33	34	46	63	82		58	2
	11	37	19					75	58	45	37	41	53	69	87	53	1
	12	39	0					90	73	57	44	39	44	57	73	51	12
March and September	7	11	80		78	56	34	15	17	37	58	80				79	5
	8	23	70		88	67	47	30	23	33	51	71				67	4
	9	33	57			80	61	45	34	35	46	63	81			57	3
	10	42	42				76	60	48	42	45	56	71	88		48	2
	11	48	23				90	75	62	52	48	52	62	75		42	1
	12	50	0					90	76	63	54	50	54	63	76	40	12
April and August	6	7	99	81	59	37	15	12	32	54	77					83	6
	7	19	89		69	48	29	19	29	48	68	89				71	5
	8	30	79		80	61	44	32	32	44	62	81				60	4
	9	41	67			74	58	46	41	46	58	73	90			49	3
	10	51	51			86	72	61	53	51	57	67	80			39	2
	11	59	29				87	75	66	60	59	63	71	82		31	1
	12	62	0					90	80	70	64	62	64	70	80	28	12
May and July	5	2	115	65	43	20	3	25	47	70						88	7
	6	13	106	75	53	32	14	20	40	61	83					77	6
	7	24	97	84	64	44	28	25	37	55	76					66	5
	8	35	87		74	57	43	36	40	53	70	88				55	4
	9	47	76		84	69	57	48	47	54	66	80				43	3
	10	57	61			82	70	62	58	59	65	75	86			33	2
	11	66	37				84	76	70	66	67	71	78	87		24	1
	12	70	0					90	82	76	72	70	72	76	82	20	12
June	5	4	117	63	40	18	6	28	50	72						86	7
	6	15	108	72	51	30	15	23	43	64	86					75	6
	7	26	100	81	61	43	29	28	40	59	79					64	5
	8	37	91	89	72	55	42	37	43	56	73					53	4
	9	49	80		82	68	56	50	50	57	69	84				41	3
	10	60	66			80	70	63	60	62	69	78	89			30	2
	11	69	42				83	76	71	69	70	75	81	89		23	1
	12	73	0					90	84	78	75	73	75	78	84	17	12

TABLE 10·7 Solar Position and Angles of Incidence for Various Latitudes (*cont.*)

Date	Solar time, A.M.	Solar position: Altitude	Solar position: Azimuth	Angles of incidence: vertical surfaces: N	NNE	NE	ENE	E	ESE	SE	SSE	S	SSW	SW	WSW	Horizontal	Solar time, P.M.
							48° north latitude										
December	8	1	53			82	60	37	15	8	30	53	75			89	4
	9	8	41				72	50	28	9	20	42	64	86		82	3
	10	14	28				84	63	41	22	15	31	52	74		76	2
	11	17	14					76	55	35	19	22	40	61	82	73	1
	12	19	20					90	69	48	29	19	29	48	69	71	12
January and November	8	3	55			80	58	36	13	10	32	55	77			87	4
	9	11	43				70	48	27	11	23	44	66	88		79	3
	10	17	29				83	62	41	23	18	34	54	75		73	2
	11	21	15					76	55	36	22	25	42	62	83	69	1
	12	22	0					90	69	49	31	22	31	49	69	68	12
February and October	7	2	72		86	63	41	18	5	27	49	72				88	5
	8	11	60			75	53	32	13	19	39	61	83			79	4
	9	19	47			88	67	46	27	19	31	50	71			71	3
	10	25	33				81	61	42	28	27	41	59	79		65	2
	11	30	17					75	56	40	30	34	48	66	85	60	1
	12	31	0					90	71	53	38	31	38	53	71	59	12
March and September	7	10	79		79	57	35	15	15	35	57	79				80	5
	8	20	67			70	49	30	20	29	48	68	89			70	4
	9	28	53			83	63	45	31	29	41	58	78			62	3
	10	35	38				78	60	45	36	38	50	66	84		55	2
	11	40	20					75	59	46	40	44	56	71	88	50	1
	12	42	0					90	73	58	47	42	47	58	73	48	12
April and August	6	9	98	82	60	38	17	12	31	53	75					81	6
	7	19	87		72	51	31	19	27	45	66	87				71	5
	8	29	75		84	64	46	32	29	40	58	77				61	4
	9	38	61			77	60	46	38	41	52	68	85			52	3
	10	46	45				75	61	50	46	50	60	74	90		44	2
	11	51	24				89	75	63	54	52	55	65	77		39	1
	12	54	0					90	77	65	57	54	57	65	77	36	12
May and July	5	5	114	66	43	21	6	25	47	69						85	7
	6	15	104	77	55	34	17	20	39	60	81					75	6
	7	25	93	87	67	47	31	25	35	53	72					65	5
	8	35	82		78	61	45	36	37	49	65	83				55	4
	9	44	68		89	74	59	48	44	49	60	75				46	3
	10	53	51			86	73	62	55	53	58	68	80			37	2
	11	59	29				87	76	67	61	60	64	71	82		31	1
	12	62	0					90	80	71	64	62	64	71	80	28	12
June	5	8	117	64	42	20	9	28	50	72						82	7
	6	17	106	75	53	33	18	23	42	63	84					73	6
	7	27	96	85	65	46	31	28	38	56	75					63	5
	8	37	85		76	59	45	37	40	52	68	86				53	4
	9	47	72		87	72	59	50	47	52	63	78				43	3
	10	56	55			85	73	63	57	56	62	71	83			34	2
	11	63	31				86	76	68	64	63	67	74	84		27	1
	12	65	0					90	81	73	67	65	67	73	81	25	12

56° north latitude

				N	NNW	NW	WNW	W	WSW	SW	SSW	S	SSE	SE	ESE	Horizontal	
December	9	2	40				72	50	27	5	18	41	63	85		88	3
	10	7	27				85	63	40	19	8	28	50	73		88	2
	11	10	14					76	54	32	13	17	37	59	82	80	1
	12	11	0					90	68	46	25	11	25	46	68	79	12
January and November	9	5	42				71	48	26	6	20	42	64	87		85	3
	10	10	28				84	62	40	19	12	30	52	74		80	2
	11	13	14					76	54	33	15	19	39	60	82	77	1
	12	14	0					90	68	47	26	14	26	47	68	76	12
February and October	8	7	59			76	54	32	11	16	37	59	82			83	4
	9	13	46			89	68	46	26	13	27	47	69			77	3
	10	19	31				82	61	40	23	21	36	56	77		71	2
	11	22	16					75	55	36	23	27	43	63	84	68	1
	12	23	0					90	69	49	32	23	32	49	69	67	12
March and September	7	8	77		80	58	36	15	13	33	55	78				82	5
	8	16	64			71	50	30	17	25	44	66	87			74	4
	9	23	50			85	65	45	29	24	36	54	74			67	3
	10	29	35				79	60	43	31	31	44	62	81		61	2
	11	33	18					75	57	41	33	37	50	67	86	57	1
	12	34	0					90	72	54	40	34	40	54	72	56	12
April and August	5	1	109	71	49	26	4	19	41	64	86					89	7
	6	10	97	84	61	39	19	12	30	52	74					80	6
	7	18	84		74	53	33	19	24	42	63	84				72	5
	8	26	71		87	67	48	32	26	36	53	73				64	4
	9	34	56			81	62	46	35	35	46	62	81			56	3
	10	40	40				77	61	47	40	43	54	69	86		50	2
	11	44	21					75	61	49	44	48	58	73	89	46	1
	12	46	0					90	74	60	50	46	50	60	74	44	12
May and July	4	1	126	54	32	10	13	36	58	81						89	8
	5	8	113	67	45	23	9	25	47	69						82	7
	6	16	102	79	58	37	20	20	37	58	79					74	6
	7	25	89		70	51	33	25	33	50	69	89				65	5
	8	33	76		83	64	47	36	34	44	60	79				57	4
	9	41	62			78	62	48	41	44	54	69	86			49	3
	10	48	44				76	62	52	48	51	61	75	89		42	2
	11	52	23				89	76	64	55	52	56	65	77		38	1
	12	54	0					90	77	65	57	54	57	65	77	36	12
June	4	4	127	53	31	9	15	37	60	82						86	8
	5	11	115	65	43	23	12	28	49	71						79	7
	6	28	92	89	69	50	34	28	36	53	72					62	6
	7	28	92	89	69	50	34	28	36	53	72					62	5
	8	36	79		81	63	48	37	37	48	63	81				54	4
	9	44	64			76	61	50	44	47	57	72	88			46	3
	10	51	46			89	75	63	54	51	55	64	77			39	2
	11	56	25				89	76	65	58	56	59	68	79		34	1
	12	57	0					90	78	68	60	57	60	68	78	33	12

SOURCE: *ASHRAE Handbook and Product Directory—1977 Fundamentals Volume*, American Society of Heating, Refrigerating and Air-Conditioning Engineers, Inc., New York, 1977, p. 26.4. Reprinted by permission.

TABLE 10-8 Mean Sky Cover, Sunrise to Sunset

Station	Years	January	February	March	April	May	June	July	August	September	October	November	December	Annual
Fairbanks, Alaska	16	0.65	0.63	0.62	0.62	0.70	0.73	0.73	0.78	0.79	0.79	0.71	0.71	0.71
Phoenix, Arizona	14	0.51	0.45	0.43	0.38	0.29	0.20	0.38	0.35	0.20	0.28	0.31	0.36	0.35
Los Angeles, California	19	0.46	0.48	0.48	0.53	0.48	0.41	0.28	0.27	0.28	0.39	0.34	0.45	0.40
San Francisco, California	49	0.57	0.55	0.50	0.45	0.44	0.37	0.42	0.46	0.38	0.40	0.45	0.56	0.46
Washington, D.C.	70	0.61	0.56	0.56	0.54	0.54	0.51	0.51	0.51	0.48	0.47	0.54	0.58	0.53
Miami, Florida	48	0.50	0.46	0.47	0.49	0.54	0.62	0.61	0.58	0.62	0.58	0.52	0.52	0.54
Atlanta, Georgia	25	0.63	0.62	0.61	0.55	0.55	0.58	0.63	0.57	0.53	0.45	0.51	0.62	0.57
Honolulu, Hawaii	13	0.53	0.60	0.59	0.60	0.60	0.55	0.50	0.51	0.48	0.54	0.55	0.54	0.55
Chicago, Illinois	84	0.64	0.62	0.61	0.58	0.53	0.52	0.43	0.46	0.47	0.50	0.63	0.66	0.55
New Orleans, Louisiana	44	0.60	0.60	0.58	0.53	0.51	0.54	0.61	0.58	0.52	0.40	0.47	0.59	0.54
Boston, Massachusetts	64	0.60	0.56	0.56	0.58	0.58	0.57	0.56	0.53	0.51	0.53	0.60	0.60	0.57
Minneapolis, Minnesota	24	0.65	0.62	0.67	0.65	0.64	0.60	0.49	0.51	0.51	0.54	0.69	0.69	0.61
Kansas City, Missouri	66	0.54	0.54	0.55	0.55	0.53	0.49	0.41	0.41	0.42	0.41	0.50	0.55	0.49
New York, New York	69	0.62	0.58	0.59	0.52	0.58	0.57	0.56	0.52	0.50	0.50	0.58	0.60	0.57
Houston, Texas	46	0.61	0.61	0.59	0.57	0.54	0.48	0.52	0.50	0.47	0.42	0.52	0.62	0.54
Seattle, Washington	24	0.80	0.77	0.74	0.69	0.64	0.64	0.49	0.53	0.56	0.72	0.80	0.81	0.68
San Juan, Puerto Rico	57	0.49	0.45	0.45	0.50	0.58	0.58	0.55	0.51	0.58	0.54	0.52	0.51	0.52
St. Croix, Virgin Islands	6	0.56	0.58	0.57	0.59	0.72	0.69	0.70	0.61	0.70	0.65	0.60	0.58	0.63

SOURCE: *Local Climatological Data*, U.S. Weather Bureau, Washington.

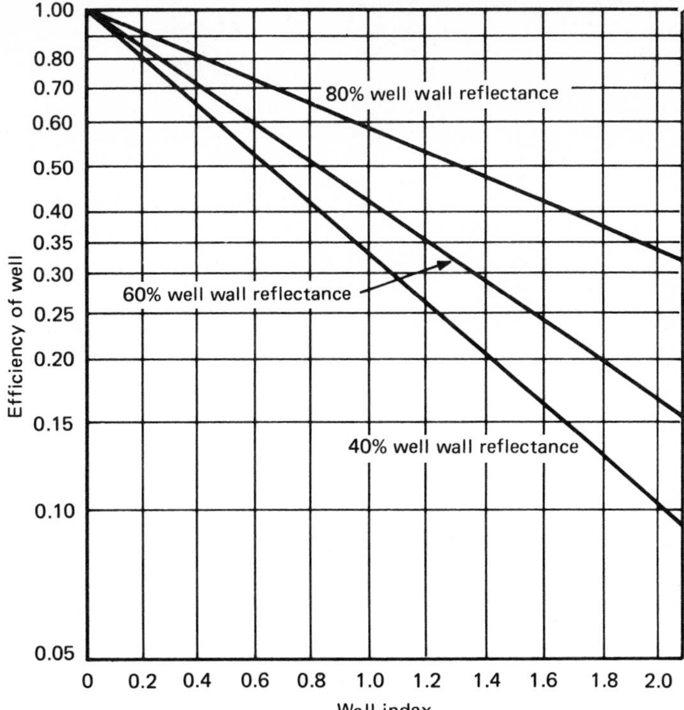

FIGURE 10-13 Efficiency factors for various depths of skylight wells. [Recommended Practice of Daylighting, *Illuminating Engineering Society, New York, 1979, p. 31.*]

NG = net-to-gross ratio (Typically this ranges from 0.6 to 0.9. The gross area includes the frame of the skylight; the net area is simply the area of the light-transmitting glazing within the frame of the skylight.)

L_e = light well efficiency, a function of the well index where

$$\text{Well index} = \frac{\text{well height} \times (\text{well width} + \text{well length})}{2 \times \text{well length} \times \text{well width}}$$

(See Figure 10-13 after the well index has been calculated.)

τ_g = transmittance of the glazing (This may be given by the manufacturer or by Table 7-16.)

τ_c = transmittance of glare or the shading control part of the skylight (The following are the transmittance factors for some of the more commonly used controls: prismatic or patterned lens, 0.90; translucent white louvers, 0.70; white translucent diffusers, 0.50.)

2 Determine the room ratio from Table 10-9.

3 Determine the coefficient of utilization by using the net toplight transmittance from Step 2 and selecting it from Table 10-10.

EXAMPLE

A designer wishes to use domed skylights in the ceiling of a single-story office building. For purposes of analysis, he decides to examine a typical interior room of 20 by 20 feet

TABLE 10-9 Room Ratios for Toplighting

Room length, ft	Room width, ft	Ceiling height above floor, ft					
		8	10	12	15	19	23
12	12	1.1	0.8	0.6	0.5		
	16	1.3	0.9	0.7	0.6		
	20	1.4	1.0	0.8	0.6	0.5	
	24	1.5	1.1	0.8	0.7	0.5	
	30	1.6	1.1	0.9	0.7	0.5	
	40	1.7	1.2	1.0	0.7	0.6	0.5
20	20	1.8	1.3	1.1	0.8	0.6	0.5
	24	2.0	1.5	1.2	0.9	0.7	0.5
	30	2.2	1.6	1.3	1.0	0.7	0.6
	40	2.4	1.8	1.4	1.1	0.8	0.7
	60	2.7	2.0	1.6	1.2	0.9	0.7
	80	2.9	2.1	1.7	1.3	1.0	0.8
30	30	2.7	2.0	1.6	1.2	0.9	0.7
	40	3.1	2.3	1.8	1.4	1.0	0.8
	60	3.6	2.7	2.1	1.6	1.2	1.0
	80	4.0	2.9	2.3	1.7	1.3	1.1
	100	4.2	3.1	2.4	1.9	1.4	1.1
	120	4.4	3.2	2.5	1.9	1.5	1.2
40	40	3.6	2.7	2.1	1.6	1.2	1.0
	60	4.4	3.2	2.5	1.9	1.5	1.2
	80	4.9	3.6	2.8	2.1	1.6	1.3
	100	5+	3.8	3.0	2.3	1.7	1.4
	120	5+	4.0	3.2	2.4	1.8	1.5
	140	5+	4.1	3.3	2.5	1.9	1.5

SOURCE: *Recommended Practice of Daylighting*, Illuminating Engineering Society, New York, 1979, p. 32.

(see Figure 10-14). There would be a 3-foot-wide skylight running down the middle of the room for its entire length. The rest of the building components involved in the design are listed below, along with information required to perform a cost-benefit analysis of the design:

Dome transmittance	0.70
U roof	0.112, winter; 0.102, summer
U skylight	0.70, winter; 0.46, summer
Well height	3 ft
Well width	3 ft
Well length	20 ft
Well reflectance	80 percent
Skylight spacing	20 ft on center
Cost for 3-ft double-dome skylight	\$25/ft^2, or \$1500
Tributary ceiling area	400 ft^2
Cost of roof construction	\$9/ft^2
Total area of interior space of building	15,000 ft^2
Room width, RW	20 ft
Room height, RH	9 ft
Task height, TH	3 ft

Room length, RL	20 ft
Desired task lighting level	50 fc
Building heating fuel	Oil at $1.25/gal
Building cooling system	50-ton central water-cooled system using electricity at $0.15/kWh
Electrical power required by lighting system	2 W/ft^2

TABLE 10-10 Coefficients of Utilization for Toplighting

		Ceiling reflectance			
		75 percent		50 percent	
		Wall reflectance			
Net toplight transmittance (including light well effect, controls, etc.)	Room ratio	50 percent	30 percent	50 percent	30 percent
70%	0.6	.37	.34	.36	.34
	0.8	.45	.42	.44	.41
	1.0	.49	.46	.48	.45
	1.25	.52	.50	.51	.49
	1.5	.55	.53	.53	.51
	2.0	.58	.56	.57	.55
	2.5	.61	.59	.60	.58
	3.0	.63	.61	.62	.60
	4.0	.65	.62	.63	.61
50%	0.6	.26	.24	.26	.24
	0.8	.32	.30	.31	.29
	1.0	.35	.33	.34	.32
	1.25	.37	.36	.36	.35
	1.5	.39	.38	.38	.36
	2.0	.41	.40	.41	.39
	2.5	.44	.42	.43	.41
	3.0	.45	.44	.44	.43
	4.0	.46	.44	.45	.44
30%	0.6	.16	.15	.16	.15
	0.8	.19	.18	.19	.18
	1.0	.21	.20	.21	.19
	1.25	.22	.21	.22	.21
	1.5	.24	.23	.23	.22
	2.0	.25	.24	.24	.24
	2.5	.26	.25	.26	.25
	3.0	.27	.26	.27	.26
	4.0	.28	.27	.27	.26
10%	0.6	.05	.05	.05	.05
	0.8	.06	.06	.06	.06
	1.0	.07	.07	.07	.06
	1.25	.07	.07	.07	.07
	1.5	.08	.08	.08	.07
	2.0	.08	.08	.08	.08
	2.5	.09	.08	.09	.08
	3.0	.09	.09	.09	.09
	4.0	.09	.09	.09	.09

SOURCE: *Recommended Practice of Daylighting*, Illuminating Engineering Society, New York, 1979, p. 32.

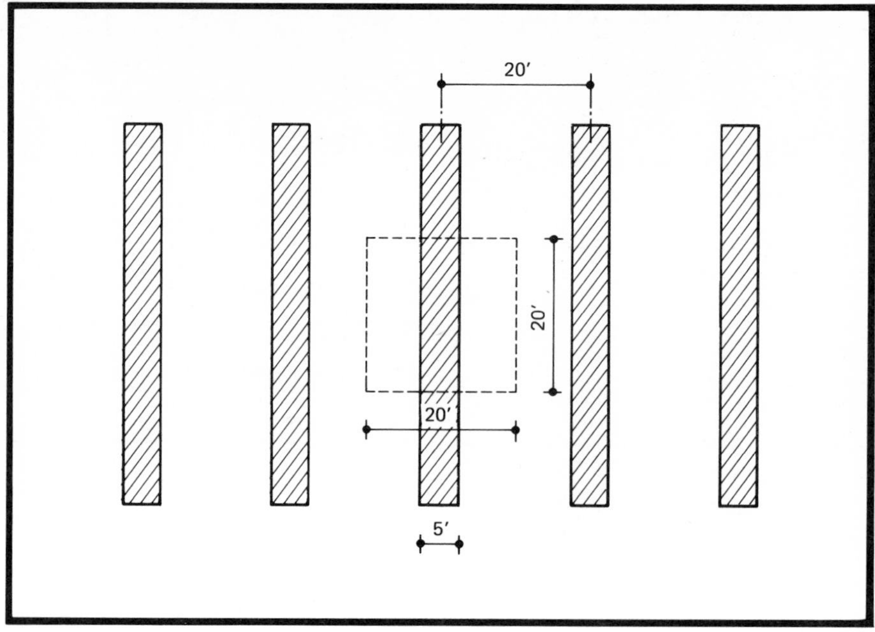

FIGURE 10-14 Plan of an example one-story office building and skylight.

Demand charges	\$20/(kW·month)
Income tax bracket	45 percent
Roof construction	4-in heavyweight concrete with 2-in insulation

$$E_o = \frac{50 \text{ fc} \times 400 \text{ ft}^2}{60 \text{ ft}^2 \times 0.75 \times 0.24} = 1852 \text{ fc} \tag{10-3}$$

where well index $= \dfrac{3 \text{ ft} \times (3 \text{ ft} + 20 \text{ ft})}{2 \times 20 \text{ ft} \times 3 \text{ ft}} = 0.575$

$L_e = 0.73$

$\tau_g = 0.53$ (interpolated from Table 10-15)

$\tau_c = 0$ (no controls)

$T_n = 0.75 \times 0.73 \times 0.53 = 0.29$

Room ratio $= 1.55$ (interpolated from Table 10-9)

$C_u = 0.24$ (from Table 10-10)

From Figure 10-13 for clear-sunny skies and for overcast conditions, the following are the minimum altitudes that the sun must attain to provide 1852 footcandles on the surface of the skylight:

Clear-sunny	Overcast
17°	53°

Using data from Table 10-7, the table below lists the times of day when the clear-sunny altitude of 17° and the overcast altitude of 53° are exceeded, thus providing more than 50 footcandles of interior illumination and allowing the overhead fluorescent lights to be shut off. The designer should note that a credit for adequate interior light is given only for hours within the normal workday. That range for this example problem is from 9:00 A.M. to 6:00 P.M.

Month	17° altitude, clear-sunny (Table 10-7)	53° altitude, overcast (Table 10-7)	Overcast fraction (Table 10-8)	Weighted average, h/day
December	9:30 to 2:30 (5 h)	. . .	0.60	2.00
January	9:00 to 3:00 (6 h)	. . .	0.62	2.28
February	9:00 to 3:30 (6½ h)	. . .	0.58	2.73
March	9:00 to 4:30 (7½ h)	. . .	0.59	3.08
April	9:00 to 5:00 (8 h)	10:30 to 1:30 (3 h)	0.52	5.40
May	9:00 to 5:30 (8½ h)	9:30 to 2:30 (5 h)	0.58	6.47
June	9:00 to 6:00 (9 h)	9:15 to 2:45 (5½ h)	0.57	6.95
July	9:00 to 5:30 (8½ h)	9:30 to 2:30 (5 h)	0.56	6.54
August	9:00 to 5:00 (8 h)	10:30 to 1:30 (3 h)	0.52	5.40
September	9:00 to 4:30 (7½ h)	. . .	0.50	3.75
October	9:00 to 3:30 (6½ h)	. . .	0.50	3.25
November	9:00 to 3:00 (6 h)	. . .	0.58	2.52
Overall average				4.20

The numbers in the third column represent the fraction of overcast sky typical for each month for New York City. These data are extracted from Table 10-8, "Mean Sky Cover, Sunrise to Sunset." This fraction was used to calculate a weighted average of hours between overcast and clear-sunny skies, during which lights may be turned off in each month. For example, in April,

$$8\text{ h} \times (1 - 0.52) + 3\text{ h} \times 0.52 = 5.40\text{ h}$$

The savings in electrical energy may then be calculated as follows:

$$T_L = 4.20\text{ h/day} \times 260\text{ workdays/year} = 1092\text{ h/year}$$

$$B_L = \$0.15/\text{kWh} \times 1092\text{ h/year} \times 2\text{ W/ft}^2 \times 400\text{ ft}^2 \div 1000\text{ W/kWh} \qquad (10\text{-}1)$$

$$B_L = \$131/\text{year}$$

Adding a skylight to an office building will, of course, decrease the need for interior artificial lighting, but it will also increase conducted heat loss through the roof and increase solar radiation heat gains, especially during the summer.

During the winter daytime, the building will be occupied and will have internal heat gains of people and lights, and since skylights are typically placed over the interior zones of office buildings, of equipment loads also. Typical office buildings have the following heat gains from equipment such as elevators, fans, and pumps:

$$\text{Typical internal equipment heat loads in offices} = 0.5\text{ W/ft}^2 \text{ or } 1.707\text{ Btu/(h}\cdot\text{ft}^2)$$

As in previous examples presented in this book, the designer must conduct a heat balance analysis for the winter daytime period to determine whether or not the proposed design will affect heating fuel costs. Tables 10-11 and 10-12 present the daily heat gains and heat losses for each month on the assumption that the skylight has been included in the roof of the building in this example.

TABLE 10-11 Daytime Heat Gains Next to an Office Roof, New York City Heating Season, after a Skylight Has Been Installed

	Solar radiation, Btu/(day·ft²)				Solar heat gain, Btu/day				Lighting		Internal heat gains, total Btu/day	
Month	Clear day	Cloudy day	τ_g	Skylight area, ft²	Clear day	Cloudy day	People	Equipment*	Clear day	Cloudy day	Clear day	Cloudy day
November	694	252	0.70	60	29,148	10,584	18,360	6,143	8,190	24,570	61,841	59,657
December	558	214	0.70	60	23,436	8,988	18,360	6,143	10,920	24,570	58,859	58,061
January	694	252	0.70	60	29,148	10,584	18,360	6,143	8,190	24,570	61,841	59,657
February	1,049	297	0.70	60	44,058	12,474	18,360	6,143	6,825	24,570	75,386	61,547
March	1,417	396	0.70	60	59,514	16,632	18,360	6,143	4,095	24,570	88,112	45,705
April	1,719	414	0.70	60	72,198	17,388	18,360	6,143	2,730	16,380	99,431	58,271

*Equipment load is 0.5 W/ft².

The results of these tables for the month of December are presented below:

	Sky condition	
Heat flows, Btu/day	Cloudy day	Clear day
Internal heat gains	58,061	58,859
Heat losses	20,664	19,224

Internal gains on clear days when compared with cloudy days are characterized by more solar radiation but lower heat gains from the artificial-lighting system because lights are off during a greater number of hours. Heat losses on cloudy days are somewhat greater than on clear days because on sunny days sol-air temperatures decrease the inside-to-outside surface temperature difference.

The comparison of daytime heat gains with heat losses for December yields the same conclusion for all heating-season months. The office building in this example has greater winter daytime heat gains than heat losses even after the skylight has been installed and even on cloudy days. Heating system costs during this period will not be affected one way or the other because of the skylight during the winter *daytime*.

During the winter nighttime, all internal and solar heat gains are gone from the building. The sun has set, the occupants have departed, the lights are off, and the equipment has been shut down. Changes in conducted heat loss therefore must be considered in evaluating the skylight's thermal and luminous performance:

$$\Delta Q_h = [0.70 \text{ Btu/(h·ft}^2\text{·°F)} - 0.112 \text{ Btu/(h·°F·ft}^2)] \times 60 \text{ ft}^2 \times 47{,}303 \text{ (°F·h)/year}^6$$

$$= 1{,}668{,}850 \text{ Btu/year [See Equation (7-7).]}$$

$$C_h = \frac{\$1.25/\text{gal} \times 1{,}668{,}850 \text{ Btu/year}}{0.55 \times 140{,}000 \text{ Btu/gal}}$$

$$= \$27.09/\text{year [See Equation (6-1).]}$$

[6]From Table 6-6; note that degree-hour data for a wall are the same for a roof condition at night because the sol-air temperature effect is absent from both wall and roof at night.

Additional infiltration heat loss during the winter night is calculated below:

$$\Delta Q_h = 0.018 \text{ Btu/(°F·ft}^3) \times [3 \text{ ft}^3/(\text{h·ft}) \times 46 \text{ ft}] \times 47{,}303 \text{ (°F·h)/year}$$
$$= 117{,}501 \text{ Btu/year [See Equation (7-12).]}$$

$$C_h = \frac{\$1.25/\text{gal} \times 117{,}501 \text{ Btu/year}}{0.55 \times 140{,}000 \text{ Btu/gal}}$$
$$= \$1.91/\text{year [See Equation (6-1).]}$$

The additional conducted and convected heat loss will increase the *peak* heat loss condition of the building, so the possible cost of larger heating equipment must be considered. Change in peak heat loss must first be calculated:

Conduction:

$$\Delta q_h = [0.70 \text{ Btu/(h·°F·ft}^2) - 0.112 \text{ Btu/(h·°F·ft}^2)] \times 60 \text{ ft}^2 \times (55°\text{F} - 15°\text{F})$$
$$= 1411 \text{ Btu/h [See Equation (7-6).]}$$

Convection:

$$\Delta q_h = 0.018 \text{ Btu/(ft}^3\text{·°F)} \times [3 \text{ ft}^3/(\text{h·ft}) \times 46 \text{ ft}] \times (55°\text{F} - 15°\text{F})$$
$$= 99 \text{ Btu/h [See Equation (7-10).]}$$

$$\text{Total } \Delta q_h = 1510 \text{ Btu/h}$$

For the entire interior space of the building, this becomes

$$\Delta q_h = 1510 \text{ Btu/h} \times (15{,}000 \text{ ft}^2 \div 400 \text{ ft}^2)$$
$$= 56{,}625 \text{ Btu/h}$$

Since this is greater than 10,000 Btus per hour, the following will be the impact of the additional peak heat loss on added heating equipment when using data from Table 5-8:

$$C_0 = 56{,}625 \text{ Btu/h} \times (\$8 \div 1000 \text{ Btu/h})$$
$$= \$453$$

TABLE 10-12 **Daytime Heat Loss from an Office Roof, New York City Heating Season, after a Skylight Has Been Installed**

Month	Median daytime temperature*	Difference from 70°F†				Average daily heat loss (Btu/day)	
		Cloudy day (A)	Clear day (with sol-air temperature) (B)	UA‡ (Btu/day) (C)	0.018 V (Btu/day) (D)	Cloudy day 9 (A · C + C · D)	Clear day 9 (B · C + A · D)
November	52	18	13	80	2	13,284	9,684
December	42	28	26	80	2	20,664	19,224
January	32	38	35	80	2	28,044	25,884
February	37	33	25	80	2	24,354	18,594
March	42	28	14	80	2	20,664	10,584
April	47	23	8	80	2	16,974	6,174

*Observed from Table 6-4.

†$t_{sa} = t_o + 0.15\,(I_H - 7°\text{F})$; to simplify the calculation, sol-air temperatures for the glass and the wall are assumed to be the same.

‡$UA = (0.112 \times 340) + 0.70 \times 60) = 80$ Btu/(h·°F); $0.018\ V = 0.018 \times 3 \times 46 = 2$ Btu/(h·°F).

TABLE 10-13 Degree-Hours for Roofs, an 80°F Indoor Temperature, and a 65°F Cooling System Activation Temperature on Weekdays in Nonresidential Buildings, Mitchel Air Force Base, Nassau County, New York, Cooling Season

Average bin temperature	Difference from 80°F	Sol-air adjustment* (A)	Hours of occurrence, 8 A.M.–6 P.M. (B)	Adjustment for 5-day week (C)	(°F·h)/year (A · B · C)
102	22	32	1	0.714	23
97	17	27	9	0.714	174
92	12	22	33	0.714	518
87	7	17	111	0.714	1347
82	2	12	218	0.714	1868
77	−3	7	290	0.714	1449
72	−8	2	243	0.714	347
67	−13	−3	166	0.714	....
					5726

*$t_{sa} = t_o + [116\text{Btu/(h·ft}^2) \times 0.15] - 7°\text{F} = t_o + 10°\text{F}$
(Figure 8-1 with data from Table 7-13)

SOURCE: Calculated by the author from data in Table 6-4.

or for the portion of building being evaluated,

$$C_0 = \$453 \times (400 \text{ ft}^2 \div 15{,}000 \text{ ft}^2)$$
$$= \$12$$

During the summer cooling season, all heat flows are heat gains, but since air-conditioning systems are on during the day only,[7] additional costs or benefits attributable to the skylight need be evaluated only for the daytime period.[8]

Additional conducted heat gain is calculated as follows:

$$\Delta Q_c = [0.46 \text{ Btu/(h·°F·ft}^2) - 0.102 \text{ Btu/(h·°F·ft}^2)] \times 60 \text{ ft} \times 5726 \text{ (°F·h)/year}$$
$$= 122{,}994 \text{ Btu/year [See Equation (8-3).]}$$

Sensible and latent infiltration gains are estimated below:[9]

$$\Delta Q_{c,s} = 0.018/(\text{°F·ft}^3) \times [3 \text{ ft}^3/(\text{h·ft}) \times 46 \text{ ft}] \times -2283 \text{ (°F·h)/year}$$
$$= -\ 5671 \text{ Btu/year [See Equation (8-8).]}$$
$$\Delta Q_{c,l} = 80.7 \text{ Btu/ft}^3 \times [3 \text{ ft}^3/(\text{h·ft}) \times 46 \text{ ft}] \times 1.807 \text{ (lb·h)/(lb·year)}$$
$$= 20{,}124 \text{ Btu/year [See Equation (8-10).]}$$

[7]Some of the daytime energy consumption in nonresidential buildings during the cooling season typically comes from so-called pickup loads: energy required to cool down the interior after it has warmed up overnight. This energy is usually relatively small compared with other loads and will be ignored in the analysis.

[8]The figure of 5726 (°F·h)/year is taken from Table 10-13.

[9]The figure of −2283 (°F·h)/year is taken from Table 8-14.

Radiation gains are estimated as follows:[10]

$$\Delta Q_c = 116 \text{ Btu/(h}\cdot\text{ft}^2) \times 60 \text{ ft}^2 \times 0.70 \times 9 \text{ h/day} \times 5 \text{ days/week} \times 26 \text{ weeks/year} = 5{,}700{,}240 \text{ Btu/year [See Equation (8-4).]}$$

The average time during the months of May through October when lights may be turned off is 6.3 hours (see analysis on page 299). The reduced internal heat load that results is estimated below:

$$\Delta Q_L = 400 \text{ ft}^2 \times 2 \text{ W/ft}^2 \times 3.413 \text{ Btu/Wh} \times 6.3 \text{ h/day} \times 5 \text{ days/week} \times 26 \text{ weeks/year} = 2{,}236{,}198 \text{ Btu/year}$$

A summary of increases and decreases in summer heat gains due to addition of the skylight is presented below:

Increases in heat gain:

Conduction	122,994 Btu/year
Infiltration:	
Sensible	......
Latent	20,124 Btu/year
Radiation	5,700,240 Btu/year

Decreases in heat gain:

Lighting	(2,236,198 Btu/year)
Infiltration, sensible	(5,671 Btu/year)
Net increase	3,601,489 Btu/year

The monetary value of this increase is estimated below:

$$C_c = \$0.15/\text{kWh} \times 0.94 \text{ kW/ton} \times [3{,}601{,}489 \text{ Btu/year} \div 12{,}000 \text{ Btu/(ton}\cdot\text{h)}] = \$42.32/\text{year [See Equation (6-5).]}$$

The increases in peak cooling load are estimated below:

Conduction:[11]

$$\Delta q_c = [0.46 - 0.102 \text{ Btu/(h}\cdot{}^\circ\text{F}\cdot\text{ft}^2)] \times 60 \text{ ft}^2 \times 46^\circ\text{F} = 988 \text{ Btu/h [See Equation (8-1).]}$$

Sensible convection:

$$\Delta q_{c,s} = 0.018 \text{ ft}^3/({}^\circ\text{F}\cdot\text{Btu}) \times [3 \text{ ft}^3/(\text{h}\cdot\text{ft}) \times 46 \text{ ft}] \times (80^\circ\text{F} - 89^\circ\text{F}) = 22 \text{ Btu/h [See Equation (8-6).]}$$

[10]The figure of 116 Btu/(h·ft²) is derived from Table 7-13.

[11]From Table 8-1 for flat roofs without suspended ceilings, adjusted as indicated on page 207, for an 80°F inside temperature in August and a 75°F average outdoor temperature.

Latent convection:

$$\Delta q_{c,l} = 80.7 \text{ Btu/ft}^3 \times [3 \text{ ft}^3/(\text{h}\cdot\text{ft}) \times 46 \text{ ft}]$$
$$\times (0.0142 \text{ lb/lb} - 0.0112 \text{ lb/lb})$$
$$= 33 \text{ Btu/h [See Equation (8-9).]}$$

Solar radiation:[12]

$$\Delta q_c = 60 \text{ ft}^2 \times 223 \text{ Btu/(h}\cdot\text{ft}^2) \times 0.67 \times 0.46$$
$$= 4124 \text{ Btu/h [See Equation (8-3).]}$$

The impact of lighting in terms of *reducing* peak cooling load is estimated below:

$$\Delta q_e = 2 \text{ W/ft}^2 \times 400 \text{ ft}^2 \times 3.413 \text{ Btu/Wh} \qquad (10\text{-}2)$$
$$= 2730 \text{ Btu/h}$$

A summary of the changes in peak heat load is presented below:

Peak cooling load increases:

Conduction	988 Btu/h
Convection:	
Sensible	22 Btu/h
Latent	33 Btu/h
Radiation	4125 Btu/h

Peak cooling load decreases:

Lighting	(2730 Btu/h)
Net increase	2438 Btu/h

The impact of this increase on demand charges is estimated below:

$$C_c = [2438 \text{ Btu/h} \div 12{,}000 \text{ Btu/(ton}\cdot\text{h)}] \times 0.94 \text{ kW/ton}$$
$$\times \$20/(\text{kW}\cdot\text{month}) \times 6 \text{ months/year}$$
$$= \$23/\text{year}$$

The effect of the increased cooling load on cooling equipment costs is calculated as follows. The change in peak cooling load for the entire interior space of the building is

$$\Delta q_c = 2429 \text{ Btu/h} \times (15{,}000 \text{ ft}^2 \div 400 \text{ ft}^2)$$
$$= 91{,}088 \text{ Btu/h}$$

or

$$\Delta q_c = 91{,}088 \text{ Btu/h} \div 12{,}000 \text{ Btu/(ton}\cdot\text{h)}$$
$$= 7.6 \text{ tons}$$

By using data in Table 5-8,

$$C_0 = 7.6 \text{ tons} \times \$450/\text{ton} = \$3420$$

[12]The figure of 223 Btu/(h·ft²) is taken from Table 8-5, that of 0.67 from Table 8-6, and that of 0.46 from Table 8-12.

or for the portion of building being analyzed,

$$C_0 = \$3420 \times (400 \text{ ft}^2 \div 15{,}000 \text{ ft}^2)$$
$$= \$91$$

The cost of the skylight and lighting controls is estimated below:

Skylight, 60 ft² × \$25/ft²	\$1500
Roof, 60 ft² × \$9/ft²	(\$ 540)
Additional cost C_0	\$ 960

$$\text{Daylight controls, } C_0 = 400 \text{ ft}^2 \times 0.75/\text{ft}^2$$
$$= \$300$$

A summary of annual costs and benefits is presented below:

Winter heating season:

Daytime	. . . . .
Nighttime	(\$29/year) (cost)

Summer cooling season:

Daytime	(\$ 42/year)
Nighttime	. . . . .
Demand charges	(\$ 23/year)
Lighting savings	\$131/year (benefit)
Net benefit, B_t	\$ 37/year

Or on an aftertax basis,

$$B_t = \$37/\text{year} \times (1 - 0.45) = \$20/\text{year}$$

The cost of the skylight plus the lighting controls and increases in heating and cooling equipment costs is presented below:

Skylight	\$ 960
Daylight controls	300
Heating system	12
Cooling system	91
Total	\$1363

A simple cost-benefit analysis shows that the skylight as designed is not cost-effective:

$$\text{Simple payback period: } \frac{\$1363}{\$20/\text{year}} = 68.2 \text{ years}$$

$$\text{Simple return on investment: } \frac{\$20/\text{year}}{\$1363} = 1.5 \text{ percent/year}$$

The skylight might well be made more cost-effective if some of the major thermal-related costs could be reduced. For example, insulating the skylight during winter nights and shading it from solar heat gain during the summer would help considerably. However, shading would also reduce to some extent the lighting-related electrical savings in summer because the lights could not be turned off during as many hours.

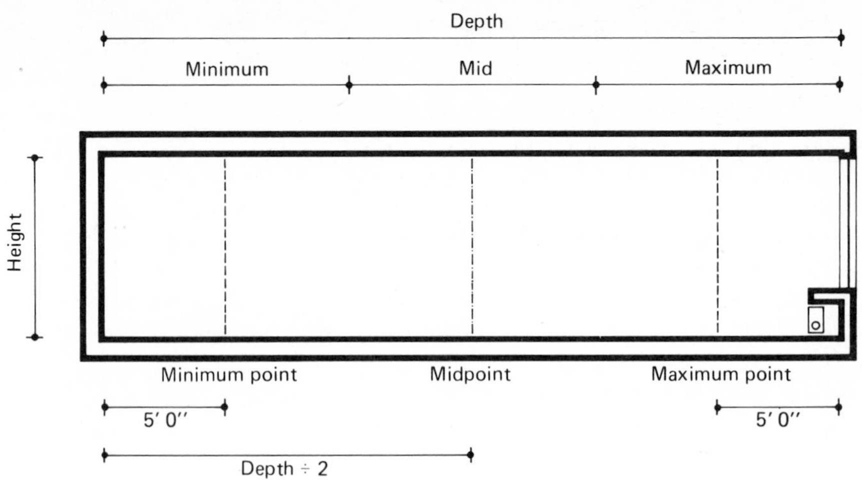

FIGURE 10-15 **Diagram of a typical office building section showing points for estimating interior natural-light levels.**

Minimum-point tributary area = 10 ft x room length
Midpoint tributary area = (room depth − 20 ft) x room length
Maximum-point tributary area = 10 ft x room length

[How to Predict Interior Daylight Illumination, *Libbey-Owens-Ford Company, Toledo, Ohio, 1976, p. 13.*]

NATURAL LIGHTING FROM WINDOWS

The procedure for estimating hours of adequate natural light from windows is based on a method developed by J. W. Griffith at Libbey-Owens-Ford Company and documented in *How to Predict Interior Daylight Illumination* (Toledo, Ohio, 1976). It assumes that the top of a window is at the ceiling level and the sill at desk height, that is, 3 feet above the floor level. The length of the window is assumed to be continuous. The area of the window is not officially a variable. By assuming various ceiling heights ranging between 8 and 14 feet, however, the designer can, in effect, vary window area and use this method to estimate the results.

The analysis procedure requires that the designer examine three representative points in a room: a maximum point 5 feet from the window, a midpoint halfway between the window and the far wall parallel to the window, and a minimum point 5 feet from the far wall (see Figure 10-15). Each prediction point represents a tributary floor area. Figure 10-15 presents the equations for calculating each tributary area.

The designer must determine the interior light level required for carrying out the functions for which the room or building was designed and then estimate the exterior light levels required to provide that illumination.

As mentioned earlier, the light that a window receives comes from three sources: the sun, the sky, and the ground. The estimating method described here requires the designer to make an assumption of the amount of interior light contributed by the ground; 20 percent is suggested for that assumption. A more conservative designer would, of course, assume that no interior light comes from ground reflectances.

The equation that the designer may then use for estimating the exterior illumination required to achieve a particular interior illumination level at each of the prediction points is presented below:

$$E_o = E_i \div (A_w \times \tau_g \times C_s \times K_s \times V_s) \tag{10-4}$$

where E_o = outside illumination, fc

E_i = inside illumination level desired on a task area surface, fc

A_w = area of window, excluding area of window frames and mullions, ft^2

C_s = coefficient of utilization which accounts for room lengths and depths, wall surface reflectances, and their impact on light distribution and intensity, no units

K_s = coefficient of utilization which accounts for ceiling heights and wall reflectances and their impact on light distribution and intensity, no units (See Tables 10-14, 10-15.)

V_s = venetian blind coefficient of utilization, which is used only if blinds are present next to the window; factor to be used for windows exposed to direct solar radiation, no units (See Table 10-15.)

τ_g = transmittance of the glazing, no units (See Table 7-16.)

TABLE 10-14 Coefficients of Utilization without Window Controls

Overcast Sky

Room length		20 ft		30 ft		40 ft	
Wall reflectance	Room depth, ft	70 percent	30 percent	70 percent	30 percent	70 percent	30 percent
Maximum	20	0.0276	0.0251	0.0191	0.0173	0.0143	0.0137
	30	0.0272	0.0248	0.0188	0.0172	0.0137	0.0131
	40	0.0269	0.0246	0.0182	0.0171	0.0133	0.0130
Mid	20	0.0159	0.0117	0.0101	0.0087	0.0081	0.0071
	30	0.0058	0.0050	0.0054	0.0040	0.0034	0.0033
	40	0.0039	0.0027	0.0030	0.0023	0.0022	0.0019
Minimum	20	0.0087	0.0053	0.0063	0.0043	0.0050	0.0037
	30	0.0032	0.0019	0.0029	0.0017	0.0020	0.0014
	40	0.0019	0.0009	0.0016	0.0009	0.0012	0.0008

C_{os}: Coefficients of utilization for room length and width, illuminated by overcast sky

Ceiling height		8 ft		10 ft		12 ft		14 ft	
Wall reflectance	Room depth, ft	70 percent	30 percent	70 percent	30 percent	70 percent	30 percent	70 percent	30 percent
Maximum	20	0.125	0.129	0.121	0.123	0.111	0.111	0.0991	0.0973
	30	0.122	0.131	0.122	0.121	0.111	0.111	0.0945	0.0973
	40	0.145	0.133	0.131	0.126	0.111	0.111	0.0973	0.0982
Mid	20	0.0908	0.0982	0.107	0.115	0.111	0.111	0.105	0.122
	30	0.156	0.102	0.0939	0.113	0.111	0.111	0.121	0.134
	40	0.106	0.0948	0.123	0.107	0.111	0.111	0.135	0.127
Minimum	20	0.0908	0.102	0.0951	0.114	0.111	0.111	0.118	0.134
	30	0.0924	0.119	0.101	0.114	0.111	0.111	0.125	0.126
	40	0.111	0.0926	0.125	0.109	0.111	0.111	0.133	0.130

K_{os}: Coefficients of utilization for ceiling height and room width, illuminated by overcast sky

Clear Sky

Room length		20 ft		30 ft		40 ft	
Wall reflectance	Room depth, ft	70 percent	30 percent	70 percent	30 percent	70 percent	30 percent
Maximum	20	.0206	.0173	.0143	.0123	.0110	.0098
	30	.0203	.0173	.0137	.0120	.0098	.0092
	40	.0200	.0168	.0131	.0119	.0096	.0091
Mid	20	.0153	.0104	.0100	.0079	.0083	.0067
	30	.0082	.0054	.0062	.0043	.0046	.0037
	40	.0052	.0032	.0040	.0028	.0029	.0023
Minimum	20	.0106	.0060	.0079	.0049	.0067	.0043
	30	.0054	.0028	.0047	.0023	.0032	.0021
	40	.0031	.0014	.0027	.0013	.0021	.0012

C_{cs}: Coefficients of utilization for room length and width, illuminated by clear sky (with or without direct sun)

Ceiling height		8 ft		10 ft		12 ft		14 ft	
Wall reflectance	Room depth, ft	70 percent	30 percent	70 percent	30 percent	70 percent	30 percent	70 percent	30 percent
Maximum	20	.145	.155	.129	.132	.111	.111	.101	.0982
	30	.141	.149	.125	.130	.111	.111	.0954	.101
	40	.157	.157	.135	.134	.111	.111	.0964	.0991
Mid	20	.110	.128	.116	.126	.111	.111	.103	.108
	30	.106	.125	.110	.129	.111	.111	.112	.120
	40	.117	.118	.122	.118	.111	.111	.123	.122
Minimum	20	.105	.129	.112	.130	.111	.111	.111	.116
	30	.0994	.144	.107	.126	.111	.111	.107	.124
	40	.119	.116	.130	.118	.111	.111	.120	.118

K_{cs}: Coefficients of utilization for ceiling height and room width, illuminated by clear sky (with or without direct sun)

SOURCE: *How to Predict Interior Daylight Illumination*, Libbey-Owens-Ford Company, Toledo, Ohio, 1976, p. 38.

TABLE 10.15 Coefficients of Utilization with Window Controls

With diffuse shade (uniform sky)

Room length		20 ft		30 ft		40 ft	
Wall reflectance		70%	30%	70%	30%	70%	30%
	Room depth						
Max	20 ft	0.0247	0.0217	0.0174	0.0152	0.0128	0.0120
	30 ft	0.0241	0.0214	0.0166	0.0151	0.0120	0.0116
	40 ft	0.0237	0.0212	0.0161	0.0150	0.0118	0.0113
Mid	20 ft	0.0169	0.0122	0.0110	0.0092	0.0089	0.0077
	30 ft	0.0078	0.0060	0.0067	0.0048	0.0044	0.0041
	40 ft	0.0053	0.0033	0.0039	0.0028	0.0029	0.0024
Min	20 ft	0.0108	0.0066	0.0080	0.0052	0.0063	0.0047
	30 ft	0.0047	0.0026	0.0042	0.0023	0.0029	0.0020
	40 ft	0.0027	0.0013	0.0022	0.0012	0.0018	0.0011

C_{us}: Coefficients of utilization for room length and width, illuminated by uniform skylight through diffuse window shade

Ceiling height		8 ft		10 ft		12 ft		14 ft	
Wall reflectance		70%	30%	70%	30%	70%	30%	70%	30%
	Room depth								
Max	20 ft	0.145	0.154	0.123	0.128	0.111	0.111	0.0991	0.0964
	30 ft	0.141	0.151	0.126	0.128	0.111	0.111	0.0945	0.0964
	40 ft	0.159	0.157	0.137	0.127	0.111	0.111	0.0973	0.0964
Mid	20 ft	0.101	0.116	0.115	0.125	0.111	0.111	0.101	0.110
	30 ft	0.0952	0.113	0.105	0.122	0.111	0.111	0.110	0.122
	40 ft	0.111	0.105	0.124	0.107	0.111	0.111	0.130	0.124
Min	20 ft	0.0974	0.111	0.107	0.121	0.111	0.111	0.112	0.119
	30 ft	0.0956	0.125	0.103	0.117	0.111	0.111	0.115	0.125
	40 ft	0.111	0.105	0.125	0.111	0.111	0.111	0.133	0.124

K_{us}: Coefficients of utilization for ceiling height and room width, illuminated by uniform skylight through diffuse window shade

With venetian blinds

Room length		20 ft		30 ft		40 ft	
Wall reflectance		70%	30%	70%	30%	70%	30%
	Room depth						
Max	20 ft	0.0556	0.0556	0.0392	0.0397	0.0298	0.0317
	30 ft	0.0522	0.0533	0.0367	0.0389	0.0278	0.0311
	40 ft	0.0506	0.0528	0.0359	0.0381	0.0270	0.0306
Mid	20 ft	0.0556	0.0556	0.0418	0.0411	0.0320	0.0364
	30 ft	0.0372	0.0339	0.0278	0.0286	0.0220	0.0256
	40 ft	0.0217	0.0211	0.0192	0.0186	0.0139	0.0164
Min	20 ft	0.0556	0.0556	0.0422	0.0456	0.0320	0.0409
	30 ft	0.0294	0.0233	0.0222	0.0203	0.0189	0.0194
	40 ft	0.0139	0.0110	0.0133	0.0108	0.0120	0.0100

C_{sv}: Coefficients of utilization for room length and width, illuminated by sun and sky through horizontal louvers

Ceiling height		8 ft		10 ft		12 ft		14 ft	
Wall reflectance		70%	30%	70%	30%	70%	30%	70%	30%
	Room depth								
Max		0.154	0.170	0.129	0.131	0.107	0.112	0.091	0.091
Mid	20 ft	0.100	0.106	0.101	0.106	0.099	0.102	0.091	0.091
	30 ft	0.074	0.080	0.086	0.090	0.091	0.093	0.091	0.091
	40 ft	0.070	0.074	0.079	0.084	0.088	0.091	0.091	0.091
Min	20 ft	0.080	0.080	0.091	0.091	0.093	0.093	0.091	0.091
	30 ft	0.068	0.068	0.079	0.079	0.087	0.087	0.091	0.091
	40 ft	0.064	0.064	0.076	0.076	0.084	0.084	0.091	0.091

K_{sv}: Coefficients of utilization for ceiling height and room width, illuminated by sun and sky through horizontal louvers

Venetian blind setting		30°		45°		60°	
Wall reflectance		70%	30%	70%	30%	70%	30%
15° sun Altitude	Max	0.0687	0.0554	0.0426	0.0346	0.0218	0.0162
	Mid	0.0488	0.0341	0.0371	0.0218	0.0195	0.0110
	Min	0.0376	0.0228	0.0276	0.0156	0.0142	0.0078
30° sun Altitude	Max	0.0630	0.050	0.0394	0.0312	0.0208	0.0156
	Mid	0.0462	0.0324	0.0337	0.0216	0.0176	0.0110
	Min	0.0342	0.0204	0.0250	0.0143	0.0130	0.0071
45° sun Altitude	Max	0.0553	0.0434	0.0345	0.0274	0.0198	0.0141
	Mid	0.0416	0.0301	0.0304	0.0211	0.0158	0.0105
	Min	0.0308	0.0182	0.0225	0.0127	0.0117	0.0064
60° sun Altitude	Max	0.0464	0.0362	0.0313	0.0236	0.0190	0.0135
	Mid	0.0370	0.0264	0.0270	0.0185	0.0140	0.0092
	Min	0.0274	0.0159	0.0199	0.0111	0.0104	0.0056

V_s: Coefficients of utilization for venetian blind angle and sun altitude, illuminated by sun and sky

SOURCE: *How to Predict Interior Daylight Illumination*, Libbey-Owens-Ford Company, Toledo, Ohio, 1976, p. 38.

Once the required exterior illumination has been estimated, the designer must determine the minimum solar altitude at which the exterior light intensity under overcast-sky and clear-sunny sky conditions will reach the level required inside. This is done by using the graphs in Figures 10-16 and 10-17.

When considering a clear-sunny-sky condition (Figure 10-17), the designer must make an adjustment to the exterior illumination figure. The curve in Figure 10-17 represents surfaces perpendicular to the sun's rays. To determine the exterior illumination required on a perpendicular surface so that the same intensity, when subjected to a vertical surface *not* perpendicular to the sun, will yield the desired exterior illumination, E_o must be adjusted by the angle of incidence θ of the sun on the surface. That angle varies throughout the day, so an average angle of incidence must be used (see Table 10-16 for 40° north latitude average-incidence angles or Table 10-7 for other latitudes).

The following equation allows for the angle-of-incidence adjustment in exterior illumination requirements:

$$E_{op} = E_o \div \cos\theta \tag{10-5}$$

where E_{op} = outside solar illumination on a surface perpendicular to the sun's rays, fc

E_o = actual outside illumination on a window surface, fc

θ = angle of incidence of solar radiation on window

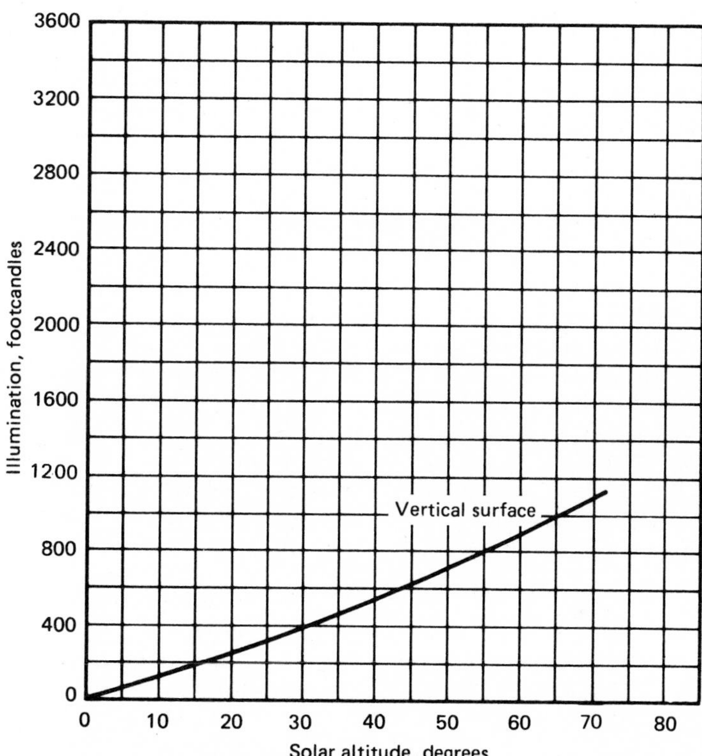

FIGURE 10-16 Overcast-sky illumination on a vertical surface as a function of solar altitude. [How to Predict Interior Daylight Illumination, *Libbey-Owens-Ford Company, Toledo, Ohio, 1976, p. 36.*]

A

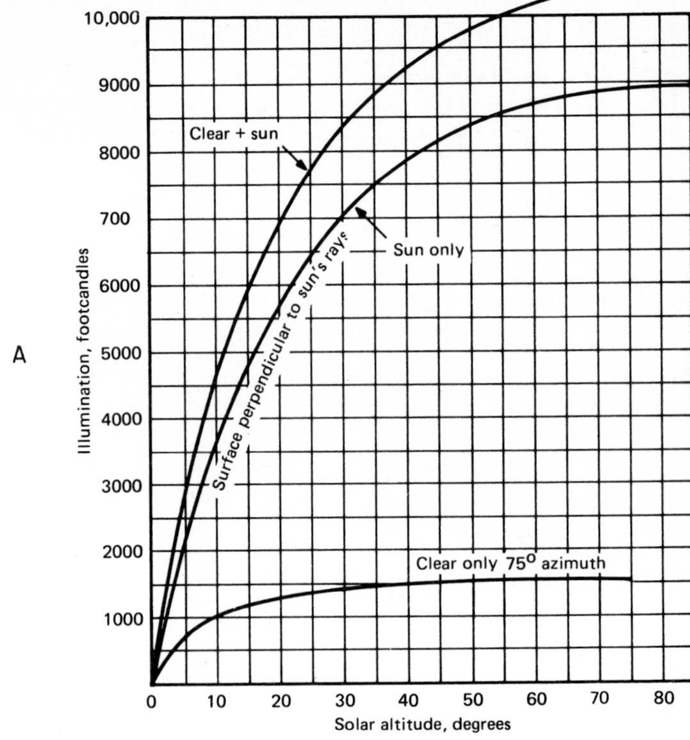

FIGURE 10-17 Clear-sky and solar illumination on a vertical surface for various seasons. *A*, summer; *B*, winter; *C*, autumn or spring. [How to Predict Interior Daylight Illumination, *Libbey-Owens-Ford Company, Toledo, Ohio, 1976, p. 36.*]

EXAMPLE

A designer proposes to increase the glass area on the south side of his office building, in which daylighting controls are already in place, in order to increase natural lighting and save electricity. In addition, he proposes to add an overhang on the south side to keep out summer sun and horizontal venetian blinds on the inside to reduce glare from direct sunlight. The east and west walls are opaque because neighboring buildings are on the lot line of the site for the new building. The building is 90 feet wide, 160 feet long, and 20 stories high. The windowsill is 3 feet above the floor, and the top of the window will increase in height from 8 to 10 feet (see Figure 10-19).

Location	New York City
Latitude	40°N
U glass	0.407, winter; 0.405, summer
U wall	0.049
Electrical cost	\$0.12/kW
Oil cost	\$1.00/gal
Demand charge	\$20/(kW·month)

B

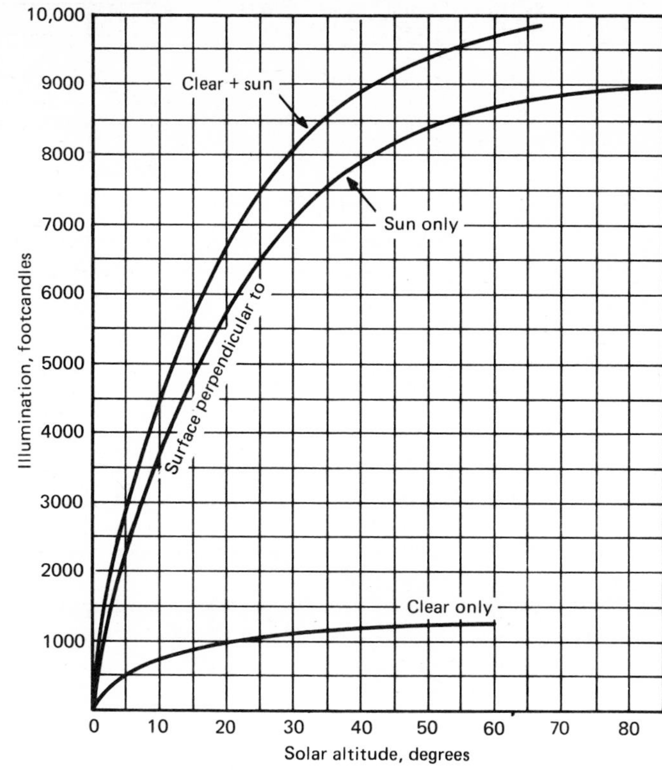
Illumination, footcandles
Solar altitude, degrees
Clear + sun
Sun only
Surface perpendicular to
Clear only

C

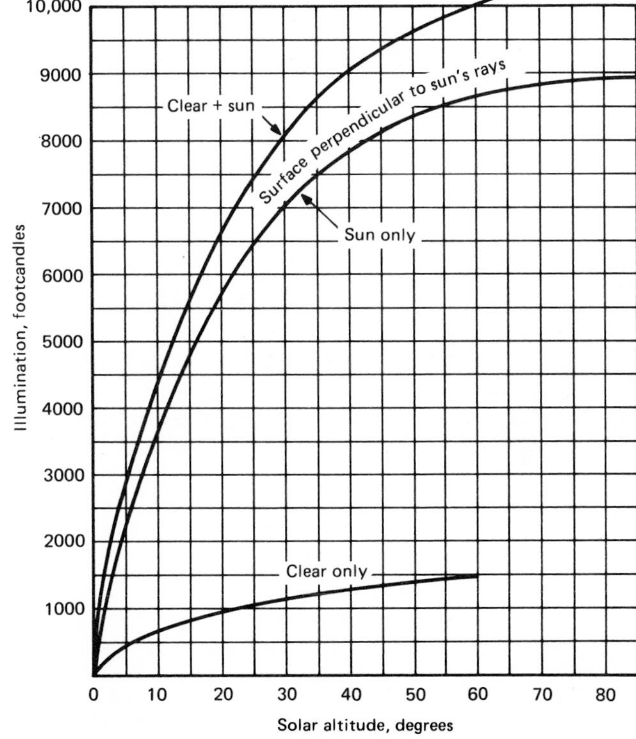
Illumination, footcandles
Solar altitude, degrees
Clear + sun
Surface perpendicular to sun's rays
Sun only
Clear only

TABLE 10·16 Average Solar Angles of Incidence for a South-Facing Vertical Wall, 9 A.M.–5 P.M., 40° North Latitude*

Month	Solar time 9	10	11	12	1	2	3	4	5	Monthly average	Seasonal average†	Season	Seasonal midpoint‡
December	44	35	29	27	29	35	44	53	. .	37.0			
January	46	38	32	30	32	38	46	56	. .	39.8	42.5	Winter	45.3
February	54	46	41	39	41	46	54	63	72	50.7			
March	63	56	52	50	52	56	63	71	80	60.3			
April	73	67	63	62	63	67	73	81	89	70.9	69.2	Spring	73.6
May	80	75	71	70	71	75	80	88	. .	76.3			
June	84	78	75	73	75	78	84	. .	. .	78.1			
July	80	75	71	70	71	75	80	88	. .	76.3	75.1	Summer	73.6
August	73	67	63	62	63	67	73	81	89	70.9			
September	63	56	52	50	52	56	63	71	80	60.3			
October	54	46	41	39	41	46	54	63	72	50.7	50.3	Autumn	45.3
November	46	30	32	30	32	38	46	56	. .	39.8			

*Data selected from Table 10-7.

†Seasonal averages were calculated by using the following monthly groupings: winter = December, January, and February; spring = March, April, and May; summer = June, July, and August; and autumn = September, October, and November.

‡The seasonal midpoint is defined as the point halfway between the beginning of the season and the end of the season. The winter season midpoint, for example, would be halfway between December 21 and March 21 or, on the table above, halfway between the months of January and February.

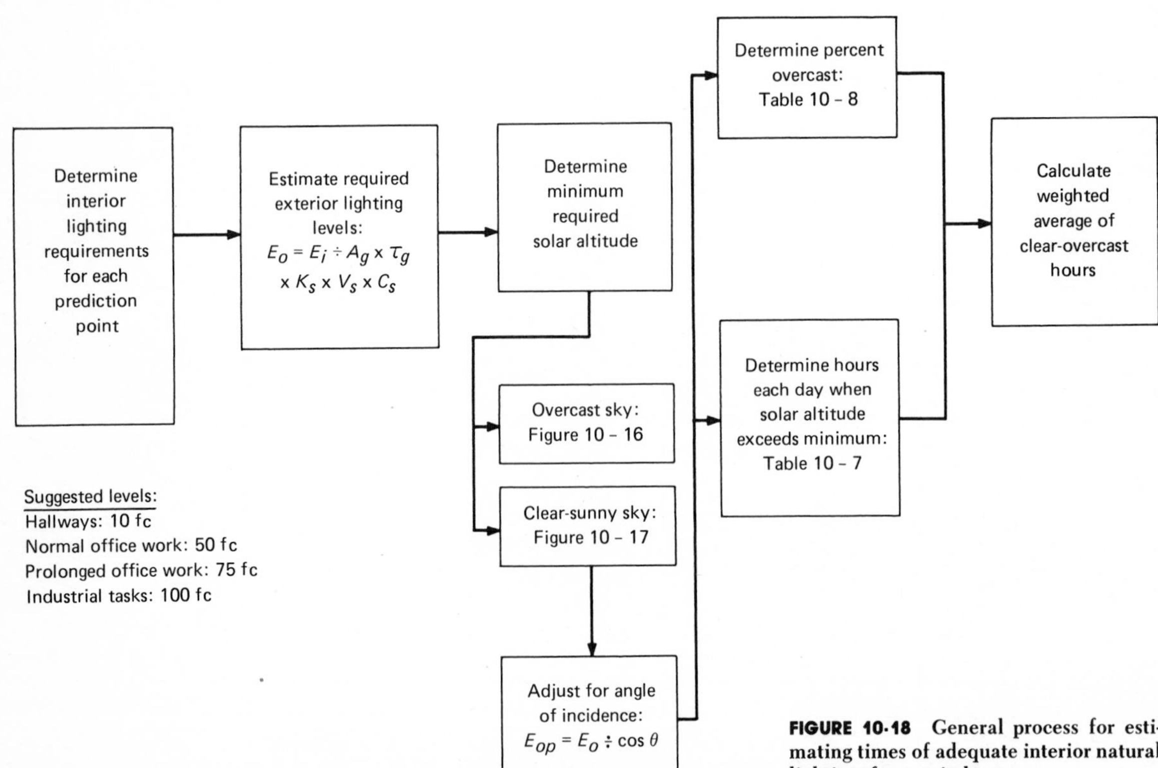

FIGURE 10·18 General process for estimating times of adequate interior natural lighting from windows.

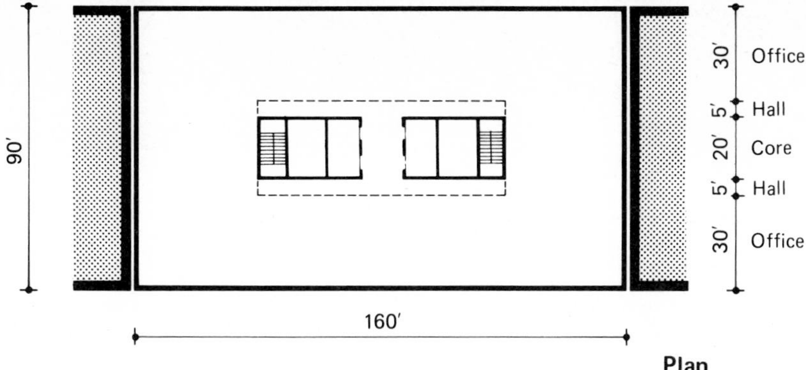

FIGURE 10·19 Plan and section of an example office building.

Income tax bracket	45 percent
Power required by lighting system	2 W/ft
Cooling system	Central
Wall construction, C_0	\$5/ft^2
Glazing construction cost, C_0	\$6/ft^2
Daylight controls	In place
Ground reflectance (for concrete)	0.55
Wall reflectance	70 percent
Daylight transmittance (for 3/16-in Thermopane insulating glass)	0.79
Solar transmittance	0.60
Frames	10 percent of glazing area
Added crack length	50 ft

Estimates for the 8-Foot-High Window

$$A_g = 40 \text{ ft} \times (8 \text{ ft} - 3 \text{ ft}) \times 0.90 = 180 \text{ ft}^2$$

$$= \text{room width} \times (\text{ceiling height} - \text{desk height}) \times \text{framing factor}$$

Assuming that 20 percent of the light on the window comes from the ground,

$$\text{Sky-source light} = 50 \text{ fc} \times (1 - 0.20)$$
$$= 40 \text{ fc}$$

Minimum-point illumination:[13]

$$E_o = 40 \text{ fc} \div (180 \text{ ft}^2 \times 0.79 \times 0.0189 \times 0.068 \times 0.0325)$$
$$= 6735 \text{ fc}$$

From Figure 10-16, one may see that overcast illumination never reaches the required 6735 footcandles no matter what the altitude of the sun.

Figure 10-17 is a graph of solar and clear-sky illumination levels on surfaces perpendicular to the sun. Therefore, to determine the illumination required on such a surface to achieve 50 footcandles at the minimum point of the room, one must use Equation (10-5). Table 10-16 has average angles of incidence for solar radiation on south-facing walls between the hours of 9 A.M. and 5 P.M. for 40° north latitude locations for use with Equation (10-5).[14]

		Minimum altitude, clear-sunny sky
Winter:	$E_{op} = 6735 \text{ fc} \div \cos 42.5° = 9135 \text{ fc}$	37°
Spring:	$E_{op} = 6735 \text{ fc} \div \cos 69.2° = 18{,}966 \text{ fc}$	. . .
Summer:	$E_{op} = 6735 \text{ fc} \div \cos 75.1° = 26{,}193 \text{ fc}$	. . .
Autumn:	$E_{op} = 6735 \text{ fc} \div \cos 50.3° = 10{,}544 \text{ fc}$	. . .

From Table 10-7, one can see the hours of the day during which the altitude of the sun reaches at least 37° for 40° north latitude locations in the winter months. One may also determine the hours of each month and season when a solar altitude at which exterior clear-sunny-sky illumination is sufficient to achieve 40 footcandles of natural light on an interior task surface at the minimum point of the room is reached:

Month	Minimum altitude	Time of day	Elapsed time	Clear-sunny fraction*	Clear-sunny hours/day
December	37	. . . .			
January	37	. . . .			
February	37	11 A.M.–1 P.M.	2	0.42	0.8

*The fraction of time in each month when the sky will be clear and sunny may be inferred from sky cover data presented in Table 10-8.

Midpoint illumination:

$$E_o = 40 \text{ fc} \div 180 \text{ ft}^2 \times 0.79 \times 0.0220 \times 0.074 \times 0.0434$$
$$= 3981 \text{ fc}$$

[13]The minimum point is the measurement point farthest from the window. The figures of 0.0189 and 0.068 are taken from Table 10-15, "With Venetian Blinds." The figure of 0.0325 is an average of all V_s for a 30° blind setting and a 70 percent wall reflectance.

[14]The figure of 37° is the minimum altitude from Figure 10-17 derived from the required illumination E_{op}.

From Figure 10-16, it is apparent that overcast illumination levels do not reach the required 3981 footcandles.

By using data from Table 10-16, the following calculation may be made for clear-sunny conditions:

	Minimum altitude, clear-sunny sky
Winter: E_{op} = 3981 fc ÷ cos 42.5° = 5400 fc	14°
Spring: E_{op} = 3981 fc ÷ cos 69.2° = 11,211 fc	. . .
Summer: E_{op} = 3981 fc ÷ cos 75.1° = 15,482 fc	. . .
Autumn: E_{op} = 3981 fc ÷ cos 50.3° = 6232 fc	17°

From Table 10-7, the following calculations may be made:

Month	Minimum altitude	Time of day	Elapsed time, h (A)	Clear-sunny fraction (B)	Clear-sunny hours/day (A · B)
December	14°	9 A.M.–3 P.M.	6.0	0.40	2.4
January	14°	9 A.M.–3:30 P.M.	6.5	0.38	2.5
February	14°	9 A.M.–4 P.M.	7.0	0.42	2.9
September	17°	9 A.M.–4:30 P.M.	7.5	0.50	3.8
October	17°	9 A.M.–3:45 P.M.	6.75	0.50	3.4
November	17°	9 A.M.–3 P.M.	6.0	0.42	2.5
Average					2.9

Maximum point illumination:[15] The light levels for the maximum point, 5 feet from the window, are calculated as follows:

$$E_o = 40 \text{ fc} \div 180 \text{ ft}^2 \times 0.79 \times 0.0278 \times 0.154 \times 0.0584$$
$$= 1125 \text{ fc}$$

Overcast-sky illumination will not reach 1125 fc (Figure 10-16). Calculations for the sunny-sky condition are presented below:

		Minimum altitude, clear-sunny sky
Winter:	E_{op} = 1125 fc ÷ cos 42.5° = 1526 fc	2°
Spring:	E_{op} = 1125 fc ÷ cos 69.2° = 3168 fc	6°
Summer:	E_{op} = 1125 fc ÷ cos 75.1° = 4375 fc	9°
Autumn:	E_{op} = 1125 fc ÷ cos 50.3° = 1761 fc	3°

[15]The maximum point is the measurement point closest to the windows.

Month	Minimum altitude	Time of day	Elapsed time, h (A)	Clear-sunny fraction (B)	Clear-sunny hours/day (A · B)
December	2°	9 A.M.–4 P.M.	7	0.40	2.8
January	2°	9 A.M.–4 P.M.	7	0.38	2.7
February	2°	9 A.M.–5 P.M.	8	0.42	3.4
March	6°	9 A.M.–5 P.M.	8	0.41	3.3
April	6°	9 A.M.–6 P.M.	9	0.48	4.3
May	6°	9 A.M.–6 P.M.	9	0.42	3.8
June	9°	9 A.M.–6 P.M.	9	0.43	3.9
July	9°	9 A.M.–6 P.M.	9	0.44	4.0
August	9°	9 A.M.–6 P.M.	9	0.48	4.3
September	3°	9 A.M.–5 P.M.	8	0.50	4.0
October	3°	9 A.M.–5 P.M.	8	0.50	4.0
November	3°	9 A.M.–4 P.M.	7	0.42	2.9
Average					3.6

Estimates for the 10-Foot-High Window

By increasing the height of the glass area by 2 feet, from an 8-foot ceiling height to a 10-foot ceiling height, the glass area is increased as follows:

$$A_g = 40 \text{ ft} \times (10 \text{ ft} - 3 \text{ ft}) \times 0.90 = 252 \text{ ft}^2$$

$$= \text{length} \times (\text{ceiling height} - \text{desk height}) \times \text{framing factor}$$

The minimum-point exterior illumination required is estimated below:

$$E_o = 40 \text{ fc} \div (252 \text{ ft}^2 \times 0.79 \times 0.0189 \times 0.079 \times 0.0325)$$

$$= 4141 \text{ fc}$$

Overcast-sky conditions will not reach this level.

Clear-sunny sky illumination requirements are established as follows:

		Minimum altitude, clear-sunny sky
Winter:	$E_{op} = 4141 \text{ fc} \div \cos 42.5° = 5617$	14°
Spring:	$E_{op} = 4141 \text{ fc} \div \cos 69.2° = 11{,}661$	. .
Summer:	$E_{op} = 4141 \text{ fc} \div \cos 75.1° = 16{,}105$	. .
Autumn:	$E_{op} = 4141 \text{ fc} \div \cos 50.3° = 6483$	18°

Month	Minimum altitudes	Time of day	Elapsed time, h	Clear-sunny fraction	Clear-sunny hours/day
December	14°	9 A.M.–3 P.M.	6	0.40	2.4
January	14°	9 A.M.–3:30 P.M.	6.5	0.38	2.5
February	14°	9 A.M.–4 P.M.	7	0.42	3.0
September	18°	9 A.M.–4:30 P.M.	7.5	0.50	3.8
October	18°	9 A.M.–3:30 P.M.	6.5	0.50	3.3
November	18°	9 A.M.–3 P.M.	6	0.42	2.5
Average					2.9

The midpoint exterior illumination requirement is calculated as follows:

$$E_o = 40 \text{ fc} \div 252 \text{ ft}^2 \times 0.79 \times 0.0220 \times 0.086 \times 0.0434$$
$$= 2447 \text{ fc}$$

Overcast-sky conditions on vertical surfaces will not reach this level (Figure 10-16).

Clear-sunny-sky illumination requirements are calculated below:

		Minimum altitude, clear-sunny sky
Winter:	E_{op} = 2447 fc ÷ cos 42.5 = 3319 fc	6°
Spring:	E_{op} = 2447 fc ÷ cos 69.2 = 6891 fc	23°
Summer:	E_{op} = 2447 fc ÷ cos 75.1 = 9516 fc	46°
Autumn:	E_{op} = 2447 fc ÷ cos 50.3 = 3831 fc	7°

Month	Minimum altitude	Time of day	Elapsed time, h	Clear-sunny	
				Fraction	Hours/day
December	6°	9 A.M.–4 P.M.	7	0.40	2.8
January	6°	9 A.M.–4 P.M.	7	0.38	2.7
February	6°	9 A.M.–4:30 P.M.	7.5	0.42	3.2
March	23°	9 A.M.–4 P.M.	7	0.41	2.9
April	23°	9 A.M.–4:30 P.M.	7.5	0.48	3.6
May	23°	9 A.M.–5 P.M.	8	0.42	3.4
June	46°	9 A.M.–3 P.M.	6	0.43	2.6
July	46°	9 A.M.–3 P.M.	6	0.44	2.6
August	46°	9:30 A.M.–2:30 P.M.	5	0.48	2.4
September	7°	9 A.M.–5 P.M.	8	0.50	4.0
October	7°	9 A.M.–5 P.M.	8	0.50	4.0
November	7°	9 A.M.–4 P.M.	7	0.42	2.9
Average					3.1

The maximum-point exterior illumination requirement is estimated as follows:

$$E_o = 40 \text{ fc} \div 252 \text{ ft}^2 \times 0.79 \times 0.0278 \times 0.129 \times 0.0584$$
$$= 959 \text{ fc}$$

Overcast-sky conditions on vertical surfaces will reach this level above about 63° solar altitude (see Figure 10-16).

Clear-sunny-sky illumination requirements are calculated below:

		Minimum altitude, clear-sunny sky
Winter:	E_{op} = 959 fc ÷ cos 42.5 = 1301 fc	2°
Spring:	E_{op} = 959 fc ÷ cos 69.2 = 2701 fc	4°
Summer:	E_{op} = 959 fc ÷ cos 75.1 = 3730 fc	7°
Autumn:	E_{op} = 959 fc ÷ cos 50.3 = 1501 fc	2°

The combined (weighted-average) effect of overcast-sky and clear-sunny-sky conditions on the ability to turn off artificial lights and rely on natural light to provide adequate illumination levels on work surfaces in the maximum-point measurement zone for a 10-foot-high window is predicted below:

Month	Overcast times	Overcast hours/day	Overcast fraction	Clear-sunny hours/day	Clear-sunny fraction	Weighted-average hours/day (overcast + clear-sunny)
December				7	0.40	2.8
January				7	0.38	2.7
February				8	0.42	3.4
March				8	0.41	3.3
April				9	0.48	4.3
May	10:30 A.M.–1:30 P.M.	3.0	0.58	9	0.42	5.5
June	9:45 A.M.–2:15 P.M.	4.5	0.57	9	0.43	6.4
July	10:30 A.M.–1:30 P.M.	3.0	0.56	9	0.44	5.6
August				9	0.48	4.3
September				8	0.50	4.0
October				8	0.50	4.0
November				7	0.42	2.9
Average						4.1

The additional hours annually during which artificial lights may be turned off, because of the additional window height, are estimated as follows:

8-ft minimum point: 1 month × 21.67 days/month × 0.8 h/day	= 17 h/year
10-ft minimum point: 6 months × 21.67 days/month × 2.9 h/day	= 377 h/year
Difference	360 h/year
8-ft midpoint: 6 months × 21.67 days/month × 2.9 h/day	= 377 h/year
10-ft midpoint: 12 months × 21.67 days/month × 3.1 h/day	= 806 h/year
Difference	429 h/year
8-ft maximum point: 12 months × 21.67 days/month × 3.6 h/day	= 936 h/year
10-ft maximum point: 12 months × 21.67 days/month × 4.1 h/day	= 1066 h/year
Difference	130 h/year

The reduction in electrical energy for lighting due to the extra 2 feet of window height is calculated below. This calculation assumes that the minimum point, midpoint, and maximum point each represent a floor zone 10 feet wide, measured perpendicularly to the exterior wall, and 400 square feet in area.

$$\text{Minimum point } B_L = \$0.15\ \text{kWh} \times 360\ \text{h/year} \times 2\ \text{W/ft}^2 \times 400\ \text{ft}^2 \div 1000\ \text{Wh/kWh} = \$43/\text{year}$$

$$\text{Midpoint } B_L = \$0.15/\text{kWh} \times 429\ \text{h/year} \times 2\ \text{W/ft}^2 \times 400\ \text{ft}^2 \div 1000\ \text{Wh/kWh} = \$51/\text{year}$$

$$\text{Maximum point } B_L = \$0.15/\text{kWh} \times 130\ \text{h/year} \times 2\ \text{W/ft}^2 \times 400\ \text{ft}^2 \div 1000\ \text{Wh/kWh} = \$16/\text{year}$$

$$\text{Total } B_L = \$110/\text{year}$$

This analysis will assume that during the winter daytime, as found in earlier examples, internal and solar heat gains in the south-facing exterior zones of office buildings will be significantly greater than heat losses. The impact of additional glass during this period will, therefore, be assumed to have no impact on fuel consumption.

During the winter unoccupied periods, the following is an estimate of the additional heat loss:

$$\Delta Q_h = [0.407 - 0.049 \text{ Btu/(h}\cdot{}^\circ\text{F}\cdot\text{ft}^2)] \times 80 \text{ ft}^2 \times 43{,}230\ ({}^\circ\text{F}\cdot\text{h})/\text{year}$$

$$= 1{,}238{,}107 \text{ Btu/year [See Equation (7-7).]}$$

Additional infiltration losses are estimated as follows:[16]

$$\Delta Q_h = 0.018 \text{ Btu/(}{}^\circ\text{F}\cdot\text{ft}^3) \times [3 \text{ ft}^3/(\text{h}\cdot\text{ft}) \times 50 \text{ ft}] \times 47{,}303\ ({}^\circ\text{F}\cdot\text{h})/\text{year}$$

$$= 127{,}718 \text{ Btu/year [See Equation (7-12).]}$$

Total additional winter nighttime heat loss:

$$\Delta Q_h = 1{,}238{,}107 \text{ Btu/year} + 127{,}718 \text{ Btu/year}$$

$$= 1{,}365{,}825 \text{ Btu/year}$$

$$C_h = \frac{\$1/\text{gal} \times 1{,}365{,}825 \text{ Btu/year}}{0.55 \times 140{,}000 \text{ Btu/gal}}$$

$$= \$18/\text{year [See Equation (6-1).]}$$

Additional *peak* heating load contribution is estimated below:

Conduction:

$$\Delta q_h = [0.407 - 0.049 \text{ Btu/(h}\cdot{}^\circ\text{F}\cdot\text{ft}^2)] \times 80 \text{ ft}^2 \times (55^\circ\text{F} - 15^\circ\text{F})$$

$$= 1146 \text{ Btu/h [See Equation (7-6).]}$$

Convection:

$$\Delta q_h = 0.018 \text{ Btu/(}{}^\circ\text{F}\cdot\text{ft}^2) \times (3 \text{ ft}^3/\text{h} \times 50 \text{ ft}) \times (55^\circ\text{F} - 15^\circ\text{F})$$

$$= 108 \text{ Btu/h [See Equation (7-10).]}$$

Total peak load contribution:

$$\Delta q_h = 1146 \text{ Btu/h} + 108 \text{ Btu/h} = 1254 \text{ Btu/h}$$

The 40-foot-wide strip of wall being evaluated represents one-eightieth of the entire south facade. The overall peak load contribution is, therefore,

$$\Delta q_h = 1254 \text{ Btu/h} \times 80 = 100{,}320 \text{ Btu/h}$$

Added heating system equipment costs are estimated below:

$$C_0 = 100{,}320 \text{ Btu/h} \times (\$6.75 \div 1000 \text{ Btu/h})$$

$$= \$677$$

or for the portion of building being analyzed,

$$C_0 = \$677 \div 80 = \$8$$

[16]The figure of 47,303 (°F·h)/year is taken from Table 6-6.

Thermal Analysis: Summer

Additional heat gain during the summer is calculated as follows:[17]

$$\Delta Q_c = [0.405 - 0.049 \text{ Btu}/(°\text{F}\cdot\text{ft}^2\cdot\text{h})] \times 80 \text{ ft}^2 \times 9195\ (°\text{F}\cdot\text{h})/\text{year}$$
$$= 261{,}874 \text{ Btu/year [See Equation (8-2).]}$$

Sensible convection:[18]

$$\Delta Q_{c,s} = 0.018 \text{ Btu}/(°\text{F}\cdot\text{ft}^3) \times [3 \text{ ft}^3/(\text{h}\cdot\text{ft}) \times 50 \text{ ft})] \times -2283\ (°\text{F}\cdot\text{h})/\text{year}$$
$$= -6164 \text{ Btu/year [See Equation (8-7).]}$$

Latent convection:

$$\Delta Q_{c,l} = 80.7 \text{ Btu/ft}^3 \times [3 \text{ ft}^3/(\text{h}\cdot\text{ft}) \times 50 \text{ ft}] \times 1.807\ (\text{lb}\cdot\text{h})/(\text{lb}\cdot\text{year})$$
$$= 21{,}874 \text{ Btu/year [See Equation (8-10).]}$$

Solar radiation:[19]

$$\Delta Q_c = 79 \text{ Btu}/(\text{h}\cdot\text{ft}^2) \times 80 \text{ ft}^2 \times 0.60 \times 9 \text{ h/day} \times 5 \text{ days/week}$$
$$\times\ 26 \text{ weeks/year}$$
$$= 4{,}436{,}640 \text{ Btu/year [See Equation (8-4).]}$$

By using data calculated earlier in this example, the average time during the months of May through October when lights may be turned off is calculated below:

	Minimum point			Midpoint			Maximum point		
Month	**8 ft**	**10 ft**	**Difference**	**8 ft**	**10 ft**	**Difference**	**8 ft**	**10 ft**	**Difference**
May	...	...	...	...	3.4	3.4	3.8	5.5	1.7
June	...	...	...	...	2.6	2.6	3.9	6.4	2.5
July	...	...	...	...	2.6	2.6	4.0	5.6	1.6
August	...	...	...	...	2.4	2.4	4.3	4.3	...
September	...	3.8	3.8	3.8	4.0	0.2	4.0	4.0	...
October	...	2.5	2.5	3.4	4.0	0.6	4.0	4.0	...
6-month average			1.1			2.0			1.0

For the 30-foot-deep zone of analysis, the average number of hours of additional lights off is

$$\Delta T_h = (1.1 \text{ h/day} + 2.0 \text{ h/day} + 1.0 \text{ h/day})/3 = 1.4 \text{ h/day}$$

$$\Delta Q_L = 1200 \text{ ft}^2 \times 2 \text{ W/ft}^2 \times 3.413 \text{ Btu/Wh}$$
$$\times\ 1.4 \text{ h/day} \times 5 \text{ days/week} \times 26 \text{ weeks/year} \qquad (10\text{-}2)$$
$$= 1{,}490{,}798 \text{ Btu/year}$$

[17]The figure of 9195 (°F·h)/year is taken from Table 6-10.

[18]The figure of −2283 (°F·h)/year is taken from Table 8-14.

[19]The figure of 79 Btu/(h·ft²) represents hourly solar radiation on vertical surfaces in the New York City area for the months of May through October. It is derived from data in Tables 7-13 and 7-14.

A summary of increases and decreases in summer heat gains due to the additional glass area is calculated below:

Increases in heat gain:

Conduction	261,874 Btu/year
Infiltration:	
Sensible	....
Latent	21,874 Btu/year
Radiation	4,436,640 Btu/year

Decreases in heat gain:

Lighting	(1,490,798 Btu/year)
Infiltration, sensible	(6,164 Btu/year)
Net increase	3,223,426 Btu/year

$$C_c = \$0.15/\text{kWh} \times 0.94\ \text{kW/ton} \times [3{,}223{,}426\ \text{Btu/year} \div 12{,}000\ \text{Btu/(ton}\cdot\text{h)}]$$
$$= \$38/\text{year [See Equation (6-5).]}$$

The impact of the additional window area of *peak* cooling load is calculated below:

Conduction:[20]

$$q_c\ (\text{window}) = 0.405\ \text{Btu/(°F}\cdot\text{ft}^2\cdot\text{h)} \times 80\ \text{ft}^2 \times 9°\text{F} = 292\ \text{Btu/h}$$
$$q_c\ (\text{wall}) = 0.049\ \text{Btu/(°F}\cdot\text{ft}^2\cdot\text{h)} \times 80\ \text{ft}^2 \times 22°\text{F} = 86\ \text{Btu/h}$$
$$\Delta q_c = 206\ \text{Btu/h}$$

Sensible convection:

$$\Delta q_{c,s} = 0.018\ \text{Btu/(°F}\cdot\text{ft}^3) \times [3\ \text{ft}^3/(\text{h}\cdot\text{ft}) \times 50\ \text{ft}] \times (80°\text{F} - 89°\text{F})$$
$$= 24\ \text{Btu/h [See Equation (8-6).]}$$

Latent convection:

$$\Delta q_{c,l} = 80.7\ \text{Btu/ft}^3 \times [3\ \text{ft/(h}\cdot\text{ft)} \times 50\ \text{ft}] \times (0.0142\ \text{lb/lb} - 0.0112\ \text{lb/lb})$$
$$= 36\ \text{Btu/h [See Equation (8-9).]}$$

Solar radiation:[21]

$$\Delta q_c = 80\ \text{ft}^2 \times 149\ \text{Btu/(h}\cdot\text{ft}^2) \times 0.83 \times 0.51$$
$$= 5046\ \text{Btu/h [See Equation (8-3).]}$$

The impact of turning off lights on reducing peak cooling load, if August is assumed to be the month of peak cooling load, is estimated below. During August, lights are off for a greater time only in the midpoint zone.

$$\Delta q_L = 2\ \text{W/ft}^2 \times 400\ \text{ft}^2 \times 3.413\ \text{Btu/Wh} \qquad (10\text{-}2)$$
$$= 2730\ \text{Btu/h}$$

[20]See Equation (8-1). The figure of 22°F is taken from the first example of the section "Conduction: Changes in Summer Heat Gain," Chapter 8.

[21]The figure of 149 Btu/(h·ft²) is taken from Table 8-5, that of 0.83 from Table 8-7, and that of 0.51 from Table 8-10.

The changes in peak cooling load are summarized below:

Increases:

Conduction	206 Btu/h
Convection:	
Sensible	24 Btu/h
Latent	36 Btu/h
Radiation	5046 Btu/h

Decreases:

Lighting	(2730 Btu/h)
Net increase	2582 Btu/h

The effect of the increased peak cooling load on cooling equipment costs is estimated next:

For the entire south facade:

$$\Delta q_c = (2582 \text{ Btu/h} \times 80) \div 12{,}000 \text{ Btu/(ton}\cdot\text{h)}$$
$$= 17.2 \text{ tons}$$

Using data from Table 5-8,

$$C_0 = 17.2 \text{ tons} \times \$450/\text{ton} = \$7740$$

or for the portion of building being analyzed,

$$C_0 = \$7740 \div 80 = \$97$$

The impact on demand charges is

$$C_c = [2582 \text{ Btu/h} \div 12{,}000 \text{ Btu/(ton}\cdot\text{h)}] \times 0.94 \text{ kW/ton}$$
$$\times \$20/(\text{kW}\cdot\text{month}) \times 6 \text{ months/year}$$
$$= \$24/\text{year}$$

The cost of the additional glass is:

Window cost	$6/ft^2
Wall cost	5/ft^2
Difference	$1/ft^2

$$C_0 = 80 \text{ ft}^2 \times \$1/\text{ft}^2 = \$80$$

Daylight controls are assumed to be already in place in the building.

Cost-Benefit Comparison

A summary of annual costs and benefits is presented below:

Winter heating season:

Daytime	......
Nighttime	($18/year) (cost)

Summer cooling season:

Daytime	(\$38/year)
Nighttime	. . . . . .
Demand charges	(\$24/year)
Lighting savings	\$110/year
Net benefit, B_t	\$ 30/year

On an aftertax basis,

$$B_t = \$30/\text{year} \times (1 - 0.45) = \$17/\text{year}$$

The cost of the window plus the increases in heating and cooling system costs is summarized below:

Glass	\$ 80
Heating system	8
Cooling system	97
Total	\$185

A simple cost-benefit analysis yields the following results:

$$\text{Simple payback period: } \frac{\$185}{\$17/\text{year}} = 10.9 \text{ years}$$

$$\text{Simple return on investment: } \frac{\$17/\text{year}}{\$185} = 9.2 \text{ percent/year}$$

The company's normal return on investment is 10 percent. While the analysis suggests that cost-effectiveness is not quite reached, a more detailed discounted-cash-flow analysis may prove otherwise. Also, summer shading of the additional 2 feet of glass may reduce the additional summer cooling energy and equipment costs without changing substantially the daylight savings.

Finally, it should be noted that the analysis method presented above assumes an on-off switching system, *not* a continuous-dimming approach. The answers that such a method yields are, as mentioned earlier, an underestimate of the lighting power savings potential of a dimming system. Such a system will account for at least 20 percent more power savings over the savings generated by an on-off switching system. This alone is likely to result in a more favorable cost-effectiveness assessment.

ANALYZING THE IMPACT OF AN OVERHANG

When an overhang is analyzed, the designer must assume that the new depth of the room includes the depth of the overhang. In other words, the window is assumed to be at the edge of the overhang. This will yield a new set of distances for the minimum, mid, and maximum points (see Figure 10-20):

Maximum point	5 ft from edge of overhang
Midpoint	(Length of room plus depth of overhang) ÷ 2
Minimum point	Same as before

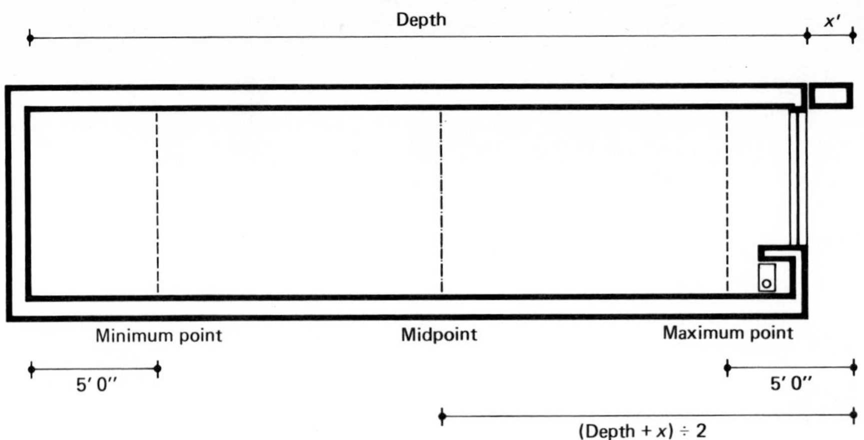

FIGURE 10-20 Positions for maximum, mid, and minimum points when analyzing an overhang. [How to Predict Interior Daylight Illumination, *Libbey-Owens-Ford Company, Toledo, Ohio, 1976, p. 15.*]

The length of the room must also be revised (see Figure 10-21). The length for each measurement-point condition must be determined by projecting lines from each measurement point through the intersection of the window and sidewalls of the room and extending out to the edge of the overhang. The new room lengths will be the following:

Maximum point: New length = old length (1 + overhang depth/5 ft)

Midpoint: New length
= old length [1 + (overhang depth/room depth ÷ 2)]

Minimum point: New length
= old length [1 + (overhang depth/room depth − 5 ft)]

The approach which may be used to calculate the tributary areas associated with overhang-related measurement points is presented in Figure 10-22.

EXAMPLE

If the designer in the previous example wishes to use an overhang over the additional 2 feet of glass added to the south side of the office building in order to reduce summer cooling loads, what is the impact on the lighting savings and what is the cost-effectiveness of such a design?

The overhang that the designer proposes to use casts a shadow over the new 2-foot strip of window during the spring and summer seasons. The depth of the overhang in this case is 1 foot (see Figure 10-23). During the autumn and winter seasons, the overhang will shade none of the windows, given the average shadow angle of those seasons, and during the spring and summer it will shade 100 percent of the additional 2 feet of glass:

30° shadow line (no shading): autumn, winter
71° shadow line (100 percent shading): spring, summer

The maximum, mid, and minimum points for the analysis become the following:

Maximum point	4 ft from window
Midpoint	14.5 ft from window
Minimum point	25 ft from window (same as before)

Because the data in Tables 10-14 and 10-15 do not accommodate minor changes in room maximum, mid, and minimum analysis points, no change will be acknowledged in these points in the following assessment of the overhang.

For the analysis the *length* of the room will stay at 40 ft, the limit that the room length may take, given the methodology's constraints. If the room had been narrower, the designer would have had to calculate "equivalent room" dimensions in accordance with the approach described in Figure 10-21.

As before, the interior natural lighting provided by ground-reflected light will be assumed to be 20 percent.

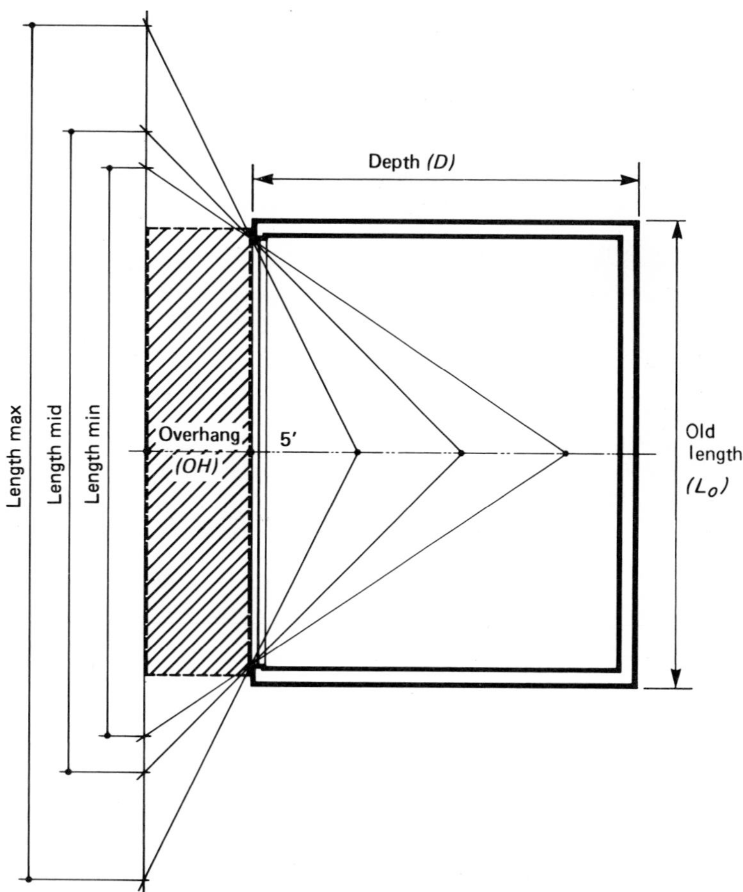

FIGURE 10-21 **Approach to adjusting room lengths when analyzing rooms with overhangs.**

$$\textbf{Maximum-point length} = L_o\,(1 + OH/5)$$

$$\textbf{Midpoint length} = L_o\left(1 + \frac{OH}{D/2}\right)$$

$$\textbf{Minimum-point length} = L_o\,(1 + OH/D - 5)$$

[*How to Predict Interior Daylight Illumination*, **Libbey-Owens-Ford Company, Toledo, Ohio, 1976, p. 14.**]

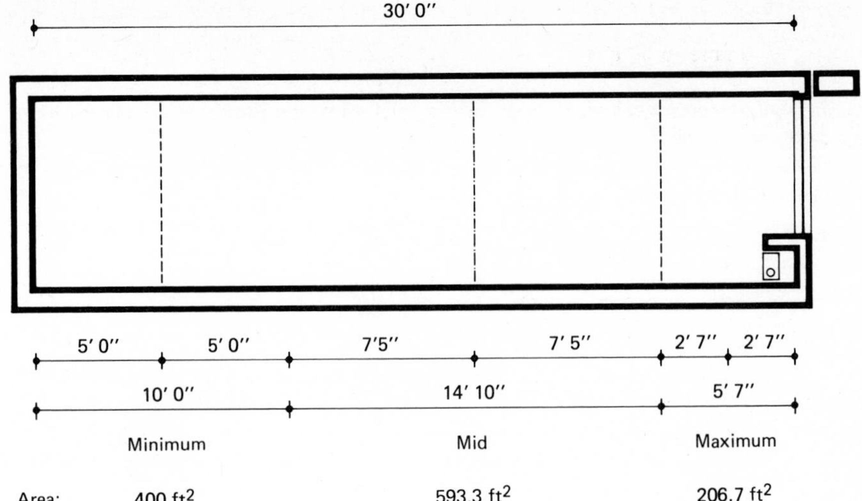

FIGURE 10-22 Tributary areas for maximum, mid, and minimum points, given an overhang condition.

Minimum Point

In the previous example, only the winter and autumn months had additional lighting benefits with the additional 2 feet of glass in window height. The overhang does not shade the window during these months, and therefore no change in interior illumination will occur.

Midpoint

Because of the overhang, the spring and summer months will have clear sky only, with no sun striking the glass. From the previous example, the midpoint exterior illumination requirement is 2447 footcandles. From Figure 10-17, one may observe that this level of illumination is never reached under solely clear-sky conditions. Summer daylight performance of the 10-foot glass would therefore be the same as that of the 8-foot glass. Winter daylight performance would remain unchanged for the 10-foot-high glass.

The table on page 317 must be revised as follows:

Month	Hours of lights off
December	2.8
January	2.7
February	3.2
March	. . .°
April	. . .°
May	. . .°
June	. . .°
July	. . .°
August	. . .°
September	4.0
October	4.0
November	2.9
6-month average	3.3

°Same as 8-foot-high window.

During the summer months the overcast-sky contribution of the 10-foot glass would be unchanged with the overhang, but the clear-sunny-sky contributions would become essentially the same as for the 8-foot window. The table on page 318 therefore becomes the following:

Month	Overcast hours	Overcast fraction	Clear-sunny hours	Clear-sunny fraction	Weighted average (overcast + clear-sunny)
December			7	0.40	2.8
January			7	0.38	2.7
February			8	0.42	3.4
March			8	0.41	3.3
April			9	0.48	4.3
May	3.0	0.58	9	0.42	5.5
June	4.5	0.57	9	0.43	6.4
July	3.0	0.56	9	0.44	5.6
August			9	0.48	4.3
September			8	0.50	4.0
October			8	0.50	4.0
November			7	0.42	2.9
Average					4.1

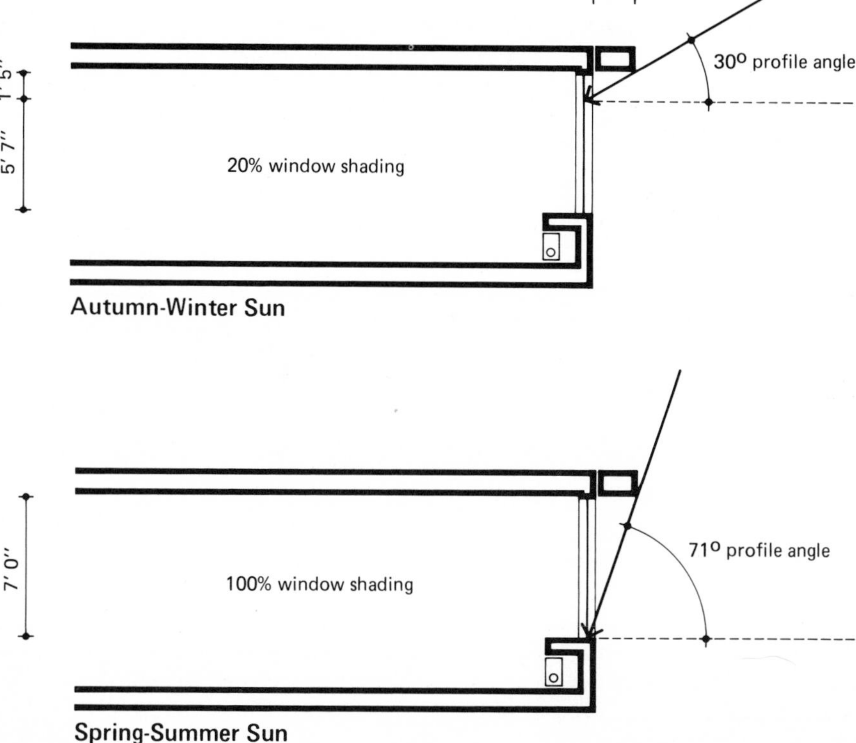

FIGURE 10-23 Section through an example office building exterior wall with an overhang.

This table is actually the same as that presented for the ***unshaded*** 2-foot strip (page 318) because the amount of clear-sunny illumination provided by the 8-foot window was already far above the 50-footcandle level.

The revised benefit of the *shaded* 2-foot strip above the base 8-foot window is presented below, indicating that only the midpoint experiences a change in benefit due to the overhang:

Minimum point: difference between 8- and 10-foot windows		360 h/year
8-ft midpoint	377 h/year	
10-ft midpoint: 6 months × 21.67 days/month × 3.3 h/day	429 h/year	
Difference		52 h/year
Maximum point: difference between 8- and 10-foot windows		130 h/year

The saving in electricity, based on the impact of the overhang, is summarized below:

Minimum point B_L	\$43/year
Midpoint, B_L = \$0.15 × 52 h/year × 2 W/ft² × 400 ft² ÷ 1000 Wh/kWh	6/year
Maximum point B_L	16/year
Total B_L	\$65/year

Thermal Effects of the Overhang

Winter thermal performance of the additional 2 feet of glass will be unchanged by the overhang. The following aspects of summer performance will, however, be changed:

- Conduction
- Solar radiation
- Demand charges
- Cooling equipment cost increases

Conduction: The sol-air temperature condition will no longer affect the outside temperature next to the glass. Overall conducted energy consumption will therefore be:

$$\text{Wall: } Q_c = 0.049 \text{ Btu/(h}\cdot{}^\circ\text{F}\cdot\text{ft}^2) \times 80 \text{ ft}^2 \times 9195\ ({}^\circ\text{F}\cdot\text{h})/\text{year}$$

$$= 36{,}044 \text{ Btu/year [See Equation (8-2).]}$$

$$\text{Shaded glass: } Q_c = 0.405 \text{ Btu/(h}\cdot{}^\circ\text{F}\cdot\text{ft}^2) \times 80 \text{ ft}^2 \times -2283\ ({}^\circ\text{F}\cdot\text{h})/\text{year}$$

$$= -73{,}969 \text{ Btu/year [See Equation (8-2).]}$$

$$\Delta Q_c = 36{,}044 \text{ Btu/year} - (-73{,}969 \text{ Btu/year})$$

$$= 110{,}013 \text{ Btu/year (improvement over the wall)}$$

Because the shaded glass reduces sol-air temperatures and the cooling system begins operating at 65°F, the shaded glass actually helps to cool the building by creating a heat loss condition between the 65 and 80°F outdoor air temperature conditions during the cooling season.

Solar radiation: The shaded glass will be subjected to diffuse solar radiation only:[22]

$$Q_c = 42 \text{ Btu/(h·ft}^2) \times 80 \text{ ft}^2 \times 0.60 \times 9 \text{ h/day} \times 5 \text{ days/week} \times 26 \text{ weeks/year} = 2{,}358{,}720 \text{ Btu/year}$$

Lighting: The table on page 320 is reconstructed below to show the effects of the overhang for the midpoint. Previous analysis shows that the minimum point and the maximum point remain unchanged.

Month	8 ft	10 ft	Difference
May	...	...	...
June	...	...	...
July	...	...	...
August	...	...	...
September	3.8	4.0	0.2
October	3.4	4.0	0.6
6-month average			0.1

$$\Delta T_L = (1.1 \text{ h/day} + 0.1 \text{ h/day} + 1.0 \text{ h/day}/3 = 0.7 \text{ h/day}$$

$$\Delta Q_L = 1200 \text{ ft}^2 \times 2 \text{ W/ft}^2 \times 3.413 \text{ Btu/Wh} \times 0.7 \text{ h/day} \times 5 \text{ days/week} \times 26 \text{ weeks/year} \quad (10\text{-}2)$$
$$= 745{,}399 \text{ Btu/year}$$

A revised summary of increases and decreases in summer heat gains is presented below (see page 321 for comparison):

Increases in heat gain:

Latent infiltration	21,874 Btu/year
Radiation	2,358,220 Btu/year

Decreases in heat gain:

Conduction	(110,013 Btu/year)
Sensible infiltration	(6,164 Btu/year)
Lighting	(745,399 Btu/year)
Net increase	1,518,518 Btu/year

$$C_c = \$0.15/\text{kWh} \times 0.94 \text{ kW/ton} \times [1{,}518{,}518 \text{ Btu/year} \div 12{,}000 \text{ Btu/(ton·h)}]$$
$$= \$18/\text{year [See Equation (6-5).]}$$

Peak cooling load changes are estimated below.

Conduction: The cooling load temperature difference for shaded glass would be the same as the outdoor air–inside air temperature difference, which in this case is 80°F − 89°F = 9°F. Since this turns out to be the same as the adjusted cooling load temperature difference used for sunlit glass, no change in peak conducted heat gain will be estimated.

[22]For the figure of 42 Btu/(h·ft²) see Table 10-6, averaged for the period May–October.

Solar radiation:

$$\Delta q_c = 80 \text{ ft}^2 \times 42 \text{ Btu/(h}\cdot\text{ft}^2) \times 0.83 \times 0.51$$
$$= 1422 \text{ Btu/h [See Equation (8-3).]}$$

Lighting: During the peak cooling load month of August, none of the spaces have a decrease in lights turned off when an overhang is used. No decrease in peak cooling load due to lighting will therefore be assessed.

The revised summary of changes in peak cooling load with the overhang in place is presented below:

Increases:

Conduction	206 Btu/h
Convection:	
Sensible	24 Btu/h
Latent	36 Btu/h
Radiation	1422 Btu/h

Decreases:

Lighting	....
Net increase	1688 Btu/h

Cooling equipment cost increases are estimated below:

For the entire south facade,

$$\Delta q_c = (1688 \text{ Btu/h} \times 80) \div 12{,}000 \text{ Btu/(ton}\cdot\text{h)}$$
$$= 11.3 \text{ tons}$$
$$C_0 = 11.3 \text{ tons} \times \$450/\text{ton} = \$5085$$

or for the portion of building being analyzed,

$$C_0 = \$5085 \div 80 = \$64$$

The impact on demand charges is

$$C_c = [1688 \text{ Btu/h} \div 12{,}000 \text{ Btu/(ton}\cdot\text{h)}] \times 0.94 \text{ kW/ton}$$
$$\times \$20/(\text{kW}\cdot\text{month}) \times 6 \text{ months/year}$$
$$= \$16/\text{year}$$

If it is assumed that the small overhang can be achieved by a minor design change in the facade causing no additional construction cost, the following is a revised summary of the costs and benefits of a *shaded* 2-foot strip of glass on top of 5 feet of unshaded glass compared with the 5-foot unshaded glass by itself:

Winter heating season:

Daytime	...
Nighttime	($18/year)

Summer cooling season:

Daytime	(\$18/year)
Nighttime	.....
Demand charges	(\$16/year)
Lighting savings	\$65/year
Net benefit, B_t	\$13/year

On an aftertax basis,

$$B_t = \$13/\text{year} \times (1 - 0.45) = \$7$$

The cost of the window plus increases in heating and cooling system costs is summarized below:

Glass	\$100
Heating system	8
Cooling system	64
Total	\$172

A simple cost-benefit analysis yields the following:

$$\text{Simple payback period: } \frac{\$172}{\$13/\text{year}} = 13.2 \text{ years}$$

$$\text{Simple return on investment: } \frac{\$13/\text{year}}{\$172/\text{year}} = 7.6 \text{ percent/year}$$

The results suggest that the overhang over the 2-foot strip of glass will actually *decrease* the cost-effectiveness of the glass rather than increase it. The reduction in the available natural light is greater than can be justified by the corresponding reduction in heat gain and peak cooling load.

SUMMARY

The previous sections describe a process for estimating the electrical savings due to reduced lighting use when adequate natural lighting is available. That process is summarized in Figure 10-24 and Table 10-17. Included are the formulas, tables, and figures needed to prepare estimates of savings for both skylight and window sources of natural light.

TABLE 10-17 **Summary of Equations to Be Used for Estimating Natural-Light Levels**

$B_L = C_e \times t \times P_L \times A_r \div 1000$	10-1 Monetary value of a reduction in artificial-lighting use
$\Delta q_L = P_L \times A_r \times 3.413$	10-2 Change in internal heat gain due to reduced artificial-lighting use
$E_o = \dfrac{E_i \times A_r}{A_s \times C_u \times C_L}$	10-3 Level of outside illumination required to maintain a given level of interior illumination by using skylights
$E_o = E_i \div (A_w \times \tau_g \times C_s \times K_s \times V_s)$	10-4 Level of outside illumination required to maintain a given level of interior illumination by using windows

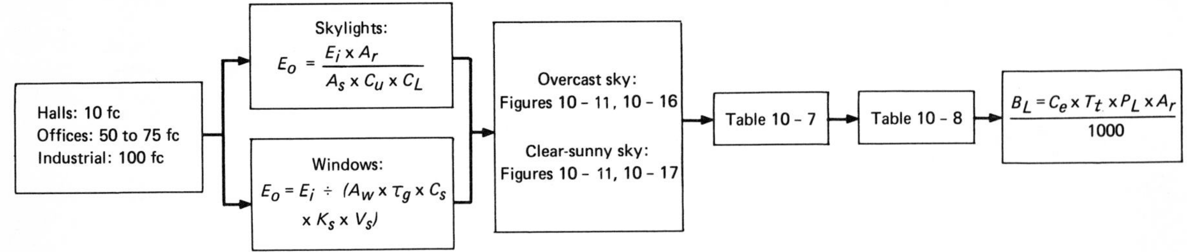

FIGURE 10-24 **General process for estimating the benefits of reduced electrical consumption due to adequate natural lighting.**

It should also be noted that some of the most effective methods for increasing interior natural illumination such as light shelves and various reflector designs (see Chapter 4) cannot be directly analyzed by the method presented in this chapter. The designer is encouraged to use scale models as a means of estimating interior light intensity for design approaches beyond the scope of this method.

BIBLIOGRAPHY

ASHRAE Handbook and Product Directory—1977 Fundamentals Volume, American Society of Heating, Refrigerating and Air-Conditioning Engineers, Inc., New York, 1977.

Recommended Practice of Daylighting, Illuminating Engineering Society of North America, New York, 1979.

Stein, Richard G.: *Architecture and Energy*, Anchor Press, Doubleday & Co., Garden City, N.Y., 1977.

APPENDIX

SYMBOLS AND ABBREVIATIONS

A	Area, usually ft^2; amplitude of temperature fluctuations, °F
A_t	Annual temperature ratio, no units
B	Benefits, $ or $/year; amplitude ratio, no units
BHLC	Building heat load coefficient, Btu/(°F·day)
c	Specific heat, Btu/(lb·°F)
C	Thermal conductance, Btu/(h·ft^2·°F) or Btu/(h·°F); also costs, $ or $/fuel unit
C_L	Coefficient of light loss, no units
CLF	Cooling load factor, no units
CLTD	Cooling load temperature difference, °F
C_u	Coefficient of light utilization, no units
d	Density of a material, lb/ft^3; also distance, ft
D	Average diffuse radiation on a horizontal surface, Btu/(h·ft^2) (also H)
DD	Degree-days, °F day/year
DH	Degree-hours, °F h/year
E	Energy, Btu (see also Q); also effectiveness, no units; intensity of surface illumination, lm/ft^2
h	Film or surface conductance, Btu/(h·ft^2·°F) (also f)
$\overline{H}$	Radiation on a horizontal surface, Btu/(h·ft^2) (also D or H)
H_o	Extraterrestrial radiation outside the earth's atmosphere, Btu/(h·ft^3)
HRH	Humidity ratio hours, (lb·h)/(lb·year)

I	Solar radiation on any surface, Btu/(h·ft²), Btu/(day·ft²); also intensity of a light source, lm
I_{cl}	Relative clothing insulation value, no units
J	Heat flow factor, Btu/(h·ft²)
k	Thermal conductivity, Btu/[h·ft²·(°F/ft)]; also year in which payback occurs, year
K_d	Correction for 65°F-based degree-days, no units
K_D	Fraction of extraterrestrial radiation which reaches the earth, no units
K_s	Coefficient of utilization for interior light distribution, no units
L	Length, ft or in typically
LCR	Load collector ratio, no units
L_e	Light well efficiency, no units
n	Useful life of an investment, years; also heating system efficiency, no units
NG	Net-to-gross ratio, no units
P	Power, W or W/ft²; also perimeter, ft
q	Hourly heat transfer rate, Btu/h
Q	Total heat transferred annually, Btu/year
r	Rate, either escalation rate (r_e) or discount rate (r_d), no units
R	Thermal resistance, (h·ft²·°F)/Btu
SC	Shading coefficient, no units
SF	Shading factor, no units
SHGF	Solar heat gain factor, Btu/(h·ft²)
SSF	Solar savings fraction, no units
Δt	Temperature difference, usually between indoors and outdoors, °F
t	Temperature, °F; or time, year typically
T	Cooling tons, Btu/h
T	Time, h/year typically
TA	Average amplitude of daily temperature fluctuations, °F
T_n	Net toplight transmittance, no units
U	Overall heat transfer coefficient, Btu/(h·ft²·°F)
v	Heating value of fuel; if oil, Btu/gal
V	Volume of air flow, typically, ft³/h or ft³/min
VE	Velocity of air flow, ft/min
V_s	Venetian blind coefficient of utilization for interior light distribution, no units
W	Power, watts or watts/ft²; also humidity ratio, lb of water per lb of dry air
α	Absorptivity or absorptance, no units; also thermal mass

α	Absorptance, no units; attenuation factor, no units
β	Solar altitude
γ	Thermal inertia index, no units
Δ	Difference or change between values, no units
ϵ	Emissivity, no units
λ	System efficiency, percent
θ	Angle of incidence, degrees
ρ	Reflectivity (decimal); also mass density, lb/ft^3
σ	Stefan-Boltzmann constant for black-body radiation, $Btu/(h \cdot ft^2 \cdot °F)$
τ	Transmissivity, no units
ϕ	Solar azimuth

CONVERSION FACTORS

U.S. customary unit	SI unit
Area	
1 ft^2	0.0929 m^2
1 yd^2	0.8361 m^2
Energy	
1 Btu	1055 J
1 $Btu/(ft^2 \cdot h)$	3.152 W/m^2
1 kcal	4186.8 J
1 kWh	3,600,000 J
1 Wh	3600 J
Heat	
1 $Btu/(h \cdot ft^2 \cdot °F)$	5.6744 $W/(m^2 \cdot K)$
1 clo	0.2004 $(K \cdot m^2)/W$
1 $(°F \cdot h \cdot ft^2)/Btu$	0.1761 $(K \cdot m^2)/W$
Length	
1 in	25.4 mm
1 ft	0.3048 m
1 yd	0.9144 m
1 mi	1.609 km
Light	
1 fc	10.7639 lx

Mass	
1 lb	0.4536 kg
1 short ton	907.18 kg
1 metric ton	1000 kg
Pressure	
1 lbf/ft^2	47.88 Pa
Velocity	
1 mi/h	0.4470 m/s
Volume	
1 ft^3	0.0283 m^3
1 yd^3	0.7645 m^3
1 qt	0.946 L
1 gal	3.785 L

NOTE: To convert °F to °C, subtract 32 from °F and divide by 1.8.

INDEX

ABOUT THE AUTHOR

William Meyer is an architect in private practice in New York with ongoing commercial and residential building projects on the east and west coasts. His firm provides both building design and analysis services: architectural design, interior design, and product design as well as energy analysis, cost-benefit analysis, and real estate analysis. Prior to establishing his own firm, Mr. Meyer was a vice president of The Ehrenkrantz Group.

In addition to his practice, Mr. Meyer is visiting associate professor at the schools of architecture of Columbia University and Pratt Institute and is a visiting lecturer at Princeton University and the New York School of Interior Design. He has master in architecture and master of management science degrees from the Massachusetts Institute of Technology and a bachelor of architecture degree from the University of Minnesota.

Mr. Meyer has published articles dealing with environmental problem solving and innovative building approaches in numerous architectural journals, and he is the recipient of awards for energy-conscious design. He is a member of the American Institute of Architects, the International Solar Energy Society, the National Trust for Historic Preservation, the American Society of Heating, Refrigerating and Air-Conditioning Engineers, and the Construction Specifications Institute.